A BRIEF HISTORY OF
VIETNAM

COLONIALISM, WAR AND RENEWAL:
THE STORY OF A NATION TRANSFORMED

BILL HAYTON

TUTTLE Publishing
Tokyo | Rutland, Vermont | Singapore

"Books to Span the East and West"

Tuttle Publishing was founded in 1832 in the small New England town of Rutland, Vermont [USA]. Our core values remain as strong today as they were then—to publish best-in-class books which bring people together one page at a time. In 1948, we established a publishing office in Japan—and Tuttle is now a leader in publishing English-language books about the arts, languages and cultures of Asia. The world has become a much smaller place today and Asia's economic and cultural influence has grown. Yet the need for meaningful dialogue and information about this diverse region has never been greater. Over the past seven decades, Tuttle has published thousands of books on subjects ranging from martial arts and paper crafts to language learning and literature—and our talented authors, illustrators, designers and photographers have won many prestigious awards. We welcome you to explore the wealth of information available on Asia at www.tuttlepublishing.com.

Published by Tuttle Publishing, an imprint of Periplus Editions (HK) Ltd.

www.tuttlepublishing.com

Copyright © 2022 by Bill Hayton

Front cover images:
TOP saiko3p, Depositphotos.com;
BOTTOM Efired, Dreamstime

Library of Congress Cataloging in Publication Data

ISBN 978-0-8048-5418-4

25 24 23 22   5 4 3 2 1   2208TP
Printed in Singapore

TUTTLE PUBLISHING® is a registered trademark of Tuttle Publishing, a division of Periplus Editions (HK) Ltd.

Distributed by:

North America, Latin America & Europe
Tuttle Publishing
364 Innovation Drive
North Clarendon VT 05759 9436, USA
Tel: 1(802) 773 8930
Fax: 1(802) 773 6993
info@tuttlepublishing.com
www.tuttlepublishing.com

Asia Pacific
Berkeley Books Pte Ltd
3 Kallang Sector #04-01
Singapore 349278
Tel: (65) 6741 2178
Fax: (65) 6741 2179
inquiries@periplus.com.sg
www.tuttlepublishing.com

Japan
Tuttle Publishing
Yaekari Building 3rd Floor
5-4-12 Osaki Shinagawa-ku
Tokyo 141 0032 Japan
Tel: 81 (3) 5437 0171
Fax: 81 (3) 5437 0755
sales@tuttle.co.jp
www.tuttle.co.jp

Ancient Sites

CHINA

Red River

Phung Nguyen ★   ● Co Loa
Hoa Binh ★   ■ **Hanoi**
                    ★ Man Bac
Ma River

Dong Son ★

Ca River

LAOS

★ Beihai

Ngang
Pass

Nhat Le
River

Mekong River

Hai Van
Pass

Thu Bon River

★ Tra Kieu
★ My Son

THAILAND

★ Sa Huynh

VIETNAM

Cu Mong
Pass

CAMBODIA

Angkor Borei ★

● Ho Chi Minh City

Mekong River

Oc Eo ★

200 km
100 miles

CONTENTS

Introduction   7

CHAPTER 1   **Bronze Drums and Brick Tombs**
             (Prehistory–900 CE)   13
             Multiple migrations bring different cultures into
             the region. Lowland areas are incorporated into
             "Chinese" empires. Revolts break out and local
             rulers take steps towards separation.

CHAPTER 2   **Other Worlds: Mountains and Coasts**   42
             Outside the northern lowlands, other cultures
             thrive: "Dong World" in the highlands, Funan
             in the Mekong Delta and Champa on the cen-
             tral coast.

CHAPTER 3   **Independence and Family Fights**
             (900–1400)   68
             The early Le dynasty creates a new state in
             the Red River Delta but also a legacy of rivalry
             between the delta, the hills and the coast with
             the Ly & Tran families fighting for control.

CHAPTER 4   **Invasion and Division (1400–1771)**   104
             A usurper takes over the kingdom and Ming
             China invades. A new alliance of uplanders and
             lowlanders expels the Ming but the alliance
             breaks apart and rival families create power
             bases in the north and the center.

CHAPTER 5   **Destruction and Unification (1771–1867)**   136
             The vicious Tay Son civil war destroys the old
             order but creates a single country from the north-
             ern mountains to the southern sea. Half a century
             of unity ends with the arrival of the French.

CHAPTER 6   **Colonialism and Resistance (1859–1907)**   163
The French take over the south, creating Cochinchina, impose protectorates on the center and
north, and create the colony of Indochina.

CHAPTER 7   **Becoming Vietnam (1907–54)**   186
Colonialism brings prosperity to some but misery
to many. Nationalism and communism spread and
after the Second World War, armed resistance
breaks out.

CHAPTER 8   **"The Vietnam War" and
"The American War" (1954–75)**   218
Partition, the creation of two rival Vietnams and
industrial warfare.

CHAPTER 9   **Peace and War and Peace
(1975–Present)**   246
Post-war crisis, confrontation with China and
economic renovation.

Further Reading   273
Bibliography   275
Index   282

Introduction

Choosing a Name

The middle months of 1802 were sweet for the new king. He had extinguished the last embers of a thirty-year uprising and his freshly unified realm was emerging from the fire. Its lands now stretched from the northern mountains to the southern sea. By defeating the rebels who had murdered his family, the king had become the first ruler to simultaneously control the Red River delta in the north and the Mekong delta in the south, together with all the territory around them and in between. The country finally had a shape—an elongated S—that modern eyes would recognize as "Vietnam." But the king knew that victory on the battlefields was not enough to ensure peace in the kingdom. It was vital to be acknowledged as the rightful ruler by all his subjects. So the king gathered around him men of letters and asked them a crucial question: did they believe there was anyone left with a rival claim to the throne? Was the previous royal dynasty still alive? To the king's pleasure, the scholars unanimously declared the old dynasty dead, allowing the new king to rightfully declare himself the founder of a new one named after his family: the Nguyen.

The king, who had been born with the name Nguyen Phuc Anh, then chose a new title for himself—Gia Long—to mark the establishment of his own royal house. The name symbolized the unity he had just created by force: Gia Dinh was the traditional name for the city we now call Saigon and Thang Long was the city that today we call Hanoi. "Gia Long" meant, in effect, "north and south." But Gia Long knew that neither symbolism nor recognition by his subjects was enough. He also needed to be recognized by neighboring rulers, and the most important neighbor of all was the ruler of the country that today we call China. In summer 1802, Gia Long sent officials on the long journey to Beijing, to request an audience with the emperor in the Forbidden City.

It was a ritual: one that gave Gia Long respectability in a world ordered by Confucian rules. Just as a son bears allegiance to a father, so the king of the smaller state pledges allegiance to the emperor of the larger one. In exchange, the emperor offers his moral support to the king. Both gain legitimacy from recognition by the other.

But there was a problem. Before they travelled to met the emperor, the delegation first had to pay their compliments to officials just over the border in Guangdong province. The envoys told the Guangdong governor that Gia Long wanted to name his new state "Nam Viet." This was also a reference to geography: "Nam" was derived from "Annam" referring to the northern part of the realm while "Viet" came from an old tribe who inhabited the south (the Viet Thuong). When he heard this, the governor was dismayed. To him, the name sounded like the name of a much older state, one that had existed in the lands of what are today northern Vietnam and southern China nearly two thousand years before. "Nam Viet" therefore sounded like it could be a claim to a part of the emperor's own lands.

After much internal debate in Beijing, the Emperor agreed to recognize the new state to his south in 1803, but with a different name. He reversed the two characters of Gia Long's choice to create "Viet Nam." This way round, the imperial court reasoned, the name only claimed the southern lands: those already under Gia Long's rule. The envoys had no choice but to accept—refusal would have denied their king the diplomatic recognition he required. So they returned home bearing a gift from the emperor: the official imperial seal, six kilograms of solid silver, bearing the newly authorized name of their state. Viet Nam was born.

On the seventeenth day of the second lunar month in 1803, Gia Long's court assembled at his palace in the central city of Hue to hear the official edict announcing the new name. Gia Long was unhappy but he was obliged to do as Confucian protocol demanded and accept the instructions from Beijing. The royal edict declared that the country's name was being changed "in order to establish the great foundations, which will be bequeathed to the distant future." But while formally making the change and accepting the recognition, Gia Long's court actually only used the name in diplomatic correspondence with Beijing.

Making matters worse, despite forcing their own choice of name on Gia Long's new country, the court in Beijing continued to use a name the Vietnamese found offensive: *An Nan* or *Annam*—"Pacified South" which dated back over a thousand years. In its internal business Gia Long's court stuck with *Nam Viet*, changing to *Dai Viet*—"Great Viet"— in 1813. In 1838, Gia Long's successor invented a new name *Dai Nam*— "Great South"—but avoided some diplomatic difficulties by choosing not to inform Beijing. *Dai Nam* continued to be the official name used by the royal court right up until the end of the dynasty in 1945.

This book then, is a brief history of a country that did not take its current shape until after 1802 nor its current name until 1945. Over the centuries this elongated S shape of territory has known many names and even more rulers, none of whom called themselves "Vietnamese." In earlier eras, kings and rebels ruled different regions, dynasties grew in strength and then retreated, rival states existed alongside each other and their frontiers ebbed and flowed, rarely coinciding with modern boundaries. Even as Gia Long was naming his country in 1803, for example, the northern and southern regions were ruled by warlords who accepted the king's authority more on paper than in practice. It would take another two or three decades to consolidate the Nguyen family's rule and only a couple of decades after that, the French Empire arrived, bringing division back to Vietnam for another century.

Questions of unity and division are still controversial in Vietnam. Reunification was the hard-won result of another thirty years war, a war that only ended when tanks crashed through the gates of the presidential palace in the southern city of Saigon in April 1975. Since then, the Vietnamese government's preferred way of writing about the country's history has been to stress unity and play down periods of division.

Who, then, are the Vietnamese? A simple answer might be: everyone who lives within Vietnam. But the word also has a more political meaning; it implies that the people who live in Vietnam today are the descendants of people who have always lived there and that those people have always thought of themselves as Vietnamese and nothing else. As we shall we, the story is more complicated than that.

Streets

Visitors who travel around Vietnam often notice a certain repetitiveness in the names of the major streets in each town and city. From Hanoi to Ho Chi Minh City, avenues and boulevards generally share a set of names drawn from the pantheon of Vietnamese national heroes. For foreigners the names can be confusing: Ly Nam De and Ly Thai To, Nguyen Trai and Nguyen Hue, Ba Trieu and Hai Ba Trung and so on. These people lived in different centuries, in different places and may not have been regarded as heroes during the times in which they lived. Nonetheless, these "street-name heroes" generally have one thing in common: they are all now portrayed as leaders or fighters in the two millennia-long struggle of the Vietnamese people for independence against China.

All of these people will appear in the pages of this book but not exactly as they appear in most books about the history of Vietnam. This book begins from the understanding that "Vietnam" and "China" and all the other countries of the region are modern creations that emerged through the interaction of local cultures with Western colonialism in the late nineteenth and early twentieth centuries. As these societies struggled to modernize and shake off foreign control, their leaders and intellectuals re-examined history to explain their predicament and navigate out of it. In the process, these leaders and intellectuals created new historical stories about the emergence of their societies: stories that emphasized independence and resistance. These stories were founded upon a sense of difference between "us" and "them" and had the effect of creating a new sense of unity among members of a new nation.

In Vietnam, the stories of nationhood were generally focused on China but not necessarily in an antagonistic way. As we shall see in later chapters, intellectuals in nineteenth century *Dai Nam* developed an idea of themselves as the "People of the Southern Country." There was a sense that the "Southern Country" was different from the "Central Country"—(*Trung Quoc*) as China is still known in Vietnamese—but the two were not regarded as enemies. Far from it: they shared many cultural similarities. Then, in the early twentieth century, as nationalist ideas grew across Asia, from Japan to the Philippines to Thailand, the next generation of intellectuals set out on a mental journey to discover the authentic roots of Vietnamese-ness. In the words of one of them, a scholar called Hoang Dao Thanh writing in 1906, "If there is a nation, then it must have a history.... All of the civilized nations in Europe, America and Japan revere the study of history.... Everyone must combine into one large group, unite into one large band."

These new Vietnamese nationalists complained that their people knew more about "Northern history" than they did about their own history. They worried that, if things did not change, the Vietnamese nation would simply disappear in the competition between other, stronger nations. As a matter of survival, they called for a new writing of history in order to make the people feel patriotic. They looked for a set of stories that explained who the Vietnamese were and how they were different from their neighbors. They found them in the annals of earlier kingdoms and the legends of leaders who had united their peoples against invaders. In Thanh's mind, the only people deserving of reverence were the "great heroes and great worthies of freedom and independence."

These stories and heroes inspired an independence movement which campaigned and fought against the French colonial governments before and after the Second World War. The more that the French tried to suppress these ideas, the more they spread. Efforts to spread "European civilization" through literacy actually ended up spreading this new sense of Vietnamese-ness among the wider population. After a long and vicious struggle, Vietnamese revolutionaries forced the French authorities to leave their colony in the mid-1950s. It was then that the main streets were renamed. In Hanoi, "Rue Henri Riviere" became Ngo Quyen Street, "Boulevard Gambetta" became Tran Hung Dao Street and "Boulevard Amiral Courbet" became Ly Thai Tho Street and so on. These names were not chosen because the heroes were "anti-Chinese," however. The Vietnamese nationalists who marched into Hanoi in October 1954 owed most of their success against the French to Chinese military aid and advice. They were not intending to offend their main sponsor. It was only in later years that heroes like Ngo Quyen, Tran Hung Dao and Ly Thai Tho were transformed into symbols of a "centuries old struggle against China."

The French colonists had maintained a thoroughly patronizing view of the people under their rule right until the very end. They had generally insisted that what little civilization they possessed had been acquired from China. As a result, once the French left, Vietnamese historians and archaeologists worked hard to create a new story of Vietnamese civilization that stood apart from China, a story of proud independence. In many cases they created stories that went far beyond what the evidence would support. However, within a few years, geopolitics also started to play a role in the way that Vietnamese history was being written. From the late 1950s onwards, the government of what became known as "South Vietnam" tried to discredit their rivals in "North Vietnam" by suggesting that they were not true nationalists because of their Chinese connections. In the process they turned the historic heroes into symbols of resistance against China. Something similar happened in the north in the late 1960s when relations with China soured, and then again in the 1980s when they became even worse.

The problem is that this way of looking at the past, which really only emerged in the late 20th century, has now become "baked in" to the standard accounts of Vietnamese history. Many modern books about Vietnam cast the entire history of the past 2,000 years (or even longer) as a permanent battle between it and a hostile China. This book will try to tell a different story.

CHAPTER 1

BRONZE DRUMS AND BRICK TOMBS (PREHISTORY-900 CE)

T he village of Dong Son sits on the southern bank of the Ma River, just north of the city of Thanh Hoa. The river's muddy brown waters flow fast between forested limestone towers: a picturesque setting for the province's pagodas and paddy fields. The river is a fickle friend: it brings fertility to these fields but, in spate, tears at the banks. Floods can bring disaster but in 1924 one brought a windfall. The torn earth revealed a collection of long-buried bronze objects and an entrepreneurial farmer quickly sold them to the local French colonial tax collector, Louis Pajot. Pajot told the French-run museum in Hanoi about his purchase, and was commissioned to organize his own excavations around the village to see what else he could dig up. Pajot had begun his career as a circus entertainer before becoming a sailor and then a civil servant. He lacked formal academic training, let alone an expertise in archaeology, so his methods were haphazard. Nonetheless, he discovered a number of skeletons and, buried alongside them, many precious objects, including several bronze drums.

Each bulbous kettledrum was blue-green in color, about a foot (30 cm) high, and a foot-and-a-half (50 cm) in diameter and too heavy to lift easily. Two pairs of handles allowed it to be moved. When Pajot scraped away the mud, it became clear that the top surfaces of the drums were beautifully decorated. Each featured a star-shaped sun at the center, around which ran concentric circles composed of geometric shapes, warriors bedecked in feathers and stylized, long-beaked birds in flight. Today, these shapes and designs can be found all across Vietnam: on T-shirts, tapestries and even tattoos. In the modern era, the "Dong Son drums," named after the village where they were first found, have become a symbol of ancient Vietnamese culture. Among archaeologists, "Dong Son culture" has become the shorthand name for a particular period of history: the time when the drums were first made.

Hundreds of bronze drums have now been found and catalogued by archaeologists, in Vietnam and also in southern China and across Southeast Asia. All the drums have the same basic shape but they come in a range of sizes and styles. At times, arguments about their origins have prompted "culture wars," particularly between researchers in Vietnam and China over which country can claim to "own" them. But what now seems clear is that they were made and owned by people on both sides of the modern border and also traded over long distances. And these people were neither "Chinese" nor "Vietnamese" as we understand those terms today.

Bronze drums like the ones found at Dong Son were large, intricately designed and difficult to make. They could only have belonged to people with wealth and power. The fact that they were buried with other prestigious items, like the sculptures, weapons, pearls and jade found in the Dong Son graves, tells us that these people belonged to settled communities with established hierarchies. Since 1924, around a hundred sites similar to Dong Son have been found across what is now northern Vietnam, concentrated in the lowland deltas of the three main rivers: the Ma River in Thanh Hoa province, the Ca River a little further south and the Red River which spreads southeast from Hanoi. The physical evidence uncovered in these settlements dates them, and the "Dong Son Culture" as a whole, to the period between 500 BCE to 300 CE: Vietnam's Bronze and Iron Ages.

The designs on the drums give us intriguing clues about daily life in this "Dong Son culture." Apart from warriors in feathers, they show water buffalo pulling plows, farmers pounding grain and people living in stilt-houses. Archaeological evidence from the places where the drums were found, confirms that all these activities once took place at the sites. But one thing that we do not know about the people who created "Dong Son Culture" was what they called themselves. Many writers assert that they were called the *Yue* (pronounced "yoo-er") because that is the most common term used in Chinese texts of the period. However, the term *Yue* actually referred to anyone who lived south of the "central states" (what is today north-central China). And in the early part of this period, that meant anywhere south of the Yangtze River: all the way from modern-day Shanghai to Hanoi and beyond. And *Yue* was not a name used by the people themselves. Its meaning when used in Chinese was more like "them" and it was used to make a distinction between the "uncivilized them" and the "civilized us." Centuries ago, the word *Yue* was pronounced more like *Ywat*, which is how, much later, it came to be rendered as *Viet* and become a foundational part of Vietnamese identity.

There were so many different groups of *Yue* that Chinese texts appear bewildered by the variety, often lumping them all together as the "Hundred *Yue*." We know very little about the languages the "*Yue*" peoples spoke: only that they were very different from the ones spoken in the "central states." It is likely that their languages came from several different roots and were related to those spoken in Southeast Asia and Oceania today ("Austroasiatic" and "Austronesian" respectively). These diverse peoples created highly organized societies in the area of what is now southern China, and for most of the period between around 1000 BCE and 600 CE were generally able to resist advances by the states to the north. That said, there were movements of people from the north to the south, particularly when conflict among the "central states" or with peoples from Inner Asia forced northerners to flee.

The stories of the drums tell us a great deal about the early history of what is now northern Vietnam. They tell us that if we want to understand this era we have to widen our lens and connect the culture of the Ma, Ca and Red river deltas with those of surrounding areas to the east and north, in present-day China. We also have to think of "layers" of culture building up over time as new arrivals brought new technologies and new ways of organizing their societies. Sometimes they mixed with the older cultures and sometimes they replaced or marginalized them. However, to put that all in context, we need to travel a bit further back in time.

Prehistory

Modern humans first walked, or paddled, into Southeast Asia around 50,000 years ago when the earth was in the middle of its "Last Glacial Period." Current theories suggest those people travelled along at least two different trajectories: an early "coastal" route via South Asia and a later "continental" route through Eurasia. At the time, ice sheets covered northern Europe and North America, sea levels were around 100 meters lower than today and dry land stretched far out into what is now the Gulf of Tonkin and the South China Sea. The climate was cooler and drier, and woods and grasslands existed where jungle forests now stand. Finding traces of human settlement from this period has been difficult, presumably because much of it now lies on the former coast, 100 meters below current sea level. But we can imagine scattered villages along the sea shore surviving through a mixture of fishing, hunting and gathering.

After around 12000 BCE the planet warmed. Ice sheets melted and sea levels rose. Peoples living along the coast were forced to adapt or go extinct. Some communities died out, some migrated inland while others paddled across the sea. For those who survived, life became easier. The warmer climate encouraged more plant growth, which supported more grazing animals and therefore more food for humans. Small groups of people established themselves in caves in the hills, far from the sea. In the 1920s, several such caves were discovered in Hoa Binh province, a hilly region southwest of Hanoi, by another French colonial archaeologist, Madeleine Colani. The French gave this Stone Age culture the name "Hoabinhian." It has since become clear that similar sites can be found all across the Southeast Asian highlands but the name "Hoabinhian" has stuck. We know that Hoabinhian people used simple flaked stone tools, and hunted and gathered products of the forest but that is about all. We don't know where they came from nor what language they spoke.

By around 6000 BCE the sea had risen to about five meters above its level today, so the coast was actually further inland than its present line. Then, as sea fell towards its current height, the coastline extended. In the delta of the Red River, southeast of modern Hanoi, the effect was exacerbated by the river itself. The river flows extremely quickly and carries huge quantities of soil and rock from upstream. As the river flattens and slows down, sediment drops out of the water creating new land. The effect is to push the coastline many meters further into the sea every year. As a result, prehistoric sites that were built right on the coast now sit several kilometers inland. Others have been covered by centuries of mud. But, as a result of all this sediment, the delta of the Red River, and the coastal strip that spreads out from it to the north and south, is now 10,000 km^2 in area and among the most fertile places in the world.

So far, eight such coastal sites have been found, concentrated in areas of modern-day Thanh Hoa and Ninh Binh provinces, south of Hanoi. They include one in the village of Da But, about 30 km further up the Ma River from Dong Son. There, archaeologists have found clear evidence of settled habitation beginning around 5000 BCE. They believe the former occupants lived by harvesting shellfish from swamps, netting fish in rivers and lagoons and gathering food in the nearby hills. The inhabitants of Da But used pottery, which was decorated with basic patterns, and they developed sophisticated stone tools and techniques of textile spinning. This Stone Age culture shows many similarities with sites discovered in the delta of the Pearl River near present-day Hong Kong.

At around the same time, but much further north in what is now central China, other groups were learning to cultivate rice and millet and to domesticate pigs. This seems to have been achieved by groups living along the banks of the Yangtze and Yellow rivers between 7000 and 4500 BCE. At around the same time, but far to the south in what is now the Philippines, other settled peoples were learning how to farm bananas and yams. It seems remarkable but there is of evidence, even in this early period, of goods, tools and technologies being traded and transported around the Southeast Asian region. Innovations were able to spread between communities over land and sea. It seems to have been this mingling of peoples and cultures—a "mosaic of popula-tions"—that led to the next phase of human development.

Another archaeological site, Man Bac in Ninh Binh province, pro-vides considerable evidence for this change. Man Bac is just south of the city of Ninh Binh and 30 km north of Dong Son. It has many sim-ilarities with the sites at both Dong Song and Da But. It occupies fertile land, is close to the sea and sits at the foot of forested limestone hills but it was occupied much more recently: between 1800 and 1500 BCE. Researchers have so far found the skeletons of 84 people buried at Man Bac and, by measuring their skulls, bones and teeth, have reached some conclusions about where they originally came from. They believe the village was home to a mixed population of both continental "East Asian" people and coastal "Southeast Asian" people. They believe it proves that population growth in the regions around the Yellow and Yangtze river regions forced some inhabitants to seek new land else-where. Between 2500 and 2000 BCE people with the skills to grow rice and look after pigs started moving south and west, eventually arriving in the Pearl and Red River deltas. There they encountered people who were already masters of their local environment: able to survive through hunting and gathering but not yet able to farm. They may have initially occupied different parts of the landscape but by the time Man Bac was inhabited, they had found ways to live and work together. The new migrants brought their domesticated plants and animals while the earlier occupiers continued to hunt and fish.

By this period, around 1800 BCE, techniques of working with bronze were being developed, initially in the mountains of what is now Yunnan province where sources of both copper and tin were easily ac-cessible. The ability to create metal tools sparked fundamental social and environmental change. As the population of these bronze-using peoples grew, some of them began to migrate into other areas, particu-larly down the valley of the Red River. In Vietnam this "Bronze Age" culture is particularly linked to a site known as Phung Nguyen, on the banks of the Red River near the present-day city of Viet Tri in moun-tainous Phu Tho province. This "Phung Nguyen Culture," as archae-ologists term it, became the dominant form of social organization in the delta for the next millennium. Genetic studies suggest that the people of Phung Nguyen culture were different from those who lived in Man Bac. They do not seem to have mixed with the Hoabinhians at all. Instead they took over. Phung Nguyen communities grew rice; farmed pigs, cattle and buffalo; hunted and gathered in the swamps and foothills; manufactured and decorated pottery; worked with bronze and iron; traded around the region and, over the following centuries, created a flourishing economy and hierarchical societies. By 500 BCE it had become a culture that had leaders who valued intricately decorated bronze drums and buried them both in places like Dong Son.

By 350 BCE, this hierarchical society had started to resemble a state. Excavations at a place now called Co Loa, 17 km north of central Hanoi, have revealed a huge site, around 600 hectares in size, that could have been its citadel. Three concentric ramparts surround Co Loa, the outermost being four meters high, twelve meters thick and eight kilometers long. The Vietnamese-American archaeologist Nam C. Kim estimates that the ramparts took at least five million person-days to build. Another archaeologist, Alice Yao, has examined the evidence from Co Loa and concluded that constructing a structure on that scale would have required the forcible mobilization of large numbers of people from surrounding areas. Co Loa's rulers must have controlled a large territory with a sizeable population, a powerful military force and, therefore, considerable revenue. Agriculture must have generated sufficient surplus to feed the citadel's construction workers, artisans, soldiers and administrators.

Exactly how this sophisticated "Co Loa state" emerged from the more disparate "Phung Nguyen Culture" is not yet understood. Given the scale of the defensive structures at Co Loa, we can assume that it must have involved raiding and fighting between rival groups throughout the period when Dong Son drums were being made, played and buried. The inscribed surfaces of the drums themselves portray scenes of battle and victory, and excavations at Co Loa have discovered plenty of weapons, including crossbows. Around the citadel's southern gate, archaeologists discovered a cache of 10,000 bronze arrowheads and elsewhere they found molds for their mass production. This suggests there were fights between rival leaders for control of territory and trade during this time (300–100 BCE).

There is plenty of evidence that agriculture was also becoming more sophisticated: combining the use of plows drawn by cattle or buffalo with bronze (and later iron) tools to make planting and harvesting more efficient. Simultaneously, the Red River Delta region was connecting to a maritime trade network that carried goods to and from other parts of Southeast Asia, the coast of what is now China and even as far as India. Waterways built in and around Co Loa connected the citadel to the main channel of the Red River and from there to the sea. The river, and its tributaries, also provided routes into the uplands that lie all around Co Loa and through those hills into what is now China's Yunnan province. The rewards for whoever controlled the nodes of this trade—the ports, markets and mountain passes—would have been immense.

Where there was reward there was also risk. Many groups were willing to fight over the wealth being generated by this regional trade. Knowledge of the wealth of the Red River Delta spread around the region. The "Co Loa state" was a source of exotic products—kingfisher feathers, peacocks, rhinoceros horns, fragrant woods and much more—all hunted and gathered in the uplands around the delta. These were then sold abroad and curiosity must have grown about their source. The citadel was a hub for regional trade and riches must have accumulated among the upper echelons of its society. This seems to have made Co Loa an object of envy and attention; particularly to an emerging empire far to the north.

✸━✦

Qin & Han (200 BCE–420 CE)

The Qin Dynasty began as a small dependency of the Zhou royal house, established alongside the Yellow River (in what is now northern China) in 987 BCE in order to raise horses. For six centuries, the Qin was just one among several "warring states" located in these plains. The dynasty gradually expanded the area under its rule but was never dominant until King Zheng finally managed to conquer the last of his rivals in 221 BCE. As a new type of ruler, with a domain occupying (albeit briefly) the central plains and the lower reaches of both the Yellow and Yangtze rivers, Zheng chose a new title: *Qin Shihuangdi*, or "first emperor of Qin." In search of immortality, he started to build a tomb outside his capital, near what is now the city of Xi'an, and surround it with an army of terracotta warriors.

But Qin Shihuangdi's ambitions for wealth and power were not yet sated. Almost immediately after declaring himself emperor, he set about expanding his realm with a new campaign of conquest. This adventure would be long and costly and fighting was particularly difficult in the south. The key to the Qin Empire's eventual success was the construction of a canal just 32 km long: the *Lingqu* or "magic trench," near the modern city of Guilin in the Chinese province of Guangxi. This piece of engineering connected a river that flowed north into the Yangtze with another that flowed south into the Pearl River. When it was completed in 214 BCE, troops and supplies could be transported 2,000 km from the heartland of the Qin state to the frontline with relative ease. The Qin could then deploy and feed a huge army (some sources talk of half a million soldiers) on its march through the southwestern mountains.

The suppression campaign was protracted and vicious. The local people, the ones the Qin called *Yue*, avoided direct confrontations and took to the hills and forests, harrying the invaders and disappearing into the trees. Qin documents recorded, somewhat miserably, that the imperial troops did not take off their armor or put down their crossbows for three years. It was only once the Qin Emperor supplemented their ranks with "criminals, banished men and parasites" that they were able to secure victory over the *Yue* and parade their leaders with "heads bowed and ropes around their necks."

After their victory, the Qin named the conquered territory *Lingnan*, literally, "south of the mountain passes." They established three "commanderies" there: Nanhai (meaning "south sea" and including most of present-day Guangdong), Guilin (most of present-day Guangxi) and Xiang (western Guangdong, southern Guangxi and some parts of the Red River delta). It was, however, a pyrrhic victory. In 206 BCE, just after the death of Qin Shihuangdi, his successors were overthrown by a rebel leader, Liu Bang, who seized the imperial throne, created his own dynasty and named it the Han. In the chaos after the coup, the Qin general in the south, the man who had led the "suppression campaign" against the *Yue*, broke away from the new empire and declared the three new commanderies to be independent. This general, Zhao Tuo, then declared himself the ruler of this state, which he called Nanyue, and his capital to be Panyu (today's Guangdong).

Zhao Tuo was originally a Qin official from the north but, like all successful Qin officials, he knew he could not rule as an outsider. He married a local woman, encouraged his subordinates to do the same and promoted local people into positions of responsibility. He may have been helped in this by all the criminals and malcontents who had been exiled to the south by the Qin and presumably had no desire to be subject to northerners' rules anymore. But Zhao Tuo went too far and declared himself "Emperor of Nanyue." This so displeased the Emperor of Han that in 188 BCE he imposed economic sanctions on Nanyue: banning the export of metal and of female (i.e., breeding) livestock. After eight years of disagreement, Zhao Tuo backed down. He agreed to stop calling himself emperor, and accepted a subordinate position to the Han. To demonstrate his new vassal status he sent tribute of "a pair of white jades, 1,000 kingfisher feathers, ten rhinoceros horns, 500 purple-striped cowrie shells and two pairs of peacocks" to the emperor. Zhao Tuo became, in effect, leader of an autonomous buffer state protecting the southern approaches to the Han Empire.

There is an account in the (Chinese) "Commentary on the Water Classic" suggesting that a decade later, in 170 BCE, Zhao Tuo attacked the lands to the southwest, captured the Red River citadel at Co Loa and incorporated it into Nanyue. At present, archaeologists do not have any direct evidence of this campaign so the story of these battles contains some conjecture. Vietnamese writers in the fifteenth century gave the southern kingdom the name of "Au Lac" and called its king "An Duong." In those Vietnamese stories, the invaders triumphed and the king's magic crossbow was captured (see "Lord Lac, Au Co and Au Lac and the Hung Kings" on p. 39 for more details). It may well be that there was an historical leader such as "King An Duong" who controlled the citadel at Co Loa until he was defeated by the forces of Zhao Tuo but there is, as yet, no clear proof.

The legends cannot be completely dismissed, however. It is possible that they are based upon some degree of truth, albeit somewhat embellished over the centuries. It is also possible that, rather than fighting, the rulers of the Red River delta area may have accepted subordinate "vassal" status to Nanyue, in the same way that Nanyue submitted to Xi'an, in return for easier trade, military protection or to have a powerful backer in the competition among local warring groups.

Whatever the details, by the time of his death in 137 BCE, Zhao Tuo appears to have expanded Nanyue into the Red River delta and around the coastal plain. After this time, Han documents refer to the delta area with the name *Jiaozhi* and the area further south (modern-day Thanh Hoa province) as *Jiuzhen*. It seems, however, that it was a very "light touch" form of rule, with local leaders left to control (and reap the rewards from) the lands around them. In return they would have been obliged to send "tribute"—probably along the lines of exotic feathers and rhino horns—to the ruler of Nanyue in Panyu. The political arrangements appear to have been relatively stable because even after Zhao Tuo's death, the region enjoyed peace for another twenty years.

In 112 BCE the fourth ruler of Nanyue, Zhao Xing, the great-great-grandson of Zhao Tuo, was assassinated and the Han emperor Wu Di took advantage of the turmoil to bring the south under his control. Han forces followed in the footsteps of the Qin armies a century before and marched into Nanyue. Within a year, the Han had captured and burned down the capital, Panyu (the remains of the palace in Guangzhou clearly show a blackened layer dating to this time) and forced Zhao Xing to capitulate. However, it seems unlikely that Han forces actually occupied the whole of Nanyue. By the time they reached Hepu (modern day Beihai), the leaders of Jiaozhi and Jiuzhen had decided not to fight. Instead, they presented the commander of the invading force with "tribute" of 100 head of cattle and 1,000 measures of wine plus their census rolls to demonstrate their loyalty. There is an intriguing story in Han documents suggesting that one local ruler, described as the "King of the Western Region" (*Xiyu*) was executed during these events and that the executioner was later given a high position by the Han. It is possible that this king had opposed the surrender but was overthrown by his officials who preferred to throw in their lot with the Han rather than fight.

This then was the moment, in 111 BC, that the northern regions of what is now Vietnam became formally incorporated into the Han Empire. This event is sometimes described by modern Vietnamese as an epochal change in the history of the country, the point at which it was forced to submit to China: the beginning of an occupation that lasted for the next thousand years. At the time, however, it is unlikely that many people in Jiaozhi and Jiuzhen actually noticed. There was no invasion: life largely carried on as before. The biggest change was symbolic: local leaders would no longer send tribute to the ruler of Nanyue in Panyu, but to the Emperor of Han in Xi'an. Local administrative districts were created, but they continued to be controlled by existing local leaders. These leaders extracted tribute from the lands under their command: sending boats of armed men out along the rivers and streams to collect tithes, perhaps summoning villagers with the deep sound of the beating of bronze drums.

Each of the two "commanderies"—Jiaozhi (the Red River delta) and Jiuzhen (modern Thanh Hoa province)—was now ruled by a Han official known as a *taishou*. Five years after the takeover, in 106 BCE, the Han Empire created a new level of government called a *cishibu*— "provincial department"—to oversee the commanderies. Jiaozhi, Jiuzhen and the rest of the former Nanyue state were put under the supervision of a provincial department also called, confusingly, Jiaozhi. By this time, Han rule had extended south along what is now the central Vietnamese coast, perhaps as far south as the modern city of Hue, and a new commandery, Rinan, was created to administer it. Rinan commandery was also placed under the Jiaozhi Department. Even more confusingly, after a brief period in Jiaozhi Commandery, the headquarters of the Jiaozhi Department was moved out of Jiaozhi and placed in Guangxin (near present-day Wuzhou in Guangxi province, China). The confusion was reduced in 203 CE, when Jiaozhi Department was renamed Jiaozhou (*zhou* means "province" in Chinese).

For the next century, insofar as we can tell from the surviving records, life in the three commanderies of Jiaozhi, Jiuzhen and Rinan (known in Vietnamese as Giao Chi, Cuu Chan and Nhat Nam respectively) was largely peaceful. Blessed with fertile soils and in possession of sophisticated agricultural technology, their populations grew. Jiaozhi was the "rice basket" of the region: exporting grain in exchange for exotic goods. Jiaozhi merchants imported pearls and cowrie shells, some of which were then exported for much higher prices to other parts of the Han Empire in return for copper coins. Jiaozhi Commandery was a trading hub, ships headed to and from there, depending upon the seasonal monsoon winds. Jiuzhen, by contrast, was less integrated and less prosperous. Some of its inhabitants still lived by hunting and collecting, although others had developed more sophisticated industries: manufacturing bricks and tiles, for example, or crafting prestigious objects such as bronze drums. By the time of a census conducted in 2 CE, the combined population of the two northern commanderies was almost a million: around twice as much as the rest of Jiaozhi Department. Although there was some immigration from other places, it seems that most of this population growth was caused by the expansion of native households. The census tells us that households were larger here than other parts of the Han Empire: containing an average of six people (compared to four or five elsewhere).

In the early years of the first century CE, however, the situation in Jiaozhi Department rapidly deteriorated because of ructions far to the north. In 9 CE, the Han dynasty was overthrown by its military commander, Wang Mang, who declared himself the founder of a new dynasty, the Xin. He introduced radical land reforms and changes in taxation. The changes were so radical that they prompted dozens of uprisings against him. In 23 CE, Wang was overthrown, killed and replaced by a descendant of the earlier Han dynasty. This man, Liu Xuan, declared himself emperor of a restored Han Empire in 25 CE. The capital was moved east from Chang'an/Xi'an to Luoyang—giving the dynasty its alternative name: the "Eastern Han."

Very little had changed in Jiaozhi during Wang Mang's 14 years as emperor: the same officials continued to run the department. However, after the Eastern Han came to power, change was dramatic. The new rulers ordered the *taishou* (the commander) in each commandery to forcibly integrate the local population. In some places, schools were established to teach the new rules; marriage rituals were changed and hunter-gathering peoples were obliged to cultivate rice. We do not know how widespread these measures were, but the dynastic history of the Eastern Han (written 400 years later) described the policy as successful, claiming that it, "transformed the people by rites and justice." In Jiuzhen, we know of one official ordering all men between 20 and 50 and all women between 15 and 40 to be married in the Han style. This seems to have been an attempt to transform the basic arrangements of domestic life, forcing traditional extended families to become nuclear ones. As a result, the dynastic history said, the people were ordered "in the proper hierarchy." It sounds very much like the typical behavior of any empire, imposing its culture on a conquered society. The final straw may have been financial. There are clues in the texts that suggest the Han imposed new taxes on the traditional rulers. Taken together, all this "ordering" and "taxing" seems to have alienated the local population. In 40 CE, this unhappiness burst into open revolt under the leadership of a pair of sisters: the "two Trung women" or as they are known in Vietnamese *Hai Ba Trung* (pronounced Hi Ba Chung).

The Trung sisters, Trung Trac and Trung Nhi, were daughters of the lord of one of the ten districts in Jiaozhi, a place called Me Linh. Trung Trac was apparently married to a man named Thi Sach, son of the lord of another of those districts: Chu Dien. According to the dynastic history, the new *taishou* of Jiaozhi, a man named Su Ding, "restrained [Thi Sach] with the law." Su Ding may have been attempting to wrest control of a large area of productive land from the hands of the local elite, but the exact situation is not known. In a later Vietnamese version of the story, Su Ding killed Trung Trac's husband, but that detail does not appear in the Chinese version. However the fighting started, the outcome was brutally swift. The dynastic history reports that "the savages"—in Jiuzhen, Rinan—and also Hepu in modern-day China—responded to the sisters' call and plundered 65 settlements in a very short period. The fighting seems to have been an ethnic war: with people described as "Luo" in the Chinese texts rising up against Han administrators, soldiers and immigrants. Su Ding was chased out of Jiaozhi and Trung Trac ruled as queen for the next two years.

In the later part of 42 CE, once the rainy season had ended, one of the most experienced Han generals, Ma Yuan, was sent by the emperor to put down the rebellion. It was a bloody fight, lasting over a year. Troops from the Han heartland had great difficulty with the climate, the terrain and the malaria. Despite the difficulties, General Ma was victorious. According to the dynastic history, "he commandeered over 2,000 large and small towered ships and conquered over 20,000 enemy troops.... He killed or captured over 5,000 people, pacifying the entire region south of the passes [Lingnan]." Ma established his headquarters at Co Loa to sit out the wet season. When his forces were able to fight again, in mid 43 CE, they won a series of battles against the rebels: eventually capturing both Trung sisters and beheading them.

The dynastic history then goes on to explain Ma's pacification strategy, "He made cities and towns orderly and built canals and irrigation systems to benefit the people.... He had the old protocols (i.e., those from before Wang Mang's usurpation) clarified and spread out to the Yue people so as to restrain them. From that time on, the Luo-yue served and carried out General Ma's traditional ways of running affairs of the state." In particular, he enforced the old Han tribute protocols. According to the eminent historian of Vietnam Keith Taylor, local leaders were hunted down and forced to pledge loyalty or be executed. Clans who resisted were deported, strategic towns were fortified into garrisons and soldiers were settled on the land. It sounds remarkably similar to the methods used by much later empires to suppress rebellions in Asia or Africa.

In the aftermath of his victory, General Ma ordered that the bronze drums, which had previously been symbols of authority for the local elite, should be confiscated. In a highly symbolic move, many of them were melted down in order to cast statues of horses, some of which General Ma presented to the emperor. In recent years several buried drums have been discovered inscribed with Chinese characters indicating their weight. One was found inside the ramparts of Co Loa citadel, stuffed with other bronze objects as if it had been dumped before it could be destroyed. Others have been found in farmers' fields. It seems likely that all were earmarked for General Ma's melting down but somehow escaped the fire.

The general spent a year pacifying the southern commanderies before returning to the north. Many of his soldiers seem to have died of malaria or other diseases but he trained a local militia and a core of officials to suppress any future challenges to Han rule. The absence of records from the fifty years after his expedition suggests that there was very little for these new administrators to write home about. Instead we have to turn to archaeology to discover more about the Han culture that became embedded in Jiaozhi, Jiuzhen and Rinan during this period. The physical legacy includes around 50 graveyards comprising one or more tombs, built of brick and often filled with precious objects. As well as statues and bronze implements, they often contained clay models of buildings, presumably models of the homesteads the tombs' occupants once inhabited. In both form and contents the tombs were almost identical to thousands of others found elsewhere in the former Han Empire. It appears highly significant, however, that no bronze drums have ever been found in these brick tombs. This suggests that two different cultures existed alongside each other—Han brick tomb builders and Luo-Yue drum owners.

The locations of the tombs also tell us something about the Han imperial administration. Almost all the graveyards have been found at strategic points alongside rivers. There are particular concentrations along the Red River around Hanoi, the Bach Dang River near Haiphong and the Ma River in Thanh Hoa. The latter site is close to where the Dong Son drums were found, suggesting that the two cultures lived alongside each other. There was also a Han citadel much further to the south, at Tra Kieu next to the Bon River, just inland from the modern town of Hoi An. The pattern suggests that, throughout the first and second centuries CE, Han rule was concentrated along lowland waterways. The few surviving documents show distances between these outposts measured by water routes not by land. In other words, people travelled between them by boat.

The most important dividing line in this period was not between "Vietnam" and "China" but between lowland and highland or, perhaps, "river" and "inland." The historian Catherine Churchman has shown how the two river deltas: that of the Red River southeast of Hanoi and of the Pearl River south of Guangzhou, had far more in common culturally than either of them did with the high hills and mountains in between. The upland areas were a different world and the fear of hostile tribes and malaria kept lowlanders away. The lowlanders may not have understood how malaria was transmitted but they associated it with the "miasmas" they saw in the uplands: water vapor rising from the forests. As a result "lowland culture" rarely climbed more than about 100 meters above sea level and never above 200 meters before the modern era. The upland areas between the two river plains lay outside the reach of imperial administrations until the beginning of sixth century. Their inhabitants remained "wild" and untaxed. In a memorial to the imperial court in 231 CE, the governor of Jiaozhi, Xue Zong, described the uplands as "still not under our control" and a "lair for rebels and escapees." The inhabitants were, he believed, "incorrigible bandits." Despite this, valuable trade continued between the two areas: exotic forest products—bird feathers, rhino horn, elephant tusks and the like were exchanged for metal tools and rice from the lowlands. And the locations of the brick tombs tell us that rivers close to the hills were a particular focus of Han settlement, presumably because of the trading opportunities.

From the perspective of Han officials, there were three kinds of people living in what is now the northern part of Vietnam. There were people like themselves who had been sent there from other parts of the empire to work as administrators or soldiers, or who had migrated there in search of profit or sanctuary. There were also "uncivilized" "barbarians" who lived beyond the reach of Han rule, mainly in the uplands. The uplanders were a source of exotic goods but also of fear because of their refusal to acknowledge the emperor's rule. The Han called them *Li* or *Lao* or *Wuhu* but we do not know what they called themselves. They were not a single group but many different tribes divided by geography, language and culture. (We will find out more about them in the next chapter.) In the middle was a third group: indigenous people willing to live under Han rule who adopted "civilized" norms of behavior and performed the roles of local leaders, auxiliaries to the Han Empire and compradors in regional trading networks. But while these three groups may have been identifiable at particular points in time, they were not fixed or exclusive. Over time, individuals and families could leave one group and join another, depending upon where they lived, who they married, how they made a living and how they behaved.

From the texts they left behind, we know the Han officials wrote in Chinese characters and spoke a Sinitic language. From traces of words still found in modern-day languages, researchers believe the hill people spoke Austroasiatic or sometimes "Tai-Kadai" languages. They may have been descendants of the Hoabinhian peoples, or the inhabitants of the Man Bac or Dong Son cultures who had been pushed into the hills, or perhaps some combination. The third group, the urbanized indigenous people, were probably descendants of the inhabitants of the Co Loa citadel and its subsidiary settlements. It is likely that they also spoke an Austroasiatic language at home but would have been able to communicate with the other groups when necessary for trade, administration or other reasons. In Xue Zong's memorial of 231 CE, he also complained that, "Customs are not uniform and languages are not mutually intelligible, so that several interpreters are needed to communicate." It was from these tangled roots that the language we call Vietnamese would eventually emerge.

This basic social and political structure continued to exist in and around the river deltas for hundreds of years. It was only after the Tang Empire took power in the seventh century that the lowland administration was finally able to extend its control into the uplands. Until then, highland peoples continued to resist: occasionally bursting into the lowlands in revolt before being sent back again with a combination of political concessions and military force. In the meantime, the fortunes of Jiaozhi, Jiuzhen and Rinan rose and fell with the fluctuations in regional trade and the political fortunes of whichever empire happened to be controlling the area at the time.

So long as sailing technology remained basic, the Jiaozhi region provided the main hub for trade between the Han empire and Southeast Asia. Small ships sailed close to the coast to avoid treacherous winds and currents but could, nonetheless, travel far. Trading networks reached India, from where merchants are recorded as having arrived in 159 and 161 CE. In 166 CE an envoy from the Roman Empire is recorded as making an appearance in Jiaozhi. All this long-distance trade brought increased prosperity, and that enabled a rise in population. By 140 CE it was almost double what it had been in 2 CE.

Written records say the region was ruled from a place called "Long Bien" but it is still not entirely clear exactly where that was. The current theory is that an ancient earthwork in the village of Lung Khe, about 22 km due east of modern Hanoi (and about 20 km southeast of Co Loa) was its site. It became the capital of both the Jiaozhi Commandery and the Jiaozhi Department in 141 CE. Six decades later, in 203 CE, the capital of the Jiaozhi Department was moved east to Guangzhou. In 262 CE, local rule came back to Long Bien. The province was split in two: the Pearl River Delta became Guangzhou and the Red River Delta became Jiaozhou. Once again, Long Bien/Lung Khe became a provincial capital—and remained so until its administrative functions were moved away by the Sui empire around 605 CE.

Today the Lung Khe citadel sits on a small hill, about 3 km south of the Duong River. Earthen banks form a large, irregular rectangle: 600 meters long by about 300 meters wide. Inside the ramparts, archaeologists have discovered roof tiles inscribed with Chinese characters dating from the Han period and objects indicating the site was once the residence of Shi Xie (known in Vietnamese as Si Nhiep). He was the governor of the Jiaozhi Department from around 187 CE until his death in 226. He is famed for having maintained some kind of order during those forty years, even as the Han empire collapsed to the north. He did this, in part, by appointing his brothers to run Jiuzhen and Guangzhou. However, even this family firm was unable to prevent the southern part of Rinan breaking away from the Han state in 192 CE. The wealth generated by long-distance trade must have been attractive for local leaders with dreams of independence. By 220 CE scribes in Jiaozhi were referring to southern parts of Rinan as the independent state of "Linyi" (or, in Sino-Vietnamese, Lam Ap).

In 220 CE, the Han Empire fragmented. A new state, called Wu, with its capital in present-day Nanjing, took control of the south. Shi Xie tried to maneuver himself into favor with the new rulers but they were not willing to tolerate such a strong rival on their southern flank. Shortly after Shi Xie died in 226, Wu sent an army to take control of the region and eliminate Shi Xie's family. Ill will seems to have lingered: surviving texts tell us there were rebellions against Wu in both Jiaozhou and Jiuzhen in 248 CE. Traditional stories say one of the rebel leaders was an extraordinarily-proportioned woman known to Vietnamese as "Ba Trieu"—Lady Trieu. There is no contemporary evidence that she ever actually existed but she has entered the pantheon of Vietnamese heroes nonetheless. Instead of a rebellion, Wu records tell us more about their officials' success in bribing the rebellious leaders to give up their fight and settle down. The real winner of the rebellion seems to have been Linyi which, in the chaos, expanded its territory by seizing the northern part of Rinan.

In 280, Wu was defeated by a rival state called Jin, which went on to occupy Wu's lands to the south, and hold them until its own demise in 420. This period saw a downturn for the fortunes of Jiaozhou and Jiuzhen. This was partly driven by improvements in sailing technology and nautical knowledge, which allowed merchants to sail more confidently across the open sea, away from the coast. Bold navigators from South and Southeast Asia, Persia and Arabia started sailing directly across the South China Sea between harbors in Linyi and Guangzhou. They travelled around the eastern end of Hainan Island, thereby avoiding the necessity of stopping in Jiaozhou. This cut the northern commanderies out of the regional trade network and they lost much of their strategic importance and wealth. We can see the consequences in population statistics. In the Jin census of 280 CE, Jiaozhi province had more tax-paying households than any other commandery in the region. By the time of another census in 464 CE, the figures had dropped by more than half. Archaeologists have also noted a decline in the number of brick tombs being constructed during this period, and their concentration in the area immediately around the modern cities of Hanoi and Bac Ninh. Taken together, this suggests that migration from the rest of the empire went into steep decline. Nonetheless, Jiaozhou province, the northern lowland part of what is now Vietnam, remained well integrated into the state to its north.

Ly Truong Nhan & Ly Nam De (420–900)

In 420 CE, the last ruler of the Jin state was overthrown by his military commander. The commander then declared himself the founder of a new dynasty: the Liu-Song. This, however, was just the first of four "southern dynasties" that ruled southern parts of what is now China over the following 170 years. Each was less successful than the one before, with palace coups taking place on average every 35 years. As a result, there was less attention paid to developments on the frontiers. In Jiaozhou, locals began to assert more independent control, taking power away from administrators sent by the imperial capital. Some officials were able to hire their relatives and pass on power to their children, creating a family-based elite. This was not, in itself, unusual for the period—other officials in other parts of the empire did similar things. The difference in Jiaozhou was that its remoteness allowed such disobedience to last longer.

The situation on Jiaozhou's southern frontier, however, became more desperate, with Linyi (land that had once been the old commandery of Rinan/Nhat Nam) making increasingly confident attacks. In 443 CE, Jiaozhou's governor was ordered by the Liu-Song emperor to prepare an invasion force to end the problem. Three years later, his army marched into Linyi, destroyed its citadels and smashed its military. The booty which the invaders carried home to Jiaozhou created the foundations for a new period of prosperity in the province. The situation in Linyi was reversed: the invasion triggered a period of decline. The war also created a *de facto* boundary between a "Sinicized" northern area and a culturally different south. The frontier was formed by an obvious dividing line: a line of hills spurring east from the main north-south axis of the Annamite mountains which reaches the sea just north of the modern city of Danang. To cross these formidable hills requires ascending to the Hai Van Pass, 500 meters above sea level: a route that was relatively easy to defend. It remained an enduring dividing line for centuries.

In 468, the centrally-appointed governor of Jiaozhou, a man called Liu Mu, died. Rather than wait for the emperor to choose a successor, a local warlord called Ly Truong Nhan killed off the remaining loyalist officials and declared himself the new governor. When Nhan died three years later, his nephew Ly Thuc Hien took power. He was still in charge when the second of the southern dynasties, the Qi, took power in 479. Rather than sending an army to punish Ly Thuc Hien, the Qi emperor decided to just recognize the usurper and formally appoint him governor. Officials noted that Jiaozhou produced valuable and exotic produce. It was better to keep the trade flowing than demand too much obedience. However, six years later in 485, the Qi emperor's patience ran out and he dispatched an army to accompany a new governor for the province. The Ly family's 17-year reign was over.

By the time the "Book of the Southern Qi" (*Nan Qi Shu*) was written, around 510 CE, Jiaozhou was being described as "a completely isolated island which controls the outer lands and as a consequence of this it frequently relies on its strategic position not to submit to authority." It was seen as an "island" because it was not connected to the rest of the empire. The central government did not control the highlands between Guangzhou and Jiaozhou (along the modern China–Vietnam border). It was not independent state so much as an insubordinate one: a naughty child that needed to be taught a lesson and returned to the family.

Some officials were more loyal than others. In the 520s, two men from elite families travelled to Nanjing to lobby the imperial court (now ruled by the Liang Dynasty) for important positions. Ly Bi (sometimes known as Ly Bon) came from a line of military commanders and Tinh Thieu was a scholar. Both were, however, snubbed by the officials in the capital. They returned home and nurtured a sense of grievance. When the Liang state attempted to impose a nephew of the emperor as inspector of Jiaozhou, others became equally aggrieved. By 541 the two men had assembled enough supporters to launch a rebellion. They drove out the imperial governor, who paid a bribe to be allowed to escape, and took over the provincial capital at Long Bien. There they began dreaming of bigger things. In 544, Ly Bi declared himself "Emperor of the South" (Rendered as *Ly Nam De* in modern Vietnamese) and named his state "Eternal Spring" or *Van Xuan*. By choosing to call himself Emperor of the *South*, Ly Bi was deliberately adopting a southern identity, but it was one that had actually been created by "Chinese" administrators and chroniclers over the previous centuries. In other words Ly Bi was both a local ruler geographically and a "Chinese" one culturally. Indeed, contemporary Chinese accounts of the events do not describe him as a foreigner, just as a rebel.

In the end, Ly Bi's reign as Ly Nam De lasted just four years. In 545 the army of the larger empire to the north marched into Jiaozhou and forced him to flee into the hills, where he was apparently killed by uplanders. A relative of Ly's asserted power in the southern part of Jiaozhou, while a rival moved to control the Red River Delta. When the (Chinese) Liang Dynasty was overthrown in 557 (by the same military commander who had dispatched Ly Bi), the two rivals reached a truce. By 570, however, the Ly family had managed to achieve domination over the whole province. It was largely left alone during the last years of the "southern Dynasties" as the Liang was displaced by the Chen, and then as the Chen was defeated by the Sui in 589. At this point, for the first time since 420 CE, a single emperor controlled most of continental East Asia, from the Inner Asian plains to the southern coast. In 602, the Sui mounted another military operation into the south—ending the sixty-year rule of the Ly clan and bringing Jiaozhou back under central control. For good measure, the Sui army headed further south and wreaked yet more devastation along the frontier with Linyi.

Despite his success in expanding territory and enforcing stability, the Sui emperor was deposed by his cousin in 618. The cousin then declared himself the founder of the Tang Dynasty. The Tang would rule for the following three centuries, the first two of which were relatively peaceful and the final one increasingly lawless. As in previous transitions, little changed in Jiaozhou at first. Sui officials simply pledged allegiance to the new rulers and the region became reintegrated into a northern empire, albeit on a new basis. In 627, the empire was reorganized and the area of Lingnan (including the modern Chinese provinces of Guangdong and Guangxi plus the lowlands of northern Vietnam) became one of ten administrative "circuits." Tang administrators set to work opening up new land for cultivation south of the Red River by building earthworks to control floods and facilitate irrigation. This new agricultural land was then distributed to a larger share of the population, in exchange for an obligation to provide troops for the imperial governor. It was a smart move: weakening the power of the established landholding families in the province and enhancing the power of the emperor.

Another sign of the shift in power was the relocation of the provincial capital, Most of the powerful families had their lands on the northern side of the Red River, whereas most of the newly-opened land was to the south of it. This seems to explain why the Tang moved their administration away from the citadel at Long Bien and, created a new one on the southern bank, on the site of what is now Hanoi. It was a good position strategically, as well as politically. It is where the Red River divides at the head of its delta, and is just upstream from the influence of sea tides, even during the dry season. The name of the location changed several times over subsequent centuries, but some of the longest-lasting were *La Thanh* and *Dai La*. As the historian Keith Taylor has noted, most of the names made reference to a wall, perhaps to the dykes that held back the river in flood.

Jiaozhou remained generally prosperous, continuing to export exotic products, but it was no longer the hub of regional trade. It became a bit of a backwater, overshadowed by its neighbor Guangzhou. The overall number of taxable households in Jiaozhou and the areas to the south remained steady at around 40,000 for the following few centuries while the number in Guangzhou increased rapidly. Since only between ten and thirty percent of households paid taxes, the census suggests a total population under Tang administration at somewhere between 150,000 and 400,000.

The empire was urban: its power was strongest in towns, garrisons and ports and it weakened with both distance from "civilization" and height above sea level. From the Tang perspective there were three main kinds of local inhabitant. There were *ren*—"people"—those who accepted imperial rule and lived peaceably in cities. There were *li*—mostly those who lived in the uplands immediately surrounding the deltas. *Li* maintained their own way of life but were willing to make arrangements with the imperial bureaucracy, such as a formal pledge of allegiance, as the price of being left alone. Thirdly, there were people described as *lao*, mainly those with independent resources and connections to the world beyond the empire, who continued to resist and rebel.

In 679, as a result of a series of crises along many different parts of the Tang empire's frontier, the province, along with several others, was recategorized as a "protectorate"—a special region requiring a combination of civilian and military rule. Jiaozhou was given a new name, one that would last for more than a millennium. It became *Annan duhu fu*—the "Protectorate of the Pacified South." *Annan*, or *Annam* in the Vietnamese spelling, endured as a name for the region as late as the twentieth century.

This special status aside, Annan was as much part of the Tang Empire as the rest of the Lingnan region. It was possible, for example, for capable officials from the protectorate to reach high positions within the imperial system. The empire's authority, was not, however, evenly distributed. At the start of the Tang period, the mountains near the deltas were largely beyond the reach of lowland administration, and were only gradually incorporated into the empire over the following centuries. The southern frontier with Linyi continued to be difficult. It was a place that required frequent "soothing" and "comforting" according to records of the time. The southern frontier situation would become even less comfortable for the Tang, particularly after the emergence of a new state, Champa, further to south. (There is more on Champa and the mountains in the following chapter.)

Bureaucrats and soldiers from northern parts of the Tang empire feared the dangers of the south: bandits, mountains and malaria were deadly; local morality could corrupt and the climate was exhausting. It was a sign of how poorly regarded the southern provinces were that disgraced officials were often sent there as a punishment for particularly egregious crimes. On the other hand, it produced gold and silver handicrafts, precious goods from the forests and other exotic treasures for sale. Bananas, shark skins (for covering sword handles), snake bile and kingfisher feathers were much prized in the imperial heartland. There was also a valuable trade in enslaved peoples: presumably uplanders who were captured and sent to work as forced labor elsewhere in the empire. A good administrator, or a corrupt one, could make a lot of money.

In the second half of the ninth century, as the Tang Dynasty weakened at its center, new challenges emerged on both the northern and southern frontiers of Annan. In what is now the Chinese province of Yunnan, an independent state known as Nanzhao started to expand its power. This area had been, many centuries before, the source of the bronze culture that had introduced drums into the region. In 860 Nanzhao expanded south from its highland base and down the Red River valley. In 863 it sacked the Annan capital, Dai La, and forced the Tang administration to leave the province. Thousands were killed, their properties were ransacked and hordes of refugees fled into Guangzhou. The situation was sufficiently desperate for the Tang to call upon one

of their most experienced commanders, Gao Pian (Cao Bien in Vietnamese) to retake Annan. He spent two years training and preparing
an army before finally defeating Nanzhao in 866. Some reports say that
in the aftermath he executed 30,000 of Nanzhao's fighters.

After his victory, Gao Pian/Cao Bien spent three years overseeing
the reconstruction of Annan. He ordered the rebuilding of the citadel,
on a much grander scale than before; the extension of the road network;
the repair of irrigation and flood protection ditches and dykes and other
improvements designed to strengthen imperial control over the whole
of Annan—including the frontier region to the south. He also seems to
have invented a series of folk tales about himself and his relationship
with the spirit world to legitimize his position of authority and
strengthen the connection between Annan and the rest of the empire.
These tales were so powerful that Gao Pian/Cao Bien is still remembered in northern Vietnam as a great social improver: one who restored
order, pacified the people and imposed a fair administration. This,
however, was the last flourish of the Tang.

Almost as soon as Gao Pian departed, in 868, a Tang garrison in the
south of Annan mutinied. It was easy to see why. Its troops, originally
from near Nanjing in China, had spent six years on active duty there.
As the empire continued to weaken, centrifugal forces continued to
strengthen. In 880, another mutiny prompted the Tang to withdraw all
its forces from Annan. Once again, local elites began to assert their
power. They may have paid formal tribute to the emperor but they were
largely left alone to rule the region in the way they saw fit. When the
Tang finally collapsed in 907, another dynasty overthrown by its own
military commander, little changed for the rulers of Annan. They made
symbolic pledges of loyalty to the successor regime, which called itself
the Liang (known by historians as the Later Liang to avoid confusion
with the first Liang dynasty) but carried on as they had done before
with little change. However, this period of autonomy would, within
decades, create the conditions for a more radical change in regional
politics: setting the Red River Delta and its surroundings on the road
to independence.

Lord Lac, Au Co and Au Lac and the Hung Kings

In Vietnamese mythology, the founders of the country were a couple: the "dragon lord" Lac Long Quan and the "fairy princess" Au Co. They are reputed to have lived well before the time of the Han Dynasty (i.e., around 2000 BCE) but to have descended from the same ancestor as the Han: Shennong, a tribal chieftain from the Yellow River region in what is now China.

According to the legend, Lord Lac Long Quan was from the lowlands, while Princess Au Co came from the hills. King Lac's father was King Duong Vuong but his mother was a dragon. Au Co was an immortal mountain fairy. The union of these two semi-magical figures produced an egg sac containing 100 sons. As a result, Vietnamese sometimes refer to themselves as "Children of the fairy, Grandchildren of the dragon."

Although the king and the queen loved one another very much, they were unable to live in each other's world. They separated and each took half their brood with them. Lord Lac and his 50 sons chose to remain in the lowlands and become fishermen while Princess Au Co and the other 50 moved to the hills

The oldest and strongest of their sons was Hung Vuong, the founder of the dynasty that became known as the "Hung Kings." He founded a kingdom called "Van Lang" which endured for 18 generations of "Hung Kings" until it was toppled by King An Duong, the ruler of "Au Lac." King An Duong then ruled until he was defeated by Zhao Tuo, the "emperor" of the state of Nanyue.

There is plenty of evidence for the historical existence of Zhao Tuo but very little for the other figures in this story. The earliest known Vietnamese account of the legend of Lord Lac and Au Co and their descendants dates from the thirteenth century and was probably created from collections of myths and stories in order to bolster the idea of a unified kingdom incorporating the lowlands and the hills.

Although modern archaeologists are very skeptical of the legend, the Vietnamese authorities teach the story of the Hung Kings in schools, celebrate an annual "Hung Kings Festival" as public holiday on the tenth day of the third lunar month and organize pilgrimages to the Hung Kings Temple in Phu Tho Province, northeast of Hanoi.

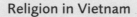

Religion in Vietnam

The divisions between religions and religious groups are far less clear in Vietnam than in Europe or the Americas. Although some Vietnamese may define themselves as, for example, purely Buddhist, others will be happy praying in a Buddhist pagoda in the morning, consulting a Daoist fortune-teller in the afternoon and making offerings on their ancestors' altar in the evening while also claiming to observe the tenets of Confucianism. There are tensions between all these belief systems but also a tacit acceptance that believers can move between them—and also others—without problem.

These days, "spirit worship" is regarded as the national belief system, something uniquely Vietnamese, although only around half the population practices it. It combines the honoring of family ancestors with prayers and offerings to the "guardian spirits" of particular places or of particular groups—such as mothers or students facing exams. It is not a fixed set of practices but varies from village to village and family to family. Some believers may consult "mediums" who claim to be able to channel spirits' voices at temple ceremonies. Others may worship the Mother Goddess.

Arguments rage over whether Confucianism and Daoism (sometimes written Taoism) are "religions" or philosophies. Both stress the importance of "heaven" but both are primarily concerned with personal behavior. Confucianism emphasizes hierarchy, order and rules whereas Daoism emphasizes simplicity, harmony and naturalness. Both sets of ideas were developed in the area of what is now the Yellow River in China and spread from there to other parts of East Asia. It is easy to see why many rulers chose to propagate Confucianism: it reinforced their political authority with the power of morality. It was introduced to Jiaozhi with the Han invasion and has been embedded in lowland areas ever since. In successive royal courts it was deployed as a tool to keep courtiers in check by obliging them to follow instructions and provided a basis for a well-ordered village society too.

Daoism was popular with rulers of the Tang Dynasty and probably arrived in Vietnam in the seventh century. Daoism can also invoke local spirits and there were many examples of Tang officials co-opting local beliefs into Daoism and fusing the two. This presumably helped officials from Tang China to exert control over potentially rebellious local people. As a result Daoism became strongly intermingled with spirit worship to the extent that these days it is hard to discern a separate Daoism in Vietnam.

Buddhism probably arrived in Funan and Champa (in what is now southern Vietnam) from India in the first century CE. Later missionary activities also brought Buddhism overland into what is now northern Vietnam from China. Buddhism became important to Vietnam's rulers with the founding of the Ly Dynasty in 1009. The Buddhist elite were the power behind the throne, facilitating the rise of the new king and enjoying a symbiotic relationship with the court. The thirteenth century Tran dynasty was also Buddhist but used Confucianism as a tool to manage government affairs.

Upland groups largely follow their own practices, often involving forms of spirit worship and shamans. Some of them have left their mark in lowland beliefs too. There is very little that can be described as a "pure" religious belief in Vietnam. Everything is in a constant state of flux, with beliefs and practices being added to, modified and hybridized according to the whim of the community or the believer.

CHAPTER 2

OTHER WORLDS: MOUNTAINS AND COASTS

Dong World

T he source of the Ma River lies in the hills northwest of the modern city of Thanh Hoa. To get there, a traveller must head upstream from the village where the Dong Son drums were discovered. Initially, they would follow the river's winding course through the wide open spaces of the river's delta. Somewhere near the town of Vinh Loc, the traveller would see low hills rising from the plain and, gradually, they would notice the river become enclosed by higher ground on both sides. The river becomes shallower and eventually unnavigable. Continuing northwest, the hills grow taller and the wide valley narrows. The main roads squeeze closer to the river banks and the names of the settlements start to change. Lowland names like Thanh, Hoa, Vinh and Loc are replaced by upland ones like Xom and Ban. The clothing of local people changes, with occasional flashes of brightly colored headdresses or embroidered tunics and, in places, houses rise up on stilts, quite distinct from the brick-built homes of the lowlands.

At a bend in the river, around 120 km from Thanh Hoa and around 100 meters above sea level, a tributary branches off to the east, running through a gap in the hills that opens out into a wide, flat-bottomed valley: a hidden world of rich rice fields and forested hills, small villages of stilt houses and a network of tracks trodden by farmers and buffalo. The river branches into small streams, one of which leads to the settlement of Mai Chau. Now a popular tourist site, just a couple of hours' drive from Hanoi, Mai Chau provides an easy glimpse into a different Vietnamese history. It demonstrates that, two thousand years after the northern lowlands were incorporated into an imperial state, the uplands still follow a different way of life.

The "hidden" valley of Mai Chau is what is known in the Tai language, as a *djong*: an area of level ground beside a stream and between cliffs. At some point over the previous two millennia, the term was adopted by imperial administrators who rendered it as *dong*. Historians now use this term to refer to a "dong world"—the upland area along what are now the borders between China and Southeast Asian countries. "Dong World," so defined, is vast: covering an area from Yunnan province in the north to Chiang Mai in Thailand in the south, and from the borders of Bangladesh in the west to Guangxi province in the east. Piecing together its history has been difficult since there are few written records but researchers now believe the peoples of Dong World maintained separate identities until they were forcibly incorporated into lowland states over the last thousand years.

Different ethnic groups seem to have found different "ecological niches" in the uplands. The Tai mastered rice growing on the valley floor. Other groups lived in the forests on the mountain sides. Some, such as the Hmong, learnt how to engineer the hills, creating the spectacular rice terraces that dominate the landscapes at higher altitudes. The difficulties of crossing the high hills between the valleys created the conditions for many separate chiefdoms to exist in a relatively small area. The result has been a patchwork of peoples, cultures and languages: some connected and others quite distinct. Living in a landscape characterized by poor access and challenging climates, they have always posed a tricky problem for lowland states, from the earliest days of imperial expansion right up until today. Fear of disease, "bad air" and bandits deterred administrators from interfering until the Mongols smashed down the door of "Dong World" in the thirteenth century. Even then, lowlanders were obliged to deal with local leaders and rule through "arms length" arrangements until they had sufficient resources and resolve to incorporate these "wild" peoples into their "civilized" states.

The Tai language is thought to have developed in what is now the mountains of Guangxi Province in China around two thousand years ago (and is closely related to languages spoken in present-day Laos and Thailand). Over the following centuries, organized groups of Tai-speakers built up sufficient resources there to form a powerful state stretching from the uplands of Yunnan in the north to the hills over-looking modern-day Thanh Hoa in the south: encircling the Red River Delta. This was the kingdom of Nanzhao, the state that sacked the An-nan capital, Dai La, in 863 and then fought a protracted campaign against the Tang administration before retreating to the hills. A Tang chronicle of the time is called the *Manshu*—literally, "The Book of Sav-ages" but while the Tai appeared as "savages" to the lowlanders, their society was actually politically and economically sophisticated.

An aristocratic elite organized food production in rice fields along valley floors. They marshaled their subjects to manage irrigation ditches and repair flood damage; they levied taxes from the hunting of animals and the gathering of forest products; and they imposed a mo-nopoly on the export of rare products such as minerals, rhino horn or rare plants. They used bronze drums as symbols of authority and, from time to time, worked with other chieftains to resist invasions from out-side. It was a form of society that had once existed in the Red River Delta but had been destroyed there by the imposition of Han control after 43 CE following the Trung Sisters' uprising.

Such societies seem to have existed for a long time in the upland areas. The archaeologist Alice Yao and her colleagues have found evi-dence of a sophisticated culture, which used pottery and bronze tools, around the shores of Lake Dian (near the modern Chinese city of Kun-ming) dating back to the sixth century BCE. There is evidence of rice paddy systems dating from the second century BCE and for less sophis-ticated cultivation of rice, wheat, barley and millet dating back much further. Excavations have also uncovered "royal" burials higher up the surrounding hills containing extravagantly-decorated containers for cowrie shells, drums and weapons, all made of bronze. They found the sites of many settlements around the edge of the lake, leading them to the conclusion that there were several different "chiefdoms" of similar power and prestige in the sixth century BCE. However, by the third century BCE they appeared to have been eclipsed by a single "capital" site. By then, according to estimates found in Han records, the ruler could command an army of 30,000 warriors.

These "prestige" burials also contained precious objects from South and Southeast Asia as well as areas to the north and east. It seems that the early inhabitants of "Dong World" were at the center of overland trading networks that extended for thousands of miles. Being high in the mountains, 1800 meters above sea level, settlements around Lake Dian were well placed to connect with routes radiating along the valleys of the Yangtze, Red, Mekong, Salween and Irrawaddy rivers. Controlling the passes through the mountains enabled Dian chieftains to impose taxes on goods and people passing through them, or to cut off supplies when they wanted to pressure those in the lowlands. For the most part, however, the uplanders thrived because of their connections with those at lower altitudes. "Dong World" was a distinct ecological and social space but it was not an economic island.

The complex geology of the uplands endowed them with considerable mineral wealth: gold, silver, tin, lead and copper. The Han period historian Sima Qian noted that people living in the area west of Lake Dian (i.e., modern-day Yunnan province) had grown rich from the trade in horses, cattle, buffalo and enslaved people. Horses had been introduced to the region from Central Asia but local people learned to breed them so successfully, that Yunnan horses became famous in South and Southeast Asia. One indication of the area's success in raising livestock was an account of a battle in 82 BCE, after which Han forces stole over 100,000 heads of cattle from the highlanders. Slaves were captured from neighboring clans or traded for other commodities or paid for in cowrie shells.

The Dian State was extinguished in 109 BCE when it was conquered by the Han, just three years after the empire had invaded the coastal state of Nanyue. A decline in traditional burials after this time suggests the Han quickly imposed lowland culture on their new subjects. However, there is also evidence that the mountain people continued to resist, with many reports of rebellions in the area over the following three centuries. It is possible that those who did not wish to be ruled by the Han moved further south and west, deeper into Dong World and closer to the hills around the Red River delta.

The end of the Han state in 220 CE led to three centuries of political fragmentation. Various successor states tried to reimpose lowland control over the uplands but only managed to do so for brief periods. One well-known effort by a commander called Zhuge Liang on behalf of the Shu Han in 225 CE resulted in his discovering that it was impossible: he didn't have the necessary manpower. Instead, he was obliged to recognize that he could not dislodge local leaders. He simply invested them with formal titles and pretended that they were ruling on behalf of the emperor. These ruling families become known as the "Great Clans of Nanzhong"—the area comprising the modern-day Chinese provinces of Yunnan, Guizhou and southern Sichuan. While most Chinese sources like to claim that these families arrived from various parts of the crumbling Han empire, leading historian of this area, Jamie Anderson believes that it is more likely that they were either native to the region and claimed distant ancestry to enhance their status, or individuals who developed ties with locally influential indigenous clans.

The Yunnan region fell under the domination of the Cuan clan, which, during the "Period of Disunion" (420 to 589 CE) accepted official alliances with a variety of lowland "Chinese" courts but abandoned them whenever they felt greater autonomy benefited them. These were not isolated mountain strongholds but polities with active trading and political links to the regions around them. They bred animals, mined minerals and produced sophisticated manufactures—such as bronze drums and textured ceramics—and earned wealth through their connections with the wider world. It is likely that the region of what is now upland Vietnam would have been characterized by similarly autonomous statelets during this period, although we know less about them. This cultural and economic pattern probably characterized the whole of the "Dong World."

Lowland imperial administrations continued to assert an official fiction that these areas were incorporated within their rule but we can tell from the absence of detailed records that actual control remained with upland leaders. In the late third century, the local governor of the area which included the uplands east of the Red River Delta estimated that they contained around 50,000 unregistered households: two-and-a-half times the size of the registered population in the delta. These upland people were generally called "bandits" or "barbarians"—*Li, Lao* or *Man*—by those writing in Chinese, and they were feared by officials. These officials left accounts of attacks by *Li* groups involving several thousand warriors. At times, alliances among chieftains could bring even larger armies to the fight.

This chieftain-based form of society had once existed in the lowlands before the Trung Sisters' revolt in 40 CE. The crushing of that uprising by General Ma Yuan led to its eradication there, whereas in the highlands it continued for at least another five centuries. It was only when the (Chinese) Southern Liang state came into existence in the early sixth century that a serious effort was made to bring the uplands under central state control. What were described as "pacification" operations slowly brought the "bandits" and "barbarians" into the "civilized" world.

In 729, a new state was formed in Yunnan, calling itself Nanzhao. It was led by people who spoke a Tai language and who were able to crush the old Cuan chief and assert control over a wide area of the highlands. Nanzhao became sufficiently powerful to threaten the lowland provinces of Tang China to both north and south. Other upland groups who were not formally part of Nanzhao sometimes allied with it for mutual protection when lowlanders attacked. As we saw in the previous chapter, Nanzhao was able to overrun and loot the Annan capital, Dai La, in 863 and force Tang administrators to leave the province. However, the revenge of the Tang army three years later resulted in the routing of Nanzhao's forces and the execution of as many as 30,000 of its fighters. Despite this reverse, Nanzhao remained in existence until 902 and Tai chieftains in the uplands to the north and west of the Red River Delta continued to pose a threat to lowland governors.

As we shall see in the next chapter, an independent state, eventually to be called Dai Viet began to emerge in the Red River Delta during the tenth century. This would have significant implications for the uplands. In 937, three decades after the demise of Nanzhao, another Tai-based upland state emerged in the same region: the Dali kingdom, led by another clan, the Duan family. Like its predecessor it operated as an independent state, although the family later pledged loyalty to the Song state and received an official title in exchange. Most of its political activity, however, was focused on managing a coalition of regional chiefdoms. In 971, 37 of them met the Dali leadership to form an alliance, which brought Dali's frontiers right to the lands of Dai Viet, an arrangement that largely endured until Dali was invaded and occupied by the Mongols in 1253.

The main exception to this was a rebellion in a part of Dong World controlled by the Nung people (also Tai-speakers) in the mountains north of the Red River plain. In 1042, a chieftain known in Vietnamese as Nung Tri Cao (Nong Zhigao in Chinese), together with his mother and their troops seized control of the prefecture of Thang Do. He declared himself to be an independent ruler of a state also called Dali (but distinct from the original) straddling the border of what is now China's Guangxi province and northern Vietnam. It was a clear challenge to both the Song Empire and Dai Viet. The Dai Viet ruler, Ly Thai Tong (about whom we will hear more in the next chapter) issued a "Proclamation to Pacify the Nung" threatening to have Nung Tri Cao and his supporters beheaded. The Dai Viet forces succeeded in capturing the Tai leader but rather than executing him, tried to bind him into their "world" by giving him an official title and making him a vassal. Almost immediately, however, Nung Tri Cao declared another independent kingdom. The Dai Viet troops drove him deeper into the hills but he returned in 1052 and made a third attempt to create a separate state, triggering a regional rebellion. His eventual fate is unknown. Chinese records say he was killed, while Nung mythology says he escaped to what is now northern Thailand. Nung Tri Cao was exceptional and his pretensions were too grand for the lowland ruler of Dai Viet to tolerate. Elsewhere in the uplands, other Tai-speaking statelets maintained their autonomy more carefully by balancing their relations between the rival lowland states and the Dali kingdom. This way of doing politics came to an end when the Mongols swept into the hills, but autonomous fiefs would continue to exist in the uplands for many centuries more.

In the early part of the fourteenth century, two Tai polities grew strong enough to once again threaten the Red River plain. One was known as the "Twelve Tai Districts" (Sipsong Chu Tai), in what is now Yen Bai Province in Vietnam to the west of Hanoi, and was ruled by the "Black Tai" people. The other was "Ai-lao" which stretched across parts of Nghe An province and Houaphanh province in Laos. Fighting began in the 1320s and, in 1335, the Dai Viet king Tran Minh Tong personally commanded six armies in an offensive against Ai Lo but they were all beaten back. With Dai Viet's weakness continuing for another century, the Tai polities were largely left to their own autonomy. Things would only begin to change in the early fifteenth century.

>⁓<

Funan

Deep in the flatlands of the Mekong Delta, a cluster of small hills breaks the horizon. The lower slopes of the southernmost park, Mount Ba The, are covered with houses. Local people have learned that this is a safe spot when the floods come. From the summit, about 200 meters high, paddy fields stretch into the distance, crisscrossed by a network of canals. On a clear day, it is possible to see the sea, 25 km to the west. Mount Ba The is an obvious reference point in this wetland plain. It is easy to understand why people have clustered here over millennia—for safety from the elements and defense against marauding strangers.

In the middle of the farmers' fields about a kilometer southeast of Mount Ba The, plastic roofing protects the remains of a 2,000-year-old settlement found beneath a small hillock known locally as "Oc Eo." Under the soil, archeologists discovered solid evidence of what has become known as the "Funan" civilization. Fu-nan is the modern pronunciation of Chinese characters that were once pronounced biu-nam—an approximation of an old word in the Khmer language *bnam*, now pronounced *phnom* and meaning "mountain." We don't know what the people called themselves, but Funan was the name used in Chinese court documents to record "tribute" missions from this faraway place on the tip of Indochina, the region where the Mekong River meets the sea. This "Funan" was once a crucial node in the trade between South, East and Southeast Asia. Ships sailing from India, blown by the monsoon winds would stop, resupply and trade here before the seasons changed and the winds could either blow them home again or onwards to the next entrepôt. Funan's fame spread around the world, perhaps as far as Europe. The Greek-Roman geographer Ptolemy mentions a port named "Cattigara" in the second century which may be a reference to Funan. The discovery of Roman coins from that period at the Oc Eo site gives the idea some credibility.

Archaeologists have now identified more than 90 sites connected to the Oc Eo/Funan culture across the Mekong Delta. These may have formed part of a single political unit or something less organized. The presence of hills may have been important for more than just flood protection. Brick structures have been discovered on the summits, suggesting they had some kind of religious or ritual meaning.

The location of Oc Eo—by waterways with good access to the open sea and, via the Mekong, to settlements inland—is very similar to that of some much older settlements discovered in the same region. Archeologists have excavated several sites, some dating from before 2000 BCE and others from the Bronze and Iron Ages (1000 BCE–500 CE) in the deltas of the Mekong, Saigon and Dong Nai rivers. These are all in areas of fertile land, a short distance (perhaps 10 km) behind where the coast would have been during the time they were occupied. Archaeologists have found many similarities between the styles of pottery and other household objects (such as beads) uncovered in these sites and those found in sites of similar age in modern-day Cambodia and Thailand. The objects appear to be significantly different from pieces found in northern Vietnam, such as the "Phung Nguyen" Bronze Age sites mentioned in Chapter 1. But the people who lived in Oc Eo may actually have migrated from such places. Skeletons discovered at the site have similarities with burials found in northern Vietnam and southern China. Preserved grains suggest the occupants of these sites grew a variety of rice originally domesticated in the Yangtze Valley. Taken together, the implication of these discoveries is that the ancestors of the people who lived in sites such as Oc Eo or An Son, northwest of Ho Chi Minh City, migrated from what is now China and initially lived alongside people already living in the flatlands. Then, from around 2500 BCE, they created what amounted to a shared "Mekong Valley" cultural community that was different to the one existing in the Red River Delta.

The archaeological evidence suggests there was trade and communication between the various settlements and the nature of the landscape suggests that most transportation would have been by boat through the marshes and along the waterways. During the first century

CE, however, the nature of the settlements appears to have changed. At Oc Eo, there is evidence that the land was cleared of trees and a dense collection of stilt houses was built on the hillock. Similar settlements emerged in a place now called Angkor Borei in present-day Cambodia, 80 km north of Oc Eo and elsewhere around the region. Something caused people to chop down trees and live more closely together. One factor may have been a local salt industry: tens of thousands of fragments from boiling pots have been discovered around the area. There is plenty of evidence of long-distance trade: Indian beads and tiles have been found at the sites. It is likely, although harder to prove, that foodstuffs and spices were also exchanged. As archaeologists such as Pierre-Yves Manguin and Michael Vickery have shown, while the Red River Delta was intimately linked to the "Sinitic World" to the northeast, the Mekong Delta was part of an Indian Ocean trading network that had been developing for several centuries.

This trade brought wealth, and that wealth enabled the Oc Eo people to build larger, denser settlements with walls, moats and canals. On present evidence it seems that by 100 CE, the people of the southern Mekong region had been formed into a coherent urbanized society based on surplus wealth produced by rice-based agriculture and trade. Other objects discovered at the site suggest that Oc Eo was a manufacturing center for pottery, beads and ornaments that were then exported via passing traders. With this surplus they could form an administration and a military to conscript a workforce that could build earthworks and waterways, some of which were long enough to connect Oc Eo with Angkor Borei and the sea. Improved drainage opened up new areas for rice growing and yet more wealth. There is still much to find out but it appears that by 240 CE, Funan had become a mature state. We do not know what language its people spoke, but the linguistic connection between "Funan" and "Phnom" suggests it was probably Mon-Khmer.

The traders of Funan looked for new markets and appear to have found them with a combination of force and diplomacy. In the third century, they may have conquered another trading kingdom on the other side of the Gulf of Thailand (called Dunxun in Chinese records) that had access to the Indian Ocean. They also turned their attention to the east, sending envoys to what was then the Wu state in southeastern China in 223 CE and then receiving envoys from Wu around 250—from whom we learn most of our knowledge of this period. These envoys almost certainly travelled on Funanese ships, which were far more advanced than their Chinese equivalents with crews well-used to long-distance navigation. The purpose of their trip was to explore potential trade routes during a period in which Wu's overland access to the west had been cut off by hostile states. Funan would remain important as a trading intermediary for some time, even after Wu was conquered by the Jin state.

Funan's primary orientation, however, remained towards India. Flat grooved, earthenware roof tiles found at Oc Eo show clear Indian origin. Other coins and medallions suggest contact with places even further west: in the Middle East and Mediterranean. It appears that Funan also imported ideas along with the tiles and coins. Around 400 CE, craftspeople began carving inscriptions in Sanskrit begin to appear on religious monuments and statues. Over the following century, the rulers of Funan started to adopt "Indian" ways of governing. An inscription found at Go Thap, 80 km northeast of Oc Eo records a King Gunavarman and his devotion to the Hindu god Vishnu. It is dated to a period when similar religious beliefs were developing among widely-spread communities across maritime Southeast Asia. There is also evidence of Buddhism spreading around the region at the same time. Some extraordinarily well-preserved wooden statues of Buddha have been recovered from waterlogged ground in the Mekong Delta and dated to a period between the fourth and seventh centuries CE.

By then, Funan formed a polity stretching across the whole of the Mekong Delta, straddling the territories of present-day Vietnam and Cambodia, with an economy built upon rice cultivation, craft manufacturing and overseas trade. Its capital seems to have been in what is now Angkor Borei in southern Cambodia. The site, about 300 hectares in size and surrounded by walls and moats, suggests a rich and powerful state. Maritime commerce boomed again during the fifth century when an Inner Asian people, the Xianbei, occupied the northern part of China, forcing the old elite of the Jin state to retreat to the south, cut off from their former trading partners. Funan became the go-between for Chinese trade with the Middle East that might have formerly travelled overland. After 420, when the new southern-based Liu-Song state replaced Jin, Funan took care to maintain diplomatic relations with it and reaped the economic rewards.

This period, the fifth and sixth centuries, was the highpoint of Funan's existence, demonstrated by a proliferation of "Indianized" religious sites and associated treasures uncovered in archaeological excavations. Religious statues, temple carvings, ritual objects and personal jewelry all demonstrate sophisticated craft techniques. Their styling connects them to the wider Indianized world across South and Southeast Asia.

All this construction and cultural creation in Funan seem to have come to a halt around 650 but it is not entirely clear why. The most likely cause was a shift in the pattern of regional trade as merchants moved to other ports. Perhaps the growth of the Cham states around the coast (see below) offered easier access to a wider range of goods and commodities. There are also suggestions that the careful environmental management of the Mekong Delta, which had enabled efficient cropping of rice, began to break down as canals silted up. At the same time, rice cultivation became more intensive in inland areas. Perhaps it became more efficient to farm inland rather than on the coast. Rather than being the core of a thriving economy and state, the Mekong Delta became peripheral to a state based higher up the river. Interestingly, even as the population moved away from places such as Oc Eo, religious sites, such as those on top of Mount Ba The continued in use for several centuries more—suggesting a continuing ritual attraction to the place even if it was no longer so economically useful.

Funan, then under a king named Rudravarman, sent a diplomatic mission to Tang China in 649, but Funan never appeared again in Chinese records. A century later, in 753, the Tang received a mission from a polity they called "Zhenla" which had apparently replaced Funan. It is not yet clear how this happened but there is plenty of evidence of continuity between the two states. Inscriptions suggest a continuous line of rulers and archaeology shows no interruptions in building or cultural styles. Whatever happened, this Zhenla was later incorporated into the expanding domain of Angkor after 802. The result for the former lands of Funan in the Mekong Delta was backwater status. They remained a relatively quiet part of the Khmer empire until the mid-eighteenth century, when the arrival of warriors and traders from the north changed everything.

><~~~><

Champa

The brick towers of central Vietnam surprise most visitors. Dozens of terracotta-colored temples dedicated to Hindu gods and incarnations of Buddha dot the coastline between the small cities of Dong Ha, just north of Hue, and Phan Rang, 700 km to the south. A few more lie further inland, like the collection at the site of My Son. Here, 30 km upriver from the estuary town of Hoi An, sits the largest known concentration of Hindu temples anywhere in the country. The remains of 70 have so far been discovered (including some that were badly damaged by American bombing during the 1965–75 war). The temples stand at the base of what the people who worshipped here regarded as the sacred mountain of Mahaparvata. For them it symbolized Mount Meru, the center of the Hindu universe, while the nearby Thu Bon River stood in for the River Ganges. Even the name that was given to this civilization, "Champa" was borrowed from an early Indian kingdom mentioned in the Hindu epic, the Mahabharata.

The temples were once richly decorated, although over the past millennium and a half almost all the sculpture has been removed. Pieces now on show in museums in Vietnam and around the world are proof of an intensely artistic culture honoring benevolent gods, fearsome warriors and curvaceous dancers. The Hindu deities Vishnu, Brahma and Shiva appear in effigy, together with large naturalistic statues of elephants, rhinoceroses and lions that once guarded the entrances to sacred sites. At the center of many of these sites are stone fertility symbols: lingas and yonis, representations of the gods Shiva and Shakti in the form of abstract male and female sexual organs, sometimes separated, sometimes connected. Steles written in Sanskrit testify to a belief system that combined religion and hierarchy.

What are these pieces of Indian culture doing in Vietnam? The people who built the temples and carved the statues were not from India, but they knew its beliefs well. Their rulers adopted Hinduism and created a series of "Indianized" societies along the coast of what is now central and southern Vietnam. With this borrowed cultural language they formed a series of independent states and confederations, collectively known as "Champa," that formed a significant power in the region from the first century until the fifteenth. In its final flourish, Champa nearly destroyed its Dai Viet rival, before collapsing in the face of its neighbor's military superiority. Its last embers were only extinguished in the early nineteenth century. Today there are still around 150,000 "Cham" people in Vietnam, descendants of this once-great civilization. Understanding the story of its rise and fall is hard because most of our evidence comes from their enemies and trading partners to the north and west. The Cham ended up on the "wrong side" of history, defeated both militarily and culturally by Dai Viet. Their temples are now tourist attractions rather than the centers of religious worship and kingly ceremony that they once were.

From the evidence currently available, historians have concluded that Champa was not a single state but many. Around 15 sizeable rivers flow through the former Cham lands, dropping sharply from the high plateau of the Central Highlands down to the sea. Each river forms a steeply-sided valley, divided from its neighbors by high hills. The societies that emerged in these valleys developed like separate islands, albeit ones connected by trade. From time to time, one valley would grow powerful enough to lead the others. Power and wealth would shift north or south, leaving behind physical reminders of historic greatness in the form of giant towers and sensuously-decorated temples.

The origins of the Cham lie overseas. They are thought to have originated as an "Austronesian" people, one spur of a branch of humanity which spread from modern-day China and Taiwan all around maritime Southeast Asia. Austronesians were accomplished sailors and voyaged as far west as Madagascar and as far east as Easter Island in the Pacific. They created a "Malay World," along the Southeast Asian archipelago from Luzon in the Philippines to Aceh in Indonesia, and implanted themselves in the Indochina mainland too. Archaeologists have found some of their earliest traces on the Vietnamese coast at a site called Sa Huynh (pronounced sa-hwing) between Hoi An and Nha

Trang. From underneath a sandy hill between the sea and a brackish lagoon, they have excavated thousands of stone age artifacts, among them axes, beads and burial jars. Similar burial jars have been found in similar sandy locations all along the "Cham coast" dating back to around 500 BCE. The sites often contain unusual forms of jewelry, particularly earrings with two animal heads and another form of intricately carved three-pointed ear decoration known as a *lingling-o*. Most interestingly, archaeologists found pottery with distinctive wave-like markings. Similar pottery designs and jewelry shapes have also been found on the other side of the South China Sea, in the Philippines, and in modern-day Thailand.

Such evidence tells us that the Austronesians arrived by sea and that they maintained their maritime connections, travelling and trading around the coasts of the region. Where they could, they settled in defendable sites like Sa Huynh: places with a safe harbor at the mouth of a river stretching from the lowland plains back into the hills. When they arrived in these places they encountered indigenous people already semi-settled there: not Austronesians but Austroasiatics. These Austroasiatics probably spoke a different kind of language: one from the Mon-Khmer group, and followed a subsistence lifestyle in the valleys and the uplands beyond. The valleys were generally steep-sided and not suitable for growing large amounts of rice. Instead, foragers would travel into the uplands to hunt and to gather rhino horn, elephant ivory and aromatic woods that could be exchanged for the necessities of life from the lowlands. It was a low-intensity way of living.

Over time, it seems, some of the Austronesian arrivals began to move out of the plains and settle in the hills—sometimes pushing out the Austroasiatic speakers and sometimes integrating with them. In the process they adapted from a coastal way of life to one better suited to the forest. Modern linguistic evidence suggests that the majority of the current "indigenous" population in the central highlands of Vietnam (incorporating the plateau around the cities of Kontum and Dalat) speak versions of Austronesian languages. The Jurai, Rhadé and Roglai groups are thought to be descendants of coastal people who moved inland. Yet this area is ringed by peoples who still speak Austroasiatic, specifically Mon-Khmer, languages. To the south, a group of Austroasiatic languages known as Bahnaric contain many "borrowings" from Cham, suggesting the two groups were in communication for a considerable period. To the north, however, the "Katuic" group of languages show fewer borrowings, suggesting less contact with Cham people. Further to the west and the south lie lands still dominated by speakers of Khmer who were, for a long period rivals of the Cham. The interactions between these groups were sometimes peaceful, orderly and profitable but at other times they could be extremely violent.

These highland-lowland connections powered an economy based upon exchange. There is evidence that, very early on, this trade covered long distances. Han Chinese records from the second century CE note an expedition from South Asia that stopped on the coast and obtained a live rhinoceros subsequently presented to the emperor. More prosaically, the presence of large numbers of beads made from glass and semi-precious stones, such as carnelian and agate, in excavated archaeological sites suggests more regular trade with South Asia. Mirrors and bronze arrowheads found in burials and roof tiles found in collapsed buildings are evidence of trade with the Han too. Over the centuries, the rise and fall of trade with the various Chinese states played a critical role in the rise and fall of the various kingdoms of Champa.

When the Han state tried to advance down the coast (as discussed in the previous chapter), perhaps seeking to capture the sources of the exotic forest products usually sent in tribute, it encountered an already settled population with its own maritime-based culture. South of the Hai Van Pass (also known as the "Pass of the Clouds" and located in the steep hills between the present-day cities of Hue and Danang) Han administrators found the local people too difficult to control directly. Instead, they created the somewhat unstable commandery of Rinan and attempted to rule through local leaders with nominal allegiance to the Han emperor. This seems to have worked for the most part but attempts to impose more direct rule—and imperial taxation—in the second century CE resulted in conflict. Rinan's southernmost district, known as Xiang-lin—literally "elephant forest" in Chinese, was the most unruly. In 144 CE and again in 192 CE there were uprisings in Xianglin. After the second rebellion, the name disappeared from Han records but a few decades later a new name with an apparently similar origin—"Lin-yi" meaning forest-town—appeared. It is likely that both names referred to the same area. The difference was that whereas Xianglin had been nominally part of the Han realm, Linyi was independent.

From this small beginning, Linyi steadily expanded northwards. Over the course of the century following 248 CE, a series of military campaigns enabled it to occupy the whole of the former Rinan commandery. Its frontiers moved 300 km north of the Hai Van Pass to the "Ngang Pass," another steep range of hills, this one on the modern-day border between the provinces of Ha Tinh and Quang Binh. In so doing, Linyi also captured Rinan's maritime trade, bringing wealth to this disobedient slice of the coast. When coastal commerce declined, as it did in the fourth century—mainly because of high customs duties and corruption in the ports of what was, by then, Jin China, Linyi turned to piracy. Under its king, Yan Wen, Linyi launched many raids along the coastline to the north. The story told of this king's biography makes him an interesting figure in his own right. He was said to have originated from Yangzhou in the delta of the Yangzi River but was kidnapped into slavery. He was then sold in Jiaozhou and taken to Linyi where he apparently rose through society and became king by 331. His reign was tumultuous. He pushed Linyi's territory further north but in 344 and 353, the northerners struck back with punitive raids on Linyi's citadels. The attacks failed, however, to subdue the kingdom.

By 420, following the collapse of the Jin state and its replacement by the first of the "southern dynasties"—the Liu-Song—trade between South Asia and China had been restored. That did not end Linyi's adventurism, however. In 446 CE, in response to continuing raids by Linyi, the Liu-Song organized a huge invasion, destroying Linyi's citadel and carrying away vast amounts of booty. This seems to have weakened Linyi sufficiently to create the conditions for a more peaceful coexistence with its northern neighbor.

Linyi's weakness created an opening for a new rival to emerge on its southern fringes. Around 480 CE, a local ruler with a powerbase in the valley of the Thu Bon River, near My Son, declared himself to be king with the name Bhadravarman. We don't know where he came from, but it is possible that his origins lay further south in the rival state of Funan, in what is now the Mekong Delta. Bhadravarman does not appear to have been Indian himself, but was clearly strongly influenced by South Asian religious and royal culture. This seems to have been transmitted by Cham and Indian traders plying the coasts between South and Southeast Asia. We know that the two regions were well integrated because in the citadel at Tra Kieu near Hoi An, archaeologists have found shards of pottery from Tamil Nadu dating from between 300 BCE and 200 CE. Traders also bought and sold sandalwood, cardamoms, camphor, cloves, jewels and precious metals. Indian writings refer to parts of Southeast Asia as the "Islands of Gold"—*swarnadvipa*—and the "Land of Gold"—*swarnabhumi*. The earliest evidence of cultural exchange yet found is an inscription in Sanskrit dated to the latter part of the third century CE and discovered near Nha Trang. It is thought to have been written in the script of the Ikshvaku dynasty, which ruled parts of what is today Andra Pradesh in India.

Both central Linyi and southern Funan had prospered as entrepôts on the trade routes between east and west and it seems that the merchants they dealt with carried new ideas as well as precious goods. King Bhadravarman and those who came after him, recognized that these South Asian beliefs could bolster their power. They established "Indian" ways of governing and worshipping. They claimed the authority of Hindu gods, notably Shiva but sometimes Vishnu, and constructed temples in which to conduct rituals that connected their earthly realm with the spiritual universe. The temples, like those King Bhadravarman ordered built at My Son, were decorated with texts in Sanskrit and striking figurative carvings in sandstone. The kingdoms they created were "mandalas": a fluid form of rule in which the king is imagined as sitting in the center of a wheel, with his power diminishing with distance from his person. In places mandalas would overlap, with rival rulers claiming the allegiance of different groups living intermingled on the same territory. Mandala rulers typically managed their relations with their neighbors through some kind of flexible federation which was mostly peaceful, but could easily become violent if conditions became harder. All this was borrowed from Indian states that the Austronesians had encountered in their voyaging, and then adapted to local circumstances.

Bhadravarman set up his own state in the lands in the Thu Bon Valley (running west from Hoi An) in the space between the rival states of Linyi and Funan. In retrospect we might call him the first Cham ruler but it was a later king, Rudravarman, who invaded Linyi and forcibly unified it with Bhadravarman's former territory. Having done so, Rudravarman opened formal diplomatic ties with the (Chinese) southern Liang state in 529 CE unlocking a new trading relationship between the two. The Chinese side recorded this as a mission from "Linyi" but this was a Linyi under new, Indianized, management. Notably, the tribute sent from Rudravarman to the Liang emperor included an image of the Buddha. Rudravarman left little physical evidence of his rule but the name of his son, Shambhuvarman, appears on a stone stele at My Son, written in Sanskrit. The inscription, dated to the late sixth century (577) , is the first on which the name "Champa" appears, "the country of he who protects the Chams."

In 605, a few decades after this inscription was made, a newly unified Sui Dynasty mounted an expedition against the place it called Linyi, plundering the citadel at Tra Kieu, a few kilometers west of the modern town of Hoi An. Among their booty, the Sui army carried away 1350 Buddhist texts written in the Austronesian language of the Chams. This little historical record adds to the somewhat limited evidence that we have about the culture of Champa. Champa was not a single unified state but a region defined by a shared culture. It comprised at least three centers: a northern one, centered on the Thu Bon Valley, initially known as Amaravati and then later as Indrapura; a central one around Nha Trang, known as Kauthara; and a southern one centered on Phan Rang, called Panduranga. Much later, during the twelfth and thirteenth centuries, another state known as Vijaya, centered on Quy Nhon—mid-way between the Thu Bon Valley and Nha Trang—became important. All of these different states presented themselves as "Champa" but they were separate. Each one controlled a port at the mouth of a river and was connected inland through the river valley to the uplands beyond. Collectively, they formed a trading system connecting inland Southeast Asia to the maritime world. Over time, power shifted between these different states and occasionally they banded together in the face of an outside threat from the Sinitic world to the north, or from the Khmer world to the west. At other times, Champa's fortunes ebbed and flowed with the regional economic tides.

Once the Tang Dynasty had taken power in China in 618 and brought that part of East Asia under a single government for the first time in 200 years, trade across the South China Sea trade seems to have taken off. A century and a half later, however, after rebels captured the Tang's northern cities in 755, demand for Southeast Asia goods dropped. Persian traders, angered by the loss of their markets and outraged by corruption, rioted in the port of Guangzhou in 758 and trade slumped. This seems to have undermined the economic base of the northernmost Cham state based in the Thu Bon Valley and the former Linyi. When the South China Sea trade resumed a few years later, it was not centered on Guangzhou but on Long Bien in Jiaozhou (modern day Hanoi). This changed the itineraries of maritime traders, bringing more trade to the southern part of the Cham world, around modern day Nha Trang.

The Cham states also had to worry about the Khmer kingdoms to the west. In 802 King Jayavarman, another "Indianized" ruler, established what became Angkor in modern-day Cambodia. Having mastered techniques of irrigation and warfare, Angkor expanded in all directions and came into conflict with Champa, as well as other states to its north, west and south. An inscription at the Po Nagar (Mother Goddess) temple in Nha Trang boasts of victorious Champa raids into Khmer lands around 813–817. At this time, Nha Trang was incorporated within the southernmost mandala of Panduranga. Its king claimed to rule "Champa" but it seems unlikely that he controlled territory much further north than Nha Trang.

Panduranga maintained its primacy among the Cham states during the ninth century while the northern mandala fell into relative decline. But during the tenth century, international trading patterns appear to have shifted again, once again sending more trade to the north. With its fortunes restored, a newly invigorated northern mandala, taking the name Indrapura, expanded further north, even beyond the Hai Van Pass, bringing its forces into conflict with the new state of Dai Viet, which had begun to emerge in the Red River Delta after 939 (see the following chapter).

Indrapura was different from its predecessor Amaravati. It chose to build its citadel 20 km to the south of Thu Bon, at a place now called

Dong Duong. Indrapura was also culturally different to My Son and the Thu Bon state. The remains of its temple sites tell us that its rulers practiced Mahayana Buddhism in preference to Hinduism. From small beginnings, Indrapura became a persistent challenger for regional hegemony. In 980, having heard of the deaths of the Dai Viet ruler Dinh Bo Linh and his son Dinh Lien, Indrapura attempted a surprise attack on the north. This might have been a decisive intervention in Vietnamese history had the invasion fleet not been struck by a huge storm and scattered before it was able to attack the Dai Viet citadel at Hoa Lu. Two years later, Dai Viet retaliated and inflicted a major defeat on Indrapura. Within a decade, however, much of the land conquered in that invasion, including the modern province of Quang Binh, had been recaptured by Indrapura, which continued to mount attacks as far north as Nghe An as late as 997. During this period Indrapura occupied, in effect, the land once controlled by Linyi several centuries before. Dai Viet attempted to push back Indrapura with two major invasions in 1044 and 1069 but they don't appear to have had much impact. Inscriptions at My Son show an uninterrupted reign of kings throughout the eleventh century.

Perhaps because of Indrapura's focus on the north during this period, a space emerged in the center of the Cham world which a new power began to fill. Located in another strategic river mouth with a well protected natural harbor, this new mandala enjoyed an excellent location from which to service coastal trade and communicate with the highlands. The seven brick towers still standing in the city of Quy Nhon, in the province of Binh Dinh, are testament to what was then called "Vijaya." Vijaya's ascent was made easier by fighting between the ruler of Panduranga in the far south and the local chief controlling the Nha Trang area which broke away under the name "Kauthara." With its rivals distracted, Vijaya was able to take advantage of the chaos. It became the dominant entrepôt on the Cham coast. Favorable trading conditions enabled it grow and then eclipse Indrapura and become the dominant mandala of the north too.

During 1160s and 1170s, the Khmer region to the west fell into internal disarray and Vijaya saw an opportunity—although there is some dispute about what happened. Some accounts suggest Vijayan forces sailed around the coast and up the Mekong River to sack the Khmer city of Angkor, prompting a revenge attack by the Angkorian king Jayavarman VII in 1190 which made Vijaya a vassal of the Khmer for over 20 years. However, the evidence for all those claims has been questioned. An alternative explanation, based on a detailed reading of inscriptions and other records, is that King Jayavarman VII may have actually originated from Vijaya. He then led a combined army of Chams and Khmers to capture Angkor. Images of such a "combined" army appear on the Bayon Temple in Angkor and it is notable that the accompanying inscriptions celebrating his victory are written in Sanskrit, which could be read by elites in both states, rather than in Khmer. He also changed the Angkorian religion to Mahayana Buddhism, which was more important for the Cham than for the Khmer. In other words, Jayavarman VII may have been a Cham who took over Angkor with the support of some Khmer and united the two for a period. His "revenge attack" in 1190 might actually be better described as his attempt to suppress a local rebellion against his rule. However once that rebellion became successful around 1220, the Cham rebels rewrote their history to appear they had been fighting against Angkor rather than a combined Angkor-Cham mandala.

Throughout the rest of the thirteenth century, the Song Empire in China—which had provided a solid market for goods from Champa—came under increasing pressure from the rival Mongol state to its north. When Song China finally collapsed in 1279, the Mongols turned their attention to areas further away. The Vijayan ruler, King Indravarman V sent them tribute but the Mongol leader, Kublai Khan, demanded complete submission rather than mere acknowledgment. Similar pressure was placed upon Dai Viet, which brought the two into some kind of alliance. In 1282, Vijaya presented Dai Viet with a precious white elephant to seal their friendly relations. That year, the Mongols demanded that Dai Viet grant them passage through their territory to invade Champa but the Dai Viet king, Tran Nhan Tong, refused. Rather than fight both armies at the same time, the Mongols decided to bypass Dai Viet and invade Champa by sea. The invasion force arrived, probably in the main Vijayan port of Sri Banoy (modern-day Quy Nhon), in early 1283.

After capturing the citadel of Sri Banoy, the Mongols attempted to move inland but were frustrated by the hills and jungle, by malaria and other diseases, and by the defenders' hit-and-run tactics. The invaders paused, built a garrison in the flat lands north of Sri Banoy and called for reinforcements. Two years later, the Mongols attempted a "pincer movement" by also invading Dai Viet from the north. They captured the Dai Viet capital, Thang Long, before being forced to retreat after about six months of fighting. At the same time, the force that had been camped out in Vijaya moved north towards Dai Viet, abandoning its attempt to control Champa but then failing to conquer Dai Viet either. The Mongols made another attack on Dai Viet late in 1287 but were again beaten back within a few months.

The two conflicts left Dai Viet in disarray: its agriculture shattered and its towns destroyed. Vijaya had suffered far less damage. Once the invasion force had departed, the new Vijayan king, Jaya Singhavarman III—son of Indravarman V, moved quickly to establish diplomatic relations with the Mongols. At the same time, the Viyayans also renewed relations with their other allies, the kingdom of Majapahit on Java (an alliance sealed earlier by the marriage of a Javan princess to the now-monarch). In 1292/3, the Mongols attempted a seaborne invasion of Majapahit—but the Vijayans refused to allow the Mongol ships to land and resupply. By the time the armada arrived off Java it was sufficiently weakened to be easily dispatched by Majapahit.

Nonetheless, Champa skillfully managed to maintain good relations with both protagonists: revitalizing the key Southeast Asian trade route between Java and China and cementing Vijaya's role as the middleman between the two. Prosperity returned and Vijaya's influence over the whole Cham world increased. Inscriptions bearing the king's name appear in temples from My Son in the north to Panduranga in the south and the highlands to the west. By 1306, Vijaya appears to have been in a strong position and Dai Viet in a relatively weak one yet, for some reason, this was the moment when Jaya Singhavarman III agreed to cede his two northernmost provinces, O (modern-day Quang Tri) and Ly (modern-day Thua Tien) to Dai Viet in exchange for the hand of a Viet princess. This region was where the Mongol invasion force had set up its temporary garrison and it is possible that the Vijayan king was unsure about its loyalty and wanted Dai Viet to take over the problem of guarding it against future interventions. There were intense diplomatic discussions between the two sides involving the abdicated king of Dai Viet, Tran Nhan Tong, spending time in a Buddhist monastery in Vijaya and then offering his daughter as a royal bride, a second wife for the king after the Javan princess.

The Dai Viet princess was delivered in 1306 and the provinces were transferred the following year—despite local protests. Unfortunately, King Jaya Singhavarman III died shortly after the deal was done. Ostensibly to prevent the new queen being burned alive on the king's funeral pyre, Dai Viet sent a flotilla of ships to rescue her. However there is evidence that the flotilla was actually used to transport Cham officials as part of a joint "pacification mission" to the provinces being transferred. The records are unclear but it seems there was conflict between the Vijaya and Dai Viet over the control of the territories, a conflict which resulted in Dai Viet installing its own preferred candidates on the Vijayan throne. In response, the Cham called on the Mongols for support. They admonished Dai Viet for its behavior but it was not until 1326 that Vijaya wriggled free of Dai Viet interference.

This set the stage for 150 years of intermittent conflict between the two states over the disputed provinces. This was a period, right at the end of the Mongol era, when regional trade was growing and the prosperity of coastal states rising. Some time around 1360, a new ruler took power in Vijaya. His Cham name is not recorded but he became known to the Vietnamese as Che Bong Nga. Starting in 1361, Che Bong Nga's forces started pushing north in a concerted manner, apparently trying to regain control of the districts Vijaya had previously ceded. At the time, Dai Viet was being ruled by a king, Tran Du Tong, generally regarded as ineffectual. When Dai Viet pushed back in 1368 their troops were defeated. Importantly, 1368 was the year in which the Mongols were pushed from power in China by what would become the Ming Dynasty, creating a vacuum in regional geopolitics. When King Tran Du Tong died without an heir, his court fell into feuding and disarray. Unlike Vijaya, Dai Viet was unable to establish proper relations with the new Ming state.

Vijaya saw an opportunity. In 1371, having sought the consent of the Ming, Che Bong Nga led an invasion of Dai Viet. Sweeping up the coast and through the Red River Delta, his forces managed to occupy the undefended capital, Thanh Long, loot the city and burn its palaces. In 1377, following another Cham attack, Dai Viet retaliated but its forces were lured into a trap and defeated, with its king being killed in battle. Once again the Cham attacked and looted Thanh Long. They did so twice more: in 1379 and 1383. Dai Viet was falling apart and Vijaya was getting ever stronger. Che Bong Nga also expanded his lands to the west, taking advantage of weakness in Angkor to push Vijayan control deep into the highlands and the delta of the Mekong. The 1380s would mark the zenith of Cham power.

From that point onwards, however, the Cham states would suffer defeat after defeat until their last vestige was extinguished 450 years later. The downward trajectory began with another raid on the north in 1390. In the fighting, Che Bong Nga was betrayed and killed. A Dai Viet noble cut off his head and took it to Thang Long, leaving the retreating Cham to carry home the rest of the body. The main Vijayan general then declared himself king, deposing the sons of Che Bong Nga, who promptly went over to the Dai Viet side and were put in charge of reconquered, former Cham territories. The "irregular" transfer of power prompted a change of sentiment towards "Champa" in the Ming court, already bothered by what it regarded as its increasing arrogance. The new king proved to be much less aggressive towards Dai Viet.

In 1400, the Tran Dynasty of Dai Viet, riven by failure and feuding, was overthrown by its most senior official, Ho Quy Ly, who shored up the authority of the state and its defenses. In 1402 Vijaya ceded large areas of the north to Dai Viet: the present-day provinces of Quang Nam and Quang Ngai. But it was Ho Quy Ly's usurpation of power that brought about the most decisive intervention in the region's politics. In 1407, the Ming invaded and deposed Ho Quy Ly and the remains of the Tran administration. For the following 20 years, the Red River Delta was ruled as part of Ming China. Power was centralized, a new state bureaucracy was constructed and governance became more sophisticated. When the Ming were eventually expelled, it was by a completely different group, one led by Le Loi, whose origins lay in the uplands of the Tai region. His Le Dynasty took over a newly invigorated

"Chinese-style" state with "early modern" political and bureaucratic structures able to gather and deploy resources much more effectively than its predecessors.

These took time to develop but, by 1471, the Le Dynasty was able to launch an overwhelming attack against Vijaya. Dai Viet pushed right the way down the coast to the capital at Qui Nhơn. The Cham were outclassed in every way: in military terms on the battlefield and in administrative arrangements off it. Dai Viet fought with gunpowder and firearms acquired from the Ming while the Cham still used spears and arrows. The campaign was a slaughter. The Vijaya citadel was breached, looted, burned and then razed to the ground. The Viet chronicles say that 60,000 people were massacred and another 30,000 captured and taken north as slaves. Chinese descriptions from ten years later still described the citadel as "a distant and dangerous place." The newly-captured territory was renamed Nam Phan by Dai Viet who placed a stone at the top of the Cu Mong Pass, just south of the now destroyed city, to mark the boundary between the new lands of Dai Viet and the remaining Cham states of Kauthara and Panduranga. Kauthara would survive at Nha Trang until 1653. Panduranga kept the name Champa alive until it was finally dissolved in 1832.

CHAPTER 3

INDEPENDENCE AND FAMILY FIGHTS (900–1400)

T he ancient capital of Hoa Lu is a brick-red jewel in an emerald setting. A small collection of ceremonial buildings nestles in a steeply-sided valley, enveloped by green-forested towers of rock. Temples, ceremonial halls, intricately carved gateways, quiet courtyards and lotus-filled pools give us clues about the site's former importance. Water passes by at a languid pace, lazily taking a short cut from the main flow of the river. It wanders between the limestone cliffs and irrigates the rice fields before rejoining the mainstream just as it reaches the sea. It is easy to see why, a millennium ago, a ruler would have chosen this site. The hills create a natural fortress around three sides, while the river provides a highway to the rest of the region. From Hoa Lu, near the city of Ninh Binh around 90 km south of Hanoi, a ruler could control the passage of traders and armies between the Red River Delta and places to the south

A millennium ago, this beautiful valley was the power base of a notorious king: Dinh Bo Linh (pronounced ding-bo-ling). He had come to power after a vicious battle for supremacy between the rival clans of Annan. The period became known as the era of the "Twelve Warlords" but for simplicity, the twelve rivals can be grouped into three. One group was based in the old heartland of imperial rule: the Red River delta, Jiao (or Giao in the Vietnamese spelling). Another was based to its west, where the Red River meets the mountains: a place known as "Feng" (Phong in Vietnamese) formerly called Me Linh. People there had strong links with the uplands, probably with speakers of Tai languages. The third group was based south of the Red River delta, an area then known as "Truong" and Hoa Lu was its citadel.

In 965, after twenty years of conflict, Truong prevailed over the other two, mainly through the utter ruthlessness of Dinh Bo Linh. One story demonstrates his iron will. Expecting an attack, he had sent out his son, Lien, as an envoy to meet the advancing army. The attackers took the son hostage and suspended him from a pole while calling on the father to surrender. Instead, Dinh Bo Linh ordered his own forces to shoot arrows at the young man, reportedly declaring that a "great man cannot compromise a great affair because of a son." The son survived and the attackers fled.

For the next fifteen years, until he was murdered in 980, Dinh Bo Linh consolidated his position as ruler of Giao, Phong and Truong with a combination of despotism and strategic weddings. Enemies were fed to tigers or boiled in cauldrons of oil, and relatives were married into other clans. The most significant result of all this torture and diplomacy was that Dinh Bo Linh managed to unite former rivals and turn Hoa Lu into the capital of a coherent state. By the end of the tenth century, single ruler controlled the lands lying within the basins of the three big northern rivers: the Ca, the Ma and the Red. Dinh Bo Linh's state was now strong enough to resist the advances of the great Song empire to the north. It was, in effect, independent.

Viciousness seems to have run in the Dinh family. At one point, Dinh Bo Linh switched the royal succession from Lien to an infant child. Lien then stabbed the younger brother to death. As a Buddhist, Lien recognized that his foul deed had burdened him with negative karma. To try to counterbalance his crime and gain merit for the next life, he erected dozens of stones around Hoa Lu inscribed with Buddhist sutras. Despite these good works, however, both Dinh Bo Linh and Lien were themselves murdered: stabbed to death while sleeping off a huge drunken meal. The assassin was caught, killed and then, apparently, eaten by the royal entourage. It is not hard to imagine such terrible events taking place in this natural citadel, hidden from outside view. But to understand how all this came about, we need to go back to the beginning of the tenth century—and final collapse of the three century-old Tang Dynasty.

>ᴙ⌒ᴚ<

Independence (907–1009)

In 907, the Tang Dynasty became yet another Chinese state to be overthrown by its own military commander. This commander then declared himself the founder of a new dynasty, known by historians as the "Later Liang." His was just the first of five families to take control of the former Tang state bureaucracy over the following half-century. At the same time, several local leaders broke away to form their own states—sometimes known as the "Ten Kingdoms." One of them was a man called Liu Yin whom the Tang Dynasty, in one of its last acts, had appointed Military Commissioner of the Lingnan region, the area "south of the mountain passes": what is now southern China and northern Vietnam. Liu Yin remained in power for a decade after the demise of the Tang. The successor state of the "Later Liang" appointed him a "prince" of Lingnan. After he died in 917, however, Liu Yin's younger brother Liu Yan declared independence from the center. For the first time in a millennium, the Lingnan region was formally free of northern control. Liu Yan initially called his new state "Great Yue," playing on Lingyan's former identity, but within year he had changed that to "Southern Han."

This put the Annan leadership in a quandary. It too had had a Tang-appointed Military Commissioner, Khuc Hao, a member of a prominent local clan. After Khuc Hao died in 908, power passed to his son, Khuc Thua My. He continued to act as if he were the representative of the northern empire, mainly to deter Liu Yan's "Southern Han" empire from invading. This worked until 923, when the Later Liang was overthrown by a successor state with much less interest in the south. Khuc Thua My then made an alliance with the Min state located in what is now Fujian province in China, bracketing the Southern Han with potentially hostile powers. It kept Annan safe until 930, when Min collapsed. Southern Han promptly invaded Annan. Khuc Thua My decided not to resist. His reward was to be spared death and, instead, exiled to the north, never to return. Liu Yan's Southern Han appointed a new governor in his place but this action prompted a series of reactions that would result in the exact opposite outcome to the one intended. Instead of being rejoined to Lingnan and the Southern Han, Annan, after much fighting, would become independent.

In 931, one of Khuc Thua My's former deputies, a leader from Hoa Lu called Duong Ding Nghe, attacked the Southern Han forces occupying Annan, expelled their officials and then defeated the reinforcements sent by Liu Yan from Guangzhou. Duong Ding Nghe then declared himself governor, ruling from Da Lai (modern Hanoi). Importantly though, he did not call himself "king": he continued to portray himself as a mere provincial leader within an empire—although exactly which empire was still unclear: was it the Southern Han, the Later Liang or perhaps something else? Six years later, however, a rival leader, originating from Phong (near the western uplands), killed Governor Nghe and called on the Southern Han to help him take control of the province. In the traditional telling, this was the moment when, for the first time, Vietnam separated from China. In this version, Duong Ding Nghe's son-in-law, a man named Ngo Quyen, defeated the invading force and declared himself the first king of an independent country. The reality is a little more complicated, although it does involve a famous military victory.

In 938, Ngo Quyen (pronounced no-kwee-yen) sallied forth from his stronghold in the Hoa Lu area and killed the man who had killed his father-in-law. Expecting retaliation from the Southern Han, he then set a trap in the mouth of the Bach Dang River, near the present-day city of Haiphong. He knew that Liu Yan would have to send forces from Guangzhou by sea in order to recapture Giao. With this in mind, he ordered his troops to bury iron-tipped stakes in the riverbed, just low enough so that boats could pass over them at high tide. He then lured the Southern Han's invading fleet up the river, waited for the tide to drop and attacked them as their boats were impaled on the spikes. The landing force was destroyed and among the dead was Liu Yan's son, the presumed heir to the Southern Han throne.

In the aftermath of the defeat, the Southern Han "empire" fragmented into several pieces, of which Annan was just one. In retrospect, Ngo Quyen's battle has been depicted as Vietnam's first war of independence but the evidence we have suggests that he really went to war to ensure his own political survival, and to defeat his rivals in Phong and their backers in the Southern Han. Even during this period, more than fifty years after the retreat of the last Tang Dynasty garrison, the rulers of Annan were still conducting themselves as autonomous but subordinate officials of a northern empire. In 938, however, it was not clear which northern empire a ruler of Annan should remain loyal to: the Tang had fallen apart and its lands become mired in battles between rival claimants. It was only in these circumstances that Ngo Quyen declared himself to be king (*vuong*) of a state. But as far as we know, he did not give that state a name. (This has not prevented many nationalist historians claiming that he called the country *Nam Viet*—or "Southern Yue").

Ngo Quyen's idea of a state was based upon those in the old imperial heartland. This was the only model he knew, and it was one that could win the allegiance of the considerable numbers of people in the province who still felt they belonged to that political and intellectual world. At the same time, however, Ngo Quyen moved his capital from the former Tang administrative center at Dai La (Hanoi) to the old citadel of Co Loa—a symbolic step linking his state to that of another regional fief 500 years earlier. It was also a good strategic move. From Co Loa he was able to bring all three regions: Giao, Phong and Truong, under his control, constructing an administration that encompassed the whole of former Annan. Ngo Quyen was well on the way to solidifying this control when in 944, just six years after his victory in the Bach Dang River, he suddenly died. His death reopened all the old questions. Ngo Quyen's brother-in-law declared himself king, backed by men from the south. Rivals from Giao, however, preferred to support the claims of Ngo Quyen's two sons. The kingdom fell into factional fighting between the elites of Giao in the lowlands and Phong in the uplands: the era traditionally known in Vietnam as the "Period of the Twelve Warlords."

It was this political mess that enabled the tyrant from Hoa Lu, Dinh Bo Linh, to take control. With support from other strongmen in the south and, it seems, clans from the uplands, he took advantage of the chaos in and around the Red River delta and forced his rivals to submit. By 965 the job was done. Twenty years of fighting ended with Dinh Bo Linh in the same position that Ngo Quyen had briefly occupied: undisputed king of a new state uniting Giao, Phong and Truong. Rather than using Co Loa or Dai La for his capital, Dinh Bo Linh ruled from his lair in Hoa Lu. He named his new state *Dai Co Viet* or "Great Viet" or "Great Yue." (*Dai* is a word of Chinese origin and *Co* is Viet vernacular but both words mean "great" so this double naming suggests an identity in transition. The *Co* part of the name was dropped a century later, in 1054.) In choosing this name, Dinh Bo Linh claimed for himself the Yue identity which had been bestowed upon southerners by northern-based empires for more than a millennium.

He then went a step further, declaring himself "emperor" in 966, equal to the rulers from the north. Dinh Bo Linh was not, however, a particularly sophisticated man and it seems his assumption of this grand title was more about his own aggrandizement than a considered statement of political development. Confirmation that Dinh Bo Linh did not see himself as leader of an entirely independent state comes from his decision to send envoys with tribute offerings to Southern Han in 965. Then, after Southern Han was taken over by a new northern empire, the Song, in 971, Dinh Bo Linh sent his own son, Dinh Lien as envoy to that court, bearing generous gifts, including elephant tusks and rhino horns, in tribute. In other words, Dinh Bo Linh did not feel his local control was secure without the recognition and endorsement of the northern empire. The Song did indeed recognize his rule but not as the ruler of *Dai Co Viet*. Instead it reverted to the former Chinese name of *Jiaozhi* Prefecture—putting him in his place within an old imperial hierarchy.

This was how things stood on the night in 980 that Dinh Bo Linh and his son Dinh Lien were stabbed to death by their courtier. Bo Linh's other son, 5-year-old Dinh Phe De, became king. Hearing of this, the Song Empire plotted to recover what they regarded as the imperial lands of Jiaozhi. Down south, the Champa court also saw an opportunity to attack. Recognizing that a state led by a 5-year-old would be unlikely to resist the impending invasions, one of Dinh Bo Linh's generals, a man named Le Hoan, seized power. He was careful to preserve the fiction that he was merely ruling in the name of the child-king but there is no doubt about who was really in charge. Le Hoan was fortunate in that a huge Champa fleet, perhaps a thousand vessels strong, was hit by a storm as it made its way to attack Hoa Lu. Most of the boats sank, forcing the attack to be aborted. Meanwhile, a Song invasion force arrived from the north. In 981, Le Hoan's forces ambushed it in the mouth of the Bach Dang River, close to where Ngo Quyen had won his famous victory 43 years earlier. The Song forces were scattered, never to return.

In the aftermath of this victory, a result that secured his de facto independence, Le Hoan was quick to resume the formalities of a subordinate imperial relationship. In 986, he told the Song that he was now the ruler, having deposed the child in whose name he was previously ruling, and offered ritual tribute. He had ended the 12 year-long "Dinh Dynasty" and created what is now known as the "Early Le (pronounced "lay") dynasty. In exchange, the Song recognized him as a vassal. It was a mutually-beneficial arrangement. From Le Hoan's perspective, it brought him a guarantee of non-interference. From the Song courts' perspective it brought legitimacy: the tribute of imperial vassals was confirmation that the "mandate of heaven" still lay with the emperor. It is clear, however, from the language of the Song communications with Dai Co Viet that something had changed. Previously, imperial missives had regarded Jiaozhou as part of the same political and cultural world as the emperor. The messages to Le Hoan are quite different. They exhort the administrators of Dai Co Viet to "conform." "Your language resembles the calls of shrikes, while we have a literature that will instruct you," they preached. It seems that in the view of the Song, Dai Co Viet was now outside the realm of civilization. The Song turned their back on the old Jiaozhou. In 986, Dai Co Viet emerged in its place.

Many developments flowed from this new political situation. With Dai Co Viet now detached from the empire, it was also cut off from the regular flow of people between the imperial center and its provincial appendage. As a result, their cultures and languages of the two areas diverged. The latest research suggests that it was during this period that people who spoke what we now call "Middle Chinese," people who were probably part of the Sinicized elite, shifted to using another language, which we now call "Proto-Viet-Muong," spoken by the majority of the population. In the process the two forms of speaking mixed with each other and perhaps other languages. Today, around seventy percent of Vietnamese words have "Chinese" origins although the underlying structure of the language is shared with Muong—a language in the Austroasiatic group still spoken by minorities from the uplands. The combination resulted, eventually, in the hybrid that we now call Vietnamese.

><del>~</del><del>~</del><

The Ly Dynasty (1009–1226)

The story of the following two centuries begins with a "temple orphan": a boy left in the care of Buddhist monks by his parents, perhaps because they did not want, or were unable, to care for him. We do not know much about the origins of this boy, Ly Cong Uan, although some Chinese sources suggest his family came from Min—today's Fujian province. Other accounts say his mother was impregnated by a "divine being," while some suggest that this "being" was actually a Buddhist leader called Van Hanh. Under the tutelage of Van Hanh and the monks, the boy grew strong and capable and was appointed to Le Hoan's palace guard in his late teens or early twenties. This was not an accident. For some time, Buddhist monks across the Red River delta had been accruing both economic and political power through the management of large areas of land donated to their temples. They used some of the profits from the harvests to educate a new class of literate administrators, men who became invaluable to the rulers of Annan. These "temple boys" had no loyalty to families or clans, they were servants of the *sangha* (the Buddhist community) and those whom the *sangha* supported.

Over the previous century, the power of each ruler had depended upon military force. Each ruler's death had triggered bloody fights over who would succeed to the throne, with wars sometimes raging for decades, to everyone's disadvantage. The three main rulers of Hoa Lu: Dinh Bo Linh, Le Hoan and Le Hoan's son Le Dinh, were typical: peasant warlords whose strengths lay in organizing military forces rather than managing a bureaucracy. The temples provided vital support to these kings by educating a cadre of administrators but the Buddhist monks came to understand that enduring peace required something more. Stability required a set of beliefs that would legitimize the ruler, bring popular consent and unite the people. They also maneuvered particularly impressive candidates into positions of importance, which is how Ly Cong Uan was given the role of keeping the Hoa Lu citadel secure.

When Le Hoan died in 1005, the pattern of previous successions continued for four years. According to an account written three and a half centuries later (known as the *Dai Viet Su Luoc* and finished in 1377), Le Hoan's son, Le Dinh, appears to have been a psychopath who "liked killing." He had his enemies burned alive, drowned in cages and bitten by snakes. He killed his older brother, "suppressed" his younger ones and lived in despotic style. Fortunately for his enemies, Le Dinh died in 1009 aged just 25 while suffering from hemorrhoids so bad that he was dubbed "the king who ruled lying down." With Le Dinh's brothers either dead or in exile there was no obvious heir: the throne was vacant and the "Early Le Dynasty" was dead.

For some time the monks had been preparing for this moment. Through their temples they had spread word of their brave and kind protégé, Ly Cong Uan. They used poems and prophesies to propagandize his right to the throne and generate an expectation that his ascent was unstoppable. They succeeded. Two days after the death of Le Dinh, Ly Cong Uan was declared king, the first ruler of the 63 year-long "Ly Dynasty." He is better known by the "temple name" (the title given to rulers after they die), a name that can still be found on streets across the country: Ly Thai To.

One of Ly Cong Uan's first moves was to transfer his capital away from the notorious citadel at Hoa Lu and return it to Dai La (Hanoi) in the heart of both the lowlands and the networks of Buddhist power. When his boat arrived there in 1010, Ly Cong Uan apparently saw a dragon flying overhead: an auspicious portent for his reign. As a result he gave the site a new name: *Thang Long* or "Rising Dragon." This date, 1010, is now regarded as the foundation of Hanoi and celebrated as such by the city authorities today. Ly Cong Uan's dragon continued to rise for the rest of his reign, and for those of his son and grandson. Those three generations are still regarded as a "golden age" today by

Vietnamese historians.

The Ly family's power had both material and ideological foundations. The Ly state benefited from the warmer and wetter climate that Southeast Asia enjoyed between 900 and 1300 CE. The rice harvest swelled, creating a surplus that could feed urban populations and be traded abroad. The court also formed a strategic alliance with the Buddhist hierarchy. The king ordered the people to support the monks and their temples and, in return, the monks organized popular support for the king. This Buddhist monarchy became so wealthy that it could afford to suspend the collection of taxes for three years after Ly came to power. Political stability returned, allowing Dai Co Viet to rejoin regional trading networks and regain some prosperity. That created a new economic base upon which a more independent polity could assert itself in the region.

The Ly family's power-base was the agricultural heartland in the middle section of the Red River centered on Thang Long/Hanoi. It stretched from Thai Nguyen (60 km north of Hanoi) to Son Tay (40 km west of Hanoi) to Thanh Hoa (150 km south of Hanoi). The areas beyond this core, particularly the coastal region to the east and the uplands to the west, were beyond the court's day-to-day control. Ly Cong Uan was willing to tolerate the power of local clans, so long as they acknowledged him as the ruler of the kingdom. In this, he was following the attitude of previous imperial regimes. Ly family control was strongest where the power of the Buddhist temples was most entrenched. However, the new king was eclectic in his approach to religion. He would travel around his kingdom establishing temples to honor local spirits, thereby gaining their blessing, at least in the eyes of local people, while also supporting Daoist priests and Confucianists. He encouraged all forms of belief so long as the various believers supported him, an attitude towards the four different belief systems that persists in Vietnam today. His priority was to neutralize all forms of organization before any could become an oppositional force. (See "Religion in Vietnam" on p. 40.)

Ly Cong Uan/Ly Thai To quickly performed the necessary rituals to establish a tributary relationship with the Song Empire, thereby ensuring security on his northern border and reducing the chances of a rival making a successful claim to his throne. The Song recognized him in the same manner they had adopted towards the rulers of Hoa Lu: conferring on him the title of "King of Jiaozhi." Facing troubles on their own northern frontier, the Song were more than happy to have a stable regime to their south. Ly Cong Uan faced the opposite problem. He now had stability in the north but instability in the south. In 1011 he launched a major campaign against rebels in the area beyond Hoa Lu, as far as modern Nghe An province. He also attempted to "pacify" the mountains to the west of his capital and suppress the influence of the upland Nanzhao kingdom: the one that had sacked Dai La in 863. He sent patrols up into the hills on "kill or capture" missions to keep Nanzhao at bay.

The 19 years that Ly Cong Uan spent on the throne created the foundations of a strong state. He had a highly personalized style of rule—upsetting his advisers by coming up with independent ideas. Rather than merely overseeing the annual plowing ceremony, he shocked the court by taking hold of the plow himself. He also continued to travel the realm and endow local temples in order to ingratiate himself with areas outside the capital. The prominent historian of Vietnam Keith Taylor describes him as "intelligent and vigorous" and constantly developing new ideas about how to command the allegiance of his people. In the later years of his reign, officials worked to codify the king's whims into laws and rules that could endure. They also ensured that the Buddhist hierarchy and its temples remained a loyal bulwark of the monarchy.

By the time that he died, in 1028, Ly Cong Uan seems to have formed Dai Co Viet into an effective and prosperous state. His reforms and his alliance with the Buddhist hierarchy created the conditions for a relatively smooth transfer of power, not because there was no resistance to his eldest son taking over but because the court and its allies snuffed out the resistance, from three relatives, almost as soon as it began. The son, Ly Phat Ma (better known today by his posthumous "temple name," Ly Thai Tong) had been born in Hoa Lu and traveled to Thang Long with his father. He was deliberately educated outside the palace, to give him a taste of ordinary life, and sent off to war against Champa at the age of 20. He had also taken part in campaigns against the Tai tribes in the uplands, giving him plenty of experience of command by the time he ascended to the throne. Court officials schooled him in the ways of law with the hope that he would then rule in a legalistic rather than an arbitrary manner when his turn came to ascend the throne.

The new king's priority was securing the state's prosperity. In 1037, the court ordered the construction of warehouses in what is now Nghe Tin province in the very southern part of the realm. This area was an entrepôt with harbors where seaborne merchants knew they could safely dock to buy goods brought down from the mountains. They also sold goods from other parts of Asia, which would then be carried over the mountains and into the basin of the Mekong River. This overland network by-passed the Champa coast and the Khmer-controlled region of the lower Mekong allowing direct trade between Dai Co Viet and Lan Xang Hom Khao (the Kingdom of Lan Sang) in what is now southern Laos, along with other states in what is Thailand today. This was the part of the coast that the Ly state cared about most. Control of its business was lucrative, and formed a mainstay of the Dai Co Viet economy.

The other foundation of the Dai Co Viet's wealth was slavery. Capturing people from neighboring societies and putting them to work was an important way for rulers to demonstrate strength and gain prestige. There are records of raids on Champa in 1044 (5,000 people captured), Ai Lo (a Tai state in the mountains) in 1048 ("many" captured), Guangxi in 1060 ("countless" men and women captured), Champa in 1069 (50,000 people captured) and Guangxi in 1079 (3,000 people captured). These people were then put to work on royal estates around the Ly heartland. After each raid there was a notable increase in the number of state construction projects around the kingdom. Between 1028 and 1054, eight palaces, 151 temples and two bridges were built. Between 1054 and 1072, these were augmented by a further six palaces and 13 temples. Archaeologists excavating the Ly citadel in central Hanoi in 2010 discovered Cham inscriptions on some of the bricks, suggesting that it was constructed by enslaved people from Champa. After the building projects were completed, the enslaved were transferred to work the estates of the aristocracy. Slavery was something that the Ly did to other peoples, but not to their own. The court explicitly banned wealthy families from taking indebted local-born able-bodied men as bonded labor (in effect, slaves) in order to ensure there were enough free men to sustain a tax base and an effective army.

There were also important sources of wealth on the northern frontier: gold mines and potential slaves. When the Tai-speaking Nung people rose up in 1039, the king sent an expedition into the hills to capture and execute its leaders (as we saw in Chapter 2). But when the leader's son, Nung Tri Cao, rebelled two years later, the king offered him a pardon and recognized him as a—subordinate—ruler of the Nung. When he rose up again, however, the king sent troops to chase him over the frontier into Song China where he disappeared. At around the same time, Ly Thai Tong decided to subdue Champa and pacify his southern borderlands. He ordered preparations for war in 1043 and, the following year, invaded by ship. His forces killed a local ruler (possibly the king of Vijaya), kidnapped 5,000 people and looted the treasury. On their return, the king was able to announce a halving of taxes. He repeated the adventure in the western highlands, capturing yet more people, along with livestock from the Tai-speaking region of what is now eastern Laos. Such was the way economic booms were engineered in eleventh century Dai Co Viet.

In his final years, Ly Thai Tong settled down and prepared for death. In 1049 he dreamed a vision of heaven in which a bodhisattva sat on a lotus throne growing out of a pond. A Buddhist monk advised the king to build a pagoda atop a single pillar in a lotus pond, around which monks would chant for his soul. This he did, and the building still stands today, near Ba Dinh Square in the ceremonial center of Hanoi. The symbolism of the lotus—a beautiful flower growing out of the mud—felt apt for a ruler attempting to remain serene above the turbulence of the world outside the palace.

In 1054, Ly Thai Tong handed power to his son, Ly Nhat Ton (temple name: Ly Thanh Tong, pronounced "Lee Tang Tong") and died shortly afterwards. It was the first peaceful royal succession since the collapse of Tang rule in Annam almost 150 years before—a sign of how successfully the court had institutionalized its laws and rules across the kingdom. Ly Thanh Tong inherited a stable kingdom with pacified frontiers and, at the age of 31, he already had experience of kingship and command.

One of his first decisions was to change the name of the state, dropping the vernacular "Co," leaving only the classical words "Dai Viet." This was one of a series of moves that indicated he was claiming to rule as a "Chinese-style" emperor, rather than merely a "king." He had his soldiers' foreheads tattooed with the words "Son of Heaven's Army," implying that he saw himself as the "Son of Heaven" and he ordered court officials to wear ceremonial hats and footwear similar to those used in the Song court. Yet in his diplomacy with the Song, Ly Thanh Tong continued to act deferentially: performing the rituals expected of a vassal ruler. He presented one face to the "northern empire" and another to his own people. Obtaining such dual recognition reinforced Ly Thanh Tong's moral authority over any potential rivals.

During this period, the monarch's power grew from his capacity to inspire belief among supporters and subjects. He, personally, had to provide military victories, bountiful harvests and popular satisfaction. There was no sense of "the world" or "nature" being separate realms from humanity: they all formed part of a single moral universe. The ruler's behavior could win or lose heaven's favor. His actions could decide whether rains fell or failed, whether foreigners submitted or prevailed, whether life was good or bad. The king could claim he had been endorsed by heaven, so long as he delivered. And a successful king attracted followers who could build a successful state. In the words of historian Keith Taylor, "The Ly Dynasty rose so spectacularly in the eleventh century because there was an unbroken series of believable kings; it faded and fell a few generations later because the Ly kings were no longer believable." So long as they maintained their aura of heavenly endorsement, things went well for the Ly. When that aura dissipated, division and rebellion spread.

The Ly kings' way of ruling was more "Southeast Asian" than "East Asian." The form of Buddhism they patronized came from Indian roots. They took care to travel around their realm, making sure that they were endorsed by all forms of religious and folk belief. They made offerings to local spirits, prayed at Buddhist pagodas and honored noble ancestors at their temples. They took part in festivals to mark the changing of the agricultural seasons: making sacrifices to ensure the fertility of the soil and taking part in ceremonies to mark the first plowing of the year. If storms came or crops failed they would make public gestures of contrition, blaming themselves and offering further sacrifices to the spirits and to heaven. All kinds of phenomena: from droughts to solar eclipses to the sightings of dragons in the sky would be regarded as portents or punishments sent from the unseen world.

The limited evidence that we have—from the analysis of the seasonal rings of ancient trees and of references in old manuscripts—suggests that the second half of the eleventh century was a time of reduced rainfall. If this diminished the size of rice harvests it may explain why Dai Viet became more aggressive in this period: the court needed alternative sources of money. In 1059, Dai Viet forces briefly invaded Song territory. Their target was the key port of Qinzhou/Ch'in-chou, the locus of "tribute trade" arriving from Southeast Asia and the Middle East. Over the following decade, Dai Viet launched a series of smaller attacks over the northern frontier, presumably bringing home booty each time. Difficulties with harvests may also explain why Champa, under Rudra-varman III, decided to push back northward around this time, in an attempt to regain Indrapura and the surrounding area. In 1068, following attacks from Champa, Ly Thanh Tong ordered preparations to begin for war. The following year, he and his leading general, Ly Thuong Kiet, and their forces sailed down the coast to raid Vijaya. After heavy fighting, they overcame the defenders: captured the citadel, enslaved part of the population, carried off the king and his household, and burned down the city. The state's coffers were refilled once again. The Champa king was only allowed to return home after ceding parts of Champa's northern region (near the Bao Pass, north of My Son) to Dai Viet. This formality seems to have been symbolically important, bestowing a veneer of legitimacy on the land grab and ending about a century of contestation over the settlements and people near Indrapura.

In the wake of this victory, and concerned about his own declining health, the king ordered the construction of a special temple in Thang Long/Hanoi to honor the philosopher Confucius, plus four of Confucius's most loyal disciples and the Duke of Zhou. This duke had been, 2,000 years before, the brother of the (Chinese) Zhou Dynasty emperor and, after the emperor's death, had acted as a regent until the imperial heir came of age. The message was clear: in 1070, King Ly Thanh Tong's son was just four years old. The temple was, in effect, an instruction to the court to administer the kingdom until his heir was ready to rule. The prince was sent there to study, placing him at the heart of the court's spiritual and temporal rituals. The temple still stands today in central Hanoi, where it is now known as the "Temple of Literature" or Van Mieu, although it did not acquire that name until the fifteenth century.

Two years later, in 1072, Ly Thanh Tong died, leaving his 6-year-old-son, Ly Can Duc (temple name: Ly Nhan Tong) nominally on the throne. In earlier eras this might have provided an opportunity for court intriguing and open conflict between rival claimants. However, over the reigns of its first three kings (the 63 years between 1009 and 1072), the Ly Dynasty had fundamentally transformed the way its realm was ruled: anchoring it with religious and philosophical beliefs and practices that emphasized order and peace. One way they did this was to endow key officials with the royal family name: many of the famous figures named "Ly" in this period (such as the general, Ly Thuong Kiet) were given the honor in reward for meritorious service.

The court chancellor Ly Dao Thanh (another official rewarded with the royal family's name), attempted to carry out Ly Thanh Tong's wishes and rule in collaboration with the late king's wife, the official queen. She was not, however, the mother of the crown prince. The future king's mother was a concubine known as Lady Y Lan who resented her lowly status. It seems likely that she plotted with General Ly Thuong Kiet to exile the queen and the queen's entourage from the court (exactly what happened to them is unknown) and forcibly retire chancellor Ly Dao Thanh. Following this successful "palace coup," Lady Y Lan officially became queen mother and the general and his officers were given promotions. Her place in the palace secure, Lady Y Lan and General Kiet recalled Chancellor Thanh who, in 1075, started to create a state bureaucracy following the Chinese model. Candidates were asked to take exams in the "Confucian classics" with the leading scholar given the role of tutor to the boy king. Lady Y Lan became the first of several "queen mothers" to exercise significant power at court,

This coup created a template for series of royal successions over the following century and a half: a symbiotic relationship between the royal family and the families of its various supporters. The male line of succession remained with the Ly while the leading families competed for influence at court so that their daughters might become the mother of the next king. If their daughter became queen and her son became king, the successful family could look forward to all the benefits of status and resources that access to the state treasury could bring. For this to happen, they needed the support of dynamic personalities in the court: chancellors, generals and other highly-placed officials. Ambitious courtiers could also become more powerful by earning favor with these high-ranking women and their families. At its heart, therefore, the Ly court became a coalition between these courtiers and the heads of the leading families. This sharing out of the spoils resulted in a long period of relative stability: there were just four kings in the years between 1072 and 1210. In 1072, Lady Y Lan's son, Ly Nhan Tong, succeeded aged seven and then ruled for over half a century. In 1128 Ly Than Tong (birth name: Ly Duong Hoan) succeeded aged 12, ruling for a decade. In 1138, Ly Anh Tong (birth name: Ly Thien To) succeeded aged three, and then ruled for 37 years. In 1175 Ly Cao Tong (birth name: Ly Long Trat) succeeded aged 3 and ruled for 35 years.

This was not, however, obvious at the start of that period. The knowledge that Dai Viet was ruled by a mere child may have encouraged insubordination along the kingdom's frontiers. In 1075, there was more trouble with the (Tai-speaking) Nung people in the northern hills near Cao Bang. The clan chieftain switched his allegiance from Dai Viet to Song China, thereby cutting off the trade route between Dai Viet and the Nanzhao kingdom in Yunnan. The court of Dai Viet took this as both an affront to its sense of status and a threat to its economic survival. Initial skirmishes in the hills turned, by the end of the year, to full-scale war. Significantly the campaign was not just directed at the Nung people, but at Song China too. General Ly Thuong Kiet took the initiative, ordering an invasion by more than eighty thousand Dai Viet fighters on both land and sea. His forces captured the crucial tributary ports, destroyed the Song ships based there, laid siege to the Song's regional capital at Nanning and, after six weeks, captured it. The army of Dai Viet slaughtered many inhabitants and then withdrew, carrying off cartloads of booty and 3,000 captives. The violence successfully intimidated many of the border chieftains to return their loyalties to Dai Viet.

In 1076, the Song retaliated; invading Dai Viet by both land and sea. Despite hurriedly replacing their naval ships, the Song were not able to inflict much damage on water. On land, a force of 150,000 poured over the frontier mountains until it reached the defenses of Dai Viet at the Cau River. There was only one place between the foothills and the delta swamps where there was a realistic chance of getting across the water. The army of Dai Viet had had many months in which to prepare their defenses. With their navy unable to penetrate inland, the Song were forced to make the river crossing in pontoon rafts. After a long standoff, some of the Song force did cross successfully but they were quickly overcome by the defenders. With that attack defeated, a stalemate ensued along the riverbank. Gradually, disease and difficulties with re-supply wore down the invasion force. With neither side able to vanquish the other, the two agreed a face-saving compromise. The 10-year-old emperor of Dai Viet, Ly Nhan Tong (the son of Lady Y Lan), ritually apologized for the earlier invasion of Song land and requested a resumption of tributary relations. The Song agreed to withdraw. Dai Viet regained control of the gold and silver mines in the hills near Cao Bang and a few of their captives from the first invasion were allowed to return home. Overall, it was a victory for Dai Viet—and one for which General Ly Thuong Kiet would still be celebrated a millennium later.

All this had been achieved while a child sat on the throne. It was only possible because, behind the scenes, key figures in the court were creating a bureaucracy to manage the affairs of state. They borrowed Chinese ideas of civil service examinations to select clever young men to run the kingdom. These new ways of working were sufficiently entrenched that they survived the death of their chief architect, Chancellor Ly Dao Thanh, in 1081 even though the king was only 15. Four years later, when the king was ready to rule in his own right, his mother surrendered her regency and he appointed his former tutor (who had been the top candidate in the first set of examinations, in 1075) to the position of chancellor. For the following decade, the new chancellor, Le Van Thinh, ran the day-to-day affairs of the country. He instigated a new set of reforms—bringing Buddhist temples under closer supervision and creating a hierarchy for different government officials. The effect was to shore up what could have been a shaky transfer of power—and it worked. None of the young king's relatives challenged his authority. In 1095, however, the king fell out with his chancellor and banished him to an official position in the remote hills, where he disappeared from recorded history.

Despite the departure of Chancellor Le Van Thinh, the kingdom appears to have remained stable for two decades—aside from some trouble on the southern frontier with rebels and another confrontation with Champa in 1103. The queen mother, Lady Y Lan, maintained a dominant position at court, seeing off plots against her son. The king's main worry was his childlessness. He had still not produced an heir by the time Lady Y Lan died, in 1116. However, just a few months after her death, King Ly Nhan Tong adopted the son of one of his key supporters and named him to be the crown prince. The fifth Ly king was not from the royal line but brought into it through necessity. His mother (i.e., the wife of the courtier who was the natural father of the prince) became a significant power in the court.

Having secured an heir, the king decided to go to war. His target would be the Tai tribes in the hills west of Thang Long in what is now Hoa Binh province. Their crime was to have "ignored royal authority," presumably by some act of insubordination such as failing to provide tribute goods. The campaign, in 1119, was successful, as was another, in 1125, against the Nung tribes to the north of Thang Long. After that, the kingdom enjoyed relative peace until the king's passing in 1127. Just a few days after his death, all the women associated with him, wives and concubines, and all associated with Lady Y Lan, were obliged to join him in his funeral flames. The court was removing any rival claimants to the throne, enabling power to transfer smoothly to the adopted 11-year-old king, Ly Duong Hoan, better known by his temple name: Ly Than Tong.

With another child on the throne, another neighboring power attempted to take advantage. The Champa armies, together with allies from Angkor to the west, harried the southern frontier in 1127, 1133, 1135, and 1137, carrying away loot and slaves. Then, in 1138, King Ly Than Tong died at the age of just 22. By then he had three sons, by different women. The stakes were high: the family of whichever child became king would enjoy power and favor at court. On his deathbed, the king succumbed to intense lobbying and agreed to choose the second-oldest child—born of a queen—in preference to the first-born who was the son of a concubine. That put the queen in a powerful position at court, together with a senior courtier called Do Anh Vu. In an echo of previous regencies, the queen and the courtier ruled in the name of the infant king for the following decade and continued to exercise significant power even after he became an adult.

During this period, climatic, environmental and regional changes forced major adjustments in the administration of Dai Viet. Tree ring data suggests that the climate shifted from drier to wetter at the end of the eleventh century. Environmental historian Li Tana has shown how this enabled the cultivation of new areas of land. Marshy areas near the coast were drained and irrigated with fresh water. The construction of dykes led to reduced flooding and increased land area for settlement. New laws were introduced in 1141 allowing, in effect, anyone who reclaimed agricultural land from the marsh to claim it as their own.

At the same time, harbors in the southern part of the realm, which had facilitated trade between the highlands and the sea for generations, silted up and declined. By then, however, there was already a push to open new ports, much closer to the capital, triggered by changes in China. In 1127, the Song court had been pushed out of its northern territories by peoples from Inner Asia and then set up a new capital in the south, initially in modern-day Nanjing and later in Hangzhou. Cut off from their overland trading routes, the Southern Song intensified their maritime connections with Southeast Asia. They were in particular need of military horses from the kingdom of Dali, the successor state to Nanzhao located in present-day Yunnan province. The easiest way to obtain them was through Dai Viet. The Southeast Asians also wanted to trade, so they sent gifts of "tribute" to ingratiate themselves with the Southern Song. In a pair of missions in 1155 and 1156, Dai Viet presented the emperor with nine tamed elephants and more than 40 kilograms of gold. Champa sent large amounts of aromatic woods and Angkor sent spices and other products sourced from the South Asia and the Middle East.

As a result of all these changes, a network of ports, collectively known as Van Don, emerged among the islands of Ha Long Bay, where the northern part of the Red River Delta meets the sea. Historically, this had been a marginal region, beyond the control of either Dai Viet or the Song. Both states regarded it as plagued by piracy. Now, with the drainage of the marshes and a stronger central government, Dai Viet was able to assert authority there—formally recognizing Van Don as a port in 1148. With the region becoming more peaceful and the Southern Song looking for more trade, merchants from the Malay world, Angkor, Champa, and Siam began sailing directly to Van Don. It became a new pillar of the economy.

From the 1170s, the population of Dai Viet started to grow again—both by natural increase and by inward migration. The coastal region became more ethnically mixed as both rice growers from the hills and traders from abroad settled in the newly-opened lands. By the end of the twelfth century, there were enough people in Dai Viet for the practice of "slave raids" to end. Relations between Dai Viet and its neighbors improved greatly, with Champa and even Angkor paying tribute, presumably to facilitate access to the markets of Van Don. As trade between them grew, so did the wealth of each state. The "golden ages" of three of the classical Southeast Asian civilizations: Dai Viet, Angkor and Champa, happened simultaneously.

Only a few decades later, however, Dai Viet would become mired in crisis, triggering major shifts in the political system. The penultimate king of the Ly Dynasty Ly Long Trat (temple name: Ly Cao Tong) succeeded to the throne in 1175 aged three. Surviving records depict him as a playboy and his advisors as objects of fun, publicly mocked for their incompetence. The court made efforts to shore up its popular support by, for example, instituting a campaign in the 1180s to teach Confucian values of loyalty to family and king to the public. But it seems to have had little effect. Instead, the rival families of the Red River Delta began to openly fight with one another. There were rebellions in areas close to the frontiers and then, in 1199, catastrophic floods followed by famine.

In the first decade of the thirteenth century, the situation grew worse. As the king descended into debauchery inside the palace, he ordered massive spending on new buildings and gardens. Corruption exploded, the court became increasingly ineffective and disorder spread. There was a rebellion in Hoa Lu, the former capital, then in Son Tay to the west of Thang Long and then in Hai Duong, the province to the east. In 1208 the king dispatched one warlord to put an end to the disobedience of another but the target of the campaign bribed the king to call off his forces. By such moves the king destroyed his credibility and his alliances. Rival clans in the Red River delta, each with a local powerbase, took up arms against one another while the king played with his concubines. The Ly ruled in name only while real power was exercised by the clans.

In 1209, the warlord who had bribed the king the year before managed to kill the warlord who had been sent against him. In revenge, the dead warlord's bodyguard seized the Crown Prince, named Ly Sam, and his mother from the palace and escaped into the region known as "Dang" (around modern day Hung Yen city), which was controlled by the Tran family. This would be the moment that power began to shift from the Ly family with its roots in the northern part of the Red River Delta, to the Tran family, with its base in the southeast.

The Tran had arrived on the coast three generations before, apparently as traders from Fujian province, in what is now southeastern China. (Had they remained in China their family name would probably have been pronounced as "Chen" in Han Chinese or "Tan" in Hokkien.) They settled in the area around what is now Nam Dinh city, became wealthy and formed alliances with other clans near the coast, particularly the To family. With the Tran-To alliance now in possession of the 15-year-old Crown Prince, the family patriarchs engineered a marriage between him and one of the Tran daughters. They then unilaterally proclaimed the Crown Prince to be king, even though his father was still alive and nominally on the throne. In response, the king sent forces to destroy the Tran-To alliance. Although the leader of that force was killed, the Tran attempt to seize power petered out and the Crown Prince returned to the royal palace. He was, nonetheless, still married to a Tran woman.

In 1210, the playboy king, Ly Cao Tong, fell ill and died. Ly Sam formally became the new monarch, at the age of 16, and his mother (the late king's wife) became the power behind the throne. However neither mother nor child had sufficient charisma or power to impose themselves on the unruly barons, who continued to feud and fight. The court continued to be run by the same ineffective chancellor with the same chaotic results. Although the politics were fiendishly complex, the following six years saw, in effect, a civil war between rival claimants to the throne. The Ly family and their supporters tried to cling on to power while the Tran family and their supporters tried to grab it. The crisis was only ended when the young king, in 1216, opted to join the Tran. The details remain obscure but one version of the story tells us that the king's mother tried to poison his pregnant wife, outraging the king so much that he defected to her rivals. Keith Taylor has suggested that this might have just been a convenient tale to make a kidnapping of the king by the Tran family look more legitimate. Whatever happened, by 1216 the last Ly king—the heir to a 200-year-old dynasty had, in effect, handed power to his family's bitter rivals, the Tran.

In 1225 the final transfer of power was orchestrated through a pair of child marriages. The leader of the Tran clan, Tran Thu Do (pronounced chun-too-dough), arranged for the sons of his brother to wed the daughters of his half-sister, Thuan Trinh, who was King Ly Sam's queen. The elder pair were married at 14 and 9 years old while the younger pair were both aged 7. Tran Thu Do thought the younger boy would make a better king, however, and so the older boy was passed over. Tran Thu Do then declared the younger boy, Tran Canh, to be king and the boy's father to be the "senior king." The actual king, Ly Sam, and his mother were dispatched to a Buddhist temple. A year later Ly Sam was encouraged to kill himself and his mother died a few years after that. His widow, Thuan Trinh, was then obliged to marry the instigator of the plot: her half-brother Tran Thu Do. All the other women associated with the Ly royal family were given as wives to upland chieftains, removing them from the capital, where they might have caused trouble, and helping to cement relations between the mountain clans and the lowland Tran. By the end of the year, the court of Dai Viet, was firmly under the control of Tran Thu Do, ruling from behind the throne. In 1232, just to make sure that he would not suffer any rebellions from the remaining members of the Ly family, Tran Thu Do organized a banquet for them. After hours of drunken celebration, he had them all tossed into a pit and buried alive.

>͏͏ͱ҉͏ͱ͏ͱ͏ͱ

The Tran (1226–1400)

These days, the town of Chi Linh is famous as the site of Vietnam's largest coal-fired power station. Its giant red and white chimneys are a prominent landmark on the old road between Hanoi and Ha Long Bay. Although well inland, the power station stands by a junction of the Thai Binh and Kinh Thay rivers that has been strategically vital for centuries. Today, dust-blackened barges are in constant motion along the river, ferrying fuel from the open-cast mines at Cam Pha near the border with China. Seven centuries ago, Chi Linh was the site of a grand estate belonging to a general still venerated as a Vietnamese national hero: Tran Hung Dao. The "Kiep Bac Temple" not far from the power station still draws huge crowds who come to honor his memory.

Tran Hung Dao (pronounced chun-hung-dow) was born in 1228, two years after his uncle, Tran Thai Tong, then just seven years old, had been placed on the throne by Tran Thu Do. As a result of the complicated succession that Tran Thu Do had engineered to transfer power from the Ly family to his own, Tran Hung Dao was also a grandson of the last Ly king, Ly Sam. The Tran were, however, quite different from the Ly. They were not from the heartland of the delta but from the coast with its ancestral and cultural links to Fujian. They were people who had settled the delta's newly-reclaimed rice fields. After Tran Thu Do's "coup by marriage" to take control of the court, the Tran clan now had the power to allocate ownership of land—and the enslaved labor to work it. Although large-scale slave raiding appears to have ended by the thirteenth century, there were still huge numbers of enslaved people, descendants of earlier captives, working the estates of the aristocracy. They were a source of cheap and pliant labor who could be set to work on whatever schemes their owners devised.

The Tran were a ruthless family who had identified where their predecessors, the Ly, had gone wrong and were determined to avoid the same fate. The Ly had maintained power by encouraging leading families by encouraging their daughters to marry into the royal line. This had worked for a long time but then collapsed into violent feuding. The Tran decided to keep the royal line "in house." For the following two centuries, Tran kings would only marry Tran women. (See "Keeping it in the Family"on p. 99.) In contrast to the Ly, who rewarded their supporters by allocating them land for a single generation, the Tran would give it to family members permanently. In 1266, the king (still Tran Thai Tong) authorized the members of his family to marshal landless people and open up vacant territory. Through such policies they attempted to entrench their ruling position in the landscape.

With plentiful supplies of free land and low-cost labor, the Tran began to accelerate the agricultural development of the Red River delta. They built thousands of dykes and drained the enclosed marshes to create new rice fields. In doing so, the Tran probably drew upon the skills of upland rice growers who had run out of land as the population increased in their traditional mountain valley homes. There is evidence from village records and family genealogies suggesting intensified migration from the hills north and west of Hanoi into the Red River Delta and the coastal regions to its south and east during this period. Even now, many words in Vietnamese relating to rice—such as those for weir, irrigation ditch, and hulled, glutinous and non-glutinous strains of grain—come from the upland Tai language.

There are records of 14 floods in the 34 years between 1236 and 1270: apparent evidence that the climate became much wetter during this period. This enabled a second rice crop—so-called "fifth month rice" because it relied on spring rainfall, to be grown in the delta area. The extra harvest made food cheaper and enabled family sizes to increase. By the end of the thirteenth century the population of Dai Viêt had swelled to around three million.

The flooding also brought about changes in the state, pushing it in the direction of a more "Chinese-style" administration. The first big flood control project on the Red River, known as the Dinh Chi ("Cauldron handle") dyke was begun in 1248. A later account recorded that it stretched from the river's source to the sea. While this may have been an exaggeration, the dyke was certainly a huge construction effort, and it had to be organized centrally by the court. Other projects re-channeled the courses of the Thai Binh, Ma, and Chu Rivers. These efforts demanded an effective administrative system, and therefore a class of literate bureaucrats, developments that strengthened the Tran family's hold on governmental power even further. Many of these bureaucrats were eunuchs: they opted to be castrated as a price of entry into the palace administration. Without testicles they could not father children and posed no threat to the royal succession of the Tran family.

New industries emerged in the delta, notably ceramic-making and boatbuilding. Archaeologists have found evidence of a large pottery complex with over 100 kilns, dating from the thirteenth century, by the river in Chi Linh. It may well have been a part of Tran Hung Dao's estate. Both industries, however, required huge amounts of wood. Each kilogram of pottery required almost a kilogram of timber to fuel the fires in the kilns. Then, as now, Chi Linh became a site of massive energy consumption. The result was deforestation. A region where royalty had hunted for wild elephants only a century before, became utterly denuded of trees. Over time, dyke-building, deforestation and (later) drought would radically change the natural environment of the northeastern part of the delta, silting up rivers and drying out fields. In the thirteenth century, however, it allowed an economic boom.

So long as the Southern Song needed trading partners, Dai Việt prospered. In the 1250s, however, peril arrived on horseback. The Mongol armies—having already conquered swathes of Asia, started pressing south. Kublai Khan, grandson of Ghenghis Khan, wanted to destroy the Southern Song but could not break through its defenses. Instead, he ordered a side-attack. In 1253 the Mongols invaded the independent state of Dali (modern-day Yunnan), finally subduing its resistance two years later. They then began demanding free passage through Dai Viet to attack the Song from the southwest but the Tran were not prepared to agree. In late 1257, the Mongols swept down the Red River Valley into Dai Viet, with thousands of Dali's troops in the vanguard. In January 1258, the invaders defeated a Dai Viet army in Vinh Phuc, northwest of Thang Long/Hanoi and then occupied the capital. After regrouping their strength, the Dai Viet forces counterattacked. Coming at the same time as an uprising in Dali and further resistance by Tai-speaking groups in the hills, this obliged the Mongols to completely withdraw from Dai Viet during the summer of 1259 and attack the Song via a different route.

The following year, Kublai Khan declared himself to be the Great

Khan of the Mongols and a year after that King Tran Thang Tong sent emissaries to him in Beijing, receiving official recognition as "King of Annan." But Dai Viet played a double game, also sending tribute to the Song court, right up until it surrendered to the Mongols in 1279. The Tran family, with its Chinese roots, saw themselves as part of the same "civilized" world as the Song, working together against a deadly threat from the "barbarian" Mongols. In fact, they referred to them as *hulu*—"despicable wretches." Concerns in Dai Viet became greater when, in 1266, Kublai Khan demanded that, rather than just sending emissaries, the Tran king himself should pay homage in Beijing, that his son or brother should remain there as a hostage and that a Mongol official be stationed in the Dai Viet court as an overseer. It was also made clear that the Mongol "Prince of Yunnan" would take Dai Viet into his care. This was too much for the Tran to accept.

In 1279, the Song Empire finally capitulated and Dai Viet found itself facing Mongol power on both its northern and eastern frontiers. This was a major challenge for the third Tran king, Tran Nhan Tong, who had just succeeded to the throne aged 20 following the retirement of his father. In response, he formed a tactical alliance with Champa. As we saw in Chapter 2, the arrangement was sealed with Vijaya's gift of a white elephant to Dai Viet in 1282, the same year that Dai Viet refused to allow the Mongols through its territory to invade Vijaya. The importance of elephants was far more than symbolic. As the environmental historian Thomas Trautmann has shown, armies that were able to use elephants effectively as weapons of war were able to block Mongol expansion. This "elephant line" obliged the Mongols to try to invade Champa by sea, which they did in early 1283, causing substantial damage but failing in their political objectives.

In 1284 Dai Viet prepared for another invasion, entrusting its defenses to General Tran Hung Dao. The Mongols came by land but not, this time, down the Red River Valley. Their forces marched through the mountains from Guangxi, overcame the first line of resistance and then consolidated their forces at Chi Linh, Tran Hung Dao's home turf. After a pause, they captured Hanoi and were joined by reinforcements arriving by sea. The Dai Viet forces dispersed around the delta, moving along the waterways they knew well, to wait out the dry winter months.

As the weather warmed and became wetter, General Tran Hung Dao employed hit-and-run tactics against the Mongols, including those who had now advanced north from Champa. They destroyed the Mongols logistics and deprived them of local supplies. Dai Viet forces were joined by soldiers from the former Song army who wreaked revenge in a crucial battle at Ham Tu, southeast of Hanoi. A month later, the Mongols decided to retreat but they were harassed and ambushed the whole way, particularly by upland allies of the Tran. Further south, the Cham cut down those who had invaded their realm.

Kublai Khan did not give up, however. In 1287 his forces invaded again, this time with the stated intention of placing King Tran Nhan Tong's uncle—who had broken with the royal family and defected—on the throne. 70,000 troops marched over the Phu Luong Pass, northwest of Thai Nguyen, while 500 warships carried thousands more men around the coast. The naval attack was stopped at the mouth of the Bach Dang River, near modern-day Haiphong but the ground assault again succeeded in capturing Hanoi, which was looted and burned. Things looked bad for the Tran. However, the Mongols once again fell victim to attacks on their logistics. Tran warships ambushed a resupply fleet in the area of the Van Don ports, preventing food and reinforcements reaching the invasion force. The Mongol generals ordered a retreat but their way home was blocked by the Dai Viet army. This was the moment that would immortalize General Tran Hung Dao.

As one group of Mongols tried to retreat downriver, another naval fleet was sent to reinforce them. Tran Hung Dao used exactly the same tactic that Ngo Quyen had deployed against the Southern Han, 350 years earlier. His forces planted metal-tipped poles in the bed of the Bach Dang River trapping the Mongol boats when the tide fell. They were sitting ducks and the flotilla was completely destroyed. Those who had tried to escape by land over the hills were harried for the entire journey and very few of them made it through the ambushes.

Despite the defeat, Kublai Khan continued to insist that King Tran Nhan Tong visit Beijing personally to pay homage. Instead, the Dai Viet court followed tradition and sent emissaries to present tribute and apologize for the recent unpleasantness. It was important to keep up the form of ritualized relations, even though it was clear that Dai Viet had established its independence from the Mongol-led Yuan state. It is possible that Kublai Khan might have attempted further invasions had he lived longer. Fortunately for Dai Viet he died in 1294 and his successors were content to implement a policy of "great forgiveness" and leave the situation as it was. King Tran Nhan Tong retired and handed the throne to his eldest son, Tran Anh Tong.

With the abating of the Mongol threat at the end of the thirteenth century, attention turned to mounting problems within Dai Viet. The effects of wartime destruction led to famine in 1290–2 and the death of a significant part of the population. Desperate people sold their fields to the rich and themselves into slavery. Although slaves were later allowed to regain their freedom (so long as they did so before 1299), their land was gone. More and more people found themselves landless and unable to survive unless they opted for serfdom on one of the large Tran estates. Tran family members, and those who had been adopted into the clan because of their loyal service to the court, benefited hugely. Over time, the aristocracy became more and more self-interested: focused more on ruling their personal fiefs and less on state affairs. It is easy to imagine general Tran Hung Dao, for example, enjoying a very comfortable retirement in the decade before his death in 1300 while his lands at Chi Linh were worked by the new underclass of rural poor.

With some stability on its northern frontiers after the victories against the Mongols, Dai Viet moved to formalize its good relations with Champa through the marriage alliance with the Cham king discussed in Chapter 2. In 1306, Dai Viet sent a princess to marry King Jaya Singhavarman III in exchange for Champa's cession of its two northernmost districts. When the Champa king died a year later, the princess had to be rescued to prevent her ending up on the funeral pyre. The new king of Champa demanded the return of the ceded districts from Dai Viet, causing the Tran to attack once again in 1311/12, depose the king and replace him with his brother who agreed to be more pliant. Another Tran invasion, in 1318, deposed that king and replaced him with one even more pliant. Even that king eventually rebelled, however. His defiance would mark the beginning of a new period of Champa assertiveness that would eventually bring disaster to Dai Viet.

BRONZE DRUM These instruments were status symbols for clan leaders across northern Vietnam and southern China between 500 BCE and 300 CE. Archaeologists coined the name "Dong Son Culture" for these peoples, after the village where the drums were first found. *(Photo: Gary Todd, Wikimedia Commons)*

ARROWHEADS Bronze arrowheads and crossbow triggers, excavated at the Co Loa citadel, about 17 km north of Hanoi, and displayed at the National Museum of Vietnamese History, Hanoi. Co Loa was a powerful center of trade and military power between 300 and 100 BCE. *(Photo: Gary Todd, Flickr)*

UPLAND LANDSCAPE Farmer with rice terraces near Mu Cang Chai in Yen Bai province, northern Vietnam. Mountainous areas are home to dozens of different ethnic and linguistic groups. Some are descendants of Tai-speaking

peoples who once controlled powerful upland states. The modern Vietnamese state categorizes people into 54 different ethnic groups. Eighty-five percent of the population is classified as "Kinh" or Viet. *(Photo: Tavarius, Shutterstock)*

HAI BA TRUNG A modern woodblock print portraying the two Trung sisters (known in Vietnamese as Hai Ba Trung) riding elephants into battle against the Han Empire in 40 CE. Their rebellion was crushed, but they are remembered as early national heroes. *(Photo: Wikimedia Commons)*

CHAM TOWERS The remains of the Po Nagar (Mother Goddess) temple in the city of Nha Trang. The temple was constructed by Cham people who built powerful trading states in what is now central Vietnam. They were strongly influenced by South Asian culture. *(Photo: saiko3p, Shutterstock)*

FUNAN The view from the top of Ba The Mountain in An Giang province, Mekong Delta. The picture shows the Oc Eo site, where archaeologists first found traces of the "Funan" civilization. Before the seventh century, Funan was an important trading center. *(Photo: Bùi Thụy Đào Nguyên, Wikimedia Commons)*

SCULPTURE OF HINDU GOD VISHNU, OC EO CULTURE Sculpture representing the Hindu god Vishnu discovered at the Oc Eo site (shown above) and on display at the Museum of Vietnamese History in Ho Chi Minh City. Probably from the fifth century CE. Vishnu, the preserver, was the most popular Hindu god during the Funan period. *(Photo: Daderot, Wikimedia Commons)*

HAI VAN PASS A French colonial guard post on the Hai Van Pass (Pass of the Clouds) between Hue and Danang. The pass crosses a spur of the Annamite Mountains that reaches the sea. For many centuries, it formed the boundary between Dai Viet in the north and Champa to the south. *(Photo: Guillermo Pis Gonzalez, Shutterstock)*

CHAM CULTURE Tenth century carving of the ten-armed Hindu deity Durga, displayed in the Museum of Cham Sculpture, Danang. Between the fifth and nineteenth centuries CE various Cham states created a rich legacy of South Asian inspired buildings and sculpture. *(Photo: Laurence Mounier, Shutterstock)*

MY SON Remains of Hindu temples at My Son, Quang Nam province. This was an important ceremonial site for the ruling dynasties of Champa from the fourth to the fourteenth centuries CE. Most are made of brick, with carvings cut directly into the walls. *(Photo: dinosmichail, Shutterstock)*

MAI CHAU The township of Mai Chau, northwest of Hanoi. Such valleys are called *djong* in the Tai language and were home to a culture that spread across the highlands of southern China and northern Southeast Asia. *(Photo: Phuong D. Nguyen, Shutterstock)*

TRAN QUOC PAGODA The oldest Buddhist pagoda in Hanoi, now located on an island in West Lake. It was originally constructed in the sixth century during the rule of Ly Nam De, who asserted the independence of his regime

against the (Chinese) Liang Empire. The building was moved to its present location in 1615 and the tower was added later. *(Photo: Vietnam Stock Images, Shutterstock)*

BACH DANG RIVER Commemorative site at Trang Kenh village near Haiphong. It was near here that Ngo Quyen defeated the Southern Han in 938 CE, that Le Hoan defeated the Song Empire in 981 and that General Tran Hung Dao defeated the Mongols in 1287. *(Photo: Dinh Chi, Shutterstock)*

HOA LU The former citadel at Hoa Lu, Ninh Binh province, once the power base of the notorious king, Dinh Bo Linh, who united the Red River Delta under his rule in 965. He reputedly had enemies boiled alive or fed to tigers. *(Photo: Mark R. Croucher, Shutterstock)*

ONE PILLAR PAGODA, HANOI In 1049, King Ly Thai Tong dreamed of heaven. A Buddhist monk advised him to build a pagoda atop a single pillar in a lotus pond. The building still stands today, near Ba Dinh Square in the ceremonial center of Hanoi. *(Photo: Jimmy Tran, Shutterstock)*

TEMPLE OF LITERATURE Originally constructed in 1070 by King Ly Thanh Tong to honor Confucius and to remind officials to guard the kingdom until his heir came of age. It was renamed the "Temple of Literature" or Van Mieu, in the fifteenth century. *(Photo: Oscar Espinosa, Shutterstock)*

KING LY THAI TO Modern statue of King Ly Thai To facing Hoan Kiem Lake in central Hanoi. Ly Thai To was brought up by Buddhist monks in the royal court and placed on the throne in 1009. He moved the capital of Dai Co Viet to Hanoi, giving it the name Thang Long or "Rising Dragon." His reign, along with that of his son and grandson are seen today as a "golden age" in Vietnamese history. *(Photo: Pattarawat Teparagul, Shutterstock)*

CITADEL OF THE HO DYNASTY – TAY DO One of the gates of Tay Do, Thanh Hoa province. After Ho Quy Ly seized power from the Tran family in 1400, he moved the capital out of Hanoi, to a site that he called Tay Do or "Western Capital." Ho was deposed by the Chinese Ming Dynasty in 1407. The Ming occupied Dai Viet until being expelled by King Le Loi in 1430.
(Photo: sirokuma, Shutterstock)

NHAT LE RIVER The Nhat Le River, Quang Bing province. During the seventeenth and eighteenth centuries, this short river formed the southern limit of a well-defended "buffer zone" between the northern state of Dang Ngoai, ruled by the Trinh family and the central-southern state of Dang Trong, ruled by the Nguyen family. *(Photo: Loner Nguyen, Shutterstock)*

HOI AN Hoi An, Quang Nam province. In the sixteenth century the Nguyen family began developing their own realm on the central coast. They took over the old trading routes between the sea and the hills and encouraged international merchants from as far as Europe and Japan to use the port at Hoi An. It remains remarkably well preserved today. *(Photo: Banana Republic, Shutterstock)*

HUE CITADEL This palace, by the Perfume River in Hue, was where the Nguyen Dynasty ruled from between 1802 and 1945. Originally constructed by the Gia Long Emperor on the model of the Forbidden City in Beijing, it also featured European style "Vauban" fortifications. *(Photo: Nguyen Quang Ngoc Tonkin, Shutterstock)*

HUE CITADEL The Hue citadel was the official home of 13 rulers of the Nguyen Dynasty. Some ruled for decades but between 1883 and 1886 six emperors came and went in quick succession as the court fought over how to respond to French imperialism. *(Photo: AlevtinaGorskaya, Shutterstock)*

In the meantime, the fifth Tran king, Tran Minh Tong, spent the 1330s fighting against Tai-speaking tribes in the western highlands of Nghe An Province: a campaign that ended with a disastrous defeat in 1335. These borderlands slipped away from Dai Viet's control.

Nonetheless, the first forty years of the thirteenth century appear to have been a period of recovery for Dai Viet, at least compared to what followed. In the 1330s, its ceramic industry found international success—reaching markets as far away as Japan and Ottoman Turkey. The trade networks connecting to Van Don enabled the scaling-up of traditional crafts and the adoption of new ones—new kinds of pottery and silk-making for example. Relations with Mongol-ruled China were still strained so most of Dai Viet's exports went elsewhere. This is not to say that everything was fine. There were drought years and occasional problems with banditry—but they were nothing like subsequent decades.

Global changes in climate appear to have had dramatic consequences in East and Southeast Asia. Surviving records suggest rainfall dramatically declined between 1340 and 1380. Drought meant the failure of "fifth month rice," which radically reduced the overall grain harvest. In 1343, this led to food shortages and then outbreaks of local disorder and even organized rebellion. After three years of counterinsurgency, the government announced an amnesty to encourage bandits to surrender and resume normal life. Famines continued regardless and the effects were felt particularly hard by slaves on the large estates. In 1354 a man claiming to be a descendant of General Tran Hung Dao occupied the family fief in Chi Linh and rallied a rebel army which controlled, for a while, a large area of the northern delta and the surrounding hills. The story of Chi Linh symbolizes the story of the Tran Dynasty: from agricultural development, aristocratic wealth and military victory to environmental crisis and social breakdown.

In 1357, the senior king, Tran Minh Tong died. With his passing, Dai Viet transitioned into a period of increasing division and chaos, exacerbated by corruption in the palace. The decline of the Tran would echo the collapse of the Ly, 200 years before. In 1368, a century of Mongol rule in China came to an end. The Yuan state, debilitated by many of the same factors of climate and famine that had weakened Dai Viet, collapsed and was overthrown by the Ming Dynasty. This would have major implications for Dai Viet and Champa in the following century.

Champa had been much less affected by the regional droughts because it continued to earn profits from international trade in rare upland and forest products. As a result, towards the end of the century, Chinese ships increasingly bypassed Dai Viet. As Dai Viet grew weaker, Champa launched ever more confident against it. It may have been this pressure from the south that obliged the Tran to break their self-imposed rule on family succession. For the first time, they took women into the court who were not from the royal line but were from a powerful family who guarded the southern hills. In 1369, King Tran Du Tong died childless. The only candidate to replace him was a boy called Nhat Le who had been adopted by the king's brother. He was presented as the legitimate heir but it was clear that the rules of succession had been broken. Nhat Le turned out to be a dissolute figure who later killed his adoptive grandmother, the woman who had argued for him to become king in the first place. Resistance to his rule split the court and another noble seized power in 1371. This man, King Tran Nghe Tong, was the son of King Tran Minh Tong but his mother was not Tran. She was one of his concubines—from the Le family of Thanh Hoa province. This appeared to be the only option for a quasi-legitimate succession but in his efforts to build political support for this coalition, Tran Phu made a hugely-fateful decision. He reached out to his mother's family and its leader, a man called Le Quy Ly. Over the following thirty years, Le Quy Ly would graduate from being the power behind the throne, to seizing the throne himself and then taking the capital south to his home province of Thanh Hoa (See "Le Quy Ly—the Vietnamese Machiavelli" on p. 101 for more details).

By the time its political dynasty collapsed, the Tran Family had ruled for almost 200 years: from 1216 until 1400. Their rise was rooted in the changing environmental and political landscape of Dai Viet. They were a family from the coast, connected to regional trading networks and allied to strongmen in the hinterland. They grew rich and powerful by developing agriculture on their large estates which enabled the population and the economy to grow. This gave them the resources to resist challenges from insiders, and attacks by outsiders, until a change in environmental fortunes combined with a collapse of the family's own internal dynamism. By the 1370s Dai Viet was unable to defend itself against Champa, which attacked in 1380, 1382, and 1383. In 1389 a ragtag army of rural poor occupied the capital for three days. The population, having doubled from approximately 1.5 million in 1200 to around three million in 1300 collapsed to only half that number in 1400 as a result of war, famine, disease and emigration.

In some ways, Dai Viet was back where it had started. One dynasty had run out of steam, another was taking power. However, the realm had changed significantly in those two centuries. A "Dai Viet culture" had emerged. A new class of educated commoners emerged who helped its rulers construct an identity for Dai Viet that was similar to the "northern empire" in many ways but also self-consciously different. This identity included roles for Confucianism, Buddhism and Daoism but also a sense of separateness based upon different myths of origin and traditions. Its court language was Chinese but it had developed ways to use Chinese characters to write down the emerging Vietnamese language—a way of writing that became known as *nôm*. This culture appreciated northern poetry and opera but found local ways to perform and develop them. The Tran family probably spoke, or at least knew, Chinese at the start of their family's rule but by the end of it, the court spoke Vietnamese. The Ly and the Tran had created a sense of difference and independence.

><~~~<

The Tran—Keeping It in the Family

The Tran patriarch Tran Thu Do was so obsessed with maintaining his family's hold over the royal line of succession that he forced some extremely unsavory arrangements upon his relations. In 1225, having engineered a marriage between the Ly crown prince (Ly Sam) and his half-sister Thuan Trinh, he ensured that the two daughters of this union, Thuan Thien and Chieu Thanh, both married sons of his brother while all were children. Tran Thu Do did not believe that the older of the two boys would make a good king, so he arranged for the younger one, Tranh Thai Tong to succeed to the throne, the first king of the Tran Dynasty. He then arranged for Crown Prince Ly Sam to meet an early death and took the royal widow (his own half-sister) Thuan Trinh as one of his wives.

Unfortunately Tranh Thai Tong's marriage to Chieu Thanh did not produce a royal heir. The other couple did, however, have children including a daughter named Thien Cam. To ensure the royal succession, Tran Thu Do ordered the two young men to swap their wives. King Tran Thai Tong then fathered a son with his new wife (and former sister-in-law) Chieu Thanh. This son, Tran Thanh Tong, was obliged to marry the daughter of his mother's previous marriage to his uncle, Thien Cam. Tran Thanh Tong became the second Tran king in 1279. The half-siblings (they shared a mother, Thuan Thien) produced a son, Tran Nhan Tong who became the third Tran king in 1294.

Tran Thu Do died in 1264. He was never king but exercised enormous power through his relatives from behind the throne and ensured that his inbred family would dominate Dai Viet for the following century and a half. Almost until the end, subsequent Tran kings were born of Tran mothers and fathers.

The Tran family also developed another innovation to avoid a key weakness of the Ly period. Rather than entrust the development of a boy king to "regents" who could manipulate the realm from behind the throne, each king chose their own heir and then "retired" when the boy came of age. As the "senior king" they could advise, counsel and guide the king and thus safeguard the dynasty while gradually handing over the reins of power. A second royal palace complex was built in the family's seat just north of the modern city of Nam Dinh, about 70 km down the Red River from Thang Long. The senior king would live here with the junior king paying visits when necessary.

Chu Van An and the Origins of the Viet

In the aftermath of the Mongol invasions and with the stability of Dai Viet under frequent challenge, the Tran court renewed its efforts to recruit educated "scholar-officials" on the Chinese model to run the machinery of government. Some of these scholar-officials would be much more than bureaucrats; they would develop ideas that would define the society they were administering and defending. Among the earliest was a scholar called Chu Van An, who declined to become an official and chose to run his own school instead. He saw himself as a Confucian and opposed what he saw as the pointless superstition of Buddhism. Politically, he advocated a return to ruling by "sage kings" based on rules derived from antiquity. Chu Van An and his disciples researched and created a history for Dai Viet, divining its ancient origins in old manuscripts and stories and providing a lineage to justify its existence as a separate state. They taught other scholars, who subsequently augmented these national stories with other ideas. In a poem of 1369, for example, Pham Su Manh borrowed elements from Chinese manuscripts to place the origins of the Viet people in the kingdom of "Van Lang." Many of the ideas about the ancient history of Vietnam actually flow from versions of history which were constructed in this period.

Le Quy Ly—the Vietnamese Machiavelli

Le Quy Ly (pronounced Lay Kwee Lee) was the court official who ended the Tran Dynasty in 1400, and made himself king by out-maneuvering all his opponents and totally remaking Dai Viet's political system. He identified all the likely obstacles to his seizure of power and neutralized them. His career was a master class in hard-nosed realpolitik, a century before Machiavelli.

Le Quy Ly grew up on the periphery of the Tran court. His family were from the area of Vinh Loc in Thanh Hoa province, about 100 km south of Thang Long/Hanoi, a long way from the Tran family base in the lower regions of the Red River Delta. Nonetheless, they had good royal connections, possibly forged in the need to resist attacks from the Cham to the south. His mother's sister had been a concubine of the fifth Tran king Tran Minh Tong in the 1330s, and was the mother of the ninth Tran king, Tran Due Tong. In 1371, the two cousins formed an alliance. Le Quy Ly was given a Tran widow as his wife and Tran Due Tong took a woman from the Le family as his queen.

Tran Due Tong became king in 1373 and from then onwards, Le Quy Ly was a key figure inside the government, particularly after Tran Due Tong was killed in battle with the Cham in 1377. As the crisis with the Cham grew worse over the following years, Le Quy Ly became a key adviser to the "senior king" Tran Nghe Tong. His first task was to generate enough money to defend the country. The huge Tran family estates were exempt from taxes so Le Quy Ly organized a massive program of land reform. He copied what the Tang Dynasty had done in China and organized local men into military units, gave them land and obliged them to pay tax on a per-head basis. At a stroke he reduced the number of serfs and increased the number of taxpayers. In so doing he also started to undermine the economic power of the Tran aristocracy.

In 1381, another move also had two useful outcomes. Le Quy Ly ordered all the Buddhist monasteries to mobilize men for the war effort. This both increased the size of the military and reduced the power of the temples. Then, by keeping the military active fighting the Cham on the southern front, he made sure they had little time or ability to intervene in court affairs, except when Le Quy Ly needed them to.

In 1383, Senior King Tran Nghe Tong moved out of the royal palace to write a book of instruction for the new king, Tran The De, a son of Tran Due Tong. When Tran Nghe Tong returned to the palace in 1387, Le Quy Ly persuaded him to depose the king and replace him with Tran Nghe Tong's youngest son, 10-year-old Tran Ngung. The boy was then married to Le Quy Ly's daughter and the deposed king, Tran The De, and his supporters were killed. Le Quy Ly then appointed a trusted group of advisers to run the court. He had networks of spies across the kingdom reporting on dissent which, using his control of the military, Le Quy Ly crushed.

In 1392, Le Quy Ly issued a book providing Confucian arguments against metaphysical Buddhism and in favor of strong central government and of kings having wise advisers. Scholars were instructed to develop their understanding of the ideas and put them into practice. Four years later Le Quy Ly introduced examinations which required successful applicants for government administrators to demonstrate their understanding of his own ideas.

In 1394, Tran Nghe Tong died, at the age of 73, leaving his youngest son Tran Thuan Tong, just 16, on the throne and at the mercy of court politics. Le Quy Ly moved into the palace, almost ready to make his final moves. First he needed to ensure that his potential opponents were destroyed. In 1396 he ordered that all remaining Buddhist monks under the age of 50 be defrocked. Thereafter, only those who passed a religious examination could be appointed to manage temples. Then, in possibly his most drastic move, he undercut the power of the wealthy by banning the use of coins and insisting that all transactions had to be made in court-issued paper money. As a result, his government came to know how much everyone owned and, more importantly, how much they owed in taxes.

In 1397, he ordered the royal palace moved to his home territory in Thanh Hoa, far from the Tran powerbase. The following year he deposed the young king Tran Thuan Tong and put his own 2-year-old grandson, the son of Tran Thuan Tong and his daughter, on the throne. He then had Tran Thuan Tong, his son-in-law, killed. In 1399, at a gathering of Tran family members, he arrested hundreds of members of the royal family, along with their retainers and slaves, and executed 370 of them. It mirrored the massacre of the Ly family, 167 years before.

With all political opposition eliminated, he introduced new laws limiting land ownership, to prevent the emergence of a new aristocracy, and reorganized local administration. Finally, in 1400, he demoted his grandson, and promoted his second son whose mother was from the Tran family—so he could claim a legitimate succession. He then declared himself senior king and the founder of a new dynasty— the Ho—not quite thirty years after he started his journey to the top.

CHAPTER 4

INVASION AND DIVISION (1400–1771)

Ho Quy Ly and the Ming (1400–27)

One of the oddest capitals in Vietnamese history still stands outside the town of Vinh Loc, close to the Ma River in Thanh Hoa province. Today it is a huge empty space, nearly a kilometer square, each of its thick stone walls pierced by a triple-arched gate. Within the walls, the palace buildings have been replaced by farmers' plots: small fields of rice and vegetables now growing in an abandoned citadel where a usurper's dreams once failed to take root. Tay Do—the name means "western capital"—was only the seat of rulers for a decade: from 1397, when the penultimate Tran king was brought here by Le Quy Ly, until 1407 when Ly, having declared himself king and the founder of a new dynasty, was deposed by an invading army from Ming China. Those ten years were, however, a critical punctuation point in the development of Dai Viet.

The shift of power to this "western capital" around 1400, and the renaming of the old capital from Thang Long to Dong Do or "eastern capital" was part of a new battle for supremacy. Rather than pitting the families of the coast against those of the middle Red River Delta, this battle would pit the families of the Red River Delta against those of the upland areas to its south, around the basins of the Ca and Ma rivers (in what is now Thanh Hoa province). This battle would continue in various forms for several centuries, only ending with the victory of the Nguyen family 400 years later. There were cultural effects too. Because

Le Quy Ly's coup against the Tran triggered the Ming invasion, it also accelerated two apparently contradictory processes: the "sinicization" (Chinese-ification) of many aspects of Dai Viet culture but also a rising hostility towards Ming China itself. Dai Viet would become more "Chinese" in its government and high culture but less so in its day-to-day attitudes and behavior.

The changes began, neatly, in 1400. Le Quy Ly, having disposed of the Tran family as a political force, declared himself the "senior king" and founder of a new dynasty called the "Ho" and changed his name to Ho Quy Ly. He needed to justify his actions and explain why he had removed the young king to a new capital. He did so by twisting a Confucian precedent from 2,400 years before. He presented himself as a modern Duke of Zhou, the man who had guarded the throne for a young king, to suggest he had no pretensions to power. In the old story, the Kingdom of Zhou had an "eastern" and a "western" capital so Ho Quy Ly borrowed the same names, even though his "Tay Do" was barely any further west than his "Dong Do" (it is actually south of Hanoi). He reinforced this claim to ancient legitimacy by changing the name of his state from Dai Viet to Dai Ngu: a reference to the mythical (Chinese) King Yu from even earlier times, a thousand years before Zhou.

Despite borrowing these historical figures, and eliminating his Tran predecessors, Ho Quy Ly was unable to win popular support in the Red River Delta. Instead, he created a police state: tracking down and punishing expressions of dissent. His attempts to build a new, reformed government came to little, mainly because his reforms had taken away much of the power of the old elite without building up an alternative. Ho Quy Ly's administration was unpopular, ineffective and vulnerable to attack.

That attack came in 1407. The third emperor of the Ming Dynasty, Zhu Di (known as the Yongle Emperor) had been persuaded by his advisers that Ho Quy Ly was a usurper without popular support. The official reason for the invasion was to eliminate Ho and restore the "legitimate" Tran Dynasty. As the scholar Kathlene Baldanza has noted, this was somewhat ironic, considering that Zhu Di had just overthrown his own nephew to seize the throne and also relocated his capital (from Nanjing to Beijing) to escape the thousands of scholars and officials who rejected his actions. In an attempt to shore up his own legitimacy, Zhu Di sent elaborate missions overseas to seek formal recognition from the various courts and statelets in Southeast Asia. Among those diplomats was Zheng He, who would became famous for his long voyages into the Indian Ocean and the Middle East. However, Zhu Di wasn't interested in seeking diplomatic recognition from Ho Quy Ly: he wanted to incorporate the lands of Dai Viet into his empire as the old province of Jiaozhou.

Ly knew the invasion was coming but he could not muster sufficient force or committed generals to stop it. Two armies amounting to a quarter of a million troops crossed over the hills from Guangxi and Yunnan, pushed aside the defenders and occupied both the old capital and the new one. The Ming invaders were welcomed by most people in the Red River Delta: both those who had been loyal to the Tran and those of Chinese descent who disliked the rule of the Ho Dynasty and the interlopers from Thanh Hoa. Ly and his family were captured and taken to China, their later fate unknown. The way was now clear for the Ming to turn the independent state of Dai Ngu back into a Chinese province.

The Ming established strongholds around the margins of the delta— from the Tay Do citadel north to Dong Do and then east towards Chi Linh and the coast. Nearly 90,000 soldiers were deployed to keep out "uncivilized" rebels, and officials were brought from other Ming provinces to create a new administration. They garrisoned the entire province, snuffing out the last embers of resistance. They built bridges, repaired roads and set up a postal system. With such technologies they pacified the delta. By 1409 they controlled Thanh Hoa, and reached as far south as Hue by 1413. They had an easier time in the lowlands where local people accepted Ming rule much more readily than those in the uplands. The lowlands and the coast had a history of contact with Guangdong and Fujian and the population there now included many who traced their family origins back to Chinese merchants and seafarers. They had been augmented by refugees from the Song who had fled the Mongols. The historian John Whitmore has shown how the area around Chi Linh, Tran Hung Dao's old redoubt which had resisted the "barbarian" Mongols over a century before, became strongly pro-Ming based upon its shared cultural orientation. This area produced many of the officials that would serve the Ming. This distinction between those who saw themselves as "civilized" and those who rejected Ming ideas of "civilization" helped to both maintain the occupation and also set up a cultural clash that would endure for centuries. Some of those who opted for "civilization" were sent away for training in other parts of the Ming empire and some of them became valuable officials. A man called Nguyen An became the chief architect of the Imperial Palace in Beijing, for example. At home, in what was now the "Province of Jiaozhi," hundreds of new "Confucian" schools were opened, together with many more shrines to the old philosopher and temples of literature. At the same time the Ming attempted to eliminate local culture. They frowned upon traditional practices such teeth blackening and re-imposed Chinese as the official language. They confiscated old texts written in Vietnamese *nôm*, destroyed documents discussing earlier dynasties and the existence of a separate "kingdom" that had once been a rival to the empire of the north. They also insisted on cultural changes: banning unmarried boys and girls from cutting their hair and imposing what they regarded as "modesty" in dress. While some people were prepared to accept these changes, perhaps even welcome them, other parts of the local population began to turn against the occupiers. Those who wanted to live outside Ming "civilization" gravitated towards the uplands on the southern fringes of the Red River Delta in the province of Thanh Hoa and further south in Nghe An.

In 1424 Emperor Zhu Di died. His successor was less concerned about the outside world and reoriented Ming policy inwards. Resources were redirected towards defending the northern borders with Inner Asia, overseas diplomacy was scrapped and the determination to hold onto Jiaozhou dissipated. In 1425 he abolished tax collections beyond those necessary to maintain the military garrisons. It was the start of a withdrawal. Into the void stepped a local leader from the uplands of Thanh Hoa, man called Le Loi (pronounced Lay Loy). We don't know too much about his origins but it is likely that Le Loi was not Viet. This area was a home to a mosaic of ethnic groups, Tai, Muong and Viet, and the historian Li Tana argues that he was probably of Muong ethnicity. A Chinese document from the following century describes him as "a barbarian among the barbarians" (i.e., he was an outsider to the

Viet population.). His family had benefited from the fall of the Tran a generation earlier, but Le Loi had initially supported the Ming before breaking with them as they tried to enforce northern cultural norms. Other leaders had tried to resist but been crushed. Le Loi became successful by combining shrewd military tactics with a very successful propaganda campaign. He avoided big battles and sieges of the cities, choosing to wage a very mobile insurgency until his units were strong enough to face the well-organized occupation forces. At the same time, he appointed a writer schooled in Chinese literature to handle his public messaging. This man, Nguyen Trai, has since become one of the heroes of Vietnamese literary history.

Nguyen Trai (pronounced Nwee-yen Chai) was a grandson of a Tran prince and the son of a famous scholar who had served Ho Quy Ly before being deported to the north by the Ming. Nguyen Trai managed to avoid capture and eventually offered his services to Le Loi. He could write in both literary Chinese and *nôm* and he helped the rebel leader to bridge the cultural gap between the peoples of the uplands and lowlands. He wrote letters to local commanders urging them to switch sides and he used his writings to mobilize the general population against the Ming. He also created stories exalting Le Loi's leadership—including one about a magical sword and a turtle. (See "The Myth of the Returned Sword" on p. 132.) Schooled in Confucian theory he also advised Le Loi how to govern in a way that would win support, rather than opposition from those who had previously welcomed Ming rule. Around this time, Le Loi claimed to have found a legitimate successor to the Tran Dynasty, a man called Tran Cao, and declared him to be the rightful king. By so doing, he was trying to have it both ways: honoring Confucian protocol *and* asserting Dai Viet independence. It also gave the Ming a fig-leaf to explain their defeat. Ming officials could pretend that they had restored the Tran dynasty and then withdraw.

With the support of Nguyen Trai's rhetoric and swelling public support, Le Loi chased the Ming forces out of the province. Local people who had supported the Ming were given the choice of departing with them or staying. Shortly after the Ming forces had departed, the "royal heir" Tran Cao disappeared, presumed poisoned, and Le Loi assumed the throne. Le Loi then petitioned the Ming with the appropriate formalities of a vassal asking to be recognized by the imperial power. Officially, he had succeeded the Tran Dynasty and Ho Quy Ly could be regarded as a mere usurper whom history could ignore. The imperial province of Jiaozhou had gone and the vassal of "Annan" had returned to the Chinese map. In the absence of any other viable options, the new Ming emperor agreed and, in 1430, he sent an official seal to confirm the arrangement. This diplomatic fiction obscured the reality that Le Loi was the ruler of an independent state which once again took the name of Dai Viet. There would be no further fighting between the "northern empire" and the "southern vassal" until the late 20th century.

The twenty years of the Ming occupation of Dai Viet had two, apparently contradictory effects. At a governmental level it entrenched "Chinese" ways of operating: officials learnt northern ways of administering and managing society, lessons that were retained even after the departure of the Ming. At the social level, however, the occupation increased local resentment towards an overbearing northern culture. The defeat of the Ming divided the Dai Viet population between those who still felt themselves part of that northern culture—not all of whom left with the occupation troops—and those who were willing to adapt to the rule of the "barbarian" uplanders. The first 30 years of the fifteenth century saw a "cultural war" between rival groups with different ideas of how society should function. The interlude between the end of the Tran and the beginning of the Le dynasties ended with a defeat for the coastal-dwellers and their old aristocracy. But it was not the last word in this cultural struggle.

Le Dynasty (1428–1527)

Le Loi (pronounced Lay Loy), also known by his temple name Le Thai To (lay-tie-toe) immediately set to work building a new state to replace the departed Ming. With the advice of Nguyen Trai and the support of many officials trained by the previous administration, he created a government in the image of the one he had just defeated. Despite his "barbarian" origins, Le Loi's court reinstated Confucian rules, starting with the propagation of the official narrative that the Le Dynasty was the legitimate successor of the Tran. It brought back literary examinations to select candidates for the bureaucracy, it organized censuses and tax codes and it promulgated laws to impose good morality on the people—banning gambling and the public consumption of alcohol, for example.

Le Loi returned the capital to its original site (modern day Hanoi), but changed its name from Dong Do to Dong Kinh to emphasize the difference with Ho Quy Ly. The meaning was the same, however: "eastern capital." Dong Kinh was the origin of the name "Tonkin" which foreigners would later use to refer to the whole northern region. At the same time, the old "western capital" Tay Do was abandoned and a new western capital, named "Tay Kinh" was established in the next river valley to the south, the native home of the Le family. The area around this new Tay Kinh, next to the Chu River, remained the spiritual home, ancestral temple and royal burial place, of the Le family until it lost the throne in 1789.

After four years of fighting, Le Loi needed to get the economy running again very quickly. Large areas of land had been abandoned by those who left with the Ming, and both food production and tax revenues had slumped. The new king was fortunate to inherit the results of Ho Quy Ly's attacks on the old Tran aristocracy, two decades before. Instead of large aristocratic or Buddhist temple estates worked by slaves and serfs, most of the fields of Dai Viet were now toiled by free peasants. The lands of officials who had served the Ming (along with their families) were confiscated and reallocated to people without land. All these farmers had the incentive to increase the production of food—and the obligation to pay taxes to the court. Le Loi also benefitted from several years of wetter weather: food supplies stabilized and unrest decreased. The population started to grow again and new villages were established. Ceramic manufacturing revived and, now that Dai Viet was outside the Ming empire, trade with the rest of the world could resume. As commerce returned, the port of Van Don thrived once more.

Le Loi only enjoyed his success for five years. He died in 1433, leaving his 10-year-old son, Le Nguyen Long, as heir. There would not be another adult king until 1460. Le Loi's former allies from the hills, illiterate warlords unfamiliar with lowland customs, filled the void while relying on the new bureaucracy to turn their instructions into actions.

The result was in-fighting within the court with rival officials jockeying for influence and stuffing government positions with their friends and relations. In 1437, to try to impose some order on the court, Nguyen Trai introduced new rules of ritual, based on those introduced by the Ming. At the same time, however, the court announced a series of regulations to reduce the influence of northern (Chinese) culture and enforce a local identity. Any remaining Ming subjects were ordered to cut their hair short and dress in "Kinh style." Court officials also insisted that subjects should only dress and speak in the Dai Viet manner and refrain from using other languages. It is possible to discern the beginnings of a Dai Viet "nationalism" during this period. Nguyen Trai wrote an account of the geography of the state in 1435 to educate the new king. It both created a sense of the territory as a "whole" and recommended that its people should not use the languages or clothing of any neighboring state but assert their own customs.

Under the influence of Confucian ideas about the superiority of "civilization"—but also local beliefs about the specialness of Dai Viet—the court's view of its place in the world changed. Rather than seeing itself as equal to the rulers to its west and south, Dai Viet came to believe it was morally superior to them. Until this time, Viet, Tai, Lao and Cham states had existed side-by-side and, although there was frequent conflict between them, there were also cultural exchanges and familial connections. The Ly had often sent princesses to wed highland chiefs including, for example, the Phuan people of eastern Laos and, as we saw earlier, the Tran had sealed a deal with the Cham with another princess bride. After 1430 this changed. The more that the Dai Viet court asserted a Confucian identity, the more it had to deny its "Southeast Asian" one. It became taboo to mention old family ties between Dai Viet and its neighbors. In its proclamations of war against Lao and Champa, Dai Viet accused their leaders of assuming too great a status, defying their rightful place in the world and therefore—justifying the punishments being dealt to them. Dai Viet had acquired a "civilizing mission."

As a result of their occupation by the Ming, Dai Viet now had the weaponry to match their sense of cultural superiority. In expeditions into the highlands around the Red River Delta its forces were able to prevail on battlefield after battlefield. They defeated various Tai groups in the hills around the Black River valley northwest of the delta in successive campaigns in 1432, 1433, 1434, 1437, 1439 and 1441. By the end of the decade, Dai Viet had established its domination further into an area (around modern-day Dien Bien Phu) inhabited by a confederation of Tai tribes known as the "Sipsong Chu Tai." From here they could block attacks from the Ai Lao people based in Hua Pan/Houaphanh in what is now eastern Laos. In effect, Dai Viet was using a classic colonial technique: sponsoring loyal chiefs to hold back hostile ones. Its forces also pushed north to win control of the trade route into Yunnan. By 1450, Dai Viet had subdued the Tai-populated areas all around its north-western and northeastern borders. As a result, Dai Viet was able to reopen direct trade with Yunnan, obtaining copper to make firearms and minerals for the production of high-class ceramics. These further increased its military and economic power.

In 1442, scandal erupted in the court. The young king, Le Nguyen Long, had been having an affair with the wife of his trusted advisor, Nguyen Trai. The wife, Nguyen Thi Lo, is described as being young and beautiful and with great influence among the women of the court. The king is said to have kept her at his side "day and night" provoking gossip and jealousy. In autumn of that year he visited the night her at Nguyen Trai's estate in Chi Linh (near the former estate of General Tran Hung Dao) but the following morning he died. There were accusations of poison and plots, none of which can be verified; he might easily have died from other causes. Nonetheless, those who now had power at court seized the moment and, just twelve days later, Nguyen Trai, his wife Nguyen Thi Lo and their entire families were executed.

The dead king's third son, only one year old, was named as the successor. Just as during the Ly Dynasty, 300 years earlier, real power lay with a coalition between the family of the queen mother and the officials at court. The queen mother, Nguyen Thi Anh, was part of a family from Thanh Hoa which was closely connected with the "barbarian" chieftains who had fought against the Ming and brought the Le Dynasty to power. Collectively, they made sure there was no opposition to the royal succession. Nonetheless, news of the king's death may have been the trigger for a new threat to emerge from Champa which, in 1444, attacked the southern provinces of Dai Viet. This initiated a new round of campaigns that would radically change the region.

The chieftains formed an army to retaliate and, the following year, marched south. They pushed all the way to Vijaya where they captured the Cham king. They put a more pliable leader on the throne and withdrew—but only as far as the Hai Van Pass (between the modern cities of Hue and Danang). Dai Viet took control of some of the key ports through which maritime traders connected with the overland routes into Southeast Asia. Military power had given the kingdom another important source of both revenue and regional influence.

Dai Viet also had internal problems to address. From 1445, there were several years in which floods alternated with droughts. Both disrupted food supplies and were interpreted, in the Confucian manner, as signs of heavenly displeasure at the behavior of the royal court. In 1451, rising unhappiness led to a palace coup and the execution or imprisonment of the old men who had ruled the state since the time of Le Loi. The queen mother also stood down from her role as regent. Exactly what happened over the following decade is unclear but in 1459 the boy-king, by then 18, was killed by his eldest brother. Eight months later, the usurper was also murdered, apparently on the orders of powerful lords who feared they were being lined up for the chop. They placed a third brother, another 18-year-old called Le Thu Thanh, on the throne. This boy, a grandson of Le Loi, was an inspired choice. He would . go on to lead Dai Viet to renewed greatness. By the end of his reign, almost four decades later, he had taken the fortunes of Dai Viet to a new high, but at the expense of its neighbors to the west and south. He was immortalized with the temple name Le Thanh Tong (pron. lay-tang-tong), a name now found on streets and statues across the country.

Surviving records portray Le Thanh Tong as an enlightened leader. An early priority was improving agriculture, increasing the number of peasant taxpayers and taking steps to prevent large landowners buying or grabbing the land of smaller farmers. He sent workers and soldiers to rebuild dykes, distribute food after flooding and provide healthcare during epidemics. In the words of the historian John Whitmore, the king "brought the Vietnamese government for the first time into the villages." Officials were posted to rural areas to keep an eye on local conditions. Timely reports allowed the court to respond to problems, preventing local difficulties from turning into national crises.

Le Thanh Tong embedded Confucian ideas into Dai Viet. He and his officials promoted ideals of Confucian morality—with its emphasis on respect for kings, fathers and husbands—to society. Women were relegated to a lower status. Examinations were reintroduced to recruit educated officials and candidates were tested in their knowledge of the "Five Classics" and the "Four Books" of Confucian thought. His support for Confucianism was paired with a disdain for Buddhism. Le Thanh Tong instituted laws restricting the rebuilding of temples and promoted, instead, the worship of local spirits. He encouraged the institution of the village *dinh* (pronounced ding)—the communal hall where noteworthy figures from the past, usually people who had done good things for the locality, were remembered and prayed to. The *dinh* became the social foundation of the Dai Viet village, bringing together the men of the main families to manage problems and disputes. Women were largely excluded and offered their devotions at Buddhist temples instead.

As historian Keith Taylor has observed, the Chinese practice was also the basis for a remodeled government. Le Thanh Tong copied the Ming by establishing six ministries: Rites, Finance, Personnel, Justice, Public Works and War. The army was also organized along Ming lines with five commands: Central (guarding the ancestral homeland in Thanh Hoa), North, South, East and West) and the same rank structure. He gave ministers high status and separated military power from civilian power to reduce the chances of a coup. He created a professional bureaucracy, so that by 1471 there were 2,400 officials registered in the court and about the same again working in the provinces. He created institutions to monitor their performance, even measuring their success by counting the numbers of peasants who had fled their jurisdictions. He also commissioned one official, Ngo Si Lien, to re-write the history of his lands and people to demonstrate their superiority over their neighbors (See "The Myth-makers" on p. 133.).

That growing sense of cultural superiority, combined with a desire to become the pre-eminent power in the region, turned into expansionism. In 1470, triggered by Cham attempts to regain control of the ports and overland trade routes, Dai Viet attacked south. The invasion was led by the 29-year-old king in person and demonstrated sophisticated tactics with modern weaponry—a result of decades of professionalization of the military. While the main force advanced along the coastal strip, seaborne troops landed behind the Cham frontline and dug in. Other units travelled through the mountains to cut off escape routes to the west. The Cham forces were encircled and destroyed by a vastly superior force. This was a new form of warfare, involving gunpowder, and Dai Viet sought a new kind of outcome. This was not a raid to gather booty. This time, Dai Viet was determined to expand the realm of civilization by annihilating the previous state and annexing its land. Vijaya was destroyed, tens of thousands of people were killed and tens of thousands more taken north as slaves.

The invasion pushed the southern boundary of Dai Viet 300 km further south, from the Hai Van Pass as far as the Cu Mong Pass just beyond Vijaya (the modern city of Qui Nhon). The kingdom now controlled all the ports of the central part of the coast, and their overland routes into the Mekong states. The conquered land was then incorporated into a new province called Quang Nam and settled with northerners. Many of them were troublesome subjects sent into what amounted to internal exile: criminals, rebellious chiefs from the borderlands, unreliable serfs and descendants of people who had served the Ming. Supervising them all were officials being punished for some infraction or other with an assignment to the "wild south." Some Cham people had remained after the conquest but they were "Viet-ized": given new names and instructed to follow northern cultural norms.

Having successfully enlarged his realm to the south, Le Thanh Tong turned his attention to the west. In 1479 his forces marched into the mountains up five separate river valleys to attack the Ai Lao/Lan Xang people in Houaphanh and the Phuan people to the south in Xiangkhouang (both in present-day Laos). The historian Li Tana tells us that almost the entire Phuan population, 90,000 households, died in the invasion. The armies then marched to Luang Prabang, 400 km from Dong Kinh and looted it, before pushing further west into what is now Myanmar. Even today that remains a formidable overland journey. The Dai Viet generals were of upland stock, probably of Muong or mixed Muong-Tai ancestry, and knew how to operate in the hills.

The campaign lasted five years until the generals were satisfied that they had smashed the ability of these Tai chiefs to threaten Dai Viet. In 1484 the armies came home, having established a series of outposts in the hills along the western border to enforce control. By the end of his campaigns, King Le Thanh Tong had made Dai Viet the pre-eminent power in eastern mainland Southeast Asia. In the absence of a threat from the Ming, it had established its dominance over the Tai statelets in the hills and Champa to the south. Its power was so great that in 1481 even Malacca, on the other side of the peninsula, complained to the Ming court that it feared annexation by Dai Viet.

Through a combination of territorial expansion and agricultural development the number of villages in the kingdom more than doubled from 3,200 recorded in the Ming census of 1417 to over 7,600 in 1490. As many as 300,000 demobilized soldiers were established on military farms—*đồn điền*—along the coast to the south of Dong Kinh/Hanoi. In the words of the king, they were ordered "to gain full use of (our) agricultural potential and to broaden the resources of the realm." They built dykes, drained swamps and turned marshlands into productive paddy fields. These units may have been replacing *ngô* (ethnic Chinese) farmers who had left the area following the end of the Ming occupation decades earlier. Those *ngô* who remained in the kingdom were a source of concern and, in 1471, the court introduced new rules to forcibly integrate them into Dai Viet society. They were given new names to make them sound more Viet. They were banned from marrying in their home districts and villages and their children and grandchildren were ordered to take different family names. In this way, the court hoped to break up any sense of community and difference among those who had previously held to a more "Chinese" culture.

Le Thanh Tong died in 1497 at the relatively young age of 55. He is said to have succumbed to a chronic disease allegedly caused by "excessively visiting women." This brought an early end to a period still regarded as a "golden age" in the history of Dai Viet. During nearly forty years on the throne he established stability at home through effective government, and a huge territorial expansion through well-planned warfare. With his propagation of both Confucianism and new national myths he had helped to create a new sense of what it meant to be Viet. He managed to integrate the wild men of the hills with the farmers of the lowlands and the Sinicized urbanites to form a united realm that would outlast him. Beneath the surface, however, cracks remained. A long period of stability was about to disintegrate.

Le Thanh Tong handed power to Le Hien Tong, one of his 14 sons, whose rule seems to have continued in the same mold as his father's. But Le Hien Tong only ruled for seven years before dying, reportedly of the same affliction as his father. Le Hien Tong's eldest son was a transvestite which ruled him out of contention for the crown. The second son was judged incompetent, so the third son was appointed king. He spent just seven months on the throne before dying a mysterious death in 1505. The second son then seized power at the age of 17. Le Uy Muc had been born of a peasant woman who had sold herself into slavery and been taken into the palace as a maid. There she caught the eye of the king and ended up as queen mother. This opened the doors of the palace to her peasant relatives who made the most of the opportunity. They were from the delta and they came to see the old royal family, with its mountain roots, as their mortal enemies. Life in the palace became chaotic and murderous.

The situation became so bad that some of the royal offspring fled to the Le family's "western capital" in Thanh Hoa. In 1509 they banded together under the command of a member of a prominent local family: the Nguyen (about whom we will hear much more in due course). From there they attacked the eastern capital, Dong Kinh, and forced King Le Uy Muc to drink poison. His body was then blasted from a cannon just to make sure. They then placed another grandson of Le Thanh Tong on the throne, 15-year-old Le Tuong Duc. But life did not settle back down. In fact there were near-continuous rebellions for the next few years. The bureaucracy collapsed and the authority of the king virtually disappeared. Instead, he retreated to a life of pleasure inside the palace and the situation outside became catastrophic.

The old social divisions of the realm reappeared. The area north of the Cau River, between Chi Linh and the Van Don ports, had been less affected by the chaos afflicting the Red River Delta and the big families from that region began to assert themselves. From among them rose a leader called Mac Dang Dung (pron. mack-dang-zung), descendant of a *ngô* (ethnic Chinese) family that had served both the Mongol Yuan

Dynasty and the Ming. Despite these roots, he passed a court examination and, in 1508, became an officer of the palace guard. Over the following two decades, he would become a power-broker at court—before taking the throne for himself.

With the power vacuum in the capital, a movement emerged in the northeast of Dai Viet claiming to represent the old Tran Dynasty and seeking its restoration. In 1516 a man claiming to be both a descendant of Tran Thai Tong, the first Tran king, and a reincarnation of the Buddhist deity Sakra/Indra, declared himself the rightful monarch. The big clans from Thanh Hoa, the Nguyen family and the Trinh family, marched against him. In the fighting, one of the Trinh leaders killed the decadent king Le Tuong Duc. The clans then declared the dead monarch's 16-year-old nephew, Le Chieu Tong, to be his successor. A civil war would rage across the region for the next decade and the Cau River would be the *de facto* frontier between the northern and southern factions. The nominal king, Le Chieu Tong, had a court in Dong Kinh under the protection of Mac Dang Dung. For a few years, the area in around the royal palace was an island of stability amid the chaos.

However, some officials began to suspect that Mac Dang Dung had personal designs on the throne. They took the king and fled into the hills. Mac Dang Dung then decided to declare the king's brother, Le Cung Hoang, the rightful ruler. Mac Dang Dung built up his forces and started to impose order around the delta: chasing the Trinh into the hills and capturing Le Chieu Tong. Several of his advisers and supporters were put to death as was King Le Chieu Tong, in 1526. All that was left was the necessary choreography to effect the transfer of dynasty from the Le family to that of Mac Dang Dung. He made public statements of his support for the king he had placed on the throne and then in 1527, with all organized opposition now suppressed, he graciously accepted Le Xuan's offer to pass the throne to him. A few months later, the ex-king and his mother were disappeared and the first incarnation of the Le Dynasty was over. Its partisans retreated to their ancestral homeland of the southern hills to lick their wounds.

Mac Dynasty (1528–93)

The 64 years in which the Mac clan ruled Dai Viet were generally miserable ones for most of the population. An initial decade of relative peace was completely overshadowed by half a century of war and the associated famines and outbreaks of disease. After a relatively bloodless transfer of dynasty, the Mac started off in control of most of the country but their opponents, who claimed to be supporters of the Le family, rebuilt their forces in the mountains of Thanh Hoa before gradually exerting control over the southern part of the realm. Decades of stalemate followed, with the rival armies sallying forth into each other's territory to wreak havoc but failing to land a decisive blow. These were good times to be a supplier of weaponry. It was not until 1592 that the Thanh Hoa chieftains finally prevailed over the Mac and were able to restore what they claimed was the legitimate Le Dynasty.

In later years, it was politically useful to write histories of the period between 1528 and 1593 that portrayed the Le family's rule as being continuous. They skipped over the extinction of the main line of Le family succession in 1528—and thereby portrayed the Mac as illegitimate usurpers. The reality was more complex. The Mac enjoyed considerable support in the flatlands of Red River Delta and the coast because of their cultural affinity with the more Sinicized populations. The Le Dynasty, on the other hand, existed in name only. The king was merely a figurehead, behind which various powerful upland clans could unite, and legitimize their power over the kingdom. During the sixteenth century, the Trinh family came to dominate this group of "Le loyalists" and their allies-turned-rivals, the Nguyen family, were obliged to migrate to the south, from where they would rise to claim the leadership of the whole country, two and a half centuries later.

In 1528, however, that all seemed highly unlikely. The Nguyen and the Trinh families had lost power to the forces of Mac Dang Dung and run away to Laos, throwing themselves upon the mercy of their mountain cousins. It demonstrates the strength of the connections between these upland groups that the Lao were prepared to grant these families a fief in which to regroup. In 1533, the refugees—led by key figures from each clan, Nguyen Kim and Trinh Kien—rallied around the 18-year-old son of Le Chieu Tong, the penultimate king of the Le lineage. By placing him at the head of their claim they were able to paint Mac Dang Dung as an illegitimate usurper. The two families' alliance was sealed by a marriage between Nguyen Kim's daughter and Trinh Kien. In 1539 the two leaders felt they were in a sufficiently strong position to start a civil war: advancing from their base in Lam Son, in the foothills of Thanh Hoa, to capture Ho Quy Ly's former capital, Tay Do, in the next river valley. A decade of peace was over, a half-century of war was just beginning.

The other part of the Nguyen-Trinh plan was to persuade Ming China to attack the Mac from the north. A century earlier, the Ming had invaded Dai Viet because a usurper had stolen the throne. The Nguyen-Trinh alliance, representing themselves as supporters of the legitimate royal succession, attempted to get the Ming to repeat that history. Some very complicated diplomacy between the Ming and Mac then ensued. The Mac may have had an advantage in their negotiations with the Ming because of their ancestral connections to China. In any case, Ming border officials had no desire to invade Dai Viet again: they saw only high costs and low rewards. However, after three years of diplomacy and maneuvering, Mac Dang Dung and his ministers made a ritual display of surrender to the Ming authorities. In 1540 they travelled through the Zhennan Pass into Guangxi where they prostrated themselves—barefooted and with ropes around their necks—before Ming officials. They presented their census rolls as any defeated power was expected to do so and announced they were ready to be subordinate to the Ming.

The historian Kathlene Baldanza has demonstrated that this was, in fact, an elaborate ruse, cooked up between the Mac and local Ming officials. Mac Dang Dung was given the official title of "Pacification Commissioner" as if he were a servant of the Ming. The independent state of "Annan" ceased to exist in Ming records, even as Dai Viet continued to exist in reality. This allowed the Ming to say that they did not recognize the usurper king while allowing the usurper king to remain in power. In effect, the Ming state accepted that its ability to intervene across its southwestern border was very limited. It was better to preserve the fig-leaf of protocol than to actually invade and be forced to sort out the resulting mess. Those claiming to represent the Le Dynasty were ignored, the Ming declared that the legitimate family line had been extinguished and the Mac family was left in a strengthened position. There was, though, a limit to the assistance that the Ming were prepared to offer. Although the Mac obtained a peaceful frontier to their north, they were left to fight the Le-loyalists without support. Just a few months after the fake surrender, Mac Dang Dung died, creating succession problems within the Mac court. Exploiting the vacuum, the Nguyen-Trinh alliance began expanding its control into Thanh Hoa. At this point, Nguyen Kim was poisoned by a supporter of the Mac and his leadership role was taken by Trinh Kien. Although still married to the sister of the man who was now head of the Nguyen family, Trinh Kien set about asserting greater control of the Le-loyalist camp. But whatever the disquiet was felt in the Trinh-Nguyen camp was outmatched by even worse splits among the Mac. The Trinh-Nguyen alliance took the initiative and, by 1546, they controlled the whole of Thanh Hoa province and all the land of Dai Viet to its south.

In 1556, after a decade and a half of inconclusive fighting, the Trinh clan and their supporters faced their own succession crisis when their chosen monarch, Ly Chieu Tong's grandson Le Trung Tong, died without an heir. Their cause only made sense if they had a legitimate member of the Ly Dynasty to rally behind. In the end they found one: a great, great, great, great nephew of Le Loi called Le Anh Tong. It was a thin connection, but just sturdy enough to hold the alliance together. Soon after, however, the Nguyen clan decided that the Trinh were becoming too strong and that it would be safer for them to leave Thanh Hoa. In 1558, Trinh Kiem appointed his brother-in-law, the head of the Nguyen family, to run the southern area under the alliance's control from a new citadel in a place then called Phu Xuan (the modern day city of Hue). This allowed the Trinh to focus on the Red River Delta but it also enabled the Nguyen to begin developing their own realm on the central coast. They took over the old trading routes between the sea and the hills and encouraged international merchants to use the port at Hoi An. By the middle of the sixteenth century, their numbers were increased by a new group of traders: the Portuguese. The result of all this commerce was rising prosperity in Nguyen-controlled territory and an absence of conflict.

The north continued to be ravaged by war for another decade. The rival armies inflicted renewed destruction on wide areas of the delta but failed to land a knockout punch. The region fell into even greater disarray when Trinh Kiem himself died in 1570. Trinh Kiem's sons and their supporters fought among themselves, handing back the advantage to the Mac. The fighting led to famine. Thousands of desperate households fled south, to the former Cham lands now ruled by the Nguyen, to escape death. According to the historian Li Tana, records from the time mention particular migrations in 1570, 1571 and 1572.

The 1570s were the highpoint of Mac military success. When the leading Mac general died in 1580, however, the situation turned. The Mac ruler was, by then, twenty years old but showed no talent for kingship. The remainder of the decade saw more fighting, more defeats for the Mac and a second refugee exodus from 1586 to 1589. Finally, in 1592, the Le-loyalists, commanded by Trinh Kiem's son Trinh Tung, succeeded in taking the Mac capital, Dong Kinh, and killing the Mac king. Accounts from the time report the Trinh-led forces cutting off the heads of ten thousand Mac soldiers in 1591, several thousand more in 1592 more thousands in February 1593 and another ten thousand in May 1593. The figures may be exaggerations but it seems likely that mass killings did take place. These displays of brutality did not change the minds of people in the delta: most continued to support the remaining Mac loyalists. Others fled to the Nguyen-controlled lands to the south.

It was at this point, mid-1593, that Trinh Tung brought his chosen Le Dynasty descendent to Dong Kinh to be formally enthroned—thus officially re-establishing the old line of Le kings. They continued to face resistance, however. It was only when the Nguyen clan sent troops to the north that the combined forces of the Le loyalists were able to impose their rule. The Nguyen had purchased European cannon and muskets from their Portuguese trading partners and they deployed their new firepower to extinguish the last embers of Mac resistance in the delta. It was not, however, the end of the conflict.

Trinh and Nguyen (1593–1771)

The Nhat Le River reaches the sea where the modern city of Dong Hoi now stands. The river breaks out of the steep, wooded hills and then flows northwards, slow and wide, for 17 km until its mouth splits a long sandy beach in two. Today, both sides of the river are lined with red–tiled two and three-story houses, punctuated by occasional tower blocks, and the beaches are home to some modest hotels. There is nothing in the landscape to suggest that, four hundred years ago, this was a bitterly-contested frontier. Yet this river was, for almost two centuries, the southern line of a buffer zone that separated a northern Viet state from a southern. To its north, the lords of the Trinh clan reigned. To the south, control was in the hands of the Nguyen family. Both, however, claimed loyalty to the same king. The defenses which the Nguyen built along the river banks were never breached, allowing two different cultures to develop within what was, in theory, a single kingdom. To the north of the zone lay a densely-populated, predominantly rice growing, Confucianized, Sinicized flatland. To its south lay a narrow land, squeezed between mountain and sea, dependent upon garden-based agriculture and regional trade, originally Chamic and resentful of northern domination. The Nhat Le River is about 70 km north of the "Demilitarized Zone" that divided Vietnam in the twentieth century. This region, between these two vastly different military barriers, was a buffer between cultural and political worlds from at least the seventeenth century into modern times.

The sixteenth century political divide began with disputes between the two clans while they fought against the Mac. Their alliance was strongest during the conquest of the Red River Delta and the subsequent "restoration" of the Le Dynasty, but deteriorated soon after. The Le king served as a unifying symbol but he was, in reality, a puppet of the Trinh. In 1600, the Trinh leader—Trinh Tung—elevated a younger child to the throne over the appointed crown prince and, despite the objections of his allies, appointed himself regent. In response, the Nguyen marched out of the delta to consolidate their own power in the south. This was not a final break, however. The Nguyen leader, Nguyen Hoang, sent his daughter back to Dong Kinh to marry Trinh Tung's son as a means of maintaining the partnership. The Trinh were in need of such support since they continued to face major problems in the delta. Its more Confucian society resented the outsiders and its loyalties remained very much with the Mac.

After their expulsion from Dong Kinh, the Mac continued to rule a fief around Cao Bang, in the northern highlands on the border with Guangxi. Ming China could not decide which court represented the genuine ruler of Dai Viet so its officials equivocated. One the one hand, they shared cultural and ancestral connections with the Mac and found the Trinh lords of Thanh Hoa too "barbarian." But on the other, the Le could argue that they represented the dynastic line—and that they controlled most of the country. The Ming decided to avoid making a decision and allowed both courts to send tribute. The Mac made the most of this tacit support, launching frequent expeditions from their stronghold into the delta over the following decades. These only ceased when their military power was finally eliminated in 1677.

Throughout this period, the Red River delta was under what amounted to military occupation. As late as 1630, almost 40 years after the Trinh-Nguyen victory, a European visitor reported that a garrison of 50,000 troops was necessary to keep order in the capital and the surrounding area. Life was hard for the peasantry. In the years after 1610, several droughts destroyed harvests, and the crisis was compounded by corruption. Honest officials petitioned the court about the problems of poverty and hunger. They reported farmers being forced to sell land to pay debts and taxes. Storms and floods made things worse and, to cap it all, in 1618 a comet appeared in the sky. The omens were clear: it was time for a new king. A murderous succession battle ended in 1623 with one of Trinh Tung's 19 sons, Trinh Trang (pronounced Ching Chang) taking power.

South of the Nhat Le River, life was better. With large parts of the earlier Chamic population expelled, there was empty land ready for cultivation. The Nguyen welcomed refugees from the north, many of whom came from the ngô (ethnic Chinese) community with its established connections to regional trading networks. After an encounter with a visiting "pirate" ship, the Nguyen opened diplomatic relations with Japan in 1609 and a thriving entrepôt developed at the port of Hoi An. Traders from all around the region traveled there to buy and sell goods transported from east and west, overland and overseas. Among them, increasingly, were Europeans. Portuguese explorers had arrived in Southeast Asia in 1511, Spanish ships came in 1521, the English and Dutch arrived in the 1600s. They bought local products and sold cannons and muskets. The Nguyen were even prepared to tolerate a Christian mission in their realm, founded in 1615, in order to keep good relations with the Portuguese. (The mission was burnt down two years later when locals blamed the Christians for a drought, but it was re-established soon afterwards.) (See "Christianity and the Vietnamese Language" on p. 134.) Openness, trade and prosperity went hand-in-hand. As Li Tana has noted, the Nguyen were unique in allowing Japanese and Chinese to become government officials, and Westerners to have positions in the court, even if only as doctors.

The Jesuit priests who served the mission called the place "Cochinchina," a European corruption of a Malay name that was a corruption of an Arabic name that was itself a corruption of the old Chinese name "Jiaozhi." This was not, however, what local people called it. The region became known as *Dang Trong*, which literally means "the inner road." The name incorporates many ideas but the most important is that people leaving the wide open spaces of the north felt like they were entering into a more confined space as they travelled south. By contrast, the north became known as *Dang Ngoai* or "the outer road" because travelling there felt like entering into a more open space. Foreigners, however, continued to refer to the north as "Tonkin," the corruption of *Dong Kinh* or "eastern capital."

The good economic fortunes being enjoyed by (southern) Dang Trong contrasted strongly with the difficult conditions in (northern) Dang Ngoai. Economic necessity, jealousy, personal ambition and an appeal to the unity of Dai Viet drove Trinh Trang to demand financial support from the Nguyen. The Nguyen refused, and prepared for war. In 1627, Trinh Trang denounced his brother-in-law's actions as "rebellion" and marched and sailed his army to the south. They got no further than the Nguyen's defensive line at the Nhat Le River. After several weeks of failing to cross the river, Trinh Trang's forces retreated north. It was the first clash in a conflict that continued in some form for another fifty years.

Chastened by the lack of victory, Trinh Trang recognized that he needed better advice from his officials and greater support from his subjects. He began to recruit talented individuals, both people who had served the Mac and representatives of influential delta families, into government. From these small moves, the Trinh began to form a new Dang Ngoai identity for the north. New efforts were made to eliminate corruption and banditry, if only to create stability and resources for further military operations against the Nguyen. The Trinh found themselves creating a coalition between those who favored Confucian-style governance and wanted to focus on improving life in the north, and the old military men who wanted to take the war to the south.

The south, meanwhile, was getting on with making money. The Portuguese were doing good business shipping Chinese silk to Hoi An where it was exchanged for Japanese silver. The Dutch East India Company, the VOC, tried to muscle in on the trade, but after several unfortunate incidents—one of which involved burning down a village, and another the murder of two Dutch traders—they gave up. They had been outsmarted by their rivals. Instead, in 1637, the Dutch did a deal with the Trinh government. Since they were not allowed to trade directly with China, the Dutch used Dang Ngoai as a base. This was just one segment of a sophisticated regional trading network. From its headquarters in Batavia (now Jakarta in Indonesia) the VOC would send ships to trade silver for Indian textiles, these would be brought back to Batavia where they would be traded for spices, which were then traded for Chinese silk purchased in Dang Ngoai. The silk and spices were then shipped to Japan where they were traded for Japanese silver, which was then shipped to India to buy more textiles so the whole cycle could begin again.

As the Ming state began to collapse in the late 1630s, the supply of Chinese silk became more erratic. The VOC turned to Tonkinese silk from Dang Ngoai instead. For more than a decade, the VOC "silk for silver" trade between Tonkin and Japan made handsome profits for all concerned. But the Trinh also had another interest in the trade: they wanted the Dutch to fight the Nguyen for them. Trinh Trang wrote letters to the VOC asking them to join an alliance against Dang Trong, even formally adopting the Dutch representative as his own son as a gesture of trust. The Dutch were initially unwilling to fight, but after the Nguyen confiscated the goods and treasure on board three wrecked ships, they changed their minds. After a series of mishaps and military defeats, however, the Dutch pulled out of the arrangement. The relationship reverted to a trading one: exchanging silk for silver was too lucrative a business to be abandoned. Nonetheless, the European impact on Dang Ngoai was significant: foreign merchants with silver to spend stimulated the development of its silk and ceramic industries. They reconnected the north to the regional trading system.

Unfortunately, trade with the north was hampered by the Confucian nature of the state. Its centralized control, the export trade monopolies given to court officials and the general suspicion towards outsiders kept trade at arms length and controlled by a relatively small number of officials—facilitating corruption and inefficiency. Trade was also hampered by geography: seagoing ships had to anchor in the estuary of the Red River and goods had to be transported inland by smaller boats. (The Dutch eventually tired of the troubles of doing business with the Trinh and would gave up completely in 1700.) In the south, by contrast, society was more open, trade was freer, handled in cash, and the economy far more successful. The harbor of Hoi An, directly on the open sea, was also far easier to access. Buoyed by economic success, the Nguyen were able to expand their control further south. In 1611, they invaded Champa as far as the Ca Pass, in the hills just north of the modern city of Nha Trang. They absorbed these lands and their inhabitants into Dang Trong. The Cham population in Nha Trang appears to have turned towards Islam around this time. In 1622 the last Hindu Cham king was replaced by one professing to be a Muslim.

In the 1620s, the Nguyen court sent troops to support the Khmer (Cambodian) monarchy against Thai attacks and, in exchange, was granted the temporary right to collect taxes from two settlements in what is now the city of Saigon, then part of the Khmer Empire. This "temporary" arrangement became more permanent as traders from Dang Trong moved to the area to take advantage of new markets. Many of them were buying rice to feed the growing number of mouths back home. The traders were followed by a military garrison, and then other trappings of state ownership.

In 1650, a new power arrived on the northern frontiers of Dang Ngoai. Manchu invaders from northeast Asia had conquered the Ming and created a new empire in its place: the Qing. This had important repercussions for the two Viet states. In the north, cross-border support for the Mac loyalists declined, allowing the Trinh to move against them in 1667 and focus their attention on other issues. In the south, thousands of Ming refugees arrived looking to join the already-established Chinese communities in Dang Trong. These people became a valuable asset for the Nguyen.

After decades of military occupation, the Trinh leadership knew they could not rule the people of Dang Ngoai in the same way as their predecessors. They had arrived as conquerors and were still resented as outsiders by many in the delta. The population had grown too large to be properly monitored by officials. Instead, the Trinh devolved authority to the heads of each village. These men were given the power to collect taxes but also the obligation to hand them over to court officials and to keep the peace. In return, villagers were left alone to run their own affairs. A well-known saying, "The king's law stops at the village gate" dates from this period. The classic northern village, with its ramparts, thick bamboo hedge and densely packed houses became the core unit of the Red River Delta. The *dinh*, the male-dominated, hierarchical, conservative assembly, which took place in the communal building of the same name, became its central pillar. Women had little place in public life, their status derived from their perceived virtues and their skills in domestic labor.

In the south, village life was different. The Viet migrants to the south mingled with the pre-existing Cham communities and, in places a hybrid culture emerged. Many chose to live in stilt houses, for example, and in villages that were open to the fields. Worship of Shiva and Po Nagar became a common practice. Viet famers learned to follow Cham agricultural techniques. Those who had been forced to leave the north were often people of lower social status. They were not steeped in Confucianism and were less concerned with maintaining old social hierarchies or rules of traditional behavior. Instead, they were more willing to incorporate different beliefs within their spiritual lives whether they be Buddhist, Hindu or animist. They were more open to

Christianity too. They saw entertainment, gambling and cockfighting more as pleasurable activities to be enjoyed than social evils to be condemned. Women also had a more prominent place in society, strengthened by their role in market trading and earning an independent living. Life was freer.

In 1651 new fighting broke out between the Cham and Dang Trong which resulted in Dang Trong annexing the land down to the Phan Rang River, 150 km further south. Cham leaders were made vassals of the Nguyen while many of Cham people fled abroad—some inland and others across the South China Sea to Hainan Island, where some of their descendants still live. This territorial expansion brought Dang Trong directly into contact, and conflict, with the Khmer (Cambodian) Empire for the first time.

As Dang Trong marched south, the two Viet states fought their final battle at the Nhat Le River. In 1672, feeling confident following their successes over the Mac, Dang Ngoai attacked. The Trinh forces came close, but failed to break through the Nguyen defenses. In the aftermath of the expedition, the Trinh lord decided that whole the effort had been a waste and should never be attempted again. He fired those who disagreed with him and formally abandoned the policy of conquering the south. This enabled him to focus more on internal matters. For the following century the boundary between what were nominally two halves of the same Le kingdom remained peaceful and two different Viet states developed side-by-side.

In 1698 Dang Trong established a new province, Gia Dinh, around Saigon and recruited new settlers to live there. Among them were many refugees from Ming China. In 1679, 3,000 of them, members of a naval flotilla and their families, were directed to settle in areas of the lower Mekong delta known today as Bien Hoa and My Tho. Through their efforts, the Nguyen continued to extend their influence into the former Khmer Empire. For the next century, the Mekong Delta became the "wild south" as various settlers, leaders and communities grabbed land, set up communities, created armies and marched against one another. Viet, Khmer, Chinese, Cham, Tai and upland peoples mingled, competed and fought. The rival governments struggled to assert their own claims amid the mayhem. Dutch and Portuguese traders and mercenaries attempted to make money and avoid betrayal. Gradually, however, the Viets asserted ever-greater control over these new, fertile lands.

But, while some were getting rich on the proceeds of the rice trade, others were starting to be hurt by economic problems. The Nguyen had never needed to produce their own currency. In the seventeenth century they had used Japanese silver coins and Chinese copper ones imported by foreign traders. However, changes in Japan, Qing China and regional trade patterns led to shortages of these coins. At the same time, the demand for coins rose in Dang Trong. In its early decades, the Nguyen had run a military administration where they could simply press subjects into service. In 1714 they were obliged by labor shortages to start paying for labor in cash. By 1725, the shortage of coinage was acute and things would be made worse by the pretensions of a young king.

In 1744, with his northern frontier secure and his southern territories expanding, the leader of Dang Trong, Nguyen Phuc Khoat, broke with the fiction of pretending to be a loyal subject of the Le Dynasty and declared himself to be king. As he did so, he instructed his officials to re-order the court in the manner of a Confucian ruler. The traditional "six ministries" were created and old rituals were reintroduced. Crucially, Nguyen Phuc Khoat didn't tell the Qing Emperor about his change of status since that would have provoked a diplomatic crisis. Nonetheless, the palace was rebuilt in a properly royal style—a huge drain on resources at a time when the court was already paying for the soldiers to fight in the Mekong Delta. Nguyen Phuc Khoat was advised that, given the shortage of silver and copper money, the easiest way to pay for this extra spending was to order the minting of new coins with a cheap and easily obtainable metal: zinc. It was convenient but it had none of the solidity of the old money. The Nguyen court had debased the currency and the result was inflation.

The people didn't trust the new zinc money and sold it cheaply to buy silver and gold. The value of zinc money collapsed while that of silver, gold and other commodities soared. In fear of the future, people who could hoard rice did so. Prices shot up across the economy. In 1755, Dan Trong introduced new maritime regulations increasing the amount of tax charged on foreign ships. International traders decided that they could no longer make sufficient profits in Dang Trong's ports. They diverted to the Bassac River at the tip of the Mekong Delta—at that time beyond the control of Viet or Khmer leaders—where trading was duty-free. The number of junks trading in Dang Trong fell from 70 in the 1740s to just 16 in 1771 and 8 in 1773. Since ship taxes had made up more than a quarter of the entire state's revenue in 1740, this was critical. In response to this loss of income, the state decided to impose greater control and taxation over its inland trade. The mountain communities were already restive but these changes imposed such a burden on them that, in 1761, open rebellion broke out. This was the spark that lit a fire that ultimately destroyed both Dang Trong and Dang Ngoai.

Dang Trong's long run of good fortune came to an end in the 1760s. It continued to expand its territory in the Mekong Delta—creating the shape of southern Vietnam as we know it today—but this only added to the court's problems. The Nguyen court encouraged what could be described as a colonial adventure in the Mekong—working in alliance with Chinese immigrants to settle areas of the delta, bring them into cultivation and form them into new provinces. Clashes with the Khmer Empire and militant minorities in the delta and the surrounding hills demanded extra military forces at a time when economic problems were depleting the court's coffers. The collapse of regional trade—both maritime and overland—fatally weakened what had been a viable independent state. This was compounded by division in the palace. After the death of Nguyen Phuc Khoan, one of his uncles took power behind the throne but proved more interested in the pleasures of office than its responsibilities.

The same combination of depressed trade, economic problems and disarray in the palace were also at work in Dang Ngoai/Tonkin. Part of the problem there was the village system. Because taxes were fixed and levied on the village as a whole, they still had to be paid even if nobles were given exemptions or military men were called away. The burden then fell more heavily on everyone else. Those who couldn't afford to pay often ran away, further increasing the burden on those who remained. In 1730 an official count discovered 527 villages that had been deserted because the inhabitants couldn't pay the tax. By the 1740s that number had risen to 1,730, with a further 1,961 partially abandoned.

Unsurprisingly, with all this immiseration, rebellions broke out across the realm. Uprisings were a near-constant feature of life in the north between 1730 and 1752. They would flare up and then be suppressed but nothing would change.

The situation was made worse by natural disasters. The Red River Delta in the 1760s alternated between floods and droughts, with occasional epidemics and blights of insects. Dykes broke because they were poorly maintained and famines occurred because land wasn't worked effectively and officials failed to maintain supplies of food. The ineffectiveness of the government led to a failure to prepare for, or cope, with the disasters, which led to falling revenues which led to even greater ineffectiveness. Some of the population simply ran away, others rebelled. Some uprisings gained enough local support to worry the Trinh but none were strong enough to overthrow them. The military men retained control but the kingdom stagnated. Change would eventually come—but from the south. In 1771, three brothers from the district of Tay Son at the foot of the mountains in Binh Dinh Province started a rebellion that would ultimately sweep along the entire coast—and in the process, create the country of Vietnam.

<hr/>

The Myth of the Returned Sword

One of the key tasks performed by Le Loi's adviser Nguyen Trai was to build myths around the rebel leader to help him win support from the population. One of the most enduring was a story about a magical sword and a talking turtle.

According to the story, the sword came to Le Loi in two halves. The blade was found in the net of a fisherman in Thanh Hoa province. While on the run from the Ming, Le Loi visited the fisherman and the blade began to shine brightly with the words "The will of Heaven" inscribed in its surface. A short time later, while travelling in the Red River Delta, Le Loi discovered the hilt of a sword in the branches of a tree. He put the two halves together and created a powerful weapon with which he led his forces in a series of victories against the occupying Ming forces in 1427.

Given that Le Loi came from Thanh Hoa and Nguyen Trai came from the Red River Delta and that both men knew that victory required uniting the two regions under a single ruler, the story had very strong political symbolism. It proved that Heaven had blessed Le Loi's campaign and that his victory and the union of the two regions was just.

The symbolism of the story went even further. Sometime after his victory over the Ming, Le Loi was travelling by boat on a lake in Thang Long (Hanoi). A great turtle rose to the surface and asked for the sword to be returned to its original owner, the Dragon King, who lived at the bottom of the lake. Recognizing that his sacred mission was complete, Le Loi threw the sword into the water where it was caught by the turtle and carried to the Dragon King.

The small lake in the middle of modern Hanoi is known as Ho Hoan Kiem (The Lake of the Returned Sword) or Ho Guom (Turtle Lake) as a reminder of this fifteenth century story.

The Myth-makers: Nguyen Trai & Ngo Si Lien

Much of what is commonly regarded as early Vietnamese history was actually written down by two court officials in the fifteenth century. The first was Nguyen Trai (pronounced Nwee-yen Chai) the adviser to Le Loi, founder of the Le Dynasty, in the 1420s and 1430s. The second was Ngo Si Lien, who performed a similar role for King Le Thanh Tong in the 1470s and 1480s. Both men wrote histories to serve the needs of their patrons.

For Nguyen Trai, the priority was to prove that Dai Viet was an independent state and the cultural equal of the "northern country" of Ming China. Ngo Si Lien took this a step further to argue that as a "civilized state," Dai Viet had the right to expand into the lands of Champa to the south.

In the process, the two men wrote down a "myth of origin" explaining how the Viet people had emerged in the distant past. They took elements from folk stories and earlier texts and wove them together in a way that legitimized the Le Dynasty.

In their writings they created a Confucian family genealogy that connected the rulers of the Viet people back to the founders of the (Chinese) Han Dynasty. As a result, they argued, the "northern country" and the "southern country" were equal and different. Dai Viet could stand on its own.

Ngo Si Lien took the story a stage further by incorporating the myth of one descendant of the Han, King Lac Long Quan, marrying Queen Au Co who gave birth to 100 sons. The oldest of these boys was the original "Hung King" from whom all other Viet rulers claimed descent.

The two histories: *Nam Viet Du Dia Chi* by Nguyen Trai (published in 1435) and *Dai Viet Su Ky Toan Thu* (Complete book of the historical records of Dai Viet) by Ngo Si Lien (published in 1479) became the source for much writing about the early history of the Viet. Now that we know more about the circumstances in which they were written, historians have learnt to regard the texts as political documents of their time rather than factual accounts. In particular, these histories helped to create a sense of cultural superiority among Viet rulers that gave them an ideological justification to extend their rule into the lands of the upland Tai peoples and the peoples of Champa to the south. They underpinned what was, in effect, a Confucian colonial ideology.

Christianity and the Vietnamese Language

The first report of anyone preaching Christianity in Vietnam has been dated to 1533. The preacher was probably called Ignatius, a priest accompanying a Portuguese vessel trading along the coast *en route* to Macau. By the 1550s, Portuguese Dominican monks were starting to evangelize among communities in Cochinchina but this effort was really a sideshow compared to their activities in China and Japan. It was the arrival of Jesuits several decades later that resulted in more determined missionary work in Indochina.

At Easter in 1615, three priests erected a simple chapel near Danang and baptized ten Vietnamese converts. The Nguyen court was willing to tolerate the Catholic presence for many reasons. Part of their calculations was the importance of gaining favor with the Portuguese in order to obtain weapons and military training.

In late 1624, two Jesuits arrived who would have major impacts on Vietnam's relations with the wider world. One was Girolamo Maiorica, from Naples, who would found dozens of churches and convert tens of thousands of people in Nghe An Province over the following 25 years. The other was Alexandre de Rhodes, born in Avignon in 1593, who would develop and publicize a "Romanized" writing system for the Vietnamese language. He would also write an introduction to the country that would become a standard reference.

Alexandre de Rhodes spent many years learning Vietnamese and in 1651 published a trilingual Vietnamese-Portuguese-Latin dictionary. He created a way of writing Vietnamese with a modified European alphabet. The script was not intended for congregations. Its purpose was to help European priests to learn Vietnamese so that they could preach directly to the people: during the seventeenth and eighteenth centuries, missionaries produced written material in *nôm* characters for their congregations to use. It was only two and a half centuries later that this way of writing the Vietnamese language started to be used for that purpose by Vietnamese people themselves. At this point it became known as *quoc ngu*—national script.

The seventeenth century saw a general rise in religious feeling. By 1650, de Rhodes estimated that the number of Christians in Dai Viet had swelled to 300,000. At the same time, others flocked to Buddhist pagodas and Daoist temples, perhaps as a means of asserting identities during a time of political turmoil. Over the subsequent decades, Christianity would go through periods of both tolerance and repression. While it was later connected with the arrival and spread of French colonialism, the two developed separately but came into cohabitation during the early twentieth century.

CHAPTER 5

DESTRUCTION AND UNIFICATION (1771–1867)

Introduction

I n early 1783, the 20-year-old future emperor of Vietnam and a few of his followers were hiding on a small island in the Gulf of Thailand, almost at the point of starvation. A few weeks earlier, Nguyen Phuc Anh and his supporters had barely escaped with their lives after a vicious battle in Saigon. They had fled to the island of Phu Quoc, but been discovered there and pursued to Koh Rong, 70 km further up the coast. Enemy ships surrounded them but were, fortuitously for Nguyen Phuc Anh, scattered by a storm. The fugitives fled 140 km further, to Koh Kut, off the coast of modern-day Thailand where they were on the verge of expiration until a chance encounter with a Chinese merchant blown off course. The merchant was married to a Viet woman and the couple traded rice along the coast from the Thai city of Chantaburi, which is how the royal refugees ended up there.

The rescued fugitives sent a message to a crucial supporter: a French Catholic bishop who had also had a narrow escape from that battle in Saigon. Pierre-Joseph-Georges Pigneau de Béhaine had known Nguyen Phuc Anh for six years. Pigneau had been in charge of a missionary settlement at Ha Tien, on the western coast of the Mekong Delta (not far from the Funan excavations mentioned in Chapter 2), when he met the then 15-year old royal claimant. Nguyen Phuc Anh was the oldest surviving son of the last adult king of Dang Trong, Nguyen Phuc Khoan, which is why he was hiding in a nearby forest at that time. A rebellion was sweeping the land and the rebels were trying to eliminate all the remaining members of the royal family. At around this time, it seems, Pigneau became a member of a multi-ethnic band of desperadoes: Viet, European, Khmer, Chinese and Thai. Missionaries, mercenaries, generals, princes, doctors and traders, all dedicated to restoring Nguyen family rule.

Looking back at this period we can see the legacy of the "four worlds" of Vietnamese history. In the far south, the watery environment in and around the Mekong Delta formed a "Funan World" with a strong Khmer influence. The central coast and its uplands were home to a "Cham World." Further north, the Trinh were a clan from the uplands of Thanh Hoa, originally part of "Dong World" and the people they ruled in the Red River lowlands constituted a rival "Delta World." The cultural and political differences between them would sustain a series of conflicts during the final thirty years of the eighteenth century. The result would create a single country, "Viet Nam," under the rule of a single emperor, incorporating all four "worlds" and stretching from the Gulf of Thailand to the Chinese border.

>~~~<

The Tay Son Rebellion (1771–1802)

In 1771, three brothers set up their own mini-state around the district of An Khe in the Central Highlands. This was an important node in the overland trade route between the valley of the Mekong River and the former Cham port at Qui Nhon. The brothers gathered support from Cham, from highlanders and from a coalition of merchants and peasants angered by the increases in taxes being forced upon them by the usurper who had taken power in Dang Trong. Truong Phuc Loan, the uncle of the last adult king Nguyen Phuc Khoan, was deeply unpopular. His subjects were suffering the consequences of military expansion into the Mekong Delta as Khmers and Thais pushed back, and local warlords asserted their own power. The result was a series of conflicts between shifting alliances of kings and commanders.

The rebellion brothers' family name was Nguyen, but they were not from the royal line. They had adopted it as a sign of loyalty to the ruling family when they had settled in the south as refugees from the north. Their home was a village called Tay Son, astride the road between An Khe and the sea. The leader of the trio, Nguyen Nhac, was a tax collector of dubious honesty. His wife was from the upland Bahnar group, a combination that gave the family extensive contacts among the traders and merchants all along this lucrative artery. Once the brothers controlled its revenues, they were able to amass enough power to rule from Qui Nhon for the next twenty years. The unorthodox and disorientating tactics used by the "Tay Son rebels" repeatedly defeated the forces of Truong Phuc Loan and, by the end of 1773, their forces controlled most of Dang Trong, with the exception of the Mekong Delta.

The disarray in Dang Trong caught the attention of the Trinh regime in the north. After almost two centuries of stalemate, its leader Trinh Sam saw an opportunity to conquer the south. Trinh Sam was, in many ways analogous to Truong Phuc Loan. He had seized power in the name of a young king, Le Chieu Thong, and pulled the strings from behind the throne. Opponents resented his usurpation, and the population was demoralized. Trinh Sam had one key advantage over Truong Phuc Loan, however: a cohesive and effective military. He also had a good excuse to intervene in the south—claiming that he was acting to save the old dynasty by putting down the Tay Son rebels. In late 1774, his army calmly passed through the defenses at the Nhat Le River that had held back the northerners for so many decades. But almost immediately after he crossed the river, the army commander announced he had come to depose Truong Phuc Loan. The southern ruler was seized by his opponents at court and delivered to the invading forces. The Trinh invasion continued: pushing south to the Dang Trong capital in Phu Xuan (modern-day Hue) forcing the remaining members of the Nguyen Phuc royal family to flee.

There were then three armies operating in the south: that of the Trinh, one loyal to the Nguyen Phuc royal family, and the Tay Son rebels. For a time the royals and the rebels contemplated an "anti-northern" alliance but neither trusted the other sufficiently to agree. Instead, the rebels offered a deal to the Trinh. The Trinh forces withdrew to the northern part of Dang Trong, controlling Phu Xuan but leaving the region south of the Hai Van Pass to the Tay Son. With their northern flank secure, the rebels focused on the south—capturing Saigon in 1776. Shortly afterwards, in a ceremony at the site of the old Cham capital of Vijaya, Nguyen Nhac declared himself to be the King of Tay Son. His two younger brothers: Nguyen Lu and Nguyen Hue were put in command of military forces.

In 1777 the rebels came close to exterminating the Nguyen family. They briefly lost Saigon but were able to recapture it after a split in the royalist leadership. Nguyen Hue's forces then tracked down, captured and executed the king—Nguyen Phuc Thuan (a son of Nguyen Phuc Khoat), the crown prince (Thuan's nephew, Nguyen Phuc Duong) and almost all of their relatives. The last survivor was the 15-year-old prince, Nguyen Phuc Anh, and it was in desperation that he turned to Bishop Pigneau and took refuge in his mission station at Ha Tien on the extreme edge of the delta. Pigneau was supposed to be converting souls to Christianity but his encounter with the prince turned him into a player in the region's political struggles. Nguyen Phuc Anh seems to have been very charismatic and by the end of the year he had rallied enough supporters to retake Saigon. Control of the city and its markets meant control of a significant slice of the Mekong economy—and those revenues were now going into the royalists' coffers. Their forces were able to hold onto the city and even start to build an administration. In 1780, having turned 18, Nguyen Phuc Anh declared himself to be king. The south now had two rival monarchs, in addition to the Le king in the north.

This was a time of great change all around the watery frontier of the south. There had already been bitter battles for the Khmer throne, with Nguyen Phuc Anh's forces invading and installing a pliant child as king in 1779. In 1782, a Thai military commander seized power as King Rama I, founder of the Chakri Dynasty (which still reigns in Thailand today). That year, the Tay Son also retook Saigon, massacring thousands of Chinese residents. In the disarray, Nguyen Anh and Pigneau fled in different directions, the king by sea and the priest by land, only meeting up once they were safely under Thai protection.

Further north, the de facto leader of Dang Ngoai, Trinh Sam, died during a time of dire drought and famine. The Trinh court fractured and its military commanders took power in what amounted to a coup. They left King Le Chieu Thong on the throne and installed Trinh Sam's eldest son, Trinh Khai, as "lord" but instituted their own reign of terror in the capital—extorting money and food and ignoring the disaster all around them. The northern realm began to collapse.

Hearing of famine, and then floods and other disasters in the north and informed about the coup, the Tay Son leaders saw an opportunity. In June 1786, the rebels invaded. Moving by both land and sea they captured the Trinh-occupied parts of Dang Trong before pressing on into Thanh Hoa and then the Red River Delta, sweeping away any resistance. Facing certain defeat, Trinh Khai killed himself and thereby ended the Trinh family's two century-old control of Dang Ngoai. On July 21, 1786, the Tay Son rebels—under the command of one of the younger brothers, Nguyen Hue—took the capital, Dong Kinh. They did so claiming to be acting as loyal subjects of the Le royal family, indeed they carried banners proclaiming this, and they made no moves against the monarchy, at least initially. However, the basic situation in the north remained just as problematic: a social crisis and a non-functioning government. Unable to rule, the rebel forces withdrew, allowing local strongmen seized power. The Tay Son invaded a further three times over the following two years.

During the course of these campaigns, the brothers at the head of the Tay Son movement fell out. The eldest, Nguyen Nhac, was content to remain king of Dang Trong and had little interest in expanding his realm to the north. He was happy to raid and plunder, but not to administer. His younger brother, Nguyen Hue, saw an opportunity. This led to an argument, a power struggle and then a physical battle between the armies of the two commanders. The result was a stalemate and a compromise that looked very much like a new version of the old partition. Nguyen Hue was given all the lands north of Hoi An, while Nguyen Nhac took everything in the center and Nguyen Lu was allocated the south. Nguyen Hue established his capital at Phu Xuan (Hue), Nguyen Nhac established his at Cha Ban (the site of the former Cham capital Vijaya, northwest of Quy Nhon), and Nguyen Lu ruled from Gia Dinh (Saigon).

Amid all the chaos in the north, the "legitimate" king Le Chieu

Thong appealed to Qing China for support. In late 1788 the Qing invaded with 200,000 troops and occupied Dong Kinh. Hearing this, Nguyen Hue had himself crowned as the "Quang Trung Emperor"— greater than a king—and set off to depose the Le Dynasty. The Qing had no desire to involve themselves any deeper in Dai Viet politics, and were preparing to withdraw in early 1789 when Nguyen Hue and his army swept into the Red River Delta. Not expecting a battle, the Qing troops celebrated the lunar new year festival. While they were doing so, Nguyen Hue launched his attack—a "Tet offensive"—catching the Chinese completely unawares. The northerners panicked and ran— thousands drowned when the bridge they were using to retreat across the Red River collapsed. The remainder fled for the border.

Nguyen Hue/Quang Trung knew that he would have trouble from the Qing if he did not immediately repair relations. He sent two eminent Confucian scholars to apologize for the disruption. Remarkably the envoys were able to persuade the Qing court to give up on the Le Dynasty and to recognize Nguyen Hue as the "King of Annan." The new king was even invited to travel to the court for an audience with the Qing Emperor. Wary of the possible dangers, however, Nguyen Hue sent a double in his place. He was reported to have enjoyed several weeks of diplomatic hospitality at the Qing court's expense. The subterfuge seemed to work because the Qing would continue to regard the Tay Son "rebels" as the legitimate rulers of Annan for another 12 years.

By 1790, Nguyen Hue ruled the territory from the border with Qing China as far south as Hoi An. Having set up his capital at Phu Xuan and solidified his power, he did what good Confucian rulers always do after a crisis: ordered a census, reduced tax rates, encouraged farmers to cultivate the land and attempted to impose stability. Remarkably for a man who had a wild reputation, Nguyen Hue also ordered the translation of the Confucian classic texts into vernacular Vietnamese characters (*nôm*) and the creation of a system of local schools. At the same time, he continued to act in ways that Confucius would not have appreciated. He had friendly relations with coastal pirates, for example. They delivered a share of their booty to him in return for official protection. He also invaded the Lao uplands to the west, reaching as far as Luang Prabang in 1791 and looting its treasures. He even started to covet the Chinese provinces of Guangxi and Guangzhou and sent envoys to ask the Qing emperor to hand them over. Fortunately for regional peace, Nguyen Hue died while the diplomats were en route and the message was recalled before it could be delivered.

In 1792, Nguyen Hue's 11-year-old son was appointed as the new monarch, with the boy's mother's half-brother overseeing his administration as regent. Nguyen Hue had only reigned for four years and had had neither the time nor the inclination to fundamentally change the way the north was run. Many of the former Trinh officials were kept in place after his death—along with their old attitudes and inefficiencies. The region continued to languish. Nguyen Hue's death was the beginning of the end for the Tay Son rebellion. He was the most talented commander of the three brothers and the rebel regime never regained its momentum. It would, however, take another decade before it finally collapsed.

The situation was very different in the south. In 1783, the young pretender Nguyen Phuc Anh had formed an alliance with the new Thai king and that year their joint force attempted to consolidate control of the Mekong Delta. Instead, it suffered several defeats at the hands of the Tay Son. It was after this disastrous performance that Nguyen Phuc Anh fled to his remote island and nearly starved to death. Having been rescued, he and the other survivors made their way to King Rama's palace in Bangkok to regroup. Over the following year he was joined by more refugees but his forces still lacked the strength necessary to resume their war against the Tay Son. In the meantime Nguyen Phuc Anh was more-or-less a prisoner of King Rama who made use of the Viet troops whenever he needed to repel invasions or subdue rebellions.

Nguyen Phuc Anh was willing to work with all kinds of foreigners in order to tip the balance against the Tay Son: Portuguese mercenaries, Chinese pirates, English traders, Siamese officers—and French priests. In 1786, Nguyen Phuc Anh asked Bishop Pigneau to request help personally from King Louis XVI of France, sending his 5-year-old son along too as a gesture of trust to be tutored by Pigneau *en route*. Pigneau hoped that the boy would convert to Catholicism and eventually lead a Christian kingdom. The French king agreed to provide soldiers and weapons in exchange for trade privileges, and French control of the port of Tourane (Danang) and the island of Poulo Condor (now known as Con Son) off the southern tip of the Mekong Delta, once the Nguyen controlled the country. Louis XVI delegated the job to the governor of the French colony of Pondicherry (in southern India), but he had little interest in adventure. Instead, Bishop Pigneau took it upon himself to organize sufficient funding from French merchants there to pay for a small force of 40 deserters from the French military and two converted merchant ships. His keenness to assist was motivated in part by Nguyen Nhac's persecution of Catholic missionaries but partly, it seems, by his admiration for Nguyen Phuc Anh.

The conflict in the Mekong Delta was extremely complex by this point. Six forces were operating in the Mekong: the Nguyen royalists and Tay Son rebels were the largest groups but there were also militias belonging to rival Khmer, Thai, Cham and Chinese warlords. Alliances were constantly being formed and fractured with the military advantage shifting between the various coalitions. The politics was made more complex still by the splits between the three brothers leading the Tay Son during 1787. Nguyen Phuc Anh saw an opportunity. With his multinational band of supporters now strong enough to take on the divided Tay Son, he left Bangkok in August 1787 and landed back at Ha Tien in the Mekong Delta. Local rulers who had supported the Tay Son started to switch sides. By October 1788 he had recaptured Gia Dinh (Saigon) and driven out the forces of the youngest Tay Son brother, Nguyen Lu, who died shortly afterwards.

Nguyen Phuc Anh now controlled the Mekong Delta and started to build his own administration there. He spent two years rebuilding his forces, gathering taxes and suppressing independent-minded warlords and bandits. His long experience of the region enabled him to manage the complex ethnic landscape with care. According to Keith Taylor, he forbade Viet people from taking land away from Khmer farmers but banned the latter from opening new land for cultivation. He ordered the two groups to remain separate. Nguyen Phuc Anh also appointed different leaders to run the five different "Chinese" communities: the Hakka and those speaking the languages of Guangdong, Fujian, Wenchang, and Chaozhou (Teochew). They were allowed to run their own affairs, so long as they paid their taxes, allowed their men to be conscripted and remained loyal to the newly-emerging state.

Now firmly in control of the south, Nguyen Phuc Anh devoted his time to preparations for an invasion of the north. Merchants were encouraged to trade in strategic commodities: sulphur for gunpowder, iron for making weapons and rice for food. Granaries were built to store grain for the armies, boatyards were established to build the invasion ships and former French naval officers were deputed to train the crews to sail them. Nguyen Phuc Anh then waited for an opportune moment to advance. In 1792, hearing that Nguyen Nhac's ships had assembled in the port of Qui Nhon, he decided the moment had arrived. A raid on the harbor destroyed the Tay Son navy. The next year, he seized Nha Trang and then Qui Nhon. The shock of the losses appears to have hastened the death of Nguyen Nhac, the last of the three rebel brothers. He collapsed and died in Phu Xuan in late 1793, leaving the throne to his 17-year-old son. Both remaining parts of the Tay Son state were formally in the hands of children.

Under the guidance of a French engineer, Olivier de Puymanel, the royalists built a large "Vauban" style fort to guard the river crossing at Dien Khanh, upstream from Nha Trang. This formed the focus of the war for three years, until the royalists were ready to move north again. The mid-1790s saw some of the heaviest fighting as the two sides struggled for control along the central coast. At a crucial moment, it was support from uplanders that enabled Nguyen Phuc Anh to outflank the Tay Son forces and tilt the balance. In later phases of the campaign, he would draw upon alliances with Lao and Siamese leaders who sent their troops over the hills and into the heart of the remaining Tay Son territory.

The campaign also led to the final extinction of Champa. Many Cham leaders had supported the Tay Son and the area of modern-day Binh Thuan province (around the beach resort of Phan Tiet) remained an independent kingdom. In 1794, the Cham king was betrayed by some of his officials who had gone over to Nguyen Phuc Anh. His royal title was abolished and a successor appointed with lower-status. He was ordered to collect taxes from his people and remit them the Nguyen court. In 1797 there were small uprisings against the new regime. Some Cham managed to flee to Cambodia but those who remained were incorporated into the new state that Nguyen Phuc Anh was steadily building.

For the following four years, there was a steady "march to the north" by Nguyen Phuc Anh's forces. Each spring, as the winds blew from the south, his ships would sail up the coast, land troops behind the enemy's frontline and take more and more territory. Victory was coming closer but it was a victory that Bishop Pigneau would never see. He died of dysentery during the campaign. The king brought his body back to Saigon where it was interred in a large mausoleum (only destroyed in the 1980s). There was still some hard fighting ahead, however. The remaining Tay Son commanders, although bitter rivals, managed to organize effective counter-attacks and hold back the advance.

In 1801, Nguyen Phuc Anh finally eliminated the southern part of the Tay Son state. In a joint advance with his Lao allies he captured the enemy capital at Phu Xuan. He quickly set about establishing his own government there while his generals prepared their forces for an invasion of the Red River Delta. The north was not yet exhausted though. Its leader, the man whom Nguyen Hue had appointed regent, made one final throw of the dice. He raised an army and marched it south to the Nhat Le River: the old dividing line between Trinh and Nguyen. In early 1802, the two sides fought the final battle of the era. The outcome was the same as in the last fight between north and south at that spot, 130 years before. The northerners threw themselves at the defenses, suffered huge casualties and were forced to retreat. This time, however, the southerners also landed behind them, blocking their escape. Most of the retreating army was captured and the war was over.

In early 1802 Nguyen Phuc Anh needed one vital constitutional question answered: were there another other claimants for the throne? The final Le king, Le Chieu Trong, had retreated to China with the Qing army in 1788 after Nguyen Hue had seized Dong Kinh for the Tay Son. Nguyen Phuc Anh's officials told him that the old king was dead and that, therefore, the Le Dynasty had ceased to exist. As a result, Nguyen Phuc Anh declared himself to be the founder of a new dynasty, the Nguyen. He declared himself to be an emperor and took an imperial title, "Gia Long" (pronounced zaa-lom). As he journeyed north behind his advancing troops, Nguyen Anh/Gia Long took care to visit the tombs of the Le kings and to meet members of their clan. It was important that proper protocol be followed. One month after leaving

Phu Xuan, he arrived in Dong Kinh, taking the city without a battle. The remaining leaders of the Tay Son, the former regent, the young king and all their family members were rounded up and killed by being pulled apart, limb from limb. After that, the north was simply too exhausted to fight anymore.

Centuries before, Dai Viet had expanded from its northern base into the former Cham lands to the south. It had then divided in two: Dang Trong in the south and Dang Ngoai in the north. Dang Trong, under the Nguyen family, had expanded even further south, eventually asserting control over the former Khmer lands of the Mekong Delta. The dynamism of this multi-cultured domain allowed the last surviving member of the Nguyen family to generate the alliances and resources that sustained his thirty-year military campaign. And the result of Nguyen Phuc Anh's campaign was, in effect, that the south took over the north. With the capture of the Red River Delta, he became the first person to rule the entire territory between the northern border with China and the flatlands of the south. The shape of Vietnam as we know it today was finally created.

><del>∙∙</del>✘

Gia Long Emperor (1802–19)

Today, the imperial palace in Hue is a shadow of its nineteenth century self. The Tết uprising in 1968, the street–fighting that followed and particularly the bombardment that concluded it, destroyed most of the old imperial buildings. Recent reconstructions give some idea of its former grandeur but modern warfare does terrible things to wooden structures. Nonetheless, the scale of the palace, and the citadel that surrounds it, remains impressive. This was the site where, in 1802, Nguyen Phuc Anh took a new imperial title—Gia Long—and where he established his capital.

In a sense, Gia Long copied the Tay Son arrangement of power. He ruled from Hue while establishing trusted generals as subordinate "viceroys" in Hanoi and Saigon. Hue had the advantage, but also the disadvantage, of being neither north nor south. Traveling to the big cities meant a multi-day journey whether by land or sea, slowing down communication in both directions. As a result, the emperor was obliged to delegate considerable powers to the military regimes that he installed in the northern citadel, Bac Thanh (Hanoi), and its southern counterpart, known as Gia Dinh (Saigon).

Gia Long wanted a new name for his country, one that recognized its greatly-expanded domain. He wanted to memorialize both his control of the region of "An Nam" and the Nguyen family's ancestry from the "Viet Thuong" people. Combining elements of the two gave him "Nam Viet." Gia Long then sent a delegation to Beijing seeking recognition of his control of the realm under this name. The governor of Guangxi province, however, objected. He suggested the name might imply a claim to the lands of the second century BCE kingdom of Nam Viet (*Nanyue* in Chinese), which included areas of Guangxi. The Qing emperor concurred and instructed that Gia Long should be recognized instead as the king of "Viet Nam." The modern name of the country was thus born, although it was not a name that either side actually chose to use. The Chinese stuck with "Annan" in regular communication while Nguyen court preferred "Nam Viet," at least until 1814 when they reverted to the old name of "Dai Viet."

Diplomatic recognition was just one step in asserting control. Gia Long needed to create a sense of unity among his disparate people but had to work within the constraints of local expectations. He ordered the building of roads linking the different regions and a postal service to circulate information. He also attempted to reduce the cultural differences between his southern "Dang Trong" people and the more Confucian population of the "Dang Ngoai" north. The realities of power, however, obliged him to allow his northern and southern viceroys considerable autonomy to manage their regions in the most appropriate way. Thus he placed limits on Buddhism—such as requiring permits for the construction of new temples—in the north, but not elsewhere. Nor did he try to enforce Confucian rules of behavior outside the north, although he did encourage the spread of its ideas. The historian Liam Kelley has highlighted how he recognized that different ways of writing had developed in the north and south and hired scribes who could write in both forms so that official edicts could be understood everywhere. The south remained different, however. In the words of Alexander Woodside, it was "more Cambodian, more Buddhist, less Confucian, less Sino-Vietnamese than the center and the north."

At this time, the population of "Viet Nam" was around seven or eight million—slightly smaller than that of Britain at the time. The establishment of the new dynasty did not mean an end of unrest; local communities continued to resist efforts by the court to create a single identity. Despite the official claim that the Le Dynasty had died out, there were still rebels who continued to assert its existence, and resist the Nguyen. They found supporters among the peasantry whose lives were not greatly improved by the change of regime. Demands both to pay taxes and to work on government construction projects became greater as the state became more organized. Many people simply refused to comply. During the 18 years of Gia Long's reign, there were well over 100 uprisings in different parts of his realm. The province of Quang Ngai, on the central coast, was in an almost permanent state of insurrection for the whole period.

Just as during the war, Gia Long continued to employ a very diverse group of people to help him run the country. Engineers and military leaders from elsewhere in Southeast Asia and from Europe remained in key positions. The dozens of geometrically-shaped "Vauban" fortifications that still exist in the key cities of Vietnam (including the Hue citadel itself), are evidence of their continuing importance. He had an equally tolerant attitude towards Christianity—so long as it did not spread to his officials. Many people had become Christians over previous decades, which was tolerable so long as their beliefs did not challenge the court. Fundamentally, Gia Long was a Confucian at heart because it provided an ideology and a structure to run the country. The ideas expressed in the classic Confucian texts were familiar to the Vietnamese elite and they stressed the importance of a single ruler and a centralized government. They were useful ideas for Gia Long to propagate. He set up the traditional six ministries, constructed his royal palace in Hue on the same model as the Forbidden City in Beijing and reinstated the practice of literary examinations to train officials to run the government. In 1812, his court adopted the "Qing Code"—in effect, the Chinese legal system, as the backbone of his administration—albeit with many modifications to take account of local customs.

In 1806, however, he broke with orthodox Confucianism by declaring himself to be the emperor—*hoang de*—of his own realm. *Hoang de* is the Vietnamese rendition of the equivalent Chinese term *huang di* but Gia Long and his descendants also used a Vietnamese word, *vua*, which has no Chinese equivalent. It combines the meanings of "ruler" and "protector," someone who is close to the people, not aloof like an emperor. In other words, although Gia Long and his court borrowed Chinese ideas of how to organize their government, they also had their own ideas of how a good ruler should behave, which was different to that in the "northern empire." Through their contact with Europeans they knew it was ridiculous to describe themselves as "sons of heaven" when there were large areas of the world beyond their imperial control. Nonetheless, the idea of the emperor receiving "tribute" and loyalty from less-powerful neighboring states remained important.

After taking the throne, Gia Long had maintained friendly relations with his ally the Thai king, Rama I, dating back to their shared campaign against the Tay Son. The Khmer kingdom in between their countries became a form of "buffer state" over which Gia Long recognized Thai authority but in which his court exercised considerable influence. When Rama I died in 1809, however, his successor, Rama II, attempted to extend his authority deeper into the Khmer territories and push out Vietnamese influence. He engineered a challenge to the Khmer throne, backed by an invasion in 1811. The incumbent Khmer king fled to Saigon and asked Gia Long for help. In response, Vietnamese sent a large force across the border to reinstall the king and force the Thais to withdraw. Gia Long then installed a garrison of around a thousand troops to both protect the Khmer court and ensure that it remained an ally. Vietnamese forces also occupied large areas to the south and east of the capital.

In 1813, Gia Long formally changed the name of the country from Viet Nam back to Dai Viet (without informing the Qing Chinese) suggesting he wanted to appeal to the power of history and recover some "greatness" from the past. It was still not certain that Nguyen family rule would endure. Rebellions erupted periodically, often led by men proclaiming allegiance to the Le kings, Trinh lords or Tay Son rebels. The northern and southern regional were only semi-attached to the central government—glued in place by the personal loyalties of their military commanders. Gia Long had created a single territory but few of its inhabitants felt connected to it. If they felt connected at all, it was to their locality and its local culture. The result was a patchwork of identities across the new country. Gia Long's solution was to rule with a "light rein," squashing rebellion when necessary but tolerating local differences.

✂︎⌇✂︎

Minh Mang (1819–40)

Unlike Gia Long's eldest son who had been tutored by Bishop Pigneau, visited France and fought with his father's multicultural coalition against the Tay Son, his fourth son—Minh Mang—was conservative, authoritarian and suspicious of foreigners. By the time of Gia Long's death, however, he was the oldest surviving child and ascended to the throne. Minh Mang (pronounced Ming Mang) inherited a kingdom of parts and set about trying to make it whole. His most effective tool was the power of Confucianism. It gave him and his officials a set of rules about how to run a central government, and a set of requirements about how the people should behave. Another tool was the management of the past. In 1820 Minh Mang ordered the court's "Historical Board" (*Quoc Su Quan*) to compile a new history of the kingdom, specifying that "the style, the way of expression and the facts are to be weighed and considered before being recorded." In other words, inconvenient facts were to be omitted in order to "tell right from wrong" and to set "good examples" for the future, thereby bolstering the idea of a unified country.

Another early act, in 1821, was to reinstate local examinations and then organize national ones to select qualified "scholar-officials" to run his court along Confucian lines. He felt it was vital to create an elite group of civil servants, loyal to the palace, who could be trusted to administer distant provinces and cities. This would enable him to centralize power within his palace in Hue and more easily impose his edicts on the people or leaders in faraway corners of the country. Gradually, whenever the opportunity arose, he removed the military leaders who had acquired positions through service with his father and replaced them with civilians loyal to him.

He then started to move against other forms of cultural difference, notably religion, whether Buddhist, Catholic or the Islam of the Cham. By 1824 Minh Mang had ejected all his father's foreign advisers and the following year he banned European missionaries from entering the country. He wanted uniformity and issued edicts that attempted to create a single culture across his whole realm. He insisted that officials use a single classical Chinese style of writing characters, rather than the separate northern and southern versions that had developed during the years of division. While the selection of educated Confucian scholars tended to increase the influence of northerners in his court, the cultural norms flowed both ways. In dress, for example, he called for northerners to wear silk trousers, in the manner of the south, rather than their traditional cotton wrap-around skirts. He also tried to suppress some local religious beliefs and sponsored ancestor worship as an alternative. He tolerated Buddhism but only as a private practice and not a state religion. Whatever beliefs people followed could not be an alternative to his own personal centrality as the emperor.

His Confucian role as "son of heaven" obliged Minh Mang to provide for his people in both spiritual and temporal ways. He had to perform the necessary rites and behave appropriately if his empire were to enjoy good fortune. His administration also had to develop the agricultural economy by building roads, repairing dykes and providing grain stores. He promoted international commerce to try to reduce smuggling. Faced with a long coastline and a poorly-developed road network, he encouraged seaborne trade. Boats carried rice from the two big river deltas to less fertile parts of the country and other goods to and from the major international harbors, particularly Saigon.

At the same time, the Hue court was also trying to control its Cambodian protectorate. Relations between the Khmer population and the Vietnamese occupation forces had deteriorated. In 1819, Gia Long had approved plans to dig the Vinh Te Canal, intended to facilitate easier transport through the Mekong Delta. The project quickly became notorious for the harsh treatment of the workers and the cruel behavior of the Vietnamese supervisors. Tens of thousands of peasants were press-ganged into service until the project was finally completed in 1824. To this day, the stories of the hardship and death involved in this construction project continue to animate ill feeling between Khmer nationalists and Vietnamese. At the same time, but on the other side of the Mekong River, a rebellion broke out against the Vietnamese-backed Khmer king and large numbers of Vietnamese soldiers and civilians were killed. It was only after the Vietnamese army joined the Khmer king's army that the rebellion could be suppressed.

The victor of this campaign was the viceroy of the southern region, Le Van Duyet. He had been a crucial friend and ally of Gia Long during the war against the Tay Son and remained in power for long afterwards. He was loyal to the court but ruled the south as a largely autonomous region. He allowed Gia Long's "heterodoxy" to flourish. Different groups—including Khmer and Cham—were allowed to continue running their own affairs so long as they remained loyal. Minh Mang had no chance of spreading Confucian orthodoxy there nor of imposing his idea of cultural uniformity. However, in 1833, Le Van Duyet died and the emperor seized the opportunity. He ordered the replacement of the old military regime with a new civilian one, bringing the south in line with measures already taken elsewhere. Dai Viet now had 31 provinces grouped into three regions, north, central and south, and each province was run by court-appointed Confucian scholar-officials. At the same time Minh Mang formally outlawed Catholicism across the entire country.

Minh Mang also attacked the "specialness" of the southern region. He started to privilege Vietnamese over other ethnic groups in the Mekong Delta. He imposed restrictions on Chinese merchants whom he accused of smuggling and began pressuring the Christian community, whom he saw as both immoral and a potential ally of European powers. He reduced the protections that Duyet had given to Khmer communities to prevent their land being taken over by Vietnamese and abolished the Cham kingdom in Binh Thanh province. He also revoked the freedom of former criminals who had been settled on the frontier. All these measures stoked up separatist feeling and led to a revolt led by Le Van Khoi, the adopted son of Le Van Duyet. Le Van Khoi took over the "Turtle Citadel" in Gia Dinh (Saigon) and mobilized supporters from all around the Mekong Delta. Among them were members of the Chinese and Catholic communities and a few European missionaries. The Thai King, Rama III, saw an opportunity to regain some of the territory lost by his predecessor, so he gave his support to the rebellion and marched a large force of soldiers into Cambodia.

A simultaneous uprising by Le Van Khoi's brother-in-law, Nong Van Van—the leader of the Tai-speaking Nong clan in the northern mountains, pulled Minh Mang's attention in two directions. The northern rebellion had been prompted by the imposition of a Vietnamese lowland administration in 1829. Court officials were put in charge of areas that had once been ruled by upland chiefs. Once installed, they demanded all the dues expected of lowland peoples: taxes, labor and "Confucian" behavior. The Nong and their upland allies resisted and, although the uprising was suppressed after two years, the imperial court backed down and reinstated the Nong family's rule. The northern hills were simply too difficult for the Hue court to administer directly. Nonetheless, by the end of his reign, Minh Mang had managed to place more of the uplands along the frontier with Laos under his—indirect—rule, through arrangements with tribal groups.

Le Van Khoi died early in 1834 during Minh Mang's siege of the Turtle Citadel in Gia Dinh, but his allies continued to hold out. Meanwhile, Vietnamese forces recaptured large areas of Cambodia, pushing out the Thais and putting their protégé back on the throne. At around the same time, Minh Mang stepped up his "Confucianization" campaign across Dai Viet. He issued the "Ten Articles Edict" instructing officials and commoners alike to follow its principles—notably respect for elders and the emperor. The last internal obstacles to his "homogenization" program were overcome in late 1835. Firstly, the final autonomous Cham statelet—Panduranga—was forcibly abolished and replaced with a Vietnamese administration. This was the sad end to a proud history of Cham independence dating back thousands of years. Secondly, the emperor's troops captured the Turtle Citadel. Its 1700 defenders, including 600 Christians, were executed. Among them were a few Europeans. A Catholic priest, Father Joseph Marchand, was taken to Hue and tortured to death. The huge fortress, which had taken 30,000 people to build in the 1790s, was razed to the ground. (These days it is hard to tell where it once was, but its center was near the Saigon Cathedral.) In 1836, with these domestic problems solved, Minh Mang formally annexed Cambodia as a new province of Dai Viet. He then tried to treat the new province just like any other part of the country. In many ways Minh Mang acted like Chinese emperors had done centuries before when they had tried to control a rebellious Jiaozhi. He attempted to make Cambodia more "civilized" by teaching its inhabitants how to behave. In fact the word he used was *hoa*—flowering—the Vietnamese equivalent of the Chinese word *hua*. The Khmer were to be taught how to farm better, how to use chopsticks, how to dress modestly and how to speak Vietnamese. Officials also tried to replace the local Theravada form of Buddhism with the Mahayana form more common in Vietnam. The result of this colonial behavior was, unsurprisingly, an anti-colonial uprising. Fighting against the Vietnamese occupation forces continued for several years. To suppress this rebellion the court was obliged to deploy large numbers of soldiers, which required conscription. To feed and pay them obliged the court to demand greater quantities of rice and higher taxes from the civilian population. Equally unsurprisingly, this created rancor among the peasantry and renewed unrest at home.

Minh Mang must have felt sufficiently confident of his mission, however, because in 1838 he ordered the name of the country to be changed once again. It became "Dai Nam" or Great South. This was, according to the imperial edict, to celebrate his empire's southward expansion. Minh Mang had expanded his rule from, in the words of the edict, "the shores of the sea to the feet of the mountains." The name change was also a means to mark the country's independence from Qing China—although the court continued to use the name "Viet Nam" in its official correspondence with Chinese officials. Minh Mang died in early 1841 (after falling off his horse) with his unifying mission still not fully completed. He had, however, achieved considerable success in imposing his ideas of uniform government and a single Confucian culture. He had confirmed an arrangement of beliefs in which the veneration of the emperor was the state religion, ancestor worship was encouraged and Buddhism was relegated to the realm of personal behavior. He had consolidated his father's achievements but some of his actions, particularly the execution of European Christian missionaries between 1833 and 1838, would eventually come to undermine them.

><del>~</del>~<del>~</del><

Thieu Tri (1841–47)

Minh Mang was succeeded, in 1841, by his eldest son Thieu Tri (pronounced T-you Chee) who attempted to rule in a similar manner to his father but without his father's charisma or political support. He continued his father's anti-Catholic policies and, just like his father, he had to cope with uprisings by groups opposed to his Confucian orthodoxy: notably Khmer communities and people in the uplands. It was, for some of them, their last stand against the tide of "Vietnamization" sweeping over them. The separate status of the Khmer, Cham, Chinese and other groups was steadily reduced. They were increasingly obliged to speak Vietnamese and accept direct rule by Viet officials. Nonetheless, a small but significant proportion of the Mekong Delta population managed to resist assimilation, particularly in areas where they formed the majority. Khmer and Cham communities continue to exist in the region to this day.

Thieu Tri's reign was dominated by two external crises: problems in Cambodia and the arrival of European gunboats. He had attempted to extricate his forces from the Cambodian quagmire in late 1841. However, two years later, the cycle of intervention started again when the Thai king Rama III intervened on the side of one of the claimants to the Khmer throne. The Vietnamese responded with military support for their preferred claimant and recaptured Phnom Penh. Another stalemate ensued until an agreement with the Thais led to what was supposed to be a mutual withdrawal in 1847 and a recognition of Viet supremacy in Cambodia. In fact, the Thais were left in the dominant position but there was little Thieu Tri could do because of larger problems emerging from the sea.

The echoes of the British attacks on China around 1840 (later known as the First Opium War) were heard all around the region. In their wake, Britain, France, the United States and other countries acquired trading rights and little pockets of territory in China. This led to much greater interest from European governments in the region and a larger presence of naval ships. Britain had Hong Kong and Singapore, Portugal had Macao, Spain had Manila and the Netherlands had Batavia (Jakarta) "Gunboat diplomacy" followed. French captains, in particular, took an interest in the fate of Catholic missionaries in Dai Nam—even though they had no formal instructions to do so. In 1843 one officer sailed his ship into Danang harbor and obtained the release of five French missionaries. Shortly afterwards a French admiral arrived in Danang, this time with orders from Paris to negotiate for a little slice of territory to use as a base. He got nowhere.

A year later, the fate of a single French missionary crystallized an international crisis. Father Dominique Lefèbvre had been sentenced to death by the court at Hue for his missionary work. The French admiral demanded, and obtained, his release. Rather than returning to Europe, however, Father Lefèbvre smuggled himself back to Saigon where he was arrested again. Rather than risk another confrontation with the French, the Dai Nam court simply expelled the missionary to Singapore. Admiral Jean Baptiste Cécille heard about the arrest, but not the release, and dispatched two warships to Danang. In April 1847, after a week of negotiations in which the French demanded the release of a man who had already been released, the French sank five Vietnamese warships and destroyed the harbor fortifications, killing perhaps 150 people. Meanwhile, Lefèbvre quietly departed Singapore and returned to Saigon, this time without being arrested. The attack on Danang destroyed whatever trust there might have been between Thieu Tri's court and France. Just as seriously, it confirmed, in the court's mind, the relationship between Christianity and European gunpowder. The result was a renewed crackdown on missionary activity. The stress may have been too much for Thieu Tri, who died shortly afterwards, at the age of 41.

❦

Tu Duc Emperor (1847–83)

The death of Thieu Tri, the third emperor of the Nguyen Dynasty, in 1847 set off factional rivalries inside the palace at a time of crisis. Thieu Tri's eldest son was passed over in favor of a slightly younger boy who was installed as the Tu Duc Emperor. The suspicion that he was a usurper dogged his efforts to rule from the outset. He suspected that his rivals were secretly supported by the Catholics. This was not a good time to be a weak emperor. As officials argued over how to respond to developments in Cambodia and Danang, a bigger danger spread across the country. Between 1848 and 1850, Dai Nam was hit by the third global cholera pandemic. Around 800,000 people died, perhaps 10% of the country's total population. In its wake, agricultural output fell, food supplies shrank and there were problems transporting rice. The result was famine, and then growing disorder.

In the middle of these overlapping crises, in an effort to shore-up Tu Duc's authority, the court invited the Qing court to formally invest him as the ruler. The ceremony took place on September 10, 1849 in the presence of an envoy sent from Beijing. This was apparently something of a hardship voyage for the Qing ambassador because he arrived with a large entourage, some of whom carried bags of soil so that the diplomat could feel close to the motherland at all times. Official recognition was not enough to stem the disorder. In 1854, a plague of locusts attacked crops in the north. This was followed by a series of rebellions among the peasantry, paralleled by a series of disasters. Amid all the troubles, officials had neglected to repair the vital dykes that channeled the rivers through the Red River Delta and prevented flooding. As a result there were floods every year. Conditions in the north were made even more precarious by the outbreak of the hugely destructive Taiping Rebellion just over the border in Guangxi in 1850. It raged for the next decade and a half, interrupting trade and sending refugees over the mountains into Dai Nam.

The royal court was far away from all these problems. Hue was still several days journey from Dong Kinh and the Red River Delta and even further from Saigon and the Mekong. Officials in Tu Duc's government struggled to make any impact at all on the spreading disorder and the social problems that caused it. Instead, the court tried to turn back to Minh Mang's policies of promoting Confucian orthodoxy and stamping out alternative beliefs. Once again Christians became the object of the government's ire. In 1852, two French missionaries were beheaded for proselytizing, along with many more Vietnamese. The combination of disorder in the provinces, dysfunction in government and discrimination against Christians created the conditions for the next phase of Vietnam's turbulent history.

The Coming of the French

Napoleon III had dreams of grandeur. He wanted to erase the shame of his uncle's military defeat at Waterloo in 1815 and give France an international status equal to that of Great Britain. France had followed in Britain's footsteps in Asia. It had established trading posts in India from the seventeenth century onwards and asserted control of Tahiti and other Pacific islands in the 1840s. In 1849, following the First Opium War, France acquired a "concession" in Shanghai. Napoleon III had been elected president in 1848 and then declared himself to be emperor after a coup in 1851. He wanted an empire. At the same time, French bankers and industrialists were looking for new markets and sources of raw material. Some were already investing in Asia and wanted more. Merchants from Lyon, Marseille and Bordeaux wanted a "French Hong Kong" as a base from which to trade—"municipal imperialism" it has been called. At the same time, activist Catholics were lobbying for the government to support beleaguered congregations in the place they still called Cochinchina. Gruesome tales of the executions by Minh Mang, particularly of Father Marchand in 1835, continued to excite the faithful, along with renewed examples of the oppression and execution of Christian believers. For its part, the French military was also keen to acquire the glory and revenues that would accompany the building of empire.

On April 22, 1857, Emperor Napoleon III convened a "Commission for Cochinchina." In its report a month later, the Commission recommended that France secure a position in Cochinchina by taking control of its three main ports. This was not, however, welcomed by members of the imperial government. The foreign minister, Alexandre Colonna-Walewski, was reluctant to go to war. The finance minister Achille Fould declared that he didn't know where Cochinchina was, and was not prepared to spend six million francs invading it. The Interior Minister Adolphe Billault warned Napoleon "not to trust priests and sailors" advocating for an invasion. Nonetheless, in one of the more fateful "non-decisions" of history the emperor decided to leave the question of whether to invade in the hands of French naval commanders already in Asia. In December 1857 they were given the freedom to intervene as they saw fit. They were to make a token attack and then use it to extract a treaty with the Dai Nam court.

The navy had several ships available. In May 1858, the French had jointly attacked Tientsin (Tianjin) with the British in the early stages of what became known as the "Second Opium War" and their swift victory meant the navy was free for other tasks. The execution of a Dominican bishop, Monsignore Diaz in Dai Nam in September 1857 gave the Spanish government a reason to join the expedition. On August 31, 1858, fourteen ships carrying 2,000 French soldiers, 500 Spanish troops and several hundred Philippine auxiliaries seized the port of Danang, just down the coast from Hue. The French had been led to believe by their missionary supporters that the local Catholic population would rise up to welcome them and overthrow their Confucian oppressors. This did not happen. Instead, the invasion force was strongly resisted by Vietnamese troops and then hit by cholera. The Dai Viet emperor refused to negotiate a treaty, and the invaders were forced to retreat.

To avoid humiliation, part of the flotilla sailed south and, on February 17, 1859, struck at an easier target, the virtually undefended port of Saigon. Once the Anglo-French alliance had achieved victory in China in October 1860, more forces were available for operations in Cochinchina. The area around Saigon was taken in February 1861 and in April, My Tho (in the Mekong Delta) was captured, along with the provincial capitals of Ba Ria, Bien Hoa and Vinh Long. The French were now able to control the export of rice from the region, placing food supplies to the whole country in jeopardy. In June 1862, facing another uprising in the north, the Dai Nam court agreed the "Treaty of Hue" with the French. It ceded Saigon and its two neighboring provinces to France, along with the island of Paulo Condor. French ships were permitted to trade up the Mekong and in the major ports of Dai Nam. Freedom of religion was to be allowed in the entire country and Spain was paid compensation for the execution of Monsignor Diaz. Dai Nam renounced its protectorate of Cambodia and the following year France took it over.

This was not, however, entirely welcomed back in France. The invasion had cost vastly more than the six million francs that the Finance Minister had objected to paying back in 1857. The final cost was around 140 million francs. There was a strong lobby for France to restrict its possessions to just the ports of Saigon, My Tho and Vung Tau and to relinquish the rest. By 1864, however, a coalition of the navy, the church and domestic business interests were pushing for full-scale occupation and administration. In 1867, Admiral Pierre de la Grandière annexed another three provinces of southern Dai Nam. A century of French colonialism had begun.

Nguyen Du & Tale of Kieu

"The Tale of Kieu" is regarded by most Vietnamese as the country's literary masterpiece. Children study it at school, most people can quote sections of it, and its characters often pop up in everyday conversation when someone needs to make a point about honesty, loyalty, jealousy or deceit. The "Tale" is the story of a beautiful young woman called Thuy Kieu forced into a life of exploitation by unscrupulous people and harsh circumstances. She endures hardship after hardship but is ultimately rewarded with freedom, and reunion with her true love.

The Tale was written by an official of the royal court called Nguyen Du (pronounced Nwee-yen Zoo) during the 1810s. He was sent as an official envoy to Beijing in 1813 where he appears to have come across a Chinese story "The Tale of Jin, Yun and Qiao" written in the mid-seventeenth century. He turned this story into a poem, 3,254 lines long, in Chu Nôm—Vietnamese written in characters. It follows a style common in traditional folk poetry where alternate lines are written with six and eight syllables.

Nguyen Du's genius was to tell a moving story of tragedy and redemption in a way that combined a very Vietnamese form of expression with references to classical Chinese texts going back centuries. He mixed abstract discussions of morality and obligation with a tragic story about a woman who is obliged to sell herself into prostitution in order to save her family from ruin.

These themes can also be found in Nguyen Du's own life. He was born in 1765 and was still in his teens when the Tay Son brothers' rebellion destroyed the old Le Dynasty. The son and brother of successful court officials, he was trained as a classical scholar but managed to avoid serving the Tay Son rulers by hiding in the hills. When the first Nguyen emperor, Gia Long, took power in 1802, Nguyen Du was summoned to court and made the "prefect" of a district near Hanoi.

Nguyen Du was conflicted about whether to serve this new southern ruler and he resigned from this and his next two posts after disputes with his fellow officials. Nonetheless, his mastery of classical learning made him a valuable asset. It was the reason why he was chosen for the mission to Beijing where he was expected to converse with officials in both the language of the court and the idioms of the classical texts. On his return he was made vice-president of the Nguyen court's "Board of Rites," in effect its foreign ministry, which handled diplomatic relations with neighboring rulers.

It was from this relatively safe position that Nguyen Du was able to write a literary classic that alluded to the problems of being forced to serve a master against one's will and the need to maintain one's personal morality in difficult circumstances. In the tale, Kieu remains virtuous despite her subjugation, just as an official can remain virtuous while serving a ruler of questionable legitimacy.

Ho Xuan Hong—the Queen of Nôm Poetry

In the early nineteenth century, Ho Xuan Huong turned her poetry into a skewer to burst the pomposity of her male-dominated Confucian society. Husbands, generals and monks became targets of her exquisite, sharply-worded critiques. We know very little about her life but Ho Xuan Hong was probably born in Nghe An province in the late eighteenth century, during the Tay Son war, and then moved with her family to Hanoi. Her father died when she was young and her mother remarried. Probably to get the girl off their hands, the family gave her as a second wife to an older man, who died shortly after. Another older husband followed, who also quickly died. She never remarried.

Ho Xuan Huong turned her experience of married life into blistering verse, such as this, entitled "Being a concubine":

One's covered with a quilt, the other freezes.
Sharing a husband, the plague of life.
Oh for only five or ten times,
He comes twice a month, if at all!
I labor for sticky rice, stale sticky rice,
As if a servant, an unpaid servant!
If I had known this,
I would have remained alone.

Ho Xuan Hong lived in Hanoi in the years after the royal court had departed to Hue. Highly educated young men (and a few women), who might once have expected to acquire a position in the palace, found their plans ruined. Without a court to attend, the cultural life of the capital moved into the streets. Once relative peace was re-established after 1802, Hanoi became a city of salons and high-brow entertainment. It was in this milieu that Ho Xuan Huong flourished.

Her poetry follows Chinese forms but with Vietnamese flourishes. It often features double entendres with sexual meaning or clever wordplays that allowed her to criticize traditional Confucian norms with its rules about wives obeying their husbands. The radical twentieth century poet Xuan Dieu described her as "the queen of Chu Nôm poetry."

CHAPTER 6

COLONIALISM AND RESISTANCE (1859-1907)

Tu Duc to Tonkin (1860–74)

In 1859 the French navy found itself running a small patch of Southeast Asia. Although France had administered colonies in India for almost two centuries, this was different. The Indian "factories" had been initially acquired with consent from local rulers. In Dai Nam, everything was taken by force. The capture of Saigon had been achieved without serious opposition but moves into its hinterland were facing stiffer resistance. There had been some debate within French ruling circles about the wisdom of trying to hold onto Saigon but the navy leadership overcame its critics and reinforced its positions with a further 2,500 troops—many of them colonial subjects from Algeria and Senegal—once the "Second Opium War" was concluded in China.

With these experienced soldiers, the French pushed outwards from Saigon, defeating one of Tu Duc Emperor's most experienced generals and then using the network of waterways through the Mekong and Saigon deltas to seize key towns. At the same time, Tu Duc was facing a more worrying threat to the north: a huge insurrection led by yet another leader claiming to be a descendant of the old Le Dynasty. By 1861 this man commanded a rebel force of 20,000 in the coastal part of the Red River Delta, the fief of the former Mac dynasty, which had never reconciled itself to being ruled by people from further south. Preferring to concentrate his forces against the northern rebels, Tu Duc agreed the Treaty of Saigon in June 1862, ceding to France the provinces of Gia Dinh (Saigon) and its neighbors Bien Hoa and Dinh Tuong. The French also pushed into Cambodia, offering the Khmer king their "protection" against both his Thai and Viet suzerains. None of this was ordered by the government back in Paris, the admirals just created a new international situation and lobbied to have it approved in retrospect. Before 1869, a return journey to Marseille by steamer took six weeks. The opening of the Suez Canal that year halved the time but it was not until the arrival of the telegraph in 1873 that speedy communication became possible between the metropole and the colony.

One immediate consequence of the Treaty of Saigon was the withdrawal of most of Tu Duc's administrators and magistrates from the ceded provinces. In their absence, social order, trade and security broke down. In places there was starvation. The French were obliged to cobble together some kind of replacement administration. Unfortunately for the French and their new subjects, many of the figures who maneuvered themselves into positions of authority under their rule were not ideally suited to their new roles. Some could barely read but were willing to put themselves at the disposal of the new authorities in order to gain local power. In this way, "rule by the indigenous"—the principle which the French government used in its north African colonies—became the norm in Cochinchina.

Naval officers were turned into local officials and given a quick introduction to the Nguyen legal code. They had great difficulty understanding how it should be applied or even how to communicate with the different communities now under their rule. Some officials wanted to completely replace Vietnamese, Khmer and Chinese with French, but others recognized the trouble that was likely to stir up. Instead, one of the earliest decisions the French made was to try to break the power of the old regime by introducing *quoc ngu*—the way of writing Vietnamese with the Western alphabet—into schools. By replacing characters with letters they made the process of administration legible to European eyes. The officials saw this as a means of both breaking the power of the old mandarin-state, and of separating "their" state from the Chinese world. Catholic-run mission schools were eager to help create a literate bilingual elite who could serve both God and France in the administration of the new colony. In 1865, the first newspaper to be printed in *quoc ngu* appeared. It was edited by a remarkably talented, missionary-educated Vietnamese civil servant born Truong Vinh Ky and baptized as Petrus Ky. The paper endured for more than forty years.

In 1865, "French Cochinchina" was formally established by the French government, which was still ambivalent about the wisdom of seizing so much territory. Colonies were expected to support themselves so, in an effort to demonstrate its utility, the Cochinchina government authorized an expedition up the Mekong in search of a river route to the interior of China. They believed success would help France compete with British colonies in Burma and Hong Kong. The expedition departed from Saigon in June 1866 but, only a few weeks later, its high hopes were disappointed. When the explorers reached the waterfalls at Khone, on the border of modern Cambodia and Laos, they recognized that the Mekong was never going to be the trade artery that they had hoped. Nonetheless, the group pressed on through difficulty and disease, eventually reaching Yunnan province sixteen months after leaving Saigon. The surviving members then travelled down the Yangtze, returning to Saigon almost exactly two years after departing. From then onwards, French hopes of river-borne access to the interior of China would shift to the Red River, and therefore the north of Dai Viet.

In spite of this disappointment, Saigon quickly attracted international trade. The French authorities cut taxes and duties and invited merchants to set up shop. The ethnic Chinese community, based just upriver in Cho Lon (the name means "big market") were encouraged to develop their regional networks and supply the colony with food and goods. One key commodity was opium, which the French authorities licensed and taxed. International shipping services started to make calls at Saigon. Entrepreneurs from France's other colonies in India and Africa arrived to test out the new commercial opportunities. Vietnamese Catholics, fleeing persecution elsewhere, also moved to Saigon. It became a polyglot entrepôt. The French literally did the ground work; draining the marshes and building the road networks along which the twin centers grew. With success came colonial infrastructure: hotels, administrative buildings, churches, parks and a botanic garden.

Armed resistance to the French in the south largely disappeared after the mid 1860s. Allowing local strongmen to control their local areas seems to have been a reasonably successful strategy. The inhabitants of the Mekong Delta had little loyalty to the Hue-based Nguyen Dynasty and seemed to be happy making a living and being left alone. Large areas remained beyond effective state control. In 1867, the French navy seized the other three provinces of the Mekong Delta—placing all of what the Nguyen court called *Nam Ky* under their control. The court, tested by other challenges elsewhere, decided not to resist. "French Cochinchina" was complete.

The navy administrators knew that the colony needed to cover its costs. They quickly recognized the potential of rice. In the early 1860s exports stood at 50,000 tons. Fifteen years later they had increased more than six times to 320,000 tons. A large part of the difference was probably rice that had previously been sent north to feed the rest of Dai Nam. Once the French were established in Cochinchina, this rice was no longer distributed within the country but sold on the international market. Land was parceled out to large farmers who were then obliged to pay tax to the Cochinchina government. The government also received income from licenses granted by the state's monopolies over salt, alcohol, opium, gambling and prostitution. Opium alone generated 1.5 million francs for the government in 1865.

By 1870, the French navy, with the support of elements of the Catholic Church, had established firm control over Cochinchina. The colony had a viable economy based upon international trade and an increasingly capitalist internal market. Large numbers of landless people were offering themselves as cheap labor on large farms or in the rapidly-growing towns and cities. The old paternalistic ways, insofar as they had existed in the south, were giving way to harsher, more atomized relationships. The French were able to rule a population that had little sense of belonging either to the royal court in Hue or to the "Confucian World" of East Asia. They had created the basics of an administrative system, the number of bilingual officials was growing and a cosmopolitan culture was taking root. They could remake Cochinchina in their own image.

The situation in Dai Nam was quite different. Here, the rule of the

Tu Duc Emperor was being increasingly challenged. The victories of the French had prompted a backlash against Europeans among court officials. In places they openly resisted the Emperor's edicts legalizing Christianity, which he had been obliged to issue by the Treaty of Saigon. In addition, large areas of the uplands around the Red River Delta were in the hands of rebels, the remnants of groups that had sprung up during the Taiping Rebellion against the (Chinese) Qing Empire and then fled into the mountains after the rebellion was crushed in 1864. As the historian of this period Bradley Camp Davis has pointed out, these groups were actually quite different from the Taiping. They were not religious and they did not have a national agenda. Nonetheless, two groups became notorious: the "Yellow Flags" led by a man called Huang Chungying and the "Black Flags" led by a rival called Liu Yongfu. Each had their own local territory and support. Some upland groups saw the arrival of the French as an opportunity to restore some measure of strength against the Nguyen court, while others would choose to fight with the Nguyen against the French. Seen from the north, the royal court in Hue was far away and out of touch: home to hundreds of Confucian-trained scholar-officials who could do little but argue among themselves about whether the Emperor had lost the mandate of heaven and how to respond to the invaders.

In 1870 France lost its own emperor. The Franco-Prussian War ended with Napoleon III deposed and his empire replaced by the "Third Republic." Little changed in Cochinchina however: the Navy continue to hold sway. If anything, the new Republican government in Paris doubled down on colonialism: seeing the development of "Greater France" as a means to assert its own status in the wake of the defeat by Prussia. Politicians increasingly talked of a "civilizing mission" to spread the benefits of progress and enlightenment around the world. This coincided with the increasing influence of commercial interests in the colonies. As French-owned businesses developed in Cochinchina they began to lobby for more support from the government at home.

Some entrepreneurs were willing to take unusual risks in the search for profit. One was Jean Dupuis, whose business activities resulted in open warfare between French and Vietnamese forces, even though neither side's government was directly involved. In 1868, Dupuis had been working as an arms trader in the Chinese city of Hangzhou and had encountered the surviving members of the French Mekong expedition as they made their way to Shanghai. From them he learned about the possibility of using the Red River as a route into China's Yunnan province. He then travelled to Yunnan and persuaded the authorities there to buy a consignment of European weapons that could be used to put down a rebellion led by the "Yellow Flags." Having agreed the deal, Dupuis then travelled down the Red River, proving its navigability, before returning to France to buy the guns. The French government agreed with the venture and Dupuis traveled back to Hong Kong and then Saigon to await their weapons' arrival. According to Dupuis, officials in Saigon advised him not to bother seeking permission for his business trip from the authorities in Hue, since it would waste considerable time and they would not be able to stop him anyway. So Dupuis set off with a few steamboats and 175 mercenaries to protect the cargo.

He sailed up the coast, into the Red River Delta and on to Hanoi. There his unofficial army made contact with Chinese businessmen in the city and took over a small part of the capital. He then proceeded upriver to deliver the weapons to the Yunnan provincial government. He returned in April 1873 with a boatful of silver and a further 150 Qing troops provided by his grateful customers. Dupuis was about to return upriver with a cargo of salt when the Hanoi authorities decided to stop his freebooting. Dupuis refused to comply, so Tu Duc appealed to the French authorities in Saigon. In response, Dupuis said he was only taking control of the Red River in order to prevent another power doing the same. Reluctantly, the Saigon governor sent a mission northwards with a vague instruction to "restore order" but without specifying whose order was to be restored. The man put in charge of the mission was Francois Garnier. Garnier had been the deputy leader of the 1866 Mekong Expedition and was probably the person who had told Dupuis about the Red River route in the first place.

Garnier stopped in Hue to collect two court officials but when he and his small flotilla of gunboats arrived in Hanoi, rather than negotiate an end to the stand-off, he announced he was there to negotiate a commercial treaty under which France would eradicate piracy along the coast. This was refused by the officials in Hanoi so, on November 20,

Garnier stormed ashore and captured the citadel. He then declared to the people of the city that he had been sent to open a trade route up the river in order to bring them commerce and wealth and had no intention of ruling them. In the following days, however, he made common cause with Dupuis and started occupying smaller settlements around Hanoi and recruiting local men to guard them. Within a few days, Hai Duong, Ninh Binh, Nam Dinh and other cities of the delta were in his hands.

Unable to stop the French, local officials called for support from the Black Flag rebels, who came sweeping into the delta. On December 21, a combined force of Dai Nam troops and rebels attacked the French-held citadel and Garnier led his troops out of the fortress to chase them away. At one point he tripped over and was jumped on by rebels who stabbed and then decapitated him. Several other senior officers were killed in other attacks nearby. Despite these losses, the French position was still reasonably secure, particularly since their gunboats could still navigate the rivers. Nonetheless, once the government in Paris heard about the battle (via the newly installed telegraph system) it ordered the governor in Saigon to suspend all hostile actions. A French envoy was sent to Hanoi to negotiate the return of the official troops and to order the arms merchant Dupuis to leave as well.

As part of the deal, the envoy also negotiated a new agreement with Tu Duc. The 1874 Treaty of Saigon formally recognized France's 1867 expropriation of the three Mekong provinces. Just as importantly, it also granted what Dupuis had been agitating for: the French right to navigate the Red River along with usage of the ports in Hanoi and in Haiphong, at the mouth of the river. It was similar to the treaties which Europeans were imposing on Qing China at around the same time. This treaty went further, however. It included language that would end the "tributary" relationship between Dai Nam (which the French still called Annam) and Qing China. It included a line stipulating "the sovereignty of the king of Annam and his complete independence from any foreign power" while also stating, in Article 3, "the King of Annam engages to conform his foreign policy to that of France." Tu Duc's court appears not to have recognized the meaning of the wording—something that became a major problem a decade later.

It was the end of an episode in which a merchant and his mercenaries, a French naval flotilla, Vietnamese officials and upland rebels—all of them acting without clear orders from any government—had caused a major conflagration for little immediate reward. Only the Black Flags seemed to have benefited: they established a maverick statelet in the hills of the borderland. Dupuis made no profit from his arms dealing adventure and the French authorities were obliged to retreat. Victims of the French attacks were buried, and revenge was exacted against Christian communities in the delta. Tu Duc's agreement to open the Red River route to Yunnan came to very little because the Black Flags continued to control the upper reaches of the valley. It was only in retrospect that the adventure would take on historic significance. At the time it was just another in a very long line of unpleasant conflicts in Tonkin.

Its legacy was much more significant. Just as France had obtained a "concession" in Shanghai in 1849 through an "unequal treaty" with the Qing, so it acquired 18.5 hectares of Hanoi through the 1874 treaty. This "concession" was a long strip of land in the area between Hoan Kiem Lake in the center of the city and the major road to its east which, at the time, ran along the bank of the Red River. Troops constructed a barracks, a customs house and diplomatic offices, along with residences, a hospital and a cemetery. The French Empire had arrived.

>━━⌒━━⌒✕

Colonization (1874–87)

Dotted in the forested hills surrounding the former imperial capital of Hue are eleven tombs built for deceased emperors of the Nguyen Dynasty. Some are far from the city, large and grand, while others are more utilitarian. A few are even squeezed into tombs previously built for one of the others. Some are decorated with elaborate mosaics while others are adorned with rougher forms of cement art. Some justify the term "royal tomb"; others do not. In general, the longer a ruler spent on the throne, the more time he had to plan his resting place and the more elaborate the result.

There are, however, two emperors missing from the Hue tombs. Both were buried in France, although under quite different circumstances. One of the missing is the last ruler of the Nguyen Dynasty, the Bao Dai Emperor, who stepped down from the throne to become president in 1945, and died in exile in 1997. The other is much less well-known: Ham Nghi who became emperor in 1884. He was the fifth ruler of Dai Nam in the space of just over a year, his three immediate predecessors had all been killed. It was the culmination of a tumultuous period in which the French colonial authorities flaunted their military strength and subjugated Dai Nam—or as they still insisted on calling it, Annam. Amid the chaos, a 14-year-old emperor was forced to sign a treaty accepting a French protectorate before dying in mysterious circumstances a month later. The relative who then took over was Ham Nghi but a year later he too was out of office: captured by French troops and sent into exile in Algeria.

The decade between the end of the ill-fated Red River expeditions in 1874 and the enthronement of Ham Nghi in 1884 saw major changes in the attitude of metropolitan France towards its colonies. The French economy was performing poorly, a new generation of secular, republican politicians was gaining power and commercial interests were pushing for the country to acquire new markets abroad. In 1875, a consortium of French banks established a new company, the "Banque de l'Indochine" (BIC) to invest in trade with Asia. In 1878, the French government awarded the BIC a monopoly over the minting of a new silver currency, the *piastre de commerce*, to unify the financial system under their control. At the time, many different currencies were being used across Cochinchina and the rest of Dai Nam. There were zinc and copper coins manufactured under the Nguyen but also Mexican silver dollars, Shanghai silver taels and Japanese yen. The piastre became dominant, although it managed to completely replace other forms of cash.

In February 1879, a new government came to power in Paris. It was ostensibly left-wing but also nationalistic and dreaming of a new overseas empire. (One of its leading members was Jules Ferry who would become Prime Minister in the critical year of 1883.) Both the commercial elite and the nationalistic government were demanding more expansionist policies. The naval authorities in Cochinchina were, however, reluctant to upset the delicate local situation. Impatient for action, the

Paris government decided to end "rule by admirals" and give the colony a new civilian governor instead. From then onwards, French law and its official secularism would apply in Cochinchina. Business needs would take priority and the protection of Catholicism would become a niche issue. Those business interests had no time for sentimentality. The imposition of French law meant little outside Saigon. Good agricultural land was simply grabbed by the powerful and lost by the weak. In 1879, 400,000 hectares of land were growing rice in Mekong Delta. Over the next 45 years that amount quintupled to more than two million hectares. Strongmen, or those in cahoots with the local authorities, became rich while others became grindingly poor. A failed harvest or some other twist of fate could mean the difference between prosperity and homelessness.

The business community was also looking for opportunities in the north and their attention turned towards its potential mineral wealth. French representatives in Hanoi and Haiphong received permission from the Dai Nam court to organize a surveying expedition, which set off into the hills in September 1881. After a month traveling up the Red River they ran into the Black Flags, who sent them back the way they had come. Two other surveyors then attempted, without official permission, to explore the hills north of Haiphong, where they also encountered members of the Black Flags who expelled them from the area. The civilian governor of Cochinchina believed he could use the incidents to enforce the provisions of the 1874 treaty and authorized some gunboat diplomacy.

From the perspective of the French authorities, the Black Flags were an illegitimate rebel force who were blocking free access along the Red River, a trade route that had been formalized in the treaty between France and Dai Nam in 1874. If the Nguyen court in Hue could not suppress the rebels and secure the river for trade, then the French would do it for them. The court had neither the resources nor the desire to take on a well-armed and deeply-entrenched statelet. Its forces in the north were barely in control of the delta and had little chance of enforcing any authority in the uplands. The Black Flags, of course, cared little about any of this. They did not regard themselves as subject to any other authority, whether Vietnamese or Chinese.

The Cochinchina governor ordered the newly-arrived head of the colony's naval division, Henri Riviere, to sail north with four gunboats and 500 marines. On April 10, 1882, Riviere's men arrived in Hanoi and delivered an ultimatum to the local authorities: if they didn't undertake to subdue the Black Flags, the French would occupy the city. Everyone knew there was no chance the local officials would be able to comply. Two weeks later the French seized the citadel, the same structure that Francois Garnier had occupied nine years earlier. The disparity between the forces is obvious from the casualty numbers: the operation took an hour and the French suffered just four soldiers injured. The Dai Viet governor the city, Hoang Dieu, wrote a final poem, entitled "Defeat" and killed himself. (These days, the street running through the center of the former citadel is named in his honor. A parallel street is named after Nguyen Tri Phuong who commanded the troops fighting against Garnier, was captured and later starved himself to death.)

As the historian Bradley Camp Davis has noted, the Dai Viet court was split—some wanted to appease the French while others wanted to use the Black Flags against them. There were also splits in the French administration—some wanted to take the fight to the Black Flags while others were worried about the risks of triggering intervention from Qing China. Caught in the middle, Henri Riviere announced to the people of Hanoi that he was only interested in crushing the bandits to open the river to commerce. He then settled in for a lengthy occupation, through the summer and winter of 1882. At this point, Qing China really did enter the game. Officials had become concerned that the French moves threatened the security of their own southern provinces so they ordered forces from Yunnan and Guangxi to cross into northern Dai Nam. The French intervention had triggered the very development that it was supposed to deter. The Chinese advance also worried the Vietnamese, who feared that the new arrivals might not go home. In November, French and Chinese representatives negotiated an agreement to disengage and to jointly work against the Black Flags. Realities on the ground would work against them.

While all this was brewing in and around Hanoi, developments far away consigned the region to war. In March 1883, Jules Ferry became Prime Minister of France and immediately ordered a more aggressive policy in Dai Nam. The deal negotiated with China was cancelled. The business lobby finally had what they had been waiting for: support for even greater intervention in the north. Two weeks after the new government was formed, Henri Riviere seized the key delta city of Nam Dinh. In response, the Chinese decided to make use of the Black Flags. There is no evidence of any formal agreement but the rebels moved their forces down into the delta and massed near the Cau Giay (Paper Bridge), in what is now a western suburb of Hanoi.

On May 19, 1883, Riviere left the citadel with around a hundred marines to reconnoiter the area. They were tracked, ambushed and around 50 members of the party, including Riviere, were killed. The following morning, the rebels displayed the dead men's heads outside the western gate of the city. The shock stunned all sides in the conflict and attracted international attention. A week later, the Paris government telegrammed the governor of Cochinchina with the message, "France shall revenge her brave children." The French became determined not just to subdue but to eradicate the Black Flags. The Vietnamese and Chinese courts, on the other hand, resolved to continue using them to fight the invaders. Just at this moment, however, another development made the situation even more complex. On July 17, the Tu Duc Emperor died in Hue.

His passing prompted fights among the senior figures at the court over which of Tu Duc's three adopted sons should succeed him. A key figure was Ton That Thuyet, a man who had requested support from the Black Flags against Garnier's forces a decade earlier and continued to do so in his role as military commander. The nominated successor, 31-year-old Duc Duc, spent just three days on the throne before Ton That Thuyet and his colleagues decided he was unfit to rule. They imprisoned him and left him to starve to death. Duc Duc was replaced by a half-brother of Tu Duc, 36-year-old Hiep Hoa, who was understandably reluctant to take the title. Within three weeks of becoming emperor he faced one of the most fateful confrontations in modern Vietnamese history.

In the aftermath of Riviere's death, the French government had decided to force the Hue court to become a protectorate. It sent a flotilla of warships to the estuary of the Perfume River, about 10 km downstream from the imperial palace. A brief ultimatum to surrender was ignored so the French shelled the coastal forts into submission. Hundreds of Vietnamese defenders were killed but just 12 French attackers were wounded. With the fleet now able to sail almost to the door of the imperial palace, its commander, Admiral Courbet, delivered an ultimatum, "We have no intention to annex your country," he declared, "but you must accept our protection." Of course, the only people from whom the palace needed protection were the ones now threatening it.

Hiep Hoa felt he had little choice. Within five days, he had agreed the "Treaty of Hue" in which "Dai Nam recognizes and accepts the protection of France. France controls all Nam's relations with foreign nations including China." The treaty also ceded an extra province to Cochinchina and gave France the right to administer the northern area it called "Tonkin" all the way from the Chinese border to Ha Tinh province. Only the central region of Dai Nam would remain under the emperor's direct rule. (Demonstrating their poor understanding of history, the French referred to these provinces alone as "Annam.") The emperor's willingness to agree these concessions heavily damaged his standing at court. Behind his back, Thuyet and allies were organizing renewed resistance in the north, working with the Black Flags and Chinese forces to attack the French. There were some early successes—300 French soldiers and Yellow Flag auxiliaries were killed west of Hanoi in September during an expedition to recover the bodies of Riviere and his patrol. In response, the French brought in thousands of reinforcements, including North African colonial troops.

Aware that enemies were plotting against him, Hiep Hoa pleaded with French diplomats for some (genuine) protection. It was not enough. In late November, Ton That Thuyet organized a coup against the emperor, forced him to abdicate and then to take an overdose of opium. On December 1, Ton That Thuyet placed Tu Duc's youngest adopted son, 14-year-old Kien Phuc, on the throne. His allies in the court then told the French, in effect, that their recently-signed treaty was as dead as Hiep Hoa. The fighting in Tonkin continued regardless. Despite thousands of Chinese regular troops joining the Black Flags, the French managed to push them all back into the uplands during early 1884. The Chinese authorities started to reconsider their involvement. Those who had advocated armed resistance to the French were losing influence. The Black Flags remained loyal only to themselves. They broke with Vietnamese officials, looted local coffers and retreated to their earlier business model: controlling the opium routes through the mountains.

In May 1884, with these successes achieved, the French persuaded the Chinese government to withdraw its forces from Tonkin. The agreement did not, however, set a timetable and renewed hostilities broke out between the two sides. On his way back from these negotiations, the French representative, Paul Patenotre sailed into Hue to formalize a revised version of the treaty forced on the court the year before. It was essentially the same as the 1883 agreement except that no provinces were transferred to Cochinchina or Tonkin. The Nguyen court's northern region of "Bac Ky" became the "French authorities"; "Tonkin" and its "Trung Ky" became "Annam." There was, however, a highly symbolic coda to the signing of the "Patrenotre Treaty." On June 6, 1884, the court, in the presence of French diplomats, destroyed the official seal given by the Qing Empire in 1804 when it recognized the kingdom of "Viet Nam." Six kilograms of beautifully engraved silver were placed into a clay stove and melted into an ugly blob. The court's tributary relationship with the Qing had been formally broken.

Less than two months later, on August 1, 1884, the Kien Phuc Emperor was poisoned, presumably by the hardline faction at the court, led by Ton That Thuyet. Those officials then placed a half-brother of Kien Phuc, 12-year-old Ham Nghi, on the throne in his place. He was just what Ton That Thuyet wanted in an emperor: an obedient boy who could become the figurehead of a national revolt organized by others. Thuyet started making plans for war.

While all this was unfolding in Hue, the French resumed their campaign against Qing China. They were demanding Chinese recognition of their protectorate in Tonkin, which required Beijing to also renounce its suzerainty over "Viet Nam." They destroyed the Qing's southeastern fleet off Fuzhou on August 23 and engaged in many months of attacks on Chinese shipping and seaports. On land, a series of poor military decisions by French commanders led to an unnecessary and chaotic withdrawal from the border town of Lang Son in March 1885 and a serious setback for the colonial campaign. It caused outrage among the political elite in Paris and the architect of the enterprise, Prime Minister Jules Ferry, was forced to resign. The French navy, however, continued to attack the Chinese and a few weeks later Beijing finally conceded. The "Treaty of Tianjin" was signed on June 9, 1885. The Qing government agreed to recognize French control of "Annam" and not to interfere in French dealings with the government in Hue. The power of European artillery had brought an end to two millennia of vassal status.

It was only after this point that the French were able to give serious thought to how they would actually implement the "Patrenôtre Treaty." The Hue court had been forced to agree that the French administration would appoint a representative to it. French officials would oversee provincial bureaucracy and the government would defend both free trade and Catholic communities. The French took over customs and were given a monopoly over certain goods (such as opium). They were, in effect, taking over the Black Flags business model. It also allowed the French to build a telegraph network connecting the protectorates with Cochinchina. Although each was officially ruled separately, the three regions were becoming part of a French-ruled whole.

But even as the French consolidated their control, Ton That Thuyet was planning to break it. He organized a store of weapons in the mountains west of Hue. In July 1885 he organized an attack on the French military camp outside the city and used it as cover to smuggle the entire royal court out of the imperial palace and 60 km north to Quang Tri. There he announced his intention to lead a revolt. Unfortunately for him, few courtiers were willing to trust a man already assumed to have been responsible for the recent deaths of three emperors, and most returned to Hue. Ton That Thuyet and his allies took Ham Nghi up into the hills and issued a proclamation calling for a general uprising against the French. Its final words Can Vuong—"Save the Emperor"—gave the rebellion its name.

Ton That Thuyet's opponents in the court did not want to provoke another war with the French occupation forces. Their response was to formally depose the absent child emperor and place his 21-year-old half-brother Dong Khanh, the last surviving adopted son of Tu Duc, on the throne instead. From September 18, 1885, there were two rival emperors in Dai Nam: one calling for resistance to the French and the other for accommodation. Unable to find sufficient French targets for their anger, many supporters of the *Can Vuong* movement turned their anger on Catholics. The historian Keith Taylor estimates that during 1885 they killed between 40,000 and 50,000 people in the area between Hue and Hanoi. The French military attempted to protect Catholic communities emphasizing, in the eyes of many Vietnamese, the links between the two.

Ham Nghi's rebel court appointed a rival government and called on other "bandit" groups, including the Black Flags, to cooperate and expel the French. However, Ton That Thuyet's rebellion failed to achieve anything like the success of previous dynastic founders such as Ly Thai To or Le Loi. The Hue court steadily whittled away his supporters politically, while French forces demolished the armed bands who tried to attack them. Ham Nghi remained in his mountain hideout with one of Tuyet's sons until his location was given away by uplanders who owed more in loyalty to Hue than they did to Ton That Thuyet. In October 1888, Ham Nghi was captured and Tuyet's son killed. Ton That Thuyet himself fled north to try to persuade the authorities in Qing China to provide support. None was forthcoming and Thuyet remained in exile there until he died many years later. The *Can Vuong* rebellion was extinguished, although its memory became an inspiration to later generations of fighters for independence. Ham Nghi, the rebel emperor, was handed over to the French who deported him to Algiers where he eventually married a local woman. He would not be buried in Hue. Instead his tomb lies in a cemetery near his former chateau in the French village of Thonac, in the valley of the Dordogne.

><~><

French Indochina (1887–1907)

Every world leader who makes an official visit to Vietnam gets a special welcome at a relic of the country's colonial past. If it were not for the bright yellow paint, the country's Presidential Palace would not look out of place in a European city. It was originally built to make a political point. In 1893, after another piece of gunboat diplomacy, Laos had become the fifth territory of the "Indochina Union" (after Cambodia, Annam and Tonkin and the colony of Cochinchina) and the dynamic governor-general, Paul Doumer, wanted an official residence that matched his new status. He chose a spot on a piece of higher ground overlooking the former site of the Hanoi citadel. There, between 1901 and 1906, a four story palace emerged, part of a plan to rebuild the city as a colonial capital. In 1897, Hanoi was a war-damaged backwater of a city but that, for Doumer, was an advantage. Saigon was the capital of French Cochinchina and Hue was the seat of the Nguyen emperor. Both had elites and officials and hierarchies already in place. Doumer wanted to make a new state and so he chose a place where he could build from the ground up.

The French "concession" was originally established in an old fort just a few streets east of Hoan Kiem lake, had been greatly expanded to include all of what is now central Hanoi. In 1888 it became a French-run city with a council that started redesigning the city along European lines. The old citadel—which Francois Garnier and Henri Riviere had captured in bloody battles in 1873 and 1883 respectively—now belonged to France. The geometrically-shaped walls, originally designed by European engineers employed by the Gia Long Emperor a century earlier, were torn down between 1894 and 1897. Tree-lined boulevards and grand villas appeared in their place. Doumer had grand ambitions for his capital. In addition to his palace, there would be schools, a theatre, banks, a supreme court and all the other trappings of modernity. There would, however, be a price to pay. To build the governor-general's new residence required the clearing of 20 hectares. Dozens of private houses and a 1,000-year-old temple were leveled. Similar things happened elsewhere. As the heritage historian William S. Logan has noted, the old Confucian examination hall was pulled down in 1883 to make a barracks, the Temple of Supreme Reason went in 1897 to create space for the city hall, and the huge Bao An pagoda was cleared to make space for the post office by Hoan Kiem lake.

Doumer's remodeling of Hanoi was just one part of a reform agenda that led to him being called the "Father of Indochina." During his five years as governor general, from 1897 until 1902, he created a central government, secured its finances, remade the civil administration and initiated a huge railway construction program. These innovations would endure beyond the French departure, half a century later. Ironically, however, Doumer's integration of the different areas under French rule would also help to promote a twentieth century "Vietnamese" national identity that would grow strong enough to bring down colonial rule.

During the 12 years preceding the appointment of Paul Doumer as governor-general, French interests in Southeast Asia had been redefined. In 1885, when the Ham Nghi Emperor was deported, policy was still run from Cochinchina, primarily in the interests of businesses based there. Over the following few years, however, Paris imposed a new, more classically imperialistic agenda based on metropolitan ideas of a *mission civilizatrice*—a "civilizing mission"—to spread the benefits of European progress to the "benighted" peoples of the newly-subjugated territories. This began with the brief governorship of Paul Bert in 1886. He instituted a new strategy for embedding French rule; working through, rather than against, the local power structures. He brought in a new group of French supervisors to oversee local officials while allowing them to work in their traditional manner. He also built a new, cooperative relationship with the royal household in which each would reinforce the position of the other. A *Résident Supérieur* was installed in the court to oversee its affairs from behind the scenes.

On October 17, 1887, the French government "regularized" its new possessions by creating the Indochinese Union to administer the colony of Cochinchina and the protectorates of Annam, Tonkin, and Cambodia. Although each had its separate status, French rule would become increasingly centralized over the next few years. This was not particularly welcomed by the Cochinchina businesses who were expected to pay for it, nor by their many supporters back in Paris. The extension of colonial rule revealed the tensions between the various interests in Indochina. Administrators, financiers, manufacturers, missionaries and military men all had different priorities. And, of course, the peoples who were to become the object of the *mission civilizatrice* had no say in the matter.

In 1889, Dong Khanh, the emperor whom the Nguyen court had placed on the throne to replace Ham Nghi, died of illness. While the French had regarded Dong Khanh as a useful puppet during his four years on the throne, his death gave them an opportunity to entirely remake the role of emperor. The *Résident Supérieur* consulted with the court and nominated as successor 10-year-old Thanh Thai, the son of Duc Duc, the emperor who had been deposed and killed by Ton That Thuyet back in 1883. With a child monarch and a pliant court, it became easier for the French administration to extend and embed its control over Tonkin and Annam. A new Governor-General, Jean Marie Antoine de Lanessan, a true believer in the *mission civilizatrice*, was appointed in 1891 and he set about pacifying the rebellious north with a mixture of military and civilian administration.

de Lanessan's most significant opponents were the last followers of Thuyet's rebellion. Chief among them was a former court official, Phan Dinh Phung (pron. Fan Ding Fung) who took to the hills of Ha Tinh province, in northern Annam, and led a small resistance army for several years after 1885. Although Phung was later made a hero of the nationalist resistance (and had several streets named after him) he was not, himself, a nationalist. He was resisting the French in the name of the true emperor, the royal court and its Confucian traditions. He saw himself as the guardian of a properly organized society and a moral culture rather than the leader of an oppressed nation. He was, fundamentally, a conservative. When he died, of dysentery in 1896, that vision of resistance to colonial, modernizing France largely died with him.

While the French were fighting these battles in Tonkin and Annam, they also had time to expand Indochina through an expedition against Siam. It was, in part, a legacy of the Black Flag conflict. The rebels had continued to maraud around the uplands after their confrontation with the French and had sacked the city of Luang Prabang (in what is northwestern Laos today). This eventually prompted the court in Luang Prabang to request assistance from the French and, in 1893, de Lanessan ordered troops to cross the frontier to try and crush the Black Flags. This, however, triggered confrontations with troops of Siam, which regarded Luang Prabang as its vassal. The French, who had long had designs on the land to the west of Tonkin and Annam, sent gunboats up the Chao Phraya River to central Bangkok where they threatened the Siam court. On October 3, 1893, Siam agreed to hand over the lands east of the Mekong River to France. Laos was added to Indochina.

This was the relatively happy situation that Paul Doumer inherited when he was installed as Governor-General of Indochina in February 1897. With peace secured, his priority was taxation. This was an area in which Doumer was expert, having been a math teacher, a Minister of Finance and an expert on colonial budgets. He knew that Annam and Tonkin were not paying their way—the costs of pacification had vastly exceeded the revenue from the protectorates and the French government had been obliged to write off their debts. Doumer needed to find money but without asking either Paris or the businesses of Cochinchina to foot the bill. Instead, he created what the historian Gerald Sasges has called, "largely imaginary sources of indirect tax revenue." His inflated predictions of future revenue from taxes on salt, alcohol and opium enabled him to issue government bonds—in effect giant IOUs—which gave him the money he required to initiate his grand plans without offering political concessions to either Paris or Cochinchina. Suddenly, out of nowhere, there was money for the railways and everything else.

The French monopolies were supposed to generate huge revenue for the government. In fact, reports from the time show that the costs of running the system—buying the alcohol, bottling and distributing it, etc.—were so high that the alcohol monopoly's actual contribution to the colony's finances were tiny—just 3% of its total income. There were, however, other reasons for keeping it in place. Under the treaties of Hue, taxation of goods, rather than people, was the preserve of the French. The French-run Department of Customs and Excise had the power to demand taxes, issue fines, arrest non-payers and even use violence. By 1908, the Department of Customs was the largest unit in the French administration, with 1,300 Europeans and 2,000 local employees based in 360 locations. By using the excuse that they were enforcing the tax rules, the French governor-general could bypass both the Vietnamese court-appointed officials and the French *residents supérieur* based in the protectorates. He had a network of civilian French agents officially employed to detect illegal distilling of alcohol and opium smuggling but who could monitor and control whatever was going on. Corruption and abuse became major problems, however, and the customs regime became a significant contributor to the deterioration of relations between the French authorities and the Vietnamese.

Meanwhile the owners of the monopolies made huge profits. Auguste-Raphaël Fontaine founded the Société des Distilleries de l'Indochine (SFDIC). With all the money he and his shareholders made, they founded the Union Commerciale Indochinoise (UCI) which, by 1914,was the biggest business in Indochina. It had government-given monopolies on the transport and sale of alcohol, opium, salt and tobacco in Tonkin plus other operations all around the French empire. Fontaine also co-founded the Société Indochinoise de Commerce, d'Agriculture et de Finance (SICAF), which made even more money from rubber, tobacco and coal. All these companies did their financing through the Banque de l'Indochine, generating yet more profits for them too. But while this small elite made money, the government's debts mounted up. By 1910, the cost of servicing the bonds that Doumer had issued rose to 18% of the total budget.

Doumer was careful to preserve the fiction of the protectorate. He maintained the appearance of the old court and its administrative system while making them increasingly subordinate to French rule. He abolished the position of "viceroy" of Bac Ky (which the French now called Tonkin) originally established by Gia Long a century earlier, and placed Tonkin under direct French rule. Although he maintained the old system of civil service exams based on knowledge of the Confucian classics, the men who passed the exams in Tonkin were set to work under French officials. He took a similar approach to the monarchy itself: appearing to uphold it while deliberately undermining it. In his early years, the child emperor Thanh Thai had been educated in conformance with the Confucian duties and rituals expected of him. However, as he became older and more independent, he became a subject of the *mission civilizatrice*.

Under the guidance of the French *Résident Supérieur* in Hue, he broke with the protocols that had given his predecessors their imperial aura. Rather than only appearing in public for particular festivals and expecting his subjects to prostrate themselves before him, he traveled around often, visited the theatre, smoked and even danced. He cut his hair short, rode a bicycle and wore western suits. In 1902, Doumer invited him to the opening of the new railway line between Hanoi and the port of Haiphong, including the huge new bridge across the Red River. It had a dramatic effect on the public audience. As one French official (and future politician) Henri Cosnier later observed, Doumer, "wished to show [Thanh Thai] to his people, and at the same time to destroy the legend which represented the Emperor of Annam as a superman, a demi-god living in the mysteries and prodigies of a palace populated by spirits, inaccessible even to the gaze, and in constant relations with the divinity.... The effect was instantaneous: The ancient prestige of the emperors of Hue had sunk in the eyes of their people."

Doumer returned to France in 1902 having transformed the French administration of Indochina. At the end of his five-year term he was able to boast that, "not a single soldier of the Indochinese troops has been killed since 1897." That was true, although he omitted to mention the number of tax collectors and other "civilian" employees who had died in the line of duty. At home, his service as governor-general was regarded as a great success, and it catapulted him back into high politics. He was elected to the Chamber of Deputies and would become President of France in 1931 (before being assassinated the following year). Back in Indochina, Doumer's legacy endured under his successor, Paul Beau. Politics was stable; Hanoi developed into a colonial city with hotels, villas and theatres; railway construction continued with lines joining major cities and Indochina started making a profit, with the surpluses shipped back home to enrich the motherland. The emperor, however, turned into a bit of a problem. While he continued to enjoy the pleasures of modernity, Thanh Thai started to chafe at the restrictions placed upon him. Lurid rumors circulated: he was alleged to have fed a wife to his tigers and to have shot dead three concubines. In July 1907, worried that he was plotting with hostile forces, the French authorities and the court's Council of Ministers declared Thanh Thai insane and persuaded his mother to formally depose him. He was dispatched to internal exile in the governor-general's beach villa at the Cochinchina resort of Cap-Saint-Jacques (today called Vung Tau). Few were sad to see him go and the French quickly appointed his 8-year-old son, Duy Tan, to rule in his place. They saw merit in having a powerless figurehead on the throne.

The French now had a docile emperor who would further undermine the prestige and mystique of the royal court by breaking with centuries-old traditions. The imperial citadel at Hue was described by a contemporary French writer as, "an immense dead city." The colonists had successfully co-opted the traditional Confucian-educated elite in the north and the center of the country by keeping them in their positions and appointing French officials to oversee them. Thousands of young men continued to take exams to join the traditional civil service into the 1900s. At the same time, the governor-general had his own, separate, intelligence-gathering and enforcement system through the Department of Customs.

Down south in Cochinchina, the entire system was now French-run, with the emperor merely a far-away figure with little relevance in day-to-day life. Taken together, this combination of French rule and cooptation destroyed popular support for the monarchy, its civil service and the traditional elite. By doing so, it opened a space for new ideas to enter society—many of which were promoted by French officials and educators. They combined European ideas of progress and nationalism with particular views about history and the proper ordering of society. Out of this collision of worldviews came the idea of being Vietnamese.

CHAPTER 7

BECOMING VIETNAM (1907-54)

Phan Boi Chau and the Emergence of Resistance

I n 1906, two Vietnamese radicals made a tour of Japan together. They met Japanese officials and Vietnamese students and urged them to support resistance against the French. The two men, 39-year-old Phan Boi Chau and 35-year-old Phan Chu Trinh (sometimes written Phan Chau Trinh), were key figures in the emergence of modern Vietnam but they had very different ideas about how the country should move forward. Although they evangelized their cause together in the 1900s they later split and went on to inspire two very different ways of being Vietnamese. Phan Boi Chau would take the revolutionary road, rejecting foreign influence and organizing armed resistance. Phan Chu Trinh would try to work with French officials to advance the cause of democracy and republicanism. The differences between them would become differences between rival political groups, rival states and then two sides in a civil war that would drag world powers into a regional inferno in which millions died.

Both men were the sons of Confucian scholars, both had been taught to read and write classical Chinese and trained to take the Nguyen Dynasty's civil service exams. Phan Boi Chau came from Nghe An Province, a region that became famous for producing many leaders of the nationalist and communist movements. It was part of Annam but far from the royal court; a poor backwater where men sought advancement and status through education and politics and a place that maintained a strong sense of tradition and was hostile to outsiders, particularly Catholics. Phan Chu Trinh, on the other hand, grew up in a wealthier family, in a village closer to Hue in a region that had always been more open to outside influence. These differences were reflected in their political ideas.

Both had grown up during the *Can Vuong* ("Save the Emperor") revolt, read the calls for political reform circulating among Chinese intellectuals and learned about the modernization taking place in Japan but each had drawn different conclusions. Phan Boi Chau wanted to expel the French and recreate a kingdom based upon traditional Confucian morality. Phan Chu Trinh wanted to embarrass the French into actually fulfilling their claims of a *mission civilizatrice* and reform Vietnamese society. After Japan beat the Russians in the war of 1904/5 hopes for an Asian challenge to Western imperialism surged. Phan Boi Chau organized a "Go East" campaign among wealthy families to send their children to Japan for study. In all, 300 students from Tonkin, Annam and Cochinchina spent time there, meeting exiled reformists and revolutionaries from all around Asia, imbibing the ideas that would transform the region. Phan Boi Chau arrived in 1905 and authored some of his most important writings there, sending back pamphlets calling for resistance against the French and sparking yet more radical discussions back in Hanoi, Hue and Saigon. Among them was "A History of the Loss of Vietnam" commissioned by the Chinese reformist Liang Qichao and published in Chinese. It was possibly the first time any writer had used "Viet Nam" as the name of the country outside diplomatic correspondence. However, this was not so much a nationalistic statement as an adoption of the formal name bestowed by the Qing Empire a century earlier. In other words, what would become the "revolutionary" name of the country, Viet Nam, was chosen by Phan Boi Chau on the basis of Liang Qichao's advice and derived from the Qing court's choice of name a century earlier.

Phan Chu Trinh wanted to get rid of the emperor, whom he saw as an obstacle on the path to reform and modernity. He wanted a republic and he believed the French would support him in his aims. In 1907, after his return from Japan, he wrote an open letter in French to the colonial governor-general, Paul Beau. He described the suffering of the people but blamed it upon a corrupt bureaucracy: the mandarins whom he called "parasites." He also warned the French that their arrogant behavior was the cause of the hate expressed towards them and called for them to recognize that reform was in everyone's best interests. That same year, Phan Boi Chau wrote his own open letter, but in a very different tone. His "Letter from abroad written in blood" was written in Chinese. It called for the killing of Westerners and those who have "forgotten their own race." It mixed Confucianism with an embryonic nationalism, containing references to figures such as the (ancient Chinese) Duke of Zhou but also to the "Southern People"—as distinct from the "Northern People" of China.

After writing his call to arms, Phan Boi Chau travelled through southern China to meet Liu Yongfu, the leader of the Black Flags who had caused so much damage to the French expeditions of 1874 and 1884. He intended to use Liu's influence in the city of Qinzhou (in Guangxi province close to the frontier with Vietnam) to create a base for operations against the French. Meanwhile, Phan Chu Trinh and few associates were founding the "Tonkin Public School" in Hanoi to promote their ideas of modernization. It was based on a Japanese example, and offered classes, lectures and pamphlets for free, funded by private donations. Its lecturers gave talks on science and society, they encouraged the learning of *quoc ngu* as an alternative to writing with characters, they discussed history and began to rehearse ideas for a nationalistic interpretation of the past. Some called for a break with the past, an abandonment of Confucianism, a change to Western ways including in dress, hairstyle and relations between men and women. In this they were following in the footsteps of reformers in both China and Japan

In 1908, all these currents combined to form a maelstrom of anti-French feeling. Ever-greater demands for taxes and *corvee* (forced) labor sparked several local uprisings that were only suppressed with deadly force. This was followed by plots to poison the food of the French garrison in Hanoi and to provoke a mutiny among Tonkinese troops. The colonial French community in Hanoi was incensed: demanding drastic action against the plotters and their supporters. Paul Beau's term of office was over and his successor—rather than address the problems of enforced taxation and labor—cracked down on both reformers and revolutionaries. Thirteen alleged plotters were executed and many others were given long prison terms. Phan Chu Trinh, the man who wanted his country to become more French, was sentenced to hard labor on Con Dao/Poulo Condor—the island that became known as the "colonial Bastille." He spent three years there before a public campaign resulted in his sentence being changed to house arrest. Since he refused to accept anything less than full freedom, the authorities deported him to France. The Tonkin Public School was closed but its influence would live on.

The French government pressured the Japanese authorities to expel Phan Boi Chau, forcing him to flee, ultimately, to China where he continued to agitate. After the Chinese revolution of 1911–12, which overthrew the Qing Empire and replaced it with the Republic of China, he formed the "Vietnam Restoration Society" modeled on Sun Yat-sen's Chinese revolutionary organization, the *Xingzhonghui*. With the support of some sympathetic Chinese officials, Phan Boi Chau trained and dispatched a few activists on assassination missions in Indochina. Two of them, in 1913, were successful, prompting panic among the French community who arrested hundreds of suspects, executing several of them and pressuring the authorities in Canton/Guangzhou to have Phan Boi Chau arrested, which they did in 1913. By the time he was released in 1917, the French had succeeded in destroying the Vietnam Restoration Society.

As well as a stick, the colonial authorities were also trying to offer their subjects a carrot to accept French rule. A new Governor-General, Albert Sarraut, arrived in post in November 1911 and served until May 1919 (with a three-year absence from 1914-17 for health reasons). In addition to creating a new political police, the Sûreté Général, he attempted to improve the image of colonial rule with small expansions of education and health provision. More significantly, he also tried to create a new French-oriented local elite by promoting a version of what he called "Annamese" culture. This attempted to embed French rule by connecting it with the royal court, its mandarins and the associated Confucianism and respect for hierarchy. At the same time it tried to separate the idea of "Annam" from China by promoting *quoc ngu* over character-based writing and emphasizing a separate cultural tradition.

Although these efforts worked for a time, they would come to worsen the problems the French faced. Despite their professed reformism, the colonial authorities were more committed to protecting the old corrupt elite than to their supposed *mission civilizatrice*, as the travails of Phan Chu Trinh demonstrated. Everyone in Indochina knew the French really called the shots and the more they promoted "Franco-Confucian" culture, the more tainted it became. From the 1920s on, modernizers would want to break with both France and Confucianism.

Even at the height of French colonialism, in 1940, there were never more than 35,000 colonists in Indochina but this relatively small group were able set the agenda far more successfully than the authorities back in Paris. While metropolitan France became more skeptical about the merits of empire, the colonists dug in against calls for reform and doubled down on exploitation. They wanted, in effect, to run the Indochina economy as a captive market. The state-backed monopolies over salt, alcohol, tobacco and opium provided easy money for some. Initially, the colonists were only able to operate because they dealt with longer-established Chinese business syndicates, particularly in Cochinchina. These syndicates connected ports in Southeast Asia, from Saigon to Singapore, with the ports of coastal China. During the early twentieth century, however, French conglomerates took over more of the economy. Companies with official monopolies over river transport or railways or other sectors of "strategic" significance such as coal mines and cement factories benefitted from the protection of the Indochina government, including subsidies. The colonists also profited from the huge increase in demand for commodities: coffee, sugar, cotton, and rubber. Three billion francs were invested in these sectors during the 1920s and yet more profits accrued to the intermediary banks. A tiny group of French financiers and businessmen reaped the largest rewards.

The 1920s were the "Belle Epoque" of French rule in Indochina. Rice exports surged, peaking at 1.8 million tons in 1928. Coal exports surpassed a million tons per year and rubber also boomed. All this fed an urban economy of increasing sophistication and a new "Indochinese" hybrid culture. An "Annamese" elite and a middle class did emerge and grow in the cities and towns. New buildings were constructed in Hanoi, Saigon and the smaller cities to accommodate the interests of the *colons* and the emerging middle classes (numbering around 900,000 people by 1930). Many French words entered the Vietnamese language such as those for coffee (*ca fe*—café), cake (*ga to*—gâteau), cheese (*pho mai*—fromage) and railway station (*ga*—gare). The addition of beef to noodle soup created the pho that became the national dish. In Saigon, local performers adapted French musical and theatrical styles to recreate traditional opera as a new form known as *cai luong*. The "Ecole des Beaux-Arts d'Indochine" was founded in Hanoi in 1925 with a brief to develop an "indigenous" style. One of its graduates, Nguyen Cat Tuong, would play a major role in creating a new way of dressing: popularizing the *ao dai* (pron. ow zei) now regarded as the "traditional" Vietnamese women's costume. From these, and many other, connections emerged the essence of what were becoming the cultural markers of Vietnamese national identity.

Life for the vast majority of Indochina's inhabitants, however, was far less rewarding: most still worked in the fields. In Cochinchina, the modernization of agriculture through irrigation and fertilizers enriched those who owned or controlled land but turned those who could not compete into landless laborers. By 1938, 45% of the Mekong Delta was controlled by big landowners. Further north, peasants worked in ways that were little different from their ancestors. The only thing that modernized was the tax collecting regime, which became more effective and coercive. The expansion of commercial crops created a demand for plantation labor. In 1908 just 200 hectares were devoted to rubber. By 1940 it was 126,000 hectares. Tens of thousands of unemployed northerners—men and, importantly, women too—were encouraged or coerced, to head south and work among the trees. The population of the south would double from 2.8 million in 1900 to 5.6 million in 1956. The mines near Haiphong became another destination for surplus labor. Coal exports rose from 200,000 tons per year in 1900 to almost 2 million tons in 1940. Tens of thousands of laborers were shipped to other French colonies in the Pacific, Africa and the Americas in conditions of semi-slavery. Overall, the expansion of cash crops, mines, railways, ports and construction began to create an immiserated working class, hundreds of thousands strong, detached from the land and open to new ideas of social justice that had nothing to do with old ideas about loyalty to rulers.

During the First World War, around 90,000 Vietnamese laborers were sent to France. Just over half worked in factories and the rest labored at or near the frontlines. They encountered a vastly different world and developed completely different expectations of life. Many of them began to hope, like Phan Chu Trinh, that France would now live up to its rhetoric of liberty, equality and fraternity. In 1919 a group of them petitioned the Versailles Peace Conference with a document entitled "The Claims of the Annamite People" which called for the French government to "grant to the native population the same judicial guarantees as the Europeans." It was not a demand for independence but a request for "protection by the French people." The document was signed with the name "Nguyen Ai Quoc," which literally translates as "Nguyen who loves his country." "Nguyen Ai Quoc" was actually a pseudonym for the drafting committee that included the venerable Phan Chu Trinh and a young man from Nghe An called Nguyen Sinh Cung. In time, Cung would actually adopt the identity of Nguyen Ai Quoc, before changing his pseudonym to one that would echo around the world: Ho Chi Minh.

Nguyen Sinh Cung/Ho Chi Minh continued his activism in France, moving steadily leftwards in his politics. He joined the French Socialist Party in late 1919 and then discovered Lenin's writings on imperialism. In the aftermath of the Russian Revolution, he found Lenin's ideas of a "dual headed" struggle against capital both in the colonial countries and the colonies made sense. The Europeans and Americans did not seem interested in giving colonial peoples their rights; the Soviets did. By February 1920, Ho Chi Minh was giving speeches on Bolshevism and by March he was urging the Socialist Party to join the Soviet-led "Third International." Towards the end of the year he helped to form the French Communist Party. In early 1923 he made the decision that committed his life to revolution: he journeyed to Moscow to begin work with the Communist International, the Comintern. He was not alone. Others who heard the call of communism while in Paris at around the same time included the future Chinese leaders Deng Xiaoping and Zhou Enlai. After a sojourn in Moscow, Ho persuaded the Comintern to dispatch him to southern China in late 1924, as a translator for its main

TOMB OF THE MINH MANG EMPEROR, HUE Minh Mang was the second emperor of the Nguyen Dynasty and imposed strict Confucian-style rule. He brought the whole country under his direct control, annexed Cambodia, and repressed minorities and "foreign" religions. *(Photo: Oleskaus, Shutterstock)*

GOVERNOR-GENERAL'S RESIDENCE Originally completed in 1906 for Governor-General Paul Doumer. He chose a spot on a piece of higher ground overlooking the former site of the Hanoi citadel. It is now the official residence of the President of Vietnam. *(Photo: Svetlana Erevmina, Shutterstock)*

THE FRENCH ATTACK The arrival of the French empire. An engraving published by the French newspaper L'Illustration in 1858 showing the failed attack by French, Spanish and Philippine troops on Danang. Note the crucifixions, an exaggeration designed to remind French readers of the persecution of Christians by the Nguyen Dynasty. The invaders withdrew from Danang a few months later and occupied Saigon instead. *(Photo: Marzolino, Shutterstock)*

Opposite:

FRENCH SAIGON An early map of French-controlled Saigon, published by the French magazine *Le Tour du Monde* in 1860. It shows the old citadel (later destroyed), a new commercial district laid out along European lines, the "Chinese bazaar" of Cho Lon to the northwest and the plantations and rice fields around the city. *(Photo: Marzolino, Shutterstock)*

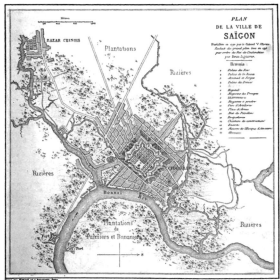

Restaurant Terrasse du Continental
Saigon (Cochinchine)

COLONIALISTS The inequality of colonial life in Saigon is obvious from this postcard of the Continental Hotel. The hotel was built in 1880 to serve the growing number of visitors to the city. While international trade made some Vietnamese wealthy, the vast majority endured poverty. *(Photo: Public Domain)*

The Grand Hotel de la Rotonde in Saigon, opposite the Continental Hotel on the old Rue Catinat around 1920. Even at the height of colonialism, in 1940, there were never more than 35,000 French in Indochina. They ruled over a population of 25 million Vietnamese in the colony of Cochinchina and the protectorates of Annam and Tonkin. *(Photo: Public Domain)*

Colonial officers and businesspeople at a café next to the department store "Aux Fabriques de France" on Rue Paul-Bert (now Trang Tien Street) in central Hanoi. Colonial enterprises dominated the economy through state-backed monopolies and commercial conglomerates, but a Vietnamese middle class began to emerge in the 1920s. *(Photo: Public Domain)*

HENRI RIVIERE The French naval officer whose actions against "bandits" resulted in France occupying northern Vietnam. He seized the Hanoi citadel in 1882. *(Photo: Wikimedia Commons)*

TON THAT THUYET Military commander of the Nguyen court and the power behind the throne in the 1880s. He ordered the killing of three emperors and the kidnapping of a fourth. *(Photo: Wikimedia Commons)*

COLONIAL ECONOMY A restaurant car in Indochina, 1928. A north-south railway line linking Hanoi with Saigon was initiated by Governor-General Doumer in 1898 but was not completed until 1936. The 1,730 km journey originally took 42 hours. Nearly a century later it still takes 34 hours. *(Photo: Public Domain)*

CON SON PRISON Entrance to the Prison Museum on Con Dao Island, 90 km off the coast of southern Vietnam. Once known as Poulo Condor, Con Dao was a French penal colony before 1954 and then used by the Republic of Vietnam during the 1960s and 1970s. Conditions were notoriously harsh. *(Photo: studioloco, Shutterstock)*

DIEN BIEN PHU Trench and crater at A1 Hill, Dien Bien Phu, northwestern Vietnam. The victory of the Vietnamese side over French imperial forces at the battle here in May 1954 led to the departure of French forces, independence and separation into two Vietnams. *(Photo: beibaoke, Shutterstock)*

HO CHI MINH CITY Ho Chi Minh City, the commercial heart of Vietnam. Formed in 1976 by combining the three districts of Saigon, Cholon and Gia Dinh, it is now home to ten million people with another ten million living in

the surrounding provinces. It is the wealthiest city in the country, accounting for around a quarter of national economy. *(Photo: Nguyen Quang Ngoc Tonkin, Shutterstock)*

CAO DAI RELIGION The Cao Dai "cathedral" in Tay Ninh province is the centre of a uniquely Vietnamese religion, officially founded on November 18, 1926 and now numbering around four million adherents. The origins of Cao

Dai lie in Daoism, but the religion also includes elements of Confucianism and Buddhism. During the 1950s it was also a powerful military force. *(Photo: Public Domain)*

PHAN BOI CHAU A fiery activist who linked nineteenth century anti-French resistance with the twentieth century nationalist movement. *(Photo: Wikimedia Commons)*

PHAN CHU TRINH Phan Chu Trinh was a reformer who hoped to persuade France to live up to its promises of liberty and equality during the early twentieth century. *(Photo: Wikimedia Commons)*

HO CHI MINH, 1921 Born Nguyen Sinh Cung in 1890, the son of a Confucian scholar-official. Seen here as the Indochinese delegate to the French Communist Congress in Marseilles. *(Photo: Wikimedia Commons)*

HO CHI MINH, 1946 Now the leader of the recently-declared Democratic Republic of Vietnam and enmeshed in complex negotiations with the French colonial administration that would end in war. *(Photo: Wikimedia Commons)*

NGO DINH DIEM President Dwight D. Eisenhower and Secretary of State John Foster Dulles (from left) greet the president of the Republic of Vietnam, Ngo Dinh Diem at Washington National Airport, May 8, 1957. Diem created the Republic but was assassinated in a American-backed plot in 1963. *(Photo: US National Archives)*

SAIGON UNIFICATION PALACE Originally called the Independence Palace. It was built in 1962 to replace the French-built residence of the Governor of Cochinchina. Its construction symbolized the sweeping-away of colonialism and the foundation of new independent country, the Republic of Vietnam. *(Photo: Hamdan Yoshida, Shutterstock)*

BATTLE OF IA DRANG VALLEY November 1965. The first pitched battle between main force units of the US Army and the People's Army of Vietnam. Fighting killed 237 American and over 1,000 Vietnamese soldiers. *(Photo: U.S. Army)*

TET OFFENSIVE US Marines move through Hue on February 11, 1968, 12 days into the Tet Offensive. Communist units had seized the city and assassinated around 3,000 officials. They held out for a month. Although a military failure, the uprising convinced many Americans the war was unwinnable. *(Photo: USMC)*

NAPALM Bombs explode on village south of Saigon, 1965. Fifty-eight thousand Americans died during the war; the number of Vietnamese killed during the same period was around 1.7 million. *(Photo: U.S. National Archives)*

MODERN VIETNAM Nguyen Phu Trong, President of Vietnam and General-Secretary of the Communist Party hosts US President Donald J. Trump at the Presidential Palace in Hanoi, February 27, 2019. Relations between the two countries are now close, although some suspicions remain. *(Photo: White House, Joyce N. Boghosian)*

STREET LIFE Women selling flowers in the early morning in a small market, Hanoi, Vietnam. Amid the noise and bustle of modern Vietnamese cities, aspects of traditional life endure. *(JunPhoto, Shutterstock)*

organizer, Mikhail Borodin. The Soviets had agreed to provide military trainers to the Whampoa Military Academy outside the city of Guangzhou, just opened by the Chinese nationalists and headed by Chiang Kai-shek. Communists and radicals from both China and Vietnam were already gathering there, bursting with revolutionary feeling.

In Guangzhou, Ho Chi Minh's communism overlapped with Phan Boi Chau's earlier "armed Confucianism." As the historian Hue-Tam Ho Tai has pointed out, the two men came from the same province—Nghe An—and Chau was a friend of Ho Chi Minh's father. It was Chau who used his contacts with leading Chinese nationalists to enable several Vietnamese revolutionaries to join the military academy in 1924. Some were the remnants of his earlier "Go East" movement, while others came from among the several thousand Vietnamese who were now working as employees of the French colonial administration at posts in southern China. Many of them came from Nghe An. By 1925 there were enough of them in Guangzhou for Ho Chi Minh to form the "Vietnamese Revolutionary Youth League" there. This prompted a split between Ho Chi Minh and Phan Boi Chau. Inadvertently, however, Chau would prompt a major rush of recruits to the revolutionary cause.

On June 30, 1925, Phan Boi Chau made a visit to Shanghai where he was kidnapped by French agents, bundled onto a warship (fittingly named after the architect of French imperialism, Jules Ferry) and taken to Hanoi. His trial turned into a sensation: Chau dragged out the proceedings for three months, turning the tables on the prosecutors and using the court as a pulpit to denounce the crimes of colonialism. Newspapers in Hanoi and Cochinchina (where French law prevailed, making censorship more difficult) printed the transcripts in French and *quoc ngu*, spreading Chau's ideas among the ranks of young eager nationalists. Adding to the febrile atmosphere, the Khai Dinh Emperor died midway through the trial. His designated successor, Bao Dai, was then just a 12-year-old student enrolled at a school in France.

In November the court convicted the 58-year-old Chau and sentenced him to hard labor for life. The country erupted. University students marched in the streets, condemnation filled the newspapers and excerpts of the trial were turned into pamphlets and widely read. The Governor-General, Alexandre Varenne had only arrived in Hanoi two weeks before the verdict. He was a Socialist Party member who claimed to be sympathetic with the reform cause and decided to defuse the anger by commuting Chau's sentence to house arrest. The street protests turned to joy. November-December 1925 was a defining moment for Vietnamese nationalism, uniting people across difference, background and outlook.

There were yet more protests in early 1926 when Phan Chu Trinh, the man who had wanted the Annamese to become more French, passed away. Trinh had, coincidentally, returned to his homeland shortly before Chau was kidnapped and died there, of natural causes, on March 24. His funeral prompted a memorial procession through Saigon of some 70,000 students from all across Cochinchina. Many of them were punished for missing school or wearing black armbands, which led to school boycotts, strikes and expulsions. Many students chose to flee the oppressive atmosphere. Those from Tonkin and Annam tended to go to China, whereas those from Cochinchina generally headed to France. In both places they encountered radical ideas and new political movements. According to Christopher Goscha, at least 200 Vietnamese studied politics and military science at the Whampoa Academy in Guangzhou between 1925 and late 1927 (when Chinese nationalists crushed an attempted Communist uprising in the city, forcing Ho Chi Minh to flee). At the Academy, the Vietnamese mingled with Chinese radicals of all stripes—among them the future premier of Communist China, Zhou Enlai, who had joined its teaching staff. The graduates would go on to become some of the most important leaders in the Vietnamese revolution. Many would spend time in the rival military forces of China, both nationalist and communist, forging the connections that, two decades later, would propel the Vietnamese revolution to victory.

〜〜〜

The 1930s

In one of Phan Chu Trinh's last pieces of writing, entitled "Monarchy and Democracy" and published in 1925, he complained that "In my opinion these 20 million people know only their family and do not know their country… if one talks about 'the loss of national independence' not a single soul cares." For Trinh, the monarchy was a corrupted legacy of an objectionable past. Its twin foundations: Confucianism and French repression, were holding back the people and hindering the spread of nationalism. He died still convinced that the way forward lay in modernization: there was still space for Franco-Vietnamese collaboration allowing colonialism to be reformed from within. Unfortunately for Phan Chu Trinh and his supporters, the colonists in Indochina did not see it that way.

Governments in Paris, particularly those which came from the left, talked of change and even of decolonization. Governor-General Alexandre Varenne created "Chambers of People's Representatives" for Tonkin and for Annam in 1926 but their function was limited to commenting on an agenda drawn up by the authorities. When a leading pro-French reformer, Pham Quynh attempted to set up a political party at around the same time, he was blocked. Varenne also attempted a series of social reforms: improving schools, regulating plantation working conditions and creating a system of agricultural credit. The Indochina *colons*, on the other hand, were determined to resist any kind of meaningful political change and to maintain their privileged and profitable status. In 1925, more than a third of the Indochina government's revenue went to pay the running costs of its own Customs Department. That was in addition to spending on the military and police. By contrast, just over one percent was spent on sanitary and medical services. In a speech in 1925, Ho Chi Minh claimed that across Tonkin there were just ten state schools but 1,500 licensed outlets for the state alcohol monopoly. In March 1927 Varenne made the mistake of suggesting that Indochina might, one day, deserve independence. The Cochinchina *colons* pulled strings in Paris, accused Varenne of corruption, and had him replaced.

French repression of the protests in 1925/26 had caused many reformists to reassess their position. Seeing no way forward with France they created a new political force in December 1927: the Vietnam Nationalist Party [Viet Nam Quoc Dan Dang/VNQDD]. Led by middle class reformers such as the schoolteacher Nguyen Thai Hoc, the VNQDD was modeled upon the ruling party in China, the Guomindang

(GMD or KMT). It borrowed its political platform from the GMD: national independence (and the unification of all three parts of Vietnam), democratic republican government and socialist economic development. Towards these ends some members were prepared to engage in violence. In one action, a man who recruited Vietnamese to work as guest laborers abroad was killed, and in another, a French garrison was attacked. This prompted a heavy-handed response from the colonial authorities who arrested and executed Nguyen Thai Hoc and 30 others in mid-1930. A further 600 were jailed. The surviving leadership fled to China where they enjoyed the protection of the GMD. But by successfully crushing the non-communist nationalist trend in Vietnamese politics, the French had opened the door to the communist version.

There was already a sizeable group of people who felt there was no chance of reformism or the VNQDD's approach actually working. Instead, they demanded the immediate overthrow of the colonial regime. A few were inspired by Phan Boi Chau's earlier activities and formed a group called Tan Viet (New Viet). Others, particularly those who had lived and worked in France, gravitated towards various flavors of communism. Some of them joined Ho Chi Minh's "Vietnamese Revolutionary Youth League" and formed secret branches of the organization in Tonkin, Amman and Cochinchina. There were, however, disagreements between them, particularly over whether to prioritize Vietnamese nationalism or, as the Soviet-led Comintern demanded, international class struggle. These differences of opinion hamstrung the communist movement during the late-1920s.

In November 1928, the American government forced Britain to end its policy of restricting the global supply of rubber. That, combined with surging production in the Dutch East Indies, led to a dramatic fall in rubber prices around the world and a crisis for plantations and exporters in Indochina. The knock-on effects led to a wave of business bankruptcies in Saigon and Cholon, in particular. This was made worse by the "Wall Street Crash" a year later and the subsequent global economic slump. Export markets collapsed, incomes for plantation owners and rice farmers dropped catastrophically, banks (mainly French-owned) and moneylenders (mainly Indian "Chettiars") foreclosed on loans and dispossessed small and medium farmers of their land. Workers were laid off and plantation wages were severely cut. That led to a major outbreak of labor unrest in 1930 when rubber tappers, dockyard workers and many others staged strikes and street protests.

The revolutionary atmosphere prompted communist activists in northern Annam to launch an anti-French uprising in May 1930. The area was the least policed region of the country and was strongly connected to the family and political networks of Phan Boi Chau and Ho Chi Minh. The local communist leadership ignored the instructions of the Comintern and turned protests against excessive taxation and the colonial salt monopoly into an all-out rebellion. They were well organized and created around 30 "soviets"—communist-ruled areas—across the provinces of Nghe An and Ha Tinh. It took French forces almost a year to destroy them through a campaign that included aerial bombing. The French brought in Foreign Legionnaires and troops from the highlands because they didn't trust their Viet forces to do the job without mutinying. By the end of the campaign, thousands of people had been killed, thousands more tortured and the communist leadership inside Indochina had been destroyed.

The historian Peter Zinoman has calculated that between the beginning of 1930 and the end of 1932, the prison population of Indochina rose by 75% to 12,000 people. Conditions in the overcrowded jails were terrible, and some of the worst were in the city of Thai Nguyen and the island of Poulo Condor—where, in 1930, 10 percent of the prisoners died of disease. The prisons became recruiting offices for the communists. The incarceration of so many activists from all over Indochina helped to create a new national sense of common purpose. Communists were no longer divided according to their home regions but were forced to work together and argue about the political future. The fact that prisoners were not segregated by type meant political prisoners could spread their message to those jailed for other crimes—and sometimes the prison guards as well. Overall, the communists' commitment to Leninism, with its rules about consensus and commitment to an agreed policy seems to have given them an advantage. The nationalists, on the other hand, seemed to have failed to organize themselves in the same way. The colonial prison system, in effect, allowed the communist movement to rebuild itself and assert political supremacy.

The upsurge in militancy prompted the Comintern to reassert its control over the various communist factions. Ho Chi Minh, having fled China for Moscow in 1927 and then travelled through Southeast Asia, summoned the surviving leaderships of all the various groups to a meeting in Hong Kong in October 1930. After some argument, they agreed to go along with the Comintern's directive, emphasizing international class struggle over national liberation and to form a single "Indochina Communist Party" (ICP). At this point, the Comintern insisted on an "Indochina" party to struggle within the French colony of Indochina. There were very few participants from Cambodia or Laos, however. It was a Vietnamese party in all but name.

The French authorities pursued their campaign against anti-colonial activists with vengeful thoroughness. By the end of 1931 they had crushed both the nationalist and the communist organizations inside the country. They persuaded the British police in Hong Kong to arrest Ho Chi Minh there in 1931. (Only intervention by a sympathetic British lawyer, Francis Loseby, prevented his extradition and almost certain execution. Ho Chi Minh was held in Hong Kong until January 1933, when he escaped to China and then to Moscow.) An uneasy peace endured during the remainder of the 1930s but beneath the surface big changes were taking place. Instead of offering meaningful reform to placate their critics, the French administration attempted to revive the role of the increasingly discredited monarchy under the new, young emperor. Bao Dai returned to Hue from France in 1932 and he was put at the head of a royal government for Annam the following year. The man appointed to be its Minister of Interior was called Ngo Dinh Diem, the son of a former court official, who would later go on to become the first president of independent South Vietnam. Despite the name, the royal government was no more independent than the earlier "Representative Councils" and Diem resigned after just two months. The experiment was abandoned shortly afterwards.

While some Vietnamese continued to side with the French, either because they supported the monarch or because they believed in talk of reform, increasingly large numbers of them were turning away. A few were active supporters of the nationalist or communist parties but most were simply disengaged. For some, the answer lay with fascism.

A desire for a "muscular" nationalism coalesced under the banner of "Dai Viet"—the name used by the state since the tenth century. These activists had no time for democracy, and formed groups such as the "Dai Viet National Socialist Party" (*Dai Viet Quoc Xa Dang*). Others turned to millenarian religious movements such as the Cao Dai founded in 1926 or the Hoa Hao founded in 1939 [see Boxes on Cao Dai and Hoa Hao]. Others found solace in opium. The colony was beset with a sense of malaise. But no matter how viciously the French tried to eliminate opposition, it kept finding ways to reappear.

In Cochinchina, where local citizens were allowed to stand for elections to the Colonial Council and the Saigon Municipal Council, leftist groups including Trotskyites and anarchists formed tactical alliances, winning seats in 1933, 1935 and 1937. Their activities were helped by the coming to power of the Popular Front in Paris, which ordered the freeing of 1,500 political prisoners in Indochina, a loosening of newspaper censorship and a reduction in controls on political activity. The release of its activists allowed the ICP to rebuild its underground networks in all three parts of the country. The party worked very successfully to build up its own "Popular Front" coalitions, working with other groups to win seats in the two Chambers of Representatives and municipal councils. This did not work everywhere, however. In 1939, the Trotskyists, who opposed the ICP and its links to the Comintern and to the Soviet leader Joseph Stalin, won 80% of the vote in elections to the Colonial Council. There was overwhelming anti-colonial sentiment but support for the ICP was still in the minority.

The effects of the economic depression lingered, particularly in rural areas where poverty reached near-famine levels. By 1930, 2.5 percent of landlords owned almost half the rice-growing land of Cochinchina. Eighty percent of the total cultivated area was leased to tenants who had to pay both rent and taxes, and could be evicted for non-payment of either. In 1939, a survey of poor villages in Tonkin calculated that eighty percent of the population ate just one inadequate meal per day. While some wealthy families owned large amounts of land, the majority had less than enough to feed themselves. Fifty-eight percent owned no land at all. Unlike the other political parties, the Indochina Communist Party recognized that these people were a vast reservoir of potential supporters, and set out to cultivate them. It was easy to blame the colonial French, corrupt bureaucrats and grasping landlords for the miseries of village life.

In 1932, one of the colony's leading financiers, Paul Bernard the boss of the *Société Financière Française et Coloniale*, wrote a book in which he noted that the only companies then able to make a profit in Indochina were those with an official monopoly or some form of state protection. In his words, French and Vietnamese "had worked for twenty years to feed a handful of usurers and pawnbrokers." In this and other writings, he criticized the dependency of the economy on rice exports and called for radical change in policy to spread the benefits of development more widely among the local population so as to increase their prosperity and stimulate local demand for goods and services. He recognized the problems caused by farmers being evicted and urged the government to buy out big landlords and share out their fields among smaller farmers. Bernard estimated that the population of Indochina was growing by around 180,000 people per year but the economy was failing to provide them with work. He argued that the colonial government's pursuit of prestige projects such as the national railway network was a colossal waste of resources. The solution to both problems, he said, was to turn the colony into an independent economy (although one still bound to France politically) by promoting industrialization. In contrast to earlier calls for political reform, these ideas for economic reform were welcomed by the *colons* but rejected by the government in Paris. The 1934–6 "Popular Front" of Socialists and Communists would not support industrial jobs being created in Indochina that would undermine the position of workers in France. The calls for reform went unheeded and the last chance for meaningful change in Indochina was lost.

><><

Annamites Become Vietnamese

In late 1938, Ho Chi Minh travelled with a convoy of aid and advisers from Moscow to the Chinese Communist Party base in the city of Yan'an. War was already underway: Japan had attacked Beijing and

Shangai the previous year and was in control of most of northeastern China. The Nationalist government had retreated to the southwestern city of Chongqing, and was maintaining an uneasy alliance with the communists. Ho arrived there in early 1939 and renewed his contacts with some of the activists he had known in Guangzhou a decade earlier including Zhou Enlai. He also met Ho Hoc Lam, another native of Nghe An, who had "gone east" with Phan Boi Chau's movement in the 1900s, trained at military school in both Japan and China with Chiang Kai-shek and then risen to become a general in the Chinese Nationalist army. In 1936, Ho Hoc Lam and a few other exiles had founded the Vietnam Independence League—the Viet Nam Doc Lap Dong Minh Hoi, known as the Viet Minh. It was formally registered with the Chinese Nationalist government, although not actually functioning. Lam agreed that Ho Chi Minh could take it over.

In the summer of 1939, war came to Europe. Developments in France would directly affect Indochina. The successor to the Popular Front government replaced the civilian governor-general with the military commander, General Georges Catroux. Catroux immediately reversed many of the earlier political reforms. The Indochina Communist Party was banned again and many activists were detained. In June 1940, after Germany occupied Paris and a "collaborationist" government was established in Vichy, Japan began to make demands of the authorities in Hanoi. The Japanese military wanted to prevent supplies reaching Chinese government forces via Haiphong and the roads and railways of Tonkin, and demanded that Catroux allow "inspectors" to monitor the border crossings. Aware that he was not going to receive any support from the British or the Americans, Catroux felt forced to agree. He was then fired by the Vichy government and replaced by the navy commander, Admiral Jean Decoux. (Politics may have played a part since Catroux was a supporter of the Free French government while Decoux supported Vichy.) But within weeks, the Vichy government had agreed to the inspections and even more.

In August 1940, Japan imposed on French Indochina a treaty that was, in many ways, similar to the ones the French had forced on the Nguyen court in 1874 and 1884. It formally recognized French sovereignty over Indochina while stipulating that Japan would be able to use

Haiphong port, several airfields and railways in Tonkin and station 6,000 troops north of the Red River. A year later, another agreement allowed Japanese forces to station huge numbers of troops across the whole of Indochina, placing them within striking distance of the rest of Southeast Asia. The "ABCD" coalition of America, Britain, China and the Dutch East Indies demanded that Japan withdraw and imposed an embargo, cutting off 90% of its oil supplies. Instead, in December 1941, the Japanese attacked south to occupy the oil fields of Borneo: invading British Malaya and the Dutch East Indies. Assuming that this would trigger American intervention, they made a pre-emptive strike against Pearl Harbor.

As Japanese military strength increased, the French found themselves competing with Japan for power within their own colony. The two played games of political chess, constantly trying to mobilize favored groups within the population to gain advantage. Decoux cracked down on political opposition but attempted to gain support by instigating a massive program of public works, equalizing salaries for Vietnamese and European officials and increasing the number of children enrolled in school by over 50%. While the French still had their supporters, the Japanese encouraged the Vietnamese population to see them as liberators from the French. Some pro-Japanese groups were supporters of the exiled pretender to the throne, Cuong De, then living in Japan, who had previously been allied with Phan Boi Chau. Cuong De had considerable support among the Cao Dai religious community in the south, many of whom rallied to the Japanese and were given weapons. The Japanese also supported and armed the Hoa Hao Buddhist movement as another counterweight to the French in Cochinchina. Other Japan-supporters came from the "Dai Viet" fascist groups, originally formed in the 1930s, and concentrated in the north. Ngo Dinh Diem founded the "Dai Viet Restoration Association" in 1942 with mainly Catholic supporters. They were nationalists, inspired by Japanese talk of "Asia for the Asians," and dogmatically opposed to the materialistic atheism of the communists.

Meanwhile, Ho Chi Minh was hiding in the northern hills, making plans to fight Japan. In February 1941, Ho crossed into Vietnam for the first time in 30 years. He set up base at a cave near Pac Bo, just a few kilometers from the Chinese border and in May the leading members of the Indochina Communist Party held their "Eighth Plenum" there. They took two key decisions. Firstly they agreed on a "national liberation first" strategy, a shift from the earlier "class struggle" strategy; talk of liberating peasants from greedy landlords disappeared. Secondly they agreed to turn the Viet Minh into a "front organization," a broad-based grouping that would include as many different groups as possible willing to liberate the country both from the Japanese and the French. The ICP would officially "disappear" although, unofficially, it would continue to exist as the guiding leadership within the Viet Minh. Many of those involved in the preparations for the plenum were veterans of the Youth League founded in Guangzhou 16 years earlier, and also of the French prison system. Significantly, most of these people were from the northern wing of the ICP and none were from Cochinchina because the French had successfully eliminated or imprisoned the southern leadership. This "northern" leadership, with its pro-Chinese orientation would remain the dominant group in the ICP for several decades.

The ICP/Viet Minh set about rebuilding their networks inside the country using the language of national liberation and unity to attract intellectuals and peasants alike. They spent four years planning how to take over the state, organizing supporters in cities, towns and villages and preparing to take power. They infiltrated non-Communist organizations, such as the Japanese-sponsored Vanguard Youth movement. They were also active in the mountains, working with Tai and other upland peoples who had hitherto been suspicious of the Viet and consequently more friendly towards the French.

The tide of war started to turn against Japan in the second half of 1942 but bitter fighting continued in Southeast Asia. Indochina became a vital supply base for Japan's frontline troops. Peasants were ordered to grow cotton and jute in place of rice, and much of the rice that was grown was requisitioned for military use. During 1944, Allied bombing destroyed road and rail connections between north and south and submarine operations disrupted coastal shipping. With the Japanese prioritizing their war efforts over local needs, it became impossible to move enough rice from the south to the northern and central areas where food was short. The result was famine. Between December 1944 and May 1945 around a million Vietnamese died of starvation: 10% of the population of Tonkin and northern Annam. After this, the population of the north was desperate for change.

On March 9, 1945, the Japanese launched a coup against the French, disarming their troops and detaining the Indochina leadership including Admiral Decoux. They then obliged the Bao Dai Emperor to renounce the treaties with France and declare the formation of a new state, called the "Empire of Viet Nam" incorporating Tonkin, Annam and, theoretically at least, Cochinchina. Bao Dai asked for Ngo Dinh Diem to become his new prime minister but the Japanese insisted upon Tran Trong Kim who, back in 1920, had been the author of *Viet Nam Su Luoc* (History of Vietnam), the first history text published in the Vietnamese alphabet. The new leadership freed political prisoners, abolished the names "Tonkin" and "Annam" and issued a new national flag of a red stripe on a golden-yellow background. However, they failed to inspire any enthusiasm among what could, for the first time, properly be called the "Vietnamese" public. More support went to the Viet Minh forces who were raiding granaries and distributing rice to the starving.

In June, Japanese forces withdrew from the border, leaving the uplands open to the Viet Minh. By early summer, its movement's leadership had moved their headquarters closer to Hanoi. They were now in contact with Allied high command and were receiving some support from American intelligence in exchange for helping to rescue shot-down airmen. There were occasional skirmishes between the now-armed Viet Minh and the Japanese. Some Vietnamese who had been enlisted in Japanese units changed sides, bringing their weapons with them. Viet Minh members were taking up positions in the cities, towns and villages ready to seize power when the moment came. They were not, however, the only ones. Belatedly, the Nationalist and Dai Viet groups were also preparing to take power but they had nowhere near the depth of support or organization displayed by the Viet Minh.

On August 15, 1945, the Japanese emperor announced his country's surrender. By coincidence, the Viet Minh had called a "People's National Congress" for the same week. Its sixty delegates claiming to represent "all social classes, associations and nationalities" voted to create a provisional government of the "Democratic Republic of Vietnam"

(DRV) with Ho Chi Minh as president. They also approved a new flag, composed of the same colors as the flag of Bao Dai's "Empire of Vietnam" but rearranged to form a yellow star on a red background. The congress was cut short and the provisional government called for a national mobilization. All over the country, the coalitions they had carefully put together over the previous months started to take power as the Japanese withdrew to their barracks and ports. The DRV forces had to work quickly before the French could seize the initiative. Hue was "liberated" on the 23rd and Saigon by the 25th.. The Viet Minh had even got to the emperor. On August 30, Bao Dai abdicated. In front of a huge crowd at the gate of the imperial palace in Hue, he formally handed over the gem-studded sword and square seal of office to Tran Huy Lieu, representing the DRV, and formally ended the 143-year-old Nguyen Dynasty.

Three days later, on September 2, 1945, on a wooden platform erected on the French-built traffic circle outside the Governor-General's Palace in Hanoi, Ho Chi Minh and his fellow Viet Minh leaders formally declared the independence of the Democratic Republic of Vietnam. This was the first time the watching crowds had ever seen their new leaders. Standing on the podium alongside Ho were the men who would direct the Viet Minh's struggle over the following decade: Truong Chinh, the First-Secretary of the ICP and therefore the most important political leader in the country and Vo Nguyen Giap, the schoolteacher turned head of the Liberation Army.

For two crucial weeks, the DRV ruled almost the whole country but on September 13 two battalions of British Gurkha troops were flown into Saigon. They were there to implement an agreement made at the Potsdam Conference that China would be responsible for military operations north of Danang while the British would operate south of that line. By the time they arrived, a Viet Minh committee had taken over the city's main buildings and ICP agents were assassinating key figures in the rival Trotskyite, nationalist and religious organizations. The British commander, General Douglas Gracey, was welcomed by the surrendering Japanese forces but was under orders not to meet the Viet Minh representatives. Gracey's orders required him to merely hold the fort in "French Indo-China" until the French could take over, which they started to do on September 23. That night, some of the French force rampaged through Saigon attacking Vietnamese. In response, a Vietnamese gang killed around 200 French and Eurasians. Gracey then re-armed the surrendered Japanese and drove the Viet Minh forces out of the city. The official British military history records that by January 1946, 3026 Vietnamese had been killed, along with 3 British, 37 Indian and Gurkha, 106 French and 110 Japanese soldiers. By that time 17,000 (white) French troops had arrived in Cochinchina allowing the British to leave, along with the Japanese. A new French ruler, given the title "High Commissioner" was installed in October: Admiral Georges Thierry d'Argenlieu, a man steeped in colonial and Catholic tradition and once described by a critic as possessing "the most brilliant mind of the twelfth century."

In the north, Chinese Nationalist forces had begun arriving in September and their presence kept the French away. They insisted that their Nationalist Vietnamese allies be included in the government. Compared to the situation in the south, this was a relatively small problem for the communists and, for several months, the two rival parties managed to work together as the DRV consolidated its administration north of Danang. The French wanted the Chinese to leave, and on March 6, 1946 the two sides reached a deal: France agreed to renounce all its colonies in China and China agreed to withdraw its forces from Indochina. In the high pressure negotiations, Ho was forced to concede that the DRV would become a "free state" within a French-aligned "Indochinese Federation" and that French troops could return. That was a setback but the Chinese withdrawal, when it came in June, allowed the Viet Minh to eliminate the Vietnamese Nationalists. Within weeks the Viet Minh attacked the forces of the VNQDD and the Dai Viet groups and either eliminated them or chased them over the border to China. As historian Brett Reilly has discovered, the fighting was vicious, with both sides referring to one another as *Viet gian*—"traitors to the Vietnamese race." With these battles in 1946 the Vietnamese civil war began.

As violence began in the north, High Commissioner d'Argenlieu, part of the *colon* community and the few remaining Vietnamese "constitutionalists" who still trusted the French took matters into their own hands. Without permission from Paris, they declared the creation of the "Republic of Cochinchina," asserting that it was a separate French colony. Then d'Argenlieu decided to take his campaign into the north. He began by challenging the DRV's leveling of customs duties in the port of Haiphong. The DRV authorities refused to back down so, on November 23, 1946, French warships shelled the city; leveling several districts and killing around 6,000 Vietnamese. Retaliation was not long coming. On December 19, Viet Minh militants launched attacks in Hanoi. d'Argenlieu now had the excuse he had been seeking, and unleashed his troops. By the end of February they had secured Hanoi, Hue and the large towns and cities. The countryside, however, was ruled by the Viet Minh. A second war, one between two rival governments—a French-led "Indochina Federation" and the Vietnamese-led DRV—was now underway. Both governments claimed authority over the whole country but neither was able to enforce it. It was a war that would overlap and interact with the intra-Vietnamese civil war for the next thirty years.

The French brought in more troops, both European and colonial. The strength of the *Corps Expéditionnaire Français d'Extrême-Orient* (CEFEO) reached 100,000 in 1947. The Viet Minh were also recruiting and could count on at least as many fighters in both regular units and guerrilla groups. Advising them were colonially-trained officers who had changed sides, Japanese soldiers who didn't want to go home and a few European deserters. Jungle warfare came no more "naturally" to the Vietnamese than it did to the French. But through the application of science and engineering—as taught in colonial colleges—the Viet Minh came to pose a formidable threat. The French recognized that they needed more help and turned to whatever local forces were available. In early 1947 they made alliances with the Cao Dai and Hoa Hao religious militias and the Binh Xuyen gang (which had been responsible for the killing of French civilians in September 1945). It was a dirty game and players repeatedly shifted sides in a constantly moving arrangement of allegiance and interests. New phrases entered the language to describe the teams. In 1948, newspapers aligned with the Nationalist parties adapted a Chinese phrase and coined the term *Viet Cong* to describe the communist-led forces. The choice implicitly linked the Viet Minh to their Chinese sponsors, with the negative implications that that carried for many on the nationalist side in the civil war. The nationalists became known as the *Viet Quoc*.

It was a very dirty war. The Viet Minh executed officials working with the French and others whose politics they did not like. Its fighters threw grenades into bars popular with *colon* civilians. CEFEO patrols routinely killed those they suspected of working for the DRV. Its soldiers were armed with flamethrowers and mortars and used them indiscriminately. Unknown, but large, numbers of people were tortured or raped. But no matter how much violence they deployed, it was never enough to defeat the DRV. Fighters disappeared into the forests or civilian clothes only to reappear. Military commanders called for more troops but war-damaged metropolitan France had other priorities. By 1952 the DRV controlled about half of Tonkin, three quarters of Annam and about a quarter of Cochinchina. Neither side was able to land a decisive blow. The French war correspondent turned historian Bernard Fall estimated that as many as a million people may have been killed during these seven brutal years. The population of Saigon tripled to 1.7 million in 1954 as villagers fled to the relative safety of the cities.

In March 1947, the French government chose a new High Commissioner to replace the medieval-minded d'Argenlieu. His successor, the Socialist Emile Bollaert, co-opted efforts by non-communist Vietnamese to create an alternative to the DRV by bringing back the abdicated emperor, Bao Dai. It was the first of many attempts to find a "third way" solution between the French and the Viet Minh. In September 1947, Bao Dai and the non-communists broke with the DRV and announced they were ready to negotiate with the colonial power. It was a critical moment. The Vietnamese Nationalists, the *Viet Quoc*, had decided to use the French to get rid of the communists. There was still no agreement on a political solution, however, and in late 1948, Bollaert was replaced as High Commissioner by Leon Pignon. At the same time, the international situation became more critical. The communists were winning the Chinese civil war, the Dutch were being forced to give up their colony in Indonesia and fighting was beginning along the border between two Koreas. Pignon recognized that he had to compromise in order to create an anti-communist "front" between France and the "third way" groups.

On July 2, 1949, the French government formally created the "Associated State of Vietnam" with Bao Dai as its head of state, bringing together Cochinchina, Annam and Tonkin under a single government. The objections of the Cochinchina *colons* were overruled. Just like the other "associated states" of Laos and Cambodia, this Vietnam remained within the French Union meaning that Paris remained in control of finances, the law and the military. Very quickly the "third way" groups and their supporters realized that they had been sold a pup. Bao Dai refused to play his part, the monarchy languished and politics descended into *ennui*.

As Chris Goscha has demonstrated, the local and international situation combined to bring the conflict to a crisis. The French authorities were able to paint themselves as leading the fight against communism in Southeast Asia, gaining support from the UK and the United States. In January 1950, China and the Soviet Union formally recognized the DRV and the following month the United States recognized the Associated State of Vietnam (ASVN). At almost the same time the Chinese and American governments sent officials to investigate their respective "Vietnams," and both returned home with requests for weapons, training and money. Chinese advisers began to arrive in the northern hills shortly afterwards and in September 1950, the United States created the Military Assistance Advisory Group (MAAG) in Saigon, partly as a *quid pro* quo for French involvement in NATO and the European Defense Community. Under Chinese tutelage, the ICP ordered a huge program of land reform and peasant mobilization and a year later, the SVN instituted a military draft. It was the beginning of a very slippery slope.

><<

Dien Bien Phu and the End of French Rule

During the first half of the 1950s, the Vietnamese communists radically reshaped the rural society they now ruled. At the behest of their Chinese advisors, they imposed drastic land reforms with a violent campaign against those they defined as landlords. They followed a Chinese model, even though conditions in Vietnam were quite different. Land was given to the landless and hundreds of thousands of peasants, both men and women, were mobilized to support the war effort. Between 10,000 and 15,000 people were executed by cadres of what was now called the "Vietnam Workers Party" (rather than the ICP) and many tens of thousands more were beaten and imprisoned. The Vietnamese leadership were admirers of China's revolutionary success and, in 1952, they launched a "rectification" campaign to ensure obedience to the new political orthodoxy. All efforts were devoted to defeating the French. Fighting raged back and forth across the northern and central regions of Vietnam involving increasingly large forces. Christopher Goscha has calculated that the DRV armed forces mobilized more than 1.7 million laborers in these campaigns and hundreds of thousands more were used by the French and SVN forces.

In April 1953, the Politburo of the Vietnam Workers Party decided upon a new strategy to defeat the French. It was a crucial moment. The Soviet leader, Stalin, had died in March, the Korean war had reached stalemate and both the Moscow and Beijing leaderships were ready to accept some kind of compromise, so long as the imperialists could be pushed back from their borders. China had created a communist "buffer state" in Korea and was looking to do the same in Indochina. The French government wanted to focus on affairs closer to home by ridding themselves of the financial burden of war in Asia. In Vietnam itself, the only rural areas under the control of the French and their allied militias were the deltas of the Red River and the Mekong, the central coast around Hue and Danang and upland regions where minority groups maintained autonomous fiefs. Outside the main cities, the Viet Minh now controlled the country but, after bitter defeats in 1951 and 1952, the Politburo recognized that they could not defeat the French through pitched battles in the lowlands. Instead, they decided to lure the French into the hills by mounting a series of diversionary attacks in Laos. Thus the stage was set for the denouement of the French presence in Indochina: the battle of Dien Bien Phu.

Shortly after the Politburo's decision, the French government appointed General Henri Navarre as commander of the CEFEO. His instructions from Paris were to inflict sufficient damage on the Viet Minh forces that their leadership would agree to negotiations and France could make an "honorable exit" from Indochina. Navarre needed a major change of fortune to have any chance of achieving this, but he hoped that American financial and materiel support would provide it. In July, he and his military colleagues approved a new plan to take the counterinsurgency fight into the enemy's heartland. This was exactly what his enemy wanted him to do. Within weeks, Viet Minh spies knew what the plan involved and their leaders were making plans to turn it to their advantage.

On November 2, Navarre and his staff chose a wide-bottomed valley in the Black River borderlands inhabited by Tai, Hmong, Lao and Chinese peoples, many of whom saw the French as allies against the lowland Vietnamese. Dien Bien Phu was a typical piece of upland *dong* world (see Chapter 2) but it controlled the road between Vietnam and Laos and possessed a rudimentary, Japanese-built airstrip. Three weeks later, the first of 14,000 troops—French, Vietnamese, Tai, Moroccan, Senegalese and Foreign Legion were dropped into the valley to be followed by thousands of tons of stores, ammunition and even light tanks. Meanwhile, the Chinese communists stepped up support for their Viet Minh allies with thousands of tons of weapons, supplies and vehicles with which to move them. Just as importantly, they trained new brigades of troops and advised their commanders. In fact, the historian Christopher Goscha has argued that "the Chinese played the determining role in choosing to take the French on at Dien Bien Phu."

The Viet Minh took their time. For four agonizing months they transported—often by foot and bicycle along monsoon-sodden mountain tracks—the war machinery necessary to defeat a modern expeditionary force. Peasants and hill peoples were pressed into service, motivated by the cadres' promises of land reform and communist nirvana. The CEFEO had badly underestimated its enemy. The novelist Graham Greene, who visited the Dien Bien Phu fortifications in early 1954, noted that "the achievement was magnificent... all was under their eye." But the hills all around the French bases were alive with hostile activity. Everyone involved recognized that this was likely to be a decisive engagement. Even as the French were digging in, the "great powers"—the UK, USA, USSR and France—called an international conference in Geneva to resolve the conflicts in both Korea and Indochina.

On March 13, while planning for that meeting continued, the Viet Minh finally launched their attack. The French were outnumbered five-to-one, outgunned and out-thought. The battle lasted two terrible months, paralleling the preparations for Geneva as representatives from the United States, the Soviet Union, China, France, and Great Britain argued over the best way to combine peace with geopolitical advantage. On May 7, the day before the conference was due to begin discussions of Indochina, the final French hold-outs at Dien Bien Phu surrendered. The world was stunned. Nothing would be the same again.

The result of the Viet Minh victory at Dien Bien Phu was a deal between France and China over the fate of Vietnam. France agreed to withdraw its troops from Indochina in exchange for stability in the region. The delegates then agreed on the *temporary* partition of Vietnam between north and south pending elections on a future government, although nothing was ever formally ratified. It has long been claimed that the leadership of the People's Republic of China pressured the DRV into accepting the partition against its wishes. However, recent discoveries in the Vietnamese archives suggest that partition was actually an outcome the DRV leadership had been prepared to accept from the outset. Its military forces were exhausted; it faced a challenging domestic political situation and needed to avoid further interventions by France and the United States. The main opponent of partition was the government of the Associated State of Vietnam. While the Geneva conference was underway, Bao Dai had invited Ngo Dinh Diem, the Dai Viet Party nationalist who disliked the French almost as much as the communists, to become prime minister. Diem condemned the Geneva agreement but there was nothing he could do about it. Instead, he used his new power to chip away at French control. On July 20, 1954 he unilaterally withdrew the "Associated State of Vietnam" from the French Union, making it the "State of Vietnam." Then, in December, he ended use of the *piastre*, the currency controlled by the Bank of Indochina, and created a new financial system, customs and border posts.

Once it became clear that the country would be partitioned into a communist north and a nationalist south, huge numbers of people found they were destined to live in a state they did not want to be a part of, and fled. Around 330,000 people left the north before the French-commanded troops marched out of Hanoi on October 9, 1954. At least another half-a-million left in the following eight months. Two-thirds of them were Catholics who feared persecution. Two hundred thousand were Buddhist believers and others were supporters or employees of the French, members of the landlord and capitalist classes or political opponents who knew full well what the communists had in store for them. There were also movements from south to north by those who feared what Ngo Dinh Diem's government would do to them. At least 80,000 people left the two main communist-ruled areas on the tip of the Mekong Delta and along the central coast. The French, meanwhile, continued to withdraw their troops: all were gone from Tonkin by May 1955. Almost all the remainder had gone from the whole of Indochina by the end of April 1956. 98 years after its first attacks on Danang, the era of French imperialism in Southeast Asia came to an end.

Ho Chi Minh

The man who became known to the world as Ho Chi Minh was born Nguyen Sinh Cung in the province of Nghe An on May 19, 1890. His father was a scholar-official in the Confucian style but one who resented the French and served the court in Hue somewhat reluctantly. His mother died in childbirth when Cung was ten and a brother died shortly afterwards.

In 1904, the boy, now known by his "adolescent name" of Nguyen Tat Thanh, met his father's friend, the radical Phan Boi Chau. He turned down the chance to join Chau's "Go East" movement and instead joined the *Quoc Hoc*, the "National College." This had been created by the French to train a new generation of officials in modern (i.e., European) methods of government but employed some nationalistically-minded teachers. (Interestingly, the first headmaster of the College was Ngo Dinh Kha, the father of Ngo Dinh Diem who would go on to become Ho's political rival as president of the Republic of Vietnam.)

In 1910, Nguyen Tat Thanh's father, by then a magistrate, ordered a landlord with whom he had differences to be caned. The beating was so severe that the landlord died and Thanh's father was sacked. The following year, Thanh left Hue and eventually took a job as a cook on a ship heading to France. There he attempted to join the *Ecole Coloniale*, intended for training colonial administrators, but was blocked, possibly because of his father's misdemeanors. It seems that, at this stage of his life, Thanh was a reformist rather than a revolutionary: hoping to learn from the French and argue for equality in Indochina.

Thanh kept travelling, working on ships travelling to French colonies, and in low-paid jobs in New York and at the Carlton Hotel in London. He witnessed discrimination against colonized peoples and became very cynical of the claims of liberal democracy. His politics became more radical, particularly after the success of the Russian Revolution in 1917.

That year he travelled to Paris, where he met the activist Phan Chu Trinh. By this stage of the First World War there were tens of thousands of Chinese and Indochinese laborers and soldiers in France. It became a laboratory for new political ideas. In 1919, Thanh, Trinh and others petitioned the Versailles Peace Conference for civil rights in Indochina. The petition was issued in the name of "Nguyen Ai Quoc"— which became Thanh's political pseudonym.

Nguyen Ai Quoc continued his journey leftwards, joining the Socialist Party and then heading to Moscow to work with the Communists. By 1924 he was a full-time revolutionary organizer on a mission to Guangzhou in southern China to set Asia ablaze with communism.

Caodaism

Caodaism is a uniquely Vietnamese religion, officially founded on November 18, 1926 and now numbering around four million adherents across the southern part of the country and around the world. At its center is a brightly colored "cathedral" in the southern city of Tay Ninh, decorated with what appears to be a collision of contradictory religious beliefs. In his book *The Quiet American*, Graham Greene memorably described it as, "Christ and Buddha looking down from the roof... on a Walt Disney fantasia of the East; dragons and snakes in Technicolor."

In reality, the Cao Dai religion is a fusion of the key beliefs of Confucianism, Daoism and Buddhism with a Vietnamese twist.

Its founder was Ngo Van Chieu, a civil servant educated in French schools, who attended spirit worship "seances" at a Daoist temple near the city of Can Tho. Among the many spirits who appeared to him in these events was one with the name "Cao Dai Tien Ong." Chieu introduced friends—many of them civil servants and teachers—to his revelation and began to spread his ideas. He also encountered a group of spiritualists who organized European-style seances. Some of them had read Victor Hugo's writings which foresaw a new religion that could unite east and west. At this point, Ngo Van Chieu seems to have broken with the growing movement and handed over the reins to another French-educated civil servant, Le Van Trung.

The movement grew fast. It attracted people from all sectors of society but had particular appeal to poor farmers scratching a living or working on plantations in the forests north of Saigon. By June 1927 it had over 100,000 followers and that number doubled the following year. This rapid growth of a strange movement worried the French authorities who feared that it might be a cover for nationalism or communism, particularly after protests broke out in 1930. Many of the religion's leaders later declared their loyalty to the exiled pretender to the imperial throne, Cuong De, increasing French hostility towards them. During the Second World War, they worked with the Japanese occupation forces and created their own militia, which became a powerful force until it was dismantled by President Diem's army in the 1950s.

Caodaism combines the three "Sino-Vietnamese" religions. Its origins lie in Daoism, particularly its use of "mediums" to communicate with spirits, but it also includes elements of Confucianism and Buddhism. Believers worship the *Cao Dai Tien Ong Dai Bo Tat Ma Ha Tat*—a name which combines the supreme beings of Confucianism (*Cao Dai* or Great Palace), Daoism (*Tien Ong* is a reference to the Jade Emperor) and Buddhism (*Dai Bo Tat Ma Ha Tat* or Bodhisattva). Believers follow the duties and the prohibitions of each of the three religions.

Much has been made of the presence of the French writer Victor Hugo among the pantheon of Cao Dai "saints." He is not, however an object of veneration so much as an early influence and a figure who is said to have appeared at early seances through the intervention of spirit mediums. The practice of seances has been suppressed in Vietnam although it continues outside the country.

Caodaism borrows Buddhism's belief in the three epochs of spiritual development but promises relief from Buddhism's endless cycle of reincarnation through the prospect of an "amnesty." There is a strong undercurrent of belief in the imminent end of the world and the prospect of salvation for its believers. It is no surprise that such beliefs emerged at a time of such profound change and conflict in Vietnam's history.

Hoa Hao Religion

In July 1939, in a village called Hoa Hao, a 19-year-old man declared himself to be the Buddha and announced the founding of a new religion. The location was significant: by the banks of the Mekong River, close to the canal linking it to the city of Ha Tien and the sea. In other words, connected to Cambodia in one direction and the Malay world in the other. The man, Huynh Phu So, melded elements of the two main forms of Buddhism: Mahayana as practiced in China and northern Vietnam and Theravada as practiced in Cambodia, and introduced some ideas from the Islam practiced by neighboring Cham communities. All this was augmented by a strong sense of Vietnamese nationalism.

He argued that Buddhism should be practiced in daily life, by everyone, not by a dedicated caste of monks. He also called for simplicity, telling his followers not to build extravagant pagodas but to worship at simple altars. Rather than spending money on supporting the clergy, he urged followers to use it to help those in need. From Islam, he borrowed the ideas of regular calls to prayer, the building of "minarets" from which to broadcast these calls, praying in a particular direction (towards Buddha's birthplace in India) and the banning of distracting images from places of worship. He chose the color brown for altar cloths and flags because, in his view, it included every other color and was therefore a symbol of human connectedness and harmony.

Within months, Huynh Phu So had attracted large numbers of sup-porters. The French regarded him as both dangerous and mad and detained him in a psychiatric institution. He might have remained there had the Japanese not occupied the country in 1942. They freed So and encouraged his organization to grow. They also trained a militia several thousand strong and by the end of the Second World War, the Hoa Hao had control of the western Mekong Delta along the border with Cambodia. There were probably around 100,000 adherents.

Once the war was over, the communist-led Viet Minh attempted to co-opt the Hoa Hao into their newly declared state and armed forces. Huynh Phu So was suspicious and refused to put his militia under Viet Minh control. In April 1947 the Viet Minh had So assassi-nated, a move that backfired spectacularly. The Hoa Hao became en-emies of the communists and kept them out of large parts of the Mekong Delta. The organization was only disarmed by President Di-em's army in 1955. Although no longer an armed movement, it re-mains a carefully-watched independent force in southern Vietnamese society to this day.

CHAPTER 8

"THE VIETNAM WAR" AND "THE AMERICAN WAR" (1954-75)

1954–63

The "Independence Palace" at the heart of Saigon remains a gleaming slice of 1960s optimism in a busy, noisy, twenty-first-century city. Its strong horizontal lines and clean, curtain-like verticals still embody old hopes for progress and a brighter future. It was on this site that the story of "South Vietnam" both began and ended. It began with the declaration of a new country in 1954, and ended, twenty one years later, with the smashing down of its front gates by a communist tank. In the course of those two decades, vast numbers of people were killed, injured or displaced in a conflict that spread over three countries and dominated the world's discussions. At its core, however, was a vicious argument about the best way to be Vietnamese. Vietnam's tragedy was that this civil war became part of a global battle of ideas, drawing in powerful countries that understood little about the intricacies of the underlying conflict but were willing to aid and arm their local partners to service their wider aims.

The building we see today replaced one completed by the French in 1875 to house the Governor of Cochinchina. It was a grand confection, built to symbolize the authority of the new rulers and demonstrate the permanence of their rule. But just 12 years later, the French created the Indochina Union and placed its capital in Hanoi. The palace became an embarrassment: too grand to be used by the junior officials in Saigon but too symbolic to be torn down. On September 9, 1954, the departing French High Commissioner handed it over to the government of the new "State of Vietnam" led by its Prime Minister Ngo Dinh Diem (pronounced no-ding-zee-em). Diem renamed the building the "Independence Palace" and made it his official residence. Eight years later, two dissident air force pilots bombed the palace, destroying its northern wing. To mark a break with the past, Diem had the whole building torn down and replaced with one that showed no signs of French imperialism and every sign of modernist confidence. By the time it was finished, Diem had been assassinated but the palace would remain the center of southern politics until the Saigon government was crushed in 1976.

Diem had come to power by enlisting the United States in his struggle against the French. He and his brothers—Ngo Dinh Thuc (Catholic bishop of Vinh Long), Ngo Dinh Nhu (leader of the secretive *Can Lao* political party), Ngo Dinh Can (a political fixer and gang boss) and Ngo Dinh Luyen (a childhood friend of the Bao Dai Emperor with good contacts in France)—persuaded American officials and politicians that they—and only they—could consolidate non-communist control in the south of Vietnam and take the fight to the communist regime in the north. At the time, officials in Saigon, largely relics of the colonial administration, were panicked by the apparent inevitability of a communist takeover. Bao Dai, although now "head of state" had chosen to set up home in Europe, the army was under the control of a general loyal to the French, hundreds of thousands of refugees were arriving from the north and the state coffers were empty. The legacy of the French counterinsurgency campaign had left Saigon police force controlled by the Binh Xuyen gang and large parts of the south under the control of warlords, mostly with allegiances to the Cao Dai or Hoa Hao sects.

As historian Ed Miller has shown, Diem was intent on eliminating all these threats to the stability of the State of Vietnam by creating a family-led dictatorship. In some ways it echoed the structure of the regime in the north. At its heart was the *Can Lao* ("personalist") Party which was the leading force in a "front organization" called the National Revolution Movement (NRM) which controlled the political system. While his brothers Nhu and Can quietly recruited army officers to their political party, Diem persuaded Bao Dai to fire the military commander. Then, on April 28, 1955, having gained the loyalty of the army and some of the Cao Dai, he turned them on the Binh Xuyen gang—killing at least 500 and driving the rest out of the city. The operation turned into a major firefight with many buildings destroyed, including the gang's prized casino.

His next target was the communists. Diem had learnt enough about how they operated during his time as a provincial chief in the 1930s to understand what needed to be done. He set up civil action teams to work on grassroots development and recruited many refugees from the north to staff them. Most were eager to root out local leftists. On July 20, 1955, the anniversary of the signing of the Geneva Accords, he set his security forces to work on a "denounce the communist" campaign that would endure for several years. Local officials were empowered to arrest anyone they suspected of having communist sympathies and jail them for two years without trial. Over the next four years, tens of thousands were detained in terrible conditions and torture became widespread. In places the campaign was very successful at disrupting communist networks but in others it just generated anti-government resentment. At around this time, the local CIA station began providing the NRM with a regular monthly subsidy, despite doubts among its officers over the movement's commitment to democracy. At around the same time, Diem created his own secret police, the Service des Études Politiques et Sociales (SEPES) to keep an eye on his rivals, allies and the various arms of the government.

In the wake of that success, Diem persuaded the elders of the former royal family (which still existed in Hue despite the emperor's abdication) to denounce Bao Dai, then living in luxury in the French city of Cannes, and to formally request Diem to become president in his place. It is likely the former royals did this to preserve their properties from the threat of confiscation. By this time, Diem had already decided that the nationwide referendum on reunification promised in the Geneva Accords should not happen. Such a vote would, in his expectation, lead to an unacceptable communist victory. To sabotage the referendum, Diem announced a snap referendum in October 1955. Voters were asked to choose their preferred president by placing a picture of either

Diem or Bao Dai into the ballot box. The 98% result in favor of Diem strongly suggested fraud, but the vote confirmed the change of leadership. Bao Dai remained in France, never to return to Vietnam. He died in 1997 and was buried in the Passy Cemetery in Paris.

Immediately after the vote, Diem declared the birth of a new state, the "Republic of Vietnam" (RVN) and promulgated a new provisional constitution. None of this had been mentioned in the referendum campaign but Diem did it anyway. He also declared that the unification referendum would not take place in the RVN. Diem's next step was to organize elections, in March 1956, for a new "National Assembly." They were relatively free, in that many parties could stand, but far from fair, in that Diem's allies won 89% of the seats. One of the first acts of the Assembly was to formally denounce the Geneva Accords, a development that was strongly welcomed by American government officials. The last French troops left Saigon the following month, leaving military training and political support in the hands of the Americans. Shortly afterwards, Diem's forces captured, tried and executed the last major Hoa Hao militia leader. To outsiders, it appeared that Diem had successfully pacified the Republic. The Assembly then drafted a permanent constitution which declared that, "The President leads the nation" and gave him the power to issue decrees and suspend laws. It was formally promulgated on October 26, 1956.

Throughout this period, Diem was bolstered by American political and financial support. By 1956 there were already 650 American personnel in the Military Assistance Advisory Group (MAAG). CIA funding was covertly bankrolling his political party and the US government had introduced a well-intentioned aid effort that had the unfortunate effect of completely distorting the development of the RVN economy, and its political system too. Under the "Commodity Import Program," well-connected businesspeople were given licenses to buy US dollars at discounted rates. The Vietnamese money they paid with was given to the RVN government, while the dollars they bought could only be used to buy American goods. Seeking easy profits, the Vietnamese businesses imported household goods for the Vietnamese middle classes, thereby destroying any chance that local firms might successfully compete with the American imports. Since taking part in the program was an easy way to make money, corruption quickly followed. Between 1955 and 1961, the scheme delivered almost $1.5 billion to the Diem government and it continued to be the main channel of American aid to the RVN right up until 1975. With such an easy flow of "free money" into its coffers, the Vietnamese government made little effort to develop an effective taxation system. Instead it developed an elite that could make easy money by bribing its way into the subsidized imports system.

With the help of the United States, Diem and his family and their supporters had, in two years, wrested control of the country from the French and made it their own. Diem was not content with just creating a "South Vietnam," however. He believed that worsening conditions in the north would prompt huge numbers to flee, causing the "other Vietnam" to collapse, enabling the RVN to expand over the entire territory of the country. At times he even spoke of organizing a "march to the north" (reversing the traditional trope of Vietnamese history) to liberate the millions now living under communism. It would never happen. The communist leadership of the Democratic Republic of Vietnam (DRV), on the other hand, was convinced of the opposite. They believed it was only a matter of time before the RVN collapsed and that *they* would lead the united country. In the meantime, the communists tried to keep Diem on the path towards reunification. In 1955 they even offered to make Diem the vice-chair of a national unity government while preparations were made for the referendum promised by the Geneva Accords. Diem's post-referendum announcement in October that year killed off such hopes

Diem had good reason to believe that the north was in trouble. The communists' land reform program, begun in 1953, was becoming more and more savage. Their leadership had sought Chinese advice and chosen to implement a rigid Maoist model. Village dwellers were categorized into different classes ranging from landlord to landless peasant with those unfortunate to find themselves in the upper categories subjected to denunciations, abuse and even execution. In many cases the real landlords had already fled but the party cadres still needed to fill their quotas. Anyone who had offended their neighbors could become the target of a denunciation campaign, with catastrophic results for the family. Reports of abuses filtered back to Hanoi but the priority of the party leadership was to destroy its political opponents—both real and imagined. In the words of historian Keith Taylor, "It eliminated anti-revolutionary class enemies in rural society, it instituted an ostensibly more equitable distribution of land usage, and it traumatized the rural population into obedience to the state." Five waves of land reform were pursued until late 1956 when the resistance to it became so strong that the 325th Division of the People's Army had to be deployed to a predominantly Catholic district of Nghe An province to suppress a full-scale peasants' revolt.

As the excesses became more widely known, a section of the party membership began demanding a greater say in policy-making. They wanted a new legal code to protect the rights of individuals, an independent judiciary and a National Assembly with proper powers. This led to a protracted debate about a new constitution for the DRV. Still-secret debates took place behind closed doors about whether Vietnam would become a truly Leninist "one party state" or something more pluralistic. At the same time, a small group of writers and artists, many of whom had served in the military at Dien Bien Phu and elsewhere, began pressing for greater cultural freedom. These people were not anti-communist but sought tolerance for alternative points of view. They created two independent publications, *Nhan Van* (Humanism) and *Giai Pham* (Fine Art), which aired the views of the reformists despite increasingly severe criticism from their political opponents.

These were the public expressions of what was, behind closed doors, a bitter fight between a dogmatic radical majority of the communist Vietnam Workers Party (VWP) and a minority of pragmatic "revisionist" critics. The land reform abuses and the arguments over culture put the radicals on the defensive but they had no intention of giving up. To rescue its reputation, the party leadership was obliged to make public apologies for the "excesses" of the land reform. Both General Giap, the hero of Dien Bien Phu, and a weeping Ho Chi Minh personally admitted to errors in the implementation of policy—but, crucially, not in the policy itself. The man who had led the VWP since 1941, Truong Chinh, was offered up as a sacrifice. He stood down in September 1956 and was replaced, temporarily, by Ho Chi Minh. At this point, the whole trajectory of Vietnam's late twentieth-century changed.

The VWP network in the south was being destroyed by Diem's "denounce the communist" campaign but party activists were under orders not to fight back. The leaders of both the USSR and China had decided that the communist world required peaceful coexistence with the capitalist countries and ordered their revolutionary comrades not to rock the boat. But in 1956, as the arrests and killings mounted and the chances of a unification referendum receded, the leader of the clandestine communist party in the south, a former railway worker named Le Duan (pronounced Lay Zwun), demanded a rethink. He was dismayed by his orders to stand aside as he watched peasants in the RVN rise up against Diem's forces only to be crushed. He and his former deputy Le Duc Tho (pronounced Lay Duck Toe) began pushing for a change of policy to allow armed resistance to begin again. The pair gradually became the dominant force in the party leadership. In November 1957 Le Duan and Ho Chi Minh attended a Moscow conference and pushed for recognition that a non-peaceful path to socialism might be acceptable in some circumstances. Everyone was aware, however, that the consequences were likely to be severe. The arguments dominated discussions in the communist leadership for over a year.

In mid-1958, the radicals asserted control. The independent publications *Nhan Van* and *Giai Pham* were suppressed and many of their writers banned from ever publishing again. Those who had argued for political reform were silenced and those who argued against resuming the war in the south were gradually sidelined. Although Le Duan was not formally in charge, he was beginning to assume all the powers of the head of the party and to push it towards war. He felt he had tacit approval from the Soviets but not yet from the Chinese so a delegation was dispatched to Beijing for consultations. The Chinese were opposed, stressing the need to develop the economy in the north instead. However, as the historian Ang Cheng Guan has shown, the southern cadres of the VWP were already moving onto a war footing in the face of continuing attacks by Diem's forces. In January 1959, the party held its 15th plenum and took the fateful decision to "liberate the south from imperialism and feudalism" using mass uprisings to seize power.

With that decision, the DRV placed itself on a war footing. By May 1959, the communist movement had been reactivated in the south and the first network of supply routes (what would become known as the "Ho Chi Minh Trail") was being developed. To facilitate this, support for the communist movement in neighboring Laos was stepped up. The DRV army intensified its training, focusing on offensive maneuvers in uplands and river deltas, and tens of thousands of southern communists who had fled north in 1954 were prepared to return home. At exactly this time, faced with a reviving communist movement in the south, Diem introduced RVN Law 10/59 creating special military tribunals empowered to execute anyone accused of an "offence against national security." Sentences could be carried out immediately, in public, by guillotine. It had the effect of escalating public fears and pushing sentiment towards the communists. It also transformed opinion in the north. Those who had previously hesitated to support renewed conflict increasingly fell into line. A week after the law was passed, the VWP published details of its plenum's decision to reunify the country, stating in a newspaper editorial that the people were ready to use "every means" to achieve their objectives. On July 8, 1959, two American military advisers to the army of the RVN (ARVN) were killed by communist guerrillas: the first of more than 58,000 US servicemen to die over the following 14 years.

Ho Chi Minh spent the August of 1959 in Beijing, negotiating Chinese support for the planned military offensive. He left with a pledge of around half a billion dollars in weapons and finance, although none of it actually appeared. Relations between the two leaderships seemed to cool off. The rest of the year was spent dispatching fighters and VWP organizers to the south, ready for a resumption of the armed struggle. In January 1960, the storm broke. In one week in one Mekong Delta province, Ben Tre, there were uprisings in 47 villages. Peasants captured weapons which they used to form more regular military units. For the first time, there were also attacks on RVN military bases. Paradoxically, the success of these actions actually worried the VWP leaders in the north. They wanted things to progress more slowly so as to avoid triggering counterstrikes before the whole movement was ready. In April, in an effort to prepare the whole DRV, the army was transferred into a professional force that could be mobilized for any contingency, military or economic. Shortly after this, relations with China seemed to improve and Zhou Enlai paid a visit to Hanoi. The "communist camp" was still far from unified, however. Disagreements between the leaderships in the USSR and China over ideology and relations with the capitalist West were becoming worse. During 1960 and 1961, this "Sino-Soviet Split" would become more obvious and the DRV leadership found itself playing a very delicate diplomatic game navigating between the two.

A full meeting of the VWP Congress in September 1960, only the third in its history, confirmed the hard-liner Le Duan as the party leader and ratified the use of armed force to overthrow the RVN. Importantly, this was not to be achieved by a direct military invasion from the north but by the resistance movement within the south. It would be important to maintain the pretense that the two campaigns were separate when, in fact, both were directed by the VWP. In December, the party created the "National Liberation Front for Southern Vietnam," or NLF, to lead a broad "united front" of anti-Diem forces in the south. It followed the old Viet Minh model of building coalitions of politically disparate groups united by a common enemy. Not all were communist but all wanted an end to the Ngo family's regime. Over the following 15 years, the NLF proved to be far better at maintaining a "national" coalition than either the Ngo family or any of their successors at the top of the RVN.

Another inflection point arrived in January 1961 when John F. Kennedy was sworn in as president of the United States and immediately adopted a new "Counterinsurgency Plan" to increase funding and training for the forces of the RVN. Direct military aid tripled to $144 million, as did the number of American military trainers. In Moscow, the Soviet leader Nikita Kruschev declared that the USSR was willing to support "national liberation movements" around the world. At the same time, the NLF formally reconstituted its leadership body, the "Central Office for Southern Vietnam" or COSVN. In February, its military wing was also formalized as the Southern Region Liberation Army (often called the People's Liberation Armed Forces or PLAF). It quickly acquired a nickname borrowed from the political fights of the previous decade: the *Viet Cong*. By March, US intelligence estimated the NLF/PLAF had 10,000 fighters under arms, was carrying out around 650 attacks each month and controlled 58% of the RVN. On January 18, 1962, DRV state media announced the foundation of another front organization, the "People's Revolutionary Party" to lead the fight against imperialism in the south of Vietnam. It was the VWP's guiding hand inside the NLF.

Military planners in both the DRV and the RVN recognized the crucial importance of controlling the Central Highlands, the upland region where the borders of the RVN, Cambodia and Laos met. Inhabited for centuries by Austroasiatic and Austronesian peoples (see Chapter 2), the uplands had always been a parallel world. The French had given the region considerable autonomy and discouraged lowland people from migrating there. As late as 1954 it was still formally the *Pays Montagnard du Sud*—the Southern Montagnard State—formally outside the State of Vietnam. On coming to power, Ngo Dinh Diem resolved to incorporate it into his state both politically and demographically. Between 1956 and 1963, his government organized the migration of a quarter of a million lowland Viet people into the hills. One consequence was the disaffection of parts of the local population who resented the privileged treatment given to the newcomers. This made it easier for the communists to open discussions with uplanders. Careful relations with the different groups were vital to the operation of the Ho Chi Minh Trail, bringing supplies and reinforcements south through the hills and forests along tracks that meandered across international borders. To counteract them, the CIA also began recruiting among the *Montagnard* peoples, creating loyal anti-communist militias. In August, American advisers introduced a new tactic in the highlands that would have devastating long term consequences. Adapting a method used by the British against communist guerrillas in Malaya, they helped RVN forces spray herbicide from a helicopter to destroy the vegetation around a military base used as cover by attackers. It was the first of 18 million gallons of chemical defoliants—given various codenames such as "Agent Orange"—to be sprayed on Vietnam over the next nine years. Some of these sprays were contaminated with dioxin, one of the most powerful poisons known to chemistry.

Throughout this period and beyond, the question of who directed the anti-communist campaign in the RVN became a political obstacle to its effective implementation. American advisors believed they had the ideal strategy but Diem had his own priorities and concerns. In September 1961, he invited a British Advisory Mission (BRIAM) to establish itself in Saigon as a counterweight to the Americans. They were veterans of the Malayan campaign and believed in focusing efforts on winning the "hearts and minds" of the rural population and isolating them from the guerrilla forces by fortifying them in "strategic hamlets." The American advisers preferred to focus on military actions taking on large forces of fighters. Arguments about which strategy to pursue would increasingly lead some on the American side to believe they could do a better job without Diem in charge.

The "strategic hamlets" policy turned into a disaster on a similar scale to the land reform campaign in the north. In 1960 the Ngo brothers had created a "Republican Youth Movement" to act as the vanguard of their ideology of "personalism." One and a half million young people were mobilized to lead the fight against communism. They set out with high-minded ideals of promoting local democracy, eliminating corruption and rooting out subversion but, unlike the DRV with its disciplined one-party state, the Diem-led RVN lacked the administrative skills to properly implement the policy. American advisers became involved but the process only became more chaotic, draconian and utterly counter-productive. Hundreds of thousands of previously non-aligned peasants were so brutalized that they became sympathetic to the state's enemies. Between 1961 and 1963, according to official reports, 8.7 million peasants were evicted from their homes and relocated in 7,000 supposedly defendable hamlets. Trapped in these hamlets by fences, formerly-productive farmers became dependent on food handouts. The policy turned into a recruitment boon for the communists.

These failures only increased the perception among American advisers and politicians that they had a better understanding of what Vietnam needed than Vietnamese leaders themselves. In October 1961, Kennedy sent his military adviser, retired general Maxwell Taylor, economic theorist Walter Rostow, CIA counterinsurgency expert Edward Lansdale and a number of other officials on a ten-day mission to Vietnam to develop a strategy to beat the communist movement. It called for a "hard commitment on the ground" with US troops. Kennedy refused the request for troops but authorized an increase in advisers and equipment. He also approved the deployment of US Air Force planes to transport ARVN troops and also to spray herbicide over forests. In February 1962, a new organization "Military Assistance Command, Vietnam" (MACV) was created to oversee the missions. By the end of the year, the number of American personnel in Vietnam had risen from 900 to 11,000. Few had any significant language or cultural training before they deployed. Misunderstandings between the two sides only grew as the numbers of advisors rose. As a result, Diem became even more suspicious of Washington.

Diem's fear of losing his nationalist legitimacy was heightened on February 27, 1962 when two RVN Air Force pilots attacked his presidential palace. They bombed and strafed the building for thirty minutes, badly damaging it but narrowly failing to kill Diem. The two men, both supporters of the former Nationalist Party, claimed that Diem needed to be removed because he was more concerned about protecting his own position than about fighting the communists. The sense of crisis only grew worse. The countryside became more contested, the fighting more destructive and the gap in understanding between the Vietnamese and American leaderships only widened. American helicopters were now transporting ARVN units into battle, American advisers were accompanying them in action and American intelligence units were monitoring Viet Cong communications. At the same time, estimates of the number of communist fighters continued rising. A critical moment came in January 1963 at a village called Ap Bac, 60 km southwest of Saigon. An ARVN attack on entrenched NLF units went so badly that the attached American adviser, John Paul Vann, briefed journalists that it was "a miserable damn performance… these people won't listen." It was an unfair characterization of what was happening in the country but it put Vietnam on the front pages of the American media and spawned the idea that the ARVN was incapable of defeating the NLF. It proved to be a powerful narrative, dominating future Western understanding of the conflict.

In both the United States and Vietnam, support grew for a "third way" between communist victory and support for Diem. It took many forms, with some seeking a "neutralist" outcome for Vietnam, while others just wanted a more effective anti-communism. One group of Buddhist monks based around Hue, a group with a tradition of nationalism and an engagement with radical politics, objected to the Ngo family's promotion of Catholicism, its repression of alternative viewpoints and its tolerance of American interference. They began to protest against restrictions on flying Buddhist flags and discrimination against Buddhists. In mid-June, one monk, Thich Quang Duc, set fire to himself in Saigon to demonstrate his opposition. The image of the believer sitting serene as he was engulfed in flame appeared in news media around the world, turning swathes of public opinion against Diem and, by extension, his American backers. A summer of demonstrations led to Diem imposing martial law and arresting large numbers of monks. At this point, American officials overcame their disagreements and came to the conclusion that they would support a coup against Diem. They communicated this to several ARVN generals who requested a clear sign of support. Washington obliged by temporarily suspending the Commodity Import Program.

On November 1, 1963, the generals made their move. While their troops took over public buildings and the airport, they called Diem and offered him safe conduct out of the country if he formally resigned. Diem then called the US ambassador Henry Cabot Lodge who declined to intervene. The president, his brother Nhu, and a few supporters then fled in the night to a church in the district of Cho Lon. The following morning they were seized by the plotters. Diem and Nhu were handcuffed in the back of an armored personnel carrier where they were killed on the orders of the coup leader, General Duong Van Minh. The American government had intervened in the most direct way possible. By sponsoring the coup they had removed the ruling clique that had held the country together since independence. Removing the Ngo family would not make life easier for the anti-communist effort. Generals would now spend more time plotting than fighting. The ramifications of all this were just beginning to unfold when President Kennedy was himself assassinated three weeks later.

Ngo Dinh Diem

The man who tried to create a non-communist Vietnam was born a decade later than Ho Chi Minh and became his opposite in many ways. Ngo Dinh Diem (pronounced No Ding Zee-em) was born in 1901 into a Catholic family from Quang Binh province in central Vietnam. His father, Ngo Dinh Kha, had studied at a missionary school in British-ruled Malaya, intending to become a priest. In the 1880s, however, the French authorities recognized his language abilities and hired him as a translator.

In 1896, Ngo Dinh Kha was appointed the first head of the *Quoc Hoc*, the National Academy, created to educate a new colonial elite comfortable with both Vietnamese and French culture. Although Ngo Dinh Kha collaborated with the French, he did so because he believed the country needed to reform and modernize. He broke with the French in 1907 when they ousted the Thanh Thai Emperor from the throne, claiming that he was mad (see Chapter 6). He resigned in protest—an act that was praised by Ho Chi Minh.

Ngo Dinh Kha clung to both his Catholic faith and his hopes for reform. He educated his three sons so they could take positions in the church and the civil service. Diem attended the French-run Pellerin School in Hue where he appeared to become a devout believer. Rather than become a priest, however, he joined the School of Public Administration and Law in Hanoi at the age of 17 and, after graduating in 1921, became a local official. Twelve years later Diem was in charge of a province: Ninh Thuan south of Hue. There, in the early 1930s, he oversaw the successful suppression of a communist-led insurgency.

Diem acquired his father's resentment of the French and, like his father, channeled it into a form of what historian Ed Miller has called "Catholic nationalism." In 1933, the French authorities appointed Diem as Interior Minister of the Nguyen government but he resigned just two months later in protest against French blocking of plans for an elected assembly. He remained living in Hue, lobbying court officials to take more nationalistic positions. He also struck up a friendship with Phan Boi Chau, then under house arrest in the city. The result was a fusion of Catholicism, nationalism and Confucianism ideas that would characterize Diem's efforts to create a new, independent, non-communist Vietnam in the 1950s.

Towards an "American War" (1963–65)

From the point of view of the communist leadership in Hanoi, developments in the RVN during 1962 and 1963 were highly encouraging. The Saigon government was in disarray, NLF guerrillas were taking control of the Mekong Delta and communist support was increasing in the highlands and along the central coast. Only the cities remained firmly under Saigon's control. This presented the Politburo of the Vietnam Workers Party with a dilemma. While communist forces could win small encounters in the south, they did not have the military strength to defeat the ARVN, particularly with the United States providing increasing amounts of aid. Research by the historian Lien-Hang Nguyen has revealed the debates taking place in Hanoi at this time. Was now the time to abandon the pretense of "non-interference" in the south and directly support the NLF with regular DRV army units? In early 1962, their Chinese comrades had agreed to provide military aid: 90,000 carbines, assault rifles and light machine guns arrived that summer. Le Duan and his allies believed the time was right for a pre-emptive DRV strike to topple the RVN before the US could intervene directly. Others, notably General Giap, believed that such a strike would trigger the unwanted US intervention and provoke a devastating war. It was better, in their view, to focus on developing the economy in the north while quietly supporting a guerrilla war in the south.

As it happened, these two positions were reflected in the attitudes of Hanoi's two main sponsors. Nikita Kruschev's Soviet Union did not want to become directly involved in a war, while Mao Zedong's China wanted to take the fight to the imperialists. As a result, the "pro-intervention" group in the VWP leadership chose to orientate towards China while the "pro-insurgency" group orientated towards the USSR. The debate was ended by the November 1963 assassination of Diem. The Party's Central Committee met immediately afterwards and opted to accelerate the fighting and mobilize the entire country to generate sufficient military force to prevail. In its aftermath, "First Secretary" Le Duan and his supporters, notably Le Duc Tho and Truong Chinh (rehabilitated after the land reform chaos), neutralized their opponents with a campaign against what they denounced as "modern revisionism." This was, ostensibly, intended to root out those who favored the Soviet Union over China, but in reality it eliminated those who prioritized the building of the economy in the north and opposed the decision to return to revolutionary war in the south. Thousands of Party members were arrested, sent for "re-education" or dismissed from their jobs. Anyone who had trained in the Soviet Union or expressed sympathy with its position was considered suspect. Internal opposition to the new strategy was eliminated. With General Giap having lost the argument, war planning was passed to General Nguyen Chi Thanh. He was put in charge of COSVN, with the previous head Nguyen Van Linh as his deputy, and sent south to the Central Highlands. Under his command, logistics were strengthened, the Ho Chi Minh Trail was expanded, soldiers were jungle-trained and the country was made war-ready.

Hanoi's choice to escalate the war was followed by a similar decision in Washington. Like General Giap, the newly-sworn-in President Lyndon Johnson would have preferred to focus on building the economy at home, and avoid sending military forces to the RVN. His predecessor's decision to support the anti-Diem coup obliged him to intervene. In late January 1964, the generals who had overthrown Diem were pushed aside by another general, 36-year-old Nguyen Khanh, with support from former leaders of the old "Dai Viet" fascist parties. In the absence of a coherent leadership in Saigon, Johnson faced a choice of "acceleration" or defeat. In an attempt to dissuade the VWP leadership from intervening in the RVN, he approved "Operational Plan 34A" (OPLAN-34A) to take the fight into the DRV. It mandated covert US military support for sabotage missions inside the north to be carried out by commandos from Vietnam and Taiwan. They would be inserted by sea and parachute and carry out attacks intended "to result in substantial destruction, economic loss and harassment." It would also allow US warships to assist with the interception of DRV boats transporting fighters and weapons south by sea. The following month, the commandos began attacking radar sites, railway bridges, petroleum storage and other economic targets. OPLAN-34A would, however, inadvertently trigger the direct intervention that both sides were trying to avoid.

By the middle of 1964, there were 23,000 American advisors in the

RVN and a few dozen Australians and New Zealanders. Around 250 Americans had died in action or from other causes. The number of Vietnamese dead since 1956 was already in the tens of thousands. MACV had been given a new commander, General William C. Westmoreland, in recognition that a new strategy was required. The NLF was steadily extending its control and American intelligence estimated its strength at around 100,000 fighters of various kinds. The NLF was running short of returnees from the north and volunteers and had just introduced its own draft in the areas it controlled. It encountered plenty of resistance and many peasants had to be pressured into joining up. Plenty of the rural poor preferred to be drafted by the ARVN where they would receive pay and their family would be compensated if they were killed. Nonetheless, tens of thousands of soldiers were deserting from the ARVN as the fighting became fiercer. It would only get worse.

On the night of July 30/31, four US-supplied but Vietnamese-crewed fast boats attacked radar facilities on the islands of Non Ngu and Hon Me, just off the DRV coast and 290 km north of the De-Militarized Zone separating the two Vietnams. As they were returning to base, they passed an American warship, the USS *Maddox* heading in the opposite direction. The *Maddox* was on a separate mission, a "DeSoto Patrol" to gather intelligence on DRV coastal defenses. At the same time other OPLAN-34A raids were taking place inland. In short, as the historian Edwin Moïse discovered, the DRV military was aware it was under attack but could not know who was responsible. On August 2, the *Maddox* was patrolling northeast of Hon Me island when it detected three approaching torpedo boats and intercepted a radioed instruction ordering them to attack. By this time, the *Maddox* was more than sixteen miles from the coast, outside Vietnamese territorial waters, and had not engaged in any hostile actions. The Vietnamese, however, believed that it was connected to the earlier raids onshore. As the torpedo boats closed, the *Maddox* began firing at them: 283 shells in all. The three Vietnamese boats then loosed their torpedos although none hit the *Maddox*. Two nights later, the *Maddox* was joined by another warship, the USS *Turner Joy*. The two ships encountered what they thought was another attack but later realized was a false alarm based on a misinterpreted radar signal.

This was the famous "Tonkin Gulf Incident" that became the *casus belli* for direct American involvement in the Vietnam War. President Johnson, three months from a general election, went on television to assert that an "unprovoked" attack on a US warship had taken place in international waters and represented an act of war by the DRV. He then asked Congress to pass a joint resolution enabling him "to take all necessary steps, including the use of armed force" in defense of the RVN, Laos, Cambodia and Thailand. As a result, the USSR ended its previous reluctance to support the DRV's war effort. When Kruschev was ousted in October, the new Soviet leader Leonid Brezhnev encouraged a more assertive foreign policy and an increase in aid to Hanoi. In November, partly on the basis of offering a strong response to communist advances, Johnson was re-elected president. The logics of the civil war within Vietnam, and the Cold War outside it, had drawn in the money and weaponry of the two ideological blocs and forced them into confrontation, regardless of the intentions of their leaders. In the words of historian Christopher Goscha, "In 1964, both Washington and Hanoi chose war and in so doing expected their respective southern [Vietnamese] allies to fall into step."

The first consequence of the "Tonkin Gulf Resolution" was an increase in communist attacks on American bases as the DRV attempted to deter Washington from greater involvement. Dramatic assaults on the Bien Hoa airbase, Binh Gia hamlet, Camp Holloway in Pleiku, a hotel-barracks in Qui Nhon and targets in Saigon generated casualties and headlines but had the opposite effect to the one intended: they increased the pressure on Johnson to intervene. Each attack was followed by retaliatory air raids and on December 14, the US secretly launched Operation Barrel Roll to bomb the routes of the Ho Chi Minh Trail in Laos. None of these "warnings" to Hanoi had any effect so Johnson's response was to increase the pressure. The two sides were locked into a cycle of escalation. The political situation in the RVN was almost a sideshow. Hardly anyone paid much attention when another military coup removed General Nguyen Khanh from the presidency and replaced him with Dr. Phan Huy Quat, a Buddhist member of the Dai Viet party but in reality a place-man for the generals.

On March 2, 1965, the first raids of Operation Rolling Thunder began: the deliberate targeting of the infrastructure of northern Vietnam in an attempt to inflict so much damage that the Hanoi leadership would end its support for war in the south. On March 4, 1965, the American embassy in Saigon asked the Vietnamese government to formally "invite" the United States to deploy combat troops in the country to defend the bases from where the airstrikes were being launched. This would, so the reasoning went, free up Vietnamese troops for war-fighting. On March 8, two battalions of Marines, 3,500 men, waded ashore at Danang in front of television cameras and a bewildered crowd of civilians. Prime Minister Phan Huy Quat had doubts but could do nothing to stop their arrival.

Back in Washington "the best and the brightest" (in the words of journalist David Halberstam) foreign policy minds were still arguing over American strategy. It was not until July that President Johnson finally announced what it was. He agreed the deployment of 125,000 troops and declared an open-ended commitment of more: whatever it would take to deter the VWP politburo from imposing communism on the south. It was intended to force the DRV to come to the negotiating table: periods of bombing were to be interspersed with pauses. Each pause would be followed by a stepped-up wave of bombing. It was a policy drawn up by theoreticians who lacked a meaningful understanding of what motivated the politburo or just how determined it was to prevail. The White House advisers believed the Vietnamese were mere puppets of Moscow and Beijing. They did not appreciate that it was in fact Hanoi dictating the pace of the war and pulling the big boys along in their wake. But they were not the only ones to underestimate their opponent. Le Doan and the Hanoi leadership had fallen into the same trap. As a result, the irresistible force of Vietnamese nationalism was about to meet the immovable object of American anti-communism and the clash would end three million lives.

Rolling Thunder kept rolling, trying to destroy the DRV's will to fight. The US Air Force launched 25,000 individual aircraft flights in 1965 alone, dropping more than 2,000 tons of bombs per month. Ammunition dumps, barracks, railways, oil storage units, electricity power stations and factories were all hit. The attacks unlocked even more aid for the DRV. Both China and the Soviet Union stepped up their supplies. The Soviets supplied aircraft, anti-aircraft missiles, radar systems and intelligence on the movement of American aircraft. Between June 1965 and March 1968, a total of 320,000 Chinese soldiers served in the DRV, with the peak troop level reaching 170,000 in 1967. Most were engineering or logistical units deployed to rebuild the damage inflicted by American bombing or anti-aircraft troops. The Chinese also passed messages to Washington that they would limit their involvement to the north but any attempt by the US to invade the DRV with ground troops, or to attack China, would lead to direct Chinese intervention, just as in Korea a decade earlier. Given that China had detonated its first nuclear weapon in October 1964, this was a serious threat. As a result there would always be limits to the American war effort in Vietnam.

1965–75: The American War and Its End

By late 1965, there were tens thousands of DRV troops encamped in the central highlands of the RVN. They had travelled south along the Ho Chi Minh trails carrying their equipment and supplies and were now formed up as fighting regiments. The central highlands were dotted with tempting targets: a series of isolated bases where US Special Forces were working with Montagnard fighters. On October 19, 1965, the 32nd and 33rd regiments of the People's Army of Vietnam (PAVN) attacked one of them, at Plei Me, about 30 km from the border with Cambodia. Their intention was to set a trap for the newly-arrived American combat troops. A month later, the commander of I Field Force took the bait. He ordered the 1st Air Cavalry Division to fly into the hills on a "search and destroy" mission. The Ia Drang Valley would become the site of the first pitched battle between main force units of the US Army and the PAVN.

The fighting began shortly after the helicopters touched down and continued for three days and nights. The Americans had landed right next to the PAVN positions and quickly found themselves outnumbered. The fighting took place in jungle clearings and the surrounding hillsides. The Vietnamese launched wave after wave of frontal attacks and came close to overrunning the American positions before artillery fire and airstrikes turned the battle. At one point B-52s carpet bombed areas of forest where the north Vietnamese troops were believed to be concentrated. By the time the fighting was done, 237 American and well over 1,000 Vietnamese soldiers had been killed. Hundreds more were wounded. The shock was profound: the number of Americans killed in Vietnam had doubled in three days. Both sides claimed victory: the Vietnamese had stood their ground but the Americans had killed vastly more. It proved to be a template for the ensuing conflict: the Americans moving by helicopter for short raiding missions and the Vietnamese fighting as close as possible to the Americans, "grabbing them by the belt" to make it hard to bring down artillery fire. PAVN commanders became more confident, Americans realized they had a long fight ahead of them.

The Battle of the Ia Drang Valley was only the first of innumerable engagements between American and PAVN forces over the following eight years. This "main force" war was, however, just one element of the conflict. All over southern Vietnam, another war was being waged between supporters of two rival states: the Republic of Vietnam and the National Liberation Front for Southern Vietnam. There were repeated attempts to find a "third way" between them. There were also battles between ethnic Viet peoples and the many minorities across the central highlands, the central coast and the Mekong delta. And in between these fights, there were business interests to advance, personal rivalries and old scores to settle. All these struggles overlapped and complicated the others connecting, for example, a struggle over land distribution in particular village with the Cold War confrontation between the United States and the Soviet Union. All of them came to be subsumed under the heading of "The Vietnam War" or, as it is known in Vietnam today, "The American War."

Vietnamese were no more "natural" at jungle fighting than Americans. Most came from families that grew rice or worked in the city. Where the PAVN excelled was in adapting the military methods they had learned from French and Chinese instructors to the battlefields of the highlands and deltas: Western science and logistics played just as important a role as communist or nationalist fervor. But little could prepare anyone for the industrial scale death that they encountered in the south. Hoang Au Phuong—better known by his writing name Bao Ninh—was one of 500 members of the 27th Youth Battalion who were sent to war in 1969. Only ten of them came home. In his epochal novel, *The Sorrow of War,* he describes the experience of air assault. "This was the dry season when the sun burned harshly, the wind blew fiercely, and the enemy sent napalm spraying through the jungle and a sea of fire enveloped them, spreading like the fires of hell. Troops in the fragmented companies tried to regroup only to be blown out of their shelters again as they went mad, became disoriented and threw themselves into nets of bullets, dying in the flaming inferno. Above them helicopters flew at tree-top height and shot them almost one by one, the blood spreading out, spraying from their backs, flowing like red mud.... After that battle no one mentioned Battalion 27 anymore."

The standard trope of this war, as portrayed in films and historical documentaries is of American boys patrolling a bewildering jungle until they are cut down by an unseen enemy. The Vietnamese experience is often assumed to be simply the reverse of this: natural-born jungle fighters waiting patiently to ambush the foreigners. While this may have been true for a small number of participants, the vast majority of Vietnamese encountered the war in utterly different ways. Death came from the sky and mostly without warning: it arrived with thousand-pound bombs dropped from B-52s in the stratosphere or from artillery shells fired from fortified positions far out of sight. The industrial scale of the violence was orders of magnitude greater than anything the communist side could throw back. The threat was constant for porters carrying supplies through the forests, for farmers tilling their fields in "free fire zones" or for rice traders navigating delta waterways. Tens of thousands of victims left no trace behind. Their bodies disappeared; their ghosts were left to wander the landscape for eternity.

In the villages, death could be more personal. The NLF targeted agents of the regime: assassinating mayors, administrators and military officials. The RVN, with American backing, did the same. Its anti-communist campaign had begun many years before, under President Diem, but in December 1967 it was reorganized as the "Phoenix Program." The program's "Provincial Reconnaissance Units" were responsible for killing around 20,000 communist activists and imprisoning a further

60,000. It was a dirty war of counterinsurgency well beyond civilian law or military rules of engagement. But even as these operations degraded the NLF's organization, the behavior of American troops created a steady flow of new recruits. Attacks on villages, abuse of civilians, destruction of houses, crops and livestock and the experience of casual cruelty, killing and rape drove more and more ordinary peasants into the arms of the revolution. The killing of around 500 people in the village of My Lai in March 1968 became globally infamous but there were many similar incidents that were only known to those involved. Troops in involved in Operation "Speedy Express" in the Mekong Delta during early 1969 claimed to have killed more than 10,000 "fighters" but only recovered 748 weapons.

58,000 Americans died during the war, of whom 48,000 were killed by the enemy (the remainder were from accidents, illness, homicides or suicides). No-one knows how many Vietnamese died; all we have are estimates. In 2008, researchers at Harvard Medical School and the University of Washington made calculations based on statistical sampling and interviews with Vietnamese households. They concluded that during its most intense period, between 1965 and 1974, the war killed an average of 170,000 people per year: a total of 1.7 million. Across the 30-year period between 1955 and 1984, they estimated total war-related deaths at 3.8 million people. The 58,000 American war deaths during the same period represent 1.5% of this total. For the vast majority of the Vietnamese population during the 1960s and 1970s, both northern and southern, the war was simply a fact of life. Decisions were taken by people far away and those on the ground had little capacity to change things or to resist. In the RVN, the best they could do was flee the countryside for the relative safety of the cities. Between 1960 and 1971, around a quarter of the southern population did so. In the north, the government moved people out of the cities to avoid the American bombing and drafted almost the entire male population, and a large part of the female population, as either soldiers or as militia forces to rebuild damaged infrastructure.

With neither side able to win nor willing to concede, the conflict continued. From Washington, President Johnson kept bombing in the hope of a negotiated solution. In Hanoi, Le Duan kept pressing for military victory. He was convinced that a general uprising in the south would bring down the RVN government and convince the Americans to leave. General Giap and his allies were less convinced but were silenced by a renewed campaign against "revisionism." Extensive preparations were made, including a long siege of a Marine base at Khe Sanh near the De-Militarized Zone and close to the border with Laos, which served to distract attention from a steady build-up of Viet Cong and PAVN guerrillas in and around the major towns and cities.

On January 30, 1968, just as the country settled down for the Tet (lunar new year) holiday, 80,000 fighters attacked military bases, population centers and key city buildings all across the RVN, expecting to trigger a popular revolution. There was no revolution but there was extensive fighting in the cities for the first time since 1946. Small groups of Special Forces attacked "spectacular" targets such as the US embassy in Saigon and the presidential palace. Television coverage ensured that the scenes reached primetime American audiences. In the city of Hue, communist units seized the old imperial citadel and systematically assassinated around 3,000 government officials and other civilians. They held out for a whole month until they were bombed into submission by a battle that devastated the city. Militarily, the assaults were a failure. Some 40,000 guerrillas were killed and all the buildings and cities they seized were recaptured. Politically, however, it was a huge success. The American public came to believe they were engaged in an unwinnable war. Robert McNamara, the Secretary of Defense, resigned on February 28 and a month later President Johnson announced he would not seek reelection. A week after that, the Hanoi leadership agreed to peace talks.

On May 13, 1968, delegations from the United States and Democratic Republic of Vietnam met at the Hotel Majestic in Paris. The Americans showed up in force with "Ambassador at Large" Averell Harriman in charge. The Vietnamese sent a Foreign Ministry bureaucrat with no authority to negotiate anything. He merely repeated the official lie that there were no DRV troops in the RVN. Hanoi was only interested in the appearance of diplomacy while the communists rebuilt their strength in the south. The Tet Offensive had destroyed the NLF's fighting strength and the Phoenix Program had severely weakened its political structures. In addition, the migration of villagers to the towns and cities was draining the "sea" in which the guerrillas were supposed to swim. In 1961 four million people were living in areas controlled by the NLF. By 1969 that was down to one and a half million (and it would crash to 230,000 by 1971). The Paris talks were supposed to expand to include the RVN government and the NLF in October, a month before the US election. However, Richard Nixon's campaign team suggested to the RVN side that they should stay away because Nixon would give them a better deal if he became president. The talks stalled.

At this point there were 492,000 American military personnel in Vietnam. There were also tens of thousands more troops from the "Free World Military Forces: 48,000 from South Korea, 40,000 from Thailand, 8,000 from Australia, 1,000 from the Philippines and 500 from New Zealand. In the wake of the Tet Offensive, the total RVN military strength had risen to 820,000, of whom about half were regular forces. But in June 1969, five months after taking office, Richard Nixon announced the first American troop withdrawals. His policy was to "Vietnamize" the war. By 1970, there were 335,000 Americans in country and by 1971, 157,000. As they departed, the Americans left behind huge quantities of military equipment for the ARVN. The plan was for the Republic's army to defend the country on the ground while American bombers would deter the DRV from the air.

On September 2, 1969—Vietnamese Independence Day—the death of Ho Chi Minh was announced in Hanoi. He was 79. Le Duan now had no rivals for influence in the politburo. At the same time, relations with the Chinese communist leadership were under severe strain. Fearing that the madness of Mao's "cultural revolution" would spread into Vietnam, and now blessed with fulsome support from the Soviet Union, the Hanoi leadership had asked China to withdraw its advisors and military personnel. In the United States, anti-war feeling had reached a crescendo, with millions of people taking part in protests on October 15. President Nixon and his National Security Adviser Henry Kissinger believed that they could arrange "an honorable end to the war" by inducing the main providers of aid to the DRV—the Soviet Union and China—to persuade Hanoi to compromise.

With the Sino-Soviet split now so deep that Beijing and Moscow were on the verge of war, there was an opportunity for the US to do deals with each one. Starting in late 1969, the Strategic Arms Limitation Talks slowed down the arms race between Russia and the US. In late February 1972, Nixon went to Beijing for "a week that changed the world," opening up a new bilateral relationship to outflank the Soviets. Neither of these developments changed the priorities of the Hanoi leadership, however. They were as determined as ever to unify the country. On March 30, they began a huge attack on the RVN—the "Nguyen Hue Offensive" (named after the eighteenth century Tay Son leader)—with 120,000 troops advancing across the DMZ, from Cambodia towards Saigon and from Laos into the Central Highlands. Fighting continued until July and the invasion was only halted with massive American bombing raids. The fighting ceased but tens of thousands of northern troops remained in the south. Nixon was livid and ordered Operation Linebacker: a campaign of retaliatory airstrikes that included the targeting of Hanoi and the mining of the harbor at Haiphong. At the same time, he continued to withdraw American troops. Numbers fell to just 24,000: the same as 1964. Nonetheless, opposition to the war—in Congress and in the streets—continued to rise

The DRV felt that it had improved its negotiating position sufficiently to begin substantive negotiations. On October 8, Henry Kissinger secretly met Le Duc Tho at a villa in Paris. Kissinger's aim was to secure stability for the RVN so the US could extract its troops. Le's aim was to maneuver the NLF—or rather its front organization, now renamed as the "Provisional Revolutionary Government of the Republic of South Vietnam" (PRG)—into power in the south. The key, in Kissinger's words, was to secure a "decent interval" between these two events. During the talks, Le Duc Tho conceded that the RVN government could form part of a "coalition" with the PRG to organize future elections in the south. Kissinger conceded to this, and to the ongoing presence of northern troops in the RVN in exchange for the release of American prisoners of war. At the end of the month, Kissinger told the world's media that "peace is at hand" and a week later Nixon won a landslide re-election victory. But when the RVN president, Nguyen Van Thieu, learned about what had been negotiated over his head, he refused to accept it. Nixon then demanded that the DRV should remove its troops before the US would sign. The communists refused to agree so Nixon ordered the "Christmas bombing" of Hanoi: 36,000 tons of bombs. The destruction was immense but it made no difference to the negotiations. On January 23, the US and the DRV signed the peace agreement originally agreed in October. Threatened with a total cut in aid if he refused, President Thieu reluctantly signed as well, as did the nominal head of the PRG, Madame Nguyen Thi Binh. The last American combat troops departed on March 23, 1973 a few days after the last Australians and South Koreans.

In hindsight, however, it is clear that the DRV had no intention of abiding by the document it had signed in Paris. It merely paused for a few weeks until conditions became more propitious. In the week the American troops left, the VWP Politburo agreed to resume fighting. Although some of the northern armed forces withdrew, in other places they continued to advance, particularly in the Central Highlands. In June, the US Congress approved the "Case–Church Amendment" banning military activity in Vietnam, Laos and Cambodia from August 15, 1973. It also voted to cut financial aid to the RVN by half. Low-level violence continued in Vietnam but with American troops now gone, few outside the country were interested. In January 1974, China seized the western half of the Paracel Islands, 200 km off the coast of central Vietnam which had been occupied by French and then Vietnamese forces since 1947. US forces stood aside as it happened. A brief flurry of anger and patriotism in the RVN focused minds on an external enemy before the conflict resumed within the country. By July, DRV forces were pushing south on several fronts.

In August, Nixon resigned to avoid impeachment in the Watergate scandal. By the end of the year, the Hanoi leadership had concluded that the United States was unlikely to intervene again in Vietnam and made preparations for a final push. In late January 1975, President Gerald Ford declared he could not foresee any circumstances in which the US would actively participate in Vietnam. In March, the DRV armed forces made their move. They swept through the Central Highlands, and then south from the DMZ region. The country panicked as refugees fled the fighting. At least 130,000 people left the country. On April 21, RVN President Nguyen Van Thieu resigned, having failed to persuade

Washington to bomb the advancing troops. Instead, the US sent a naval task force to assist with the evacuation of its defeated allies. On April 29, the Armed Forces Network broadcast Bing Crosby's White Christ-mas as the signal for the emergency withdrawal to begin. In the morning of the following day, a tank of the People's Army of Vietnam crashed through the gates of the Presidential Palace and parked on the lawn. Vietnam had been reunified.

CHAPTER 9

PEACE AND WAR AND PEACE (1975-PRESENT)

1975–1979: Post-war Crisis

C holon (pronounced cher lern) literally means "big market" but is also the Vietnamese name for the "sister city" of Saigon: originally founded about 6 km to its southwest. Today, the two cities are part of one huge conurbation but the center of Cholon still has a distinct appearance and culture. It is commonly, although inaccurately, known as "Saigon's Chinatown." Cholon's roots lie in the arrival of refugees from Ming dynasty China in the late seventeenth century (following the defeat of the Ming by the Manchu Qing). The newcomers settled in the Mekong Delta and, as we saw in Chapter 5, formed alliances with the Nguyen ruling family. A hundred years later, the Chinese community was targeted by the Tay Son rebellion precisely because of its support for the Nguyen and one group of survivors retreated to a walled settlement by the banks of a tributary of the Saigon River. Many of them were massacred by the Tay Son in 1782 but after the Nguyen retook control, Cholon rapidly became the commercial heart of the south.

By the early nineteenth century, Cholon was a key node in networks linking Southeast Asia with markets to both east and west. Its inhabitants called themselves *Hua*—literally "civilized" in Chinese—which became *Hoa* in Vietnamese. These *Viet Hoa* formed five associations or *bang*, grouping members according to their historic origins—four by region—Guangdong, Fujian, Chaozhou (Teochew) and Wenchang—and one for the Hakka people. These associations connected their members with distant relatives and traders in their ancestral homelands and helped to create the bonds of trust that facilitated long-distance trade. Silk, porcelain, pearls, paper, medicines and tea were just some of the products that passed through these networks. Over the following centuries, the goods changed but the vitality of the area continued. The "big market" of Cholon acquired a big market of its own, Binh Tay market, which still stands today: a place where local people connected with the routes of international commerce. Throughout the twentieth century and right up until 1975, Cholon continued to thrive on trade, both legal and illegal. But in the aftermath of the communist victory, the situation rapidly changed.

When the tanks of the Democratic Republic of Vietnam (DRV) occupied Saigon and the rest of the Republic of Vietnam (RVN) in the days following April 30, 1975, they maintained the fiction that they were acting as the army of an independent country called "The Republic of Southern Vietnam." But on May 15, the victors held a parade through Saigon and the reality became clear: all the troops were marching behind the flag of the northern DRV. In government offices, something similar was happening. There would be no "self-determination" or "genuinely free and democratic elections" for South Vietnam as stipulated in the 1973 Paris Peace Accords. The top officials, those who had not already fled with the Americans, were being cleared out and replaced by northerners. A single national Vietnamese state was being re-created for the first time since the annexation of Cochinchina by France in 1862. This Vietnam would not be run from the Nguyen citadel in Hue, however. One of the many legacies of French colonialism would be the shift of capital to Hanoi.

Despite the influx of northerners, the legal fiction of "Southern Vietnam" endured for a year and in some ways life continued as it had done under the RVN. The southern currency, the *piastre*, continued to be used, one independent newspaper and a monthly magazine continued to be published and in August 1975, the Communist Party Central Committee decided to allow private businesses to operate for a "transition period." At the same time, however, the northerners moved to enforce political control. More than a million former officials, soldiers and intellectuals were summoned for what was officially called *hoc tap cai tao*—re-education. For most of those called up, "re-education" was an inconvenient formality. "Level 1" re-education consisted of about a month of indoctrination. The "students" attended political classes, often in public parks in their home towns and cities. Here they were told the "truth" about the war, politics and the international situation. Having received a foundation course in the basics of socialism, they were free to go. For the remainder, former officers in the RVN military, government officials, journalists and other potential critics, re-education was much tougher. Two hundred thousand were sent away for six months and then released. Another 50,000 were detained at "collective reformatories" designed to change minds through rote learning and forced labor. Fifteen thousand particularly "problematic" inmates were still being held in "level 5" camps a decade later. An unknown number of southerners—probably several hundred—never came home. They died in the re-education camps.

With the leading advocates of non-communist, southern identity now either in exile or detention, there was little opposition as Hanoi proceeded to tear up all the commitments of the Paris Accords and merge the two Vietnams. The process would take just over a year. On November 15, 1975, the VWP leadership convened a "Political Conference on Reunification" and on April 25, 1976 they organized nation-wide elections for a single "National Assembly" to represent both halves of Vietnam. In late June, this Assembly voted to rename the country the "Socialist Republic of Vietnam" and to make Hanoi its capital. It also voted to create a single "mega-city" uniting Saigon with Cholon and the province of Gia Dinh and to give it the name of "Ho Chi Minh City." Then, finally, on July 2, 1976, the two halves of Vietnam were formally reunited.

That same month, the Politburo, with the hardline Le Duan at its head, agreed to "transform the South" and advance towards socialism by "eliminating the compradore bourgeoisie." Over the following three years, three campaigns of "socialist reconstruction" brought the south down to the level of the north. All private enterprises in the southern part of the country, collectively employing about 250,000 workers, were nationalized. The Vietnamese economist Le Dang Doanh calculates that 60,000 household enterprises were closed and another 30,000 were nationalized. In the countryside, large landholdings that had not already been reallocated by the Diem regime were taken over and redistributed. The authorities established 1,286 new cooperatives and 15,000 "production groups" in the agricultural sector, nominally covering about half the farmers in the south.

Since the most dynamic part of the southern economy was centered on Cholon and its *Viet Hoa* (Chinese) community, the campaign against capitalism increasingly took on an ethnic dimension. Seventy percent of the businesses in the south that were closed or nationalized belonged to *Viet Hoa* people. Their situation was made worse by a simultaneous decline in relations between the Vietnamese and Chinese communist parties. Small-scale clashes had been taking place along undemarcated sections of the China-Vietnam land border for a while. Vietnam said there were 90 incidents in 1974, China later claimed there had been 121. At the same time, DRV state media began talking about "the threat from the north" in an attempt to mobilize a new form of patriotic feeling among the people. Le Duan made a visit to Beijing in September 1975 but it did not go well: he reportedly resented his counterparts' "bigger brother" attitude. At the end of the year, Beijing cut its economic and military aid to Vietnam to almost nothing. The Vietnamese felt they deserved more but the Chinese felt they had already given far beyond their means. Shortly afterwards, the DRV leadership requested closer military relations with Moscow, including the transfer of more advanced weapons. These began to arrive the following year and, not coincidentally, the number of military confrontations along the border with China also increased. The Vietnamese then tried to clear the border areas of potentially disloyal minorities. Suspecting that Beijing might try to recruit *Viet Hoa* elsewhere as a "fifth column," the Vietnamese authorities pushed members of the community to repudiate their Chinese citizenship. Those who did not comply were taxed more heavily. From 1976, what was supposed to be a voluntary process became increasingly coercive. Chinese-language schools and newspapers were closed and the "hometown associations" were suppressed.

By the end of 1976, the party leadership was ready for the next stage of unification. The Fourth Party Congress in December decided to move the "whole country to socialism." The northern "Vietnam Workers Party" was merged with the southern "People's Revolutionary Party" to form a single "Communist Party of Vietnam," the CPV. There would be no more autonomy for the south. The Congress also approved a hugely ambitious "Five Year Plan" targeting 14% annual economic growth on the basis that the nationalization of thousands of private businesses and the collectivization of farms would enable a massive leap in production. In fact, the opposite happened: the southern economy tanked. While the communists took control of its "commanding heights," tens of thousands of people who used to run those businesses fled the country—leaving for China or Southeast Asia. This compounded the problems caused by the earlier departure of tens of thousands of RVN officials and business professionals. Managers were appointed to the new state-owned enterprises without the necessary skills or experience; positions were often awarded on the basis of wartime service rather than competence. Bureaucratic control of businesses and farmers fields removed the incentive to work hard and introduced inefficiencies. The overall effect was a collapse in output. After the Saigon Beer Company was nationalized, for example, it had to rely on the Ministry of Light Industry for its water supply, on the Ministry of Food Industry for its bottles and the General Department for Chemistry for carbon dioxide. Unsurprisingly Saigon's beer output failed to fizz.

More seriously, agricultural output fell. By 1978, national production of rice and other foodstuffs was down seven percent. Food began to run short, malnutrition became a problem and in places the situation came close to famine. Rationing was introduced with different categories of people given different entitlements. The party leadership placed public officials at the top of the list with ordinary citizens entitled to less. By 1981, each person in Ho Chi Minh City was limited to 2 kg of rice, 5 kg of other crops (such as manioc or sweet potatoes) and 90 grams of meat—per month. The only way to obtain more was to buy it on the black market. The economy was a post-war shambles. Rather than exploding, Gross Domestic Product per person remained stuck at less than $1 per day. The state rice reserves were exhausted, only 63%

of the government budget was funded, three million workers were unemployed and law breaking was rampant.

Making the southern situation even worse, the communist regime in neighboring Cambodia (commonly known as the Khmer Rouge) initiated a series of cross-border raids into the Mekong Delta. It was attempting to reclaim what it regarded as part of the historic lands of the Khmer people, in effect, reversing the conquests carried out by the Nguyen family in the late eighteenth century. There were more than a thousand such raids during 1977. In December, the Vietnamese hit back. A 60,000 strong invasion force failed to stop the border incursions, however, and the Cambodian raids became even more destructive. Despite Vietnamese pleas, China increased its aid and military support to the Khmer Rouge. Leaders in Beijing believed the Soviet Union was using Vietnam to encircle China. Meanwhile, Hanoi believed that China was using Cambodia to encircle Vietnam.

The Vietnamese leadership was faced with an existential crisis. Its demands that the United States should pay war reparations had come to nothing. Its economy was collapsing but it refused to relax its imposition of socialist economic policies. After being cut-off aid, its only likely source of support became Moscow. In early 1978, the Politburo came to believe the only way Vietnam could unlock the flow of Soviet aid, while simultaneously tackling its border problems, was to deliberately trigger a crisis with China. According to the historian Kosal Path, the Vietnamese leadership decided to invade Cambodia partly to eliminate the border security problem but also to deliberately place Vietnam on the frontline of the Sino-Soviet confrontation. This, it was assumed, would oblige the Soviet bloc to provide sufficient aid for Vietnam to escape a potentially fatal economic crisis. In February 1978, a full meeting of the Vietnamese Central Committee decided to invade Cambodia. Preparations for a new war began immediately.

The same Central Committee meeting also voted to abolish capitalist trade in the former RVN. On March 23, 30,000 communist party cadres cordoned off Cholon and went house-to-house, closing businesses and ransacking their premises. The following day all remaining major private businesses in the south were closed. In early May, the *piastre* was abolished, forcing anyone still holding the southern currency to change it into *dong* at an artificially-low rate. Every household was given seven hours to declare their savings. Many business-owners resisted these attacks on their wealth and in places there were battles in the streets. One report carried by a Japanese newspaper spoke of Cholon district being "full of corpses." Thousands of ethnic Chinese were forcibly moved to "New Economic Zones" in the hills. Thousands more fled the country. During 1978, 100,000 southerners arrived in other Southeast Asian countries by boat. Eighty-five percent of them were ethnic Chinese. An unknown number died at sea. A further 200,000, mainly northerners, fled overland to China.

By December 1978, Vietnam had joined the Soviet-led Council for Mutual Economic Assistance (COMECON) and signed the "Soviet-Vietnamese Treaty of Friendship and Cooperation." It was, by now, also receiving shipments of Soviet weapons. Military units were readied for action, state media talked up the "threat from the north" and the ongoing border clashes with China and Cambodia were publicized domestically and internationally. With the need to mobilize resources greater than the need to maintain socialist orthodoxy, central planning rules were relaxed to give local districts greater autonomy. Recognizing that there was a choice between allowing people to break the rules or forcing them to starve, officials in the south began to turn a blind eye to private enterprise. It was the first sign that Hanoi's socialist program would eventually be undermined from within. Then, on Christmas Day—and despite many public and private warnings from Beijing—Vietnam invaded Cambodia. It took less than two weeks to evict the Khmer Rouge from the capital Phnom Penh but this quick victory was only the beginning of a decade-long occupation that would cost thousands of lives.

The Vietnamese leadership had assumed their alliance with the Soviet Union would deter Chinese retaliation. They were wrong. In fact, the Chinese leadership was particularly determined to punish Vietnam *because* of that alliance and the United States was willing to help. In January 1979, the Chinese leader Deng Xiaoping cleared plans for an invasion of Vietnam during his meeting with US president Jimmy Carter at the White House. On February 17, 1979, the day that Vietnam's prime minister and army chief signed a friendship treaty with the government they had just installed in Cambodia, tens of thousands of Chinese troops flooded across Vietnam's northern border. The Carter administration, eager to build relations with Beijing in order to outflank the Soviet bloc, assisted the Chinese by providing information about Vietnamese military positions and the weak state of Soviet forces stationed along China's northern and western borders. Just as Hanoi hoped that its conflict with China would solidify its relations with the Soviet bloc, so Beijing expected that its conflict with Vietnam would grant it entry to a Western-led anti-Soviet community. By the time the USSR strengthened its land units along the country's far eastern borders and deployed its ships to Southeast Asian waters, the Chinese leadership had declared its military aims achieved and announced the end of fighting. The northern Vietnamese provinces of Lao Cai, Lang Son, Cao Bang and Mong Cai had been laid waste and over half a million people made homeless. This was not the end of the northern border problem, however. The two sides continued to wage a war of attrition there for the next decade. Making the situation worse, Vietnam was now also bogged down in a counterinsurgency quagmire in Cambodia.

Back in Cholon, the bright lights of private business had been extinguished. Most of the pre-war *Viet Hoa* population had fled, been expelled to the New Economic Zones, or worse. They made up at least half of the huge exodus leaving the country. In the month of June 1979 alone, 55,000 Vietnamese left by boat and another 50,000 by land. While some left illegally, others were allowed to go on payment of 10 *taels* of gold (around $3,000). In 1979, the Vietnamese government is thought to have gained $242 million from the purchase of such permits. In total, perhaps 800,000 "boat people" left Vietnam between 1975 and 1980, of whom half died at sea. It was only once the United Nations created an "Orderly Departure Program" in 1980 that the numbers began to fall. Cholon was virtually emptied of its *Hoa* population and had more-or-less ceased to be a "Chinatown." Chinese signs were taken down and its abandoned shops and houses were taken over by newcomers. It would not, however, be the end of the story.

1979–1997: From Confrontation to Reconciliation

The years after the invasion of Cambodia were a miserable period to be in Vietnam. Four decades of industrial warfare had smashed the economy, mutilated the environment and devastated families. Forests were defoliated, fields were polluted with unexploded bombs and millions were in mourning. A pall of exhaustion hung over the country. None of this deterred the leadership of what was now called the Communist Party of Vietnam (CPV). Ideologically, this period was the high point of "neo-Stalinism." The CPV believed it could direct the entire society while simultaneously standing in the vanguard of a Cold War struggle against both China and the United States. Convinced of the need to pursue the campaign in Cambodia, the invasion became a counterinsurgency quagmire entangling 180,000 soldiers. That fighting, combined with ongoing clashes on the border with China obliged impoverished Vietnam to maintain the world's fifth largest army: well over a million regular soldiers plus reserves and paramilitary forces. Nonetheless, the CPV was in full control of the country. The invasion of Cambodia had worked well for its leadership by triggering the Soviet aid that was the foundation of its political survival.

At home, hundreds of thousands of people who had run the southern part of the country and its dynamic economy had fled, annual rice production had fallen by a million tons and the economy was only being kept afloat by the infusion of the equivalent of $1.5 billion in Soviet aid each year. Even the Soviet aid was being used inefficiently. Experts sent to advise the Vietnamese calculated that factories were running at around a third of their designed capacity. Despite the claims of communist supremacy, 1979 was when the CPV leadership began to recognize the limits of state planning. Faced with another wartime crisis, they took drastic action. They hoped to preserve the communist economy they had spent a quarter of a century building, but in the process they opened the door to capitalism. In August 1979, the leadership chose to allow state-owned enterprises to sell their surplus production independently, once they had fulfilled their commitments to the government's central plan. Farmers too could also sell any rice they had left over once they'd supplied their allotted quota to the state. The results were immediate: rice production rapidly increased and the threat of famine passed. Private profit had saved the communist system. In Saigon and Cholon, the city authorities made discrete requests to the remaining Chinese entrepreneurs to reopen their food businesses. The incentives worked. A new phrase *pha rao*—"fence-breaking"—came to be used to describe the official rule-bending.

But as the economic rules relaxed, the political rules tightened. Those who criticized the leadership were silenced with censorship, sackings and demotions. A few were jailed for persistent trouble-making. A new campaign against "bad books" and "decadence" was launched and the remaining independent newspaper and magazine in the south were closed. Any threat to the "leading role" of the Communist Party was suppressed. This renewed confidence led the Vietnamese leadership to become even more belligerent towards China than its Soviet benefactor. When Le Duan visited Moscow in May 1982 it became apparent that differences between the two over their respective relations with China were becoming significant. When the Soviet leader, Leonid Brezhnev, attempted to improve ties with Beijing later that year he was told by Chinese officials that one of the three obstacles that needed to be resolved first was Vietnam's occupation of Cambodia. Vietnam, however, remained determined to eliminate the Khmer Rouge, which it saw as China's proxy.

That military aim was largely achieved by early 1985 after a Vietnamese offensive destroyed the last of the major Khmer Rouge strongholds within Cambodia. On August 16, 1985, Vietnam announced that its forces would totally withdraw from the country by 1990. By then the country was spending around a fifth of its total economic output on the military. Vietnam's foreign debt, largely owed to the Soviet Union, stood at $6 billion. A botched currency reform caused inflation to rocket from 50% to 350% in the second half of the year. It was becoming clear that the old men who had led the country through war were unable to tackle the challenges of peace. Instead, a pair of veterans of the conflict in the south who had been marginalized by Le Duan and his supporters began to gain the backing of party members. Nguyen Van Linh and Vo Van Kiet had toiled away in the communist underground during the war and then been appointed to senior posts in Ho Chi Minh City after it finished. It was they who had begun "breaking fences" during the first economic crisis, enabling the private farmers to feed the nation. Now they would bring economic reform to the whole country.

In July 1986 two things happened. Le Duan, who had led the communist party for 26 years, died. And the reforming Soviet leader Mikhail Gorbachev made a speech in Vladivostok offering China a new relationship. At this point, changes in superpower relations, the perceived failure of Vietnam's existing economic policies, the cost of maintaining a vast standing army, and a change in leadership all combined to create an opening for new thinking. By this time, inflation had hit 500% per year. The situation was getting desperate and the Communist Party was ready for the new thinking of Linh and Kiet. The model that had allowed the south to feed itself in the late 1970s was extended nationwide. With all the objections to economic reform now overcome, the CPV met for its Sixth Congress. In December 1986, it gave formal recognition to the measures which had actually already been implemented. Thus began the era of *doi moi*: literally "change to something new" but more usually translated as "renovation." The man who did more than any other to make it happen, Nguyen Van Linh, was made General-Secretary of the party.

Among the many changes he instigated was a change in attitude towards the *Viet Hoa* entrepreneurs of Cholon and the south. They were encouraged to revitalize their old connections with East and Southeast Asia and to make the city once again a node on the networks of international trade. The old *bang* networks were reactivated. A few brave investors from Taiwan and Singapore with family connections to the old Cholon began to investigate opportunities, forming joint ventures with state-owned firms and navigating the complexities of a transitioning economic system. In an effort to make these foreigners feel at home, Cholon was gradually reinvented as a "Chinatown." Little by little, a simulation of *Viet Hoa* culture was reintroduced: red lanterns, food stalls and eventually a red arch proclaiming "Chinese food street" in Chinese characters. The *Hoa* population did not return in significant numbers but enough remained to restore some of the vitality of the area.

Within the leadership of the CPV, arguments continued to rage about the way ahead. Some of the disagreements were about the economy: what role should the market play? But they overlapped with a debate about the international situation. No-one doubted the need for the party to remain in charge of the country, the discussion was about the best way to stay in power in the long term. Vietnam was still locked in confrontation with China while its main provider of aid and diplomatic support, the Soviet bloc was weakening and fracturing. In May 1987, the new Foreign Minister, Nguyen Co Thach, sponsored an article in the CPV's theoretical journal arguing, in effect, that the Soviet bloc was not going to win the economic war with capitalism and that, as a matter of survival, Vietnam needed to open relations with Western countries.

In March 1988, Vietnam's difficulties with China spread to the South China Sea. Chinese forces occupied six features in the Spratly Islands, triggering a clash at a desolate tidal rock called Johnson Reef South in which 64 Vietnamese marines were killed. The alliance with the Soviet Union had not deterred China in this instance, and in the view of the reformers, the defeat demonstrated the need for better relations with other world powers. A few months later, in May 1988, the Politburo approved "Resolution 13," its first major document on foreign policy in four years. It acknowledged, in effect, that future economic development would require international cooperation. It called for a revised position on Cambodia and a new "diversifying and multidirectional" foreign policy. Hanoi's last troops withdrew from Cambodia in September 1989. At least 55,000 Vietnamese soldiers had died during the ten years of occupation: almost as many as the number of Americans killed during the Vietnam conflict.

Immediately after the Cambodia withdrawal, the Socialist regimes in central Europe began to collapse. It was clear to the Vietnamese leadership that Soviet aid, estimated at $3 billion that year, was unlikely to be maintained. Once again, they faced a major strategic decision. To remain in power, the party needed to deliver a better standard of living to the people. But it was also vital that the party remained in power. At this point, General-Secretary Nguyen Van Linh, economic reformer that he was, slammed on the political brakes. The leadership panicked about the possibility that Vietnam could go the same way as Poland or Hungary and overthrow its communist leadership. A speech by Linh delivered to the Sixth Central Committee meeting of the Sixth Congress, in May 1989, was entitled "Why We Do Not Accept Pluralism." He was not prepared to allow liberalization to creep into the political sphere.

The Politburo's fears became more acute in February 1990 when the Soviet Communist Party abandoned the teachings of Lenin and formally renounced its constitutional leading role. By contrast, the Communist Party of China publicly reaffirmed its own Leninist leading role the following month. Coming after the June 1989 crackdown in Tiananmen Square, it demonstrated to the old men in Hanoi that the Chinese communists were deadly serious about defending their political system. In its own public statements, the Vietnamese Politburo was already following the Chinese path: asserting that Vietnam's unique history and stage of evolution required a leading role for the Communist Party. In March, the Central Committee voted to expel one member of the Politburo, Tran Xuan Bach, who had urged the party to adopt greater pluralism. The international isolation imposed on China after the Tiananmen killings created an opening for a rapprochement, and, in April 1990, Linh reached out to China via intermediaries in Laos. The timing was fortuitous. In July, the United States announced it was no longer willing to support a Cambodian coalition that included the Khmer Rouge and intended to contact Hanoi to discuss a settlement to the fighting. The Chinese leadership realized that if it did not make peace, Beijing would be left internationally exposed.

The CPV leadership had a choice to make: open to the US, as Foreign Minister Thach desired, or to China as General-Secretary Linh preferred. The guardians of Leninism won the argument. On September 2, General-Secretary Nguyen Van Linh, Prime Minister Do Muoi and another party veteran, Pham Van Dong, absented themselves from their own Independence Day celebrations and flew to Chengdu to meet Chinese leaders for the first time since the mid-1970s. The price of economic and political stability at home was to accept all China's demands in Cambodia. Years of stalemate were ended by a hard-headed assessment of what was best for the CPV. In October 1991, yet another set of "Paris Peace Accords" ended the conflict in Cambodia and led to the formal resumption of relations between Vietnam and China the following month.

Vietnam's leadership remained unwilling to put all its faith in China, however. The CPV's Seventh Congress in June 1991 called for the country to "diversify and multilateralize economic relations with all countries and economic organizations ... regardless of different socio-political systems." It was a rejection of the party's former worldview of "two camps" locked in an ideological death struggle but it was less a turn to the West and more an attempt to shore up Leninism by opening the doors to international investment and trade while maintaining strong relations with a fellow communist regime in Beijing. The Congress also saw the exit of Foreign Minister Thach: dismissed from the Politburo as part of the price for restoring relations with China.

At more-or-less the same time, the Soviet Union finally cut off its financial aid. Vietnam was forced to cut the size of the army in half: 750,000 men were rapidly demobilized. There were simply not enough jobs around to employ them. Local authorities were ordered to turn a blind eye to hundreds of thousands of illegal street workers. Many men bought a pair of scissors, a mirror and a chair and turned shady trees into barbers' shops. Others became roadside bicycle engineers. Women would take a charcoal burner, a large pot and a few stools onto the street to sell tea, *pho* noodle soup, *bun cha* mini kebabs, *lau* hotpot and all the other homemade delights for which Vietnamese food has now become justly famous. Peace with China also allowed a flood of cheap goods to cross the northern border which could be sold house-to-house by itinerant traders. But this informal economy was not enough to employ a growing population. The party needed the help of foreign capitalists. From their side, the capitalists could see the benefits of investing in a well-disciplined society with low levels of pay, reasonable levels of education and, in the south, plenty of roads and ports originally built with American tax-payers' money.

Despite all this, the CPV was determined to remain in control of the reform process. Foreign investment was directed into joint ventures so that local state-owned enterprises could benefit. By now, however, most state enterprises were operating largely without state support; so much so that their "owners," whether government ministries, provincial authorities or party organizations, treated them as private companies, albeit ones with easy access to officials and state banks. The SOEs made profits, expanded and diversified: Vietnam's exports increased fourfold between 1990 and 1996. While some of this followed the rules, there was also a lot of "fence breaking." Not everything was illegal but corruption did become endemic. State banks lent money with abandon and some of the firms tried to turn themselves into mini-empires. In the worst cases, a few corporations became outright criminals. As prices rose and salaries failed to keep up, corruption exploded. It was not so much a threat to the system as the means by which the system operated. Ever since, the CPV has been fighting a battle to control it, although with varying degrees of enthusiasm.

Despite its many problems, the Vietnamese communist system held together. More than that, it delivered impressive economic performance. Growth averaged 8% between 1991 and 1996 and the size of the economy doubled, relieving some of the political pressure on the party leadership. Foreign investment grew, exports expanded and employment rose. Poverty was dramatically reduced from nearly 60% in 1990 (using the World Bank definition) to just over 35% in 1999. Vietnam achieved this by following its own path. The leadership refused lending from the World Bank and International Monetary Fund because it was determined to maintain state control over large parts of the economy and did not wish to follow the standard prescriptions of privatization and liberalization. Instead it set about creating a "socialist oriented market economy." While some sectors were opened to foreign investment, and many firms were permitted to act like private corporations, the "commanding heights" remained under state control. The most important objective was to maintain Communist Party power. That, in turn, required sustained economic growth to deliver a rising standard of living to as many people as possible—but not at any price.

In order to sustain economic growth, Vietnam needed friendly relations with its neighbors and with as many other countries as possible. This was not easy. For two decades, the rest of Southeast Asia had regarded Vietnam as a security threat. The withdrawal from Cambodia and the peace treaty with China changed that. In June 1992, a key meeting of the CPV Central Committee ordained a hierarchy of countries. It continued to place communist friends like China, Cuba and North Korea at the top and the United States at the bottom. At the same time, however, the party also defined its top foreign policy priorities as regional co-operation and better relations with the world's economic powers. The following month, Vietnam ratified the "Treaty of Amity and Cooperation" of the Association of Southeast Asian Nations (ASEAN). That opened the door to discussions with Washington. In 1993 the United States lifted the trade embargo it had imposed in May 1975 and in 1995 the two countries normalized their diplomatic relations. That same year, Vietnam joined ASEAN and signed a cooperation agreement with the European Union. In 1989 Hanoi had diplomatic relations with only 23 non-communist states. By 1996 the number was 161.

At the same time, Vietnam worked hard to develop its relations with China. There were at least 18 meetings between senior leaders from both sides between 1991 and 2001. The most important benefit was a dramatic rise in cross-border trade: it increased almost a hundredfold from just over $30 million in 1991 to $2.8 billion in 2001. The political relationship was, however, very different to the one that existed before 1975. The Chinese leadership shocked their Vietnamese counterparts by refusing to call the two countries "allies" but merely "comrades." While the two Communist parties shared a political outlook on how to manage their own societies, they had important differences over what they regarded as their national interests. The most sensitive issue was the South China Sea. In 1992 China promulgated a new Maritime Territorial Law formalizing its claims to the Paracel and Spratly Islands—features which Vietnam also claims. On March 7, 1997, China deployed an oil-drilling platform, the Kantan III, into the Gulf of Tonkin. In response, the Vietnamese mobilized fellow members of ASEAN. When that failed to deter the Chinese, Hanoi invited the head of US Pacific Command, Admiral Joseph Prueher, to visit. A week after those discussions, the Chinese withdrew the oil rig. A new phase in Vietnam's international relations had begun.

1997–present: Booms and Busts

The Vietnam National Convention Center guards the western entrance to Hanoi. Its wave-like roof covers a building the size of a couple of sports fields and its ballroom and meeting halls are designed to impress the many heads of government and business executives who have gathered beneath it. When the Center was finished, in 2006, it stood right at the edge of the city. Farmers' fields surrounded it on three sides. The fourth side had recently been occupied by a pioneer of international capitalism, the "Big C" supermarket: a joint venture between a Thai company and the French retail giant "Groupe Casino." The Center itself had been designed by German architects as a venue to host 21 world leaders attending the annual "Asia Pacific Economic Cooperation" summit. Within just a few years of that event, the surrounding farmers" fields had given way to dozens of forty-story residential blocks. They now tower over the Convention Center, the supermarket and twelve lanes of traffic heading east-west and a further eight heading north-south. The roads were built as part of a highway system planned by Japanese consultants and paid for with lending from the World Bank and Asian Development Bank. Manicured gardens line the junctions and giant advertising hoardings encourage Vietnam's consumers to acquire American fashion, South Korean mobile phones and Swiss watches. In short, this part of Hanoi looks like a modern international city, connected to global finance and busy with the sounds of commerce. It is hard to believe that just twenty years before, peasants were planting rice and cycling along rutted paths where the middle classes now play.

For the affluent residents of the residential blocks, and the shoppers in the supermarket, life is good. Two decades of rapid economic growth have powered enormous changes in their lives and in the size and shape of their city. On its outskirts, and in industrial zones across the country, huge sheds have been built to assemble footwear and furniture, electrical machinery and electronic components. Incomes have risen, poverty has fallen and the scars of war have been covered by shopping malls, hotels and yet more residential towers. Yet, amid all this change, one thing has remained the same. Vietnam is still ruled by its Communist Party, the CPV. The rapid transformation of the country's economy and society has not led to a revolution in its politics. Vietnam's streets look capitalistic with small businesses and gaudy advertising everywhere. Behind the scenes, however, the party watches, supervises, monitors and works out how to stay one step ahead of the threat from what it calls "peaceful evolution": the idea that the people might become dazzled by foreign ideas and choose the wrong leadership.

It has taken time, but gradually the CPV has worked out ways to allow the people to enjoy more personal freedom while jealously guarding its own power. Along the way, citizens have demanded greater and faster change. Veterans of the "liberation war"—whether concerned scientists, religious believers or questioning journalists—have all run into trouble. Some have been censored, some shunned, some jailed and some exiled. Slowly, however, the party has allowed more space for discussion and expression. This struggle has paralleled an evolution in the country's political outlook and international relations. At key moments, the leadership's ingrained inclination to steer close to its communist "big brother" China, has been challenged by the demands of particular circumstances, usually economic crises. On each occasion, the result has obliged the CPV leadership to change direction, to move closer to the West and to open up the economy and society a little more. Over time, Vietnam has harnessed the power of capitalism while remaining an overtly communist state. It is a mixture that has been termed "Market-Leninism."

It has not been a smooth path. In December 1997, after many months of disagreement, the rival strands of opinion within the CPV managed to find sufficient common ground to select a new party leader: Le Kha Phieu, a political commissar from the military. He immediately initiated an enthusiastic turn towards China but at the same time oversaw a liberalizing of the economy. In May 1999, a new Enterprise Law was passed, abolishing most of the cumbersome bureaucracy which had prevented private companies from formally registering themselves. The impact, once it came into effect on January 1, 2000, was almost instantaneous: over the following five years 160,000 enterprises were registered. Most of these were existing businesses which had been operating without licenses and took advantage of the new law to register. However, the legal change meant the private sector had finally arrived in Vietnam.

At the same time, Le Kha Phieu sought an ideological partnership with China. There were 148 formal exchanges between the two communist parties during the following year, and more the year after. To his surprise, he discovered that the Chinese leadership was not interested in making a formal alliance with the CPV. An agreement between the two parties in March 1999 avoided the term "allies," or even "brothers" or "comrades." The Chinese opted instead for "long-term, stable, future-oriented, good-neighborly and all-round cooperative bilateral relations." The Chinese Communist Party was more interested in pursuing its national interests over ideological ones. The CPV leadership had little choice but to accept. Still keen to repair the relationship, Le Kha Phieu agreed to compromise on the two countries' border dispute, and agreement was reached at the end of 2000. The final settlement was presented as fair, with Vietnam awarded 114 km^2 of the disputed territory and China 114 km^2. However, no maps were published, and it seems that the "disputed territory" was ground that China had occupied after the 1979 border war. The net result was that, compared to the pre-1979 border, China gained territory. Behind closed doors in Hanoi, Phieu and his supporters were strongly criticized for having sold out Vietnam's national interest in order to win support for their conservative approach to politics. Phieu regarded it as a necessary price to pay for regime security.

In what appeared to be another attempt to demonstrate his commitment to a closer Vietnam-China relationship, Phieu unilaterally made concessions in negotiations over the maritime boundary between the two countries in the Gulf of Tonkin. He also signed up to a "Joint Statement for Comprehensive Cooperation in the New Century," which set out a framework for future bilateral relations. But that, more or less, finished Phieu's political career. The final straw came in April 2001 when he sat next to China's political heir apparent, Hu Jintao, at the CPV's Ninth Party Congress. That was just too much for his comrades. Denounced for his pro-China stance and blamed for a stagnant economy and worsening corruption, he was sacked. In his place, the Congress appointed a new General-secretary, Nong Duc Manh. Manh came from a highland background and his family were Tai-speakers. There were rumors that he was the illegitimate son of Ho Chi Minh, rumors that he did little to quash and which helped his rise to the top of the political system.

Under Nong Duc Manh, the new politburo set a new course: Vietnam's new priority was no longer ideological purity but the need to catch up economically with more developed countries. The Party Congress set a target of seven percent economic growth each year for the next two decades and agreed that this would require Vietnam to integrate more deeply into the world economy. The Congress also reaffirmed Vietnam's commitment to a diversified foreign policy. A month before the gathering, the Vietnamese leadership had agreed to a new "strategic partnership" with Russia. A few months after it, however, Russia announced that it could no longer afford to maintain the military forces that had been based at Cam Ranh Bay in central Vietnam since 1979. They withdrew in May 2002. Vietnam was suddenly alone. Worried about China's moves in the South China Sea, the country needed new friends. Its first response was to turn to its neighbors in the Association of Southeast Asian Nations. Its second was to turn to its old enemy, the United States. In July 2003, the CPV Central Committee approved "Resolution 8" stating that there was no longer a simplistic distinction between friends and enemies in Vietnam's foreign policy and that elements of both cooperation and struggle could exist within Vietnam's relationship with any one country.

With this ideological justification agreed, Vietnam was finally ready to open the door to greater military cooperation with the United States. The Vietnamese Defense Minister visited Washington in November 2003 and a week later the USS *Vandegrift* became the first American warship to visit Vietnam since 1975. In discussions between the two governments, Vietnamese diplomats made clear their growing anxiety about China's rising assertiveness and their desire to see the United States play a stronger role in ensuring a balance of power in Southeast Asia. Over the following few years, the two sides explored ways they could cooperate while Vietnam insisted on maintaining what it calls "the three noes": no to alliances, no to foreign bases on its soil and no to involving a third country in any bilateral disputes.

From 2003 onwards, China's leaders increasingly talked about their country's "peaceful rise" but Vietnamese observers became increasingly concerned about Beijing's real intentions. Perhaps even without being aware of it, the Chinese state, its agencies, corporations and the many other actors within the People's Republic, asserted their interests in and around Vietnam in ways that disconcerted the Vietnamese elite's desire for strategic autonomy. Vietnamese analysts were concerned about China's rising influence in Laos and Cambodia, its apparent lack of concern for Vietnam's interests in the Mekong River catchment, its predatory behavior in the South China Sea and its business activities within Vietnam itself. Making matters worse, in 2005 China became Vietnam's top trading partner with the balance firmly in China's favor.

Modern economic and strategic concerns mingled with historical memories of Chinese domination to produce a rising tide of anti-China sentiment. This first expressed itself on the streets of Vietnam in December 2007 with spontaneous protests against China's actions in the South China Sea. There were further protests in 2009 against a decision to allow a Chinese company to exploit bauxite reserves in Vietnam's Central Highlands. The response of the Communist Party leadership was to suppress such criticism in order to maintain smooth relations with China. There was no suggestion that Hanoi would ever break ties with Beijing. Instead it did the opposite: tightening relations but, at the same time, seeking friends and supporters in other capitals.

Vietnam stepped up its efforts to integrate into the globalized world. China had joined the World Trade Organization (WTO) in 2001 and its economy had dramatically expanded. The Vietnamese leadership knew they had to follow suit. That required intensive negotiations with the United States and the overcoming of economic, political and emotional obstacles on the American side. In late 2006, with the negotiations complete, President George W. Bush led a US delegation to the National Convention Center in Hanoi to take part in the APEC summit with the leaders of China, Russia and Japan, among many others. Under the Center's wavy roof, and dressed in traditional Vietnamese gowns and hats, the leaders of all these former enemies pledged to increase economic cooperation and build a wealthier Asia-Pacific region. A few weeks later, in January 2007, Vietnam formally joined the WTO. Its economy joined China's on the fast road to growth.

These developments prompted a stock market and real estate bubble fuelled by wild speculation and wasteful spending by some state-owned enterprises. The boom was followed by a spectacular bust in 2007/8 but after 2010, the economy settled on a more sustainable path. Growth averaged 6 percent per year, as foreign investors piled into the country.

Among the most significant was the South Korean electronics manufacturer, Samsung, which arrived in 2008. Since then it has invested at least $20 billion in Vietnam. In 2017, this one company accounted for a quarter of all Vietnam's manufacturing exports. By 2021 it was employing 170,000 people making mobile phones and other devices.

Between 2002 and 2018, according to the World Bank, Vietnam's GDP per capita almost tripled, reaching over US$2,700 in 2019. High growth was combined with a serious commitment to reducing poverty. Roads were built, electricity networks were expanded, health systems were developed and education was improved. On official Vietnamese statistics, more than 45 million people were lifted out of poverty (defined as living on less than $3 per day on a 2011 purchasing power parity basis). In 2002, 70 percent of the population were classed as poor but by 2018 that was below six percent. Government calculations in 2018 described four in five Vietnamese as economically secure. This did not mean that they were "wealthy," however. Just a quarter of the "economically secure" population lived in a permanent house with a private bathroom and piped water. But it did mean that they did not have to worry about where their next meal or housing payment would be coming from. Vietnam still has a long way to go before the majority of its people can be classed as "comfortable."

Nonetheless, on the most important indicators, Vietnamese people are better off than their equivalents in other countries. Life expectancy is 76 years, the highest in the region for countries at a similar income level. Vietnam scores 73 on the universal health coverage index: higher than regional and global averages—with 87 percent of the population covered. Ninety-nine percent of the population uses electricity as their main source of lighting, which may not sound remarkable, but the figure was just 14 percent in 1993. Seventy percent of rural residents have access to clean water, up from 17 percent in 1993. In urban areas, the figure is above 95 percent. In other words, Vietnam has done a much better job than most other countries of sharing out the benefits of economic growth among the majority of the population.

That said, there are still some gaping inequalities. Of the six percent of the population still classed as "poor," 86 percent come from ethnic minorities. To put it another way, one third of the minority population lives in poverty. The vast majority of these people live in the upland areas, the "Dong World" of earlier eras. Where once these groups ruled their own autonomous regions, now they are relegated to the status of "subject peoples," incorporated into a state dominated by lowlanders. They have been given special status: classified into groups by government anthropologists and targeted for social improvement but, as the lowland state speeds towards modernity, they are being left behind. On every indicator, people in the northwestern mountains and the Central Highlands are worse off than people in the Red River and Mekong river deltas. They have benefited less from infrastructure developments, they are discriminated against by the Viet or "Kinh" ethnic majority and they frequently lose out in the competition for investment and state support. Many minorities feel a sense of grievance and the central government tries to maintain a close watch over them. Groups close to the borders with China and Cambodia are particularly tightly observed and there are frequent complaints about harassment and abuse.

Other divisions have become less important. While the differences between people from the north, south and center provide plenty of material for jokes and arguments, there is nothing that amounts to regional "separatist" feeling in contemporary Vietnam. Jobs take people all over the country, bringing strangers into contact with one another. While some in the cities complain about these new arrivals, internal migration is creating a new sense of "Vietnameseness" and overriding once-strong regional identities. Yet, around half the population still lives in villages and about 40 percent still work in farming. As people working in towns and cities become better off, the difference between them and those still in the villages becomes greater. Despite this, the attachment to the land remains strong. The profit from growing rice on the average-sized plot still leaves a four-person household below the official poverty line. Nevertheless, village culture holds them tight. Even among the poorest 20 percent of the population, just 7 percent are classified as landless. Controlling land provides a measure of certainty. For families that experienced famine and war, the fear that such a thing could happen again is enough to make them keep at least some connection to the soil. If bad times ever come again, they might still be able to grow their own rice and survive.

Economic development is bringing new opportunities for the majority of Vietnamese but also serious problems. The World Bank classifies Vietnam among the ten countries most affected by air pollution. As the cities expand, construction, charcoal burning, waste incineration and vehicle traffic all increase. In 2019, Hanoi was the second-most polluted city in Southeast Asia. The situation in Ho Chi Minh City is better, mainly because it is closer to the sea, but even there, air quality is categorized as unhealthy for most of the year. Outside the cities, there are pressures on waterways, beaches and forests as the search for profit collides with the limits of the environment. Fields are concreted into factory zones, coastal mangrove swamps are torn up for seaside resorts, mountains are mined for cement and wild places are domesticated with cable cars and fantasy walkways. Projects like these, and many others, are being pushed by the country's most powerful private sector companies and there is little opposition to their ambition.

Vietnam also faces existential dangers from two sources beyond its immediate control: rising sea levels and falling river levels. If no defensive measures are taken, a one meter rise in average sea level will place five provinces in the Mekong Delta entirely underwater. A further five would be partially drowned. Water would lap at the edges of Ho Chi Minh City, with storm rises inundating its center and the surrounding industrial parks that generate most of the country's manufacturing output. Rice production would collapse and millions of people would be forced to migrate. The situation is being made worse by the over-extraction of groundwater, which is causing soil to shrink and land levels to fall. At the same time, dam-building along the Mekong River and its tributaries in China and Laos is cutting the amount of fresh water and sediment arriving downstream. The reduced flow is allowing salt water to intrude further inland. Arable fields are becoming salinated, forcing many farmers to give up agriculture, with some turning to shrimp production instead. Vietnam is not entirely an innocent victim in this. Since 2000, Vietnam's greenhouse gas emissions have risen by an average of five percent per year, the fastest rate in the world, albeit starting from a low base.

Environmental challenges are not the only problems Vietnam faces. The population is growing rapidly but also ageing. In 1986 Vietnam was home to about 60 million people. By 2021 that had reached 100 million and is expected to peak at 120 million by 2050. But one of the side-effects of improving life expectancy is that, before too long, there will be more old people. Over-60s make up 12 percent of the population in 2018 but that will almost double by 2040. Taken as a whole, on current trends, Vietnam's population is likely to get old before it gets rich. This is the kind of challenge that keeps Communist Party planners awake at night. While the country has done exceptionally well to stimulate and sustain economic growth, it is not clear how it will make the transition to higher levels of development. Other countries that have reached "middle income" status have typically unshackled their private sectors and reined in the state-owned sector. That has not happened in Vietnam. Most of the country's largest companies are still state-owned enterprises. The largest private conglomerates are so dominant in their home regions and so well-connected with local and national political leaders that they are acting more and more like state-owned enterprises, albeit ones that deliver huge profits for their owners. Meanwhile, small and medium-sized private companies complain about having to operate on an unfair playing field. This cozy relationship between the Communist Party elite and what are, in effect, monopoly players in the economy is creating a new form of "crony capitalism" in Vietnam, with all the attendant risks of corruption and instability.

Is there likely to be any change? For the time being, it seems unlikely. The CPV is heavily entrenched in society, it is delivering economic growth and it has more than seventy years' experience of dealing with challenges to its rule. Although its members make up only around five percent of society, the party has networks of neighborhood wardens, local militia, police and military forces to provide early warning of trouble and to eliminate it. This was the main reason why Vietnam's response to the 2020/21 COVID pandemic was so efficient. It was able to detect cases early and impose local and national lockdowns to prevent people infected with the virus passing it on to others. Its effectiveness in dealing with such threats helps to generate the public support that ultimately keeps it in office. It is also the means by which it suppresses political dissent. Time and again, the CPV has managed to overcome or suppress potentially fatal dangers to its control of the country.

It has coped with war, famine and, perhaps the most difficult of all, rapid economic development. Contrary to the expectations of outside observers and internal critics, however, it has repeatedly "failed to fail."

But current performance is not the only factor in the Communist Party's success. The historian Alexander Woodside argues that the modern country "shares a common characteristic with Vietnam's pre-industrial kingdoms: its reliance upon transnational transfers of political and legal institutions and ideas that originated elsewhere." Just as Vietnam's earlier rulers made use of Confucian ideas and the bureaucratic model of Ming China to legitimize and organize their state and society, so its current rulers make use of Leninism and the "one-party state" invented in the Soviet Union and the People's Republic of China. But there is an important difference between the old ways of ruling the country and the new ways; between the current Chinese one-party state and contemporary Vietnam. In modern Vietnam, power has been fragmented. Not since the rule of Le Duan ended in 1986 has one person been able to exert so much control over the Communist Party and the state. Governance in Vietnam today demands the constant building of coalitions between rival centers of power: different points of view within the party, different parts of the country, business and government, and so on.

Every five years, the Communist Party leadership and around 1,500 party members elected by branches all over the country gather for a Congress in the National Convention Center. In the months leading up to the big gathering, vicious political battles are fought over the loyalties of delegates and the castigation of opponents. Remarkably, given Vietnam's recent history, all this takes place behind closed doors with no actual violence. It is a secret process but one that has been highly effective at delivering stability. Then, for a week, the comrades gather under the Center's wavy roof to discuss the way ahead for the country. Some of the sessions are broadcast for the people to watch, but that is the extent of their participation. Vietnam's political system leaves the mass of the people as mere "bystanders" in their own government. Under Leninism, it is the party that has the final say, not public opinion, nor the courts or any other countervailing institution. This will be the challenge for Vietnam in the coming years: how to reconcile the Communist Party's determination to remain the sole force in politics with an increasingly prosperous population possessed of ideas of its own. Will the benefits of growth be shared equally, or will a self-serving elite become immune to the demands of the people? Will the risks be shared equally too, or will some suffer more than others from the emerging environmental and economic challenges? As we have seen in this book, if history is any guide then there is no pre-ordained route forward.

We have never been so aware of the past, so knowledgeable about the contingency of development as we are today, and yet we like to look back and see a smooth, unbroken path leading from prehistoric times to our present day. As I hope this book has demonstrated, "Vietnam" is both ancient and modern. Just like every other state, it is a product of centuries of accidents. Its inhabitants have been molded by, and molded, their environment through migration, struggle, war and culture. The result is a unique society: resilient, ingenious and dynamic. In the past century it has endured the worst of which humanity is capable. We must now hope that, in the centuries to come, it can enjoy the best.

Further Reading

R eaders wishing to dive more deeply into the history of Vietnam have three substantial books to start with. Keith Taylor's *A History of the Vietnamese* (2013) provides the best overview, Christopher Goscha's *Vietnam: A New History* (alternative title *The Penguin History of Modern Vietnam*, 2017) is the best account of the period between 1800 and 1990. Ben Kiernan's *Viet Nam: A History from Earliest Times to the Present* (2019) integrates environmental history with human history. The "big histories" of Vietnam published before the 2010s tend to be colored by a nationalistic reading of the past and have been superseded by more nuanced accounts. A Vietnamese example is Truong Buu Lam's lively *A Story of Viet Nam*.

There is a very rich tradition of Vietnamese fiction writing, stretching back to Nguyen Du's *Tale of Kieu*, which is available in several English translations including one by Huynh Sanh Thong (1987). A quick introduction to the variety of Vietnamese writing can be found in *Vietnam: a Traveler's Literary Companion* (1996) edited by John Balaban and Nguyen Qui Duc, and in *Other Moons: Vietnamese Short Stories of the American War and Its Aftermath*, edited by Quan Manh Ha and Joseph Babcock. *Dumb Luck*, a novel by Vu Trong Phong, was originally published in 1936 but only translated in 2002. Duong Thu Huong's books about the 1950s and 1960s, *Paradise of the Blind* (1993) and *Novel Without a Name* (1995), convey the hopes and tragedies of that period. Nguyen Huy Thiep interweaves the personal and political in *The General Retires* and other books. Two of the most outstanding contemporary Vietnamese writers available in English are Viet Thanh Nguyen whose novel *The Sympathiser* (2016) won the Pulitzer Prize for Fiction. More recently, *The Mountains Sing* (2020) by Nguyen Phan Que Mai is a sweeping account of Vietnam's long twentieth century.

There is an overwhelming number of books about "The Vietnam

War." Max Hastings's *Vietnam: An Epic History of a Tragic War* (2019) is an epic survey. Bernard Fall's accounts of the 1950s, *Street Without Joy: The French Debacle in Indochina* (1961) and *Hell In a Very Small Place: The Siege of Dien Bien Phu* (1966), have become classics. Graham Greene's *The Quiet American* mixes fact and fiction to evoke the same era. Some of the best accounts of the American experience can be found in *The Things They Carried* (1991) by Tim O'Brien and *A Rumor of War* (1977) by Philip Caputo. There are few Vietnamese books about the period available in English. The best-known are Bao Ninh's *The Sorrow of War* (1994) and Le Ly Hayslip's *When Heaven and Earth Changed Places*. Lesser known books include Truong Nhu Tang's *A Vietcong Memoir: An Inside Account of the Vietnam War and Its Aftermath* and Olga Dror's translation of Nha Ca's anti-war novel *Mourning Headband for Hue*. The experience of the hundreds of thousands of Vietnamese who fled after the conflict is conveyed in Jana K. Lipman's *In Camps: Vietnamese Refugees, Asylum Seekers, and Repatriates* (2020).

If you are interested in more recent developments in Vietnam, my own *Vietnam: Rising Dragon* (second edition 2020) examines the past couple of decades. Former US Ambassador to Hanoi, Ted Osius details some of the diplomacy in *Nothing is Impossible: America's Reconciliation with Vietnam* (2021).

Regular updates on books and other cultural developments in Vietnam and the rest of Southeast Asia can be found at the Mekong Review (mekongreview.com). Tim Doling's site Historic Việt Nam is a treasure trove of gems about the Vietnamese past (historicvietnam.com) and if you really want to get into the details of Vietnamese history, Liam Kelley's blog, Le Minh Khai's SEAsian History Blog, will challenge and surprise you (leminhkhai.blog).

Bibliography

R eaders should not be under any illusions that this book is entirely my own work! I have drawn on a great many books, articles and other works by a very large number of experts in Vietnamese and Asian history. All of them are far more knowledgeable than me in their own specialties but what I have done is bring their insights together in a single narrative.

My constant companion during the writing has been Keith Taylor's *A History of the Vietnamese*. For later periods Christopher Goscha's *The Penguin History of Modern Vietnam* has been immensely valuable. Writers to whom I've turned again and again include Liam Kelley, Li Tana, John Whitmore and Tim Doling's Historic Vietnam website (http://www.historicvietnam.com). I have also drawn on Ben Kiernan's *Viet Nam: A History from Earliest Times to the Present*. Many translations of key documents can be found in George Edson Dutton, Jayne Susan Werner, John K. Whitmore (eds.), *Sources of Vietnamese Tradition*.

Abuza, Zachary. "The Lessons of Le Kha Phieu: Changing Rules in Vietnamese Politics." *Contemporary Southeast Asia*, Vol. 24, No. 1 (April 2002): 121–45.

Agence France Press. "Chinese in Saigon Killed in Raid Report." *The Straits Times*, May 4, 1978, p. 26.

Allard, Francis. "Frontiers and Boundaries: The Han Empire from its Southern Periphery" in Miriam T. Stark (ed.), *Archaeology of Asia* Oxford, UK: Blackwell, 2006.

Amer, Ramses. *The Sino-Vietnamese Approach to Managing Boundary Disputes*. International Boundaries Research Unit, Department of Geography. Durham, UK: University of Durham, 2002.

_____. "Sino-Vietnamese Border Disputes" in Bruce Elleman, et. al., *Beijing's Power and China's Borders: Twenty Neighbors in Asia*. London: Routledge, 2014.

Amirell, Stefan Eklöf, *Pirates of Empire: Colonization and Maritime Violence in Southeast Asia*. Cambridge, UK: Cambridge University Press, 2019.

Anderson, Benedict. *Imagined Communities*. London: Verso, 1991.

Anderson, James A. *The Rebel Den of Nung Tri Cao: Loyalty and Identity along the Sino-Vietnamese Frontier*. Seattle: University of Washington Press, 2007.

_____. "Man and Mongols: the Dali and Đại Việt Kingdoms in the Face of the Northern Invasions" in James A. Anderson and John K. Whitmore (eds.), *China's Encounters on the South and Southwest: Reforging the Fiery Frontier over Two Millennia*. Leiden, The Netherlands: Brill, 2015.

Anderson, James A., and John K. Whitmore. "The Dong World: A Proposal for Analyzing the Highlands between the Yangzi Valley and the Southeast Asian Lowlands." *Asian Highlands Perspectives*, 44:8-71, (Spring 2017).

Ang Cheng Guan. *Vietnamese Communists' Relations with China and the Second Indochina Conflict, 1956–1962*. Jefferson, NC: McFarland, 1997.

_____. "The Vietnam War from the other Side: The Vietnamese Communists" *Perspective*. London: Routledge, 2002.

Baldanza, Kathlene. "Perspectives on the 1540 Mac Surrender to the Ming." *Asia Major*, Vol. 27, No. 2 (2014): 115–46.

Beckett, Ian F.W. "Robert Thompson and the British Advisory Mission to South Vietnam, 1961–1965." *Small Wars & Insurgencies*, Vol. 8, No. 3 (1997): 41–63.

Bellwood, Peter. "Asian Farming Diasporas? Agriculture, Languages, and Genes in China and Southeast Asia" in Miriam T. Stark (ed.), *Archaeology of Asia*. Oxford, UK: Blackwell, 2006.

Bellwood, Peter, et. al. "An Son and the Neolithic of Southern Vietnam." *Asian Perspectives*, Vol. 50, No. 1/2, (Spring/Fall 2011).

Berry, Matthew A. *Confucian Terrorism: Phan Bội Châu and the Imagining of Modern Vietnam*. (PhD thesis). University of California, Berkeley, 2019.

Boudarel, Georges. "Intellectual Dissidence in the 1950s: the Nhan Van Giai. Pham Affair." Council on Southeast Asia Studies at Yale University, *Vietnam Forum*, Vol. 13 (1990): 154–74.

_____. *Cent Fleurs écloses dans la nuit du Vietnam—Communisme et Dissidence 1954–1956*. Paris: Jacques Bertoin, 1991.

Bradley, Mark Philip. *Imagining Vietnam and America: The Making of Postcolonial Vietnam, 1919–1950*. Chapel Hill: University of North Carolina Press, 2000.

Brindley, Erica. *Ancient China and the Yue: Perceptions and Identities on the Southern Frontier, C.400 BCE–50 CE*. Cambridge, UK: Cambridge University Press, 2015.

Brocheux, Pierre, and Daniel Hémery. *Indochina: An Ambiguous Colonization, 1858–1954*. Berkeley: University of California Press, 2011.

Bulbeck, David. "Dong Son" in Keat Gin Ooi (ed.), *Southeast Asia: A Historical Encyclopedia, from Angkor Wat to East Timor*. Santa Barbara, CA: ABC-CLIO, 2004.

Buu Hoan. "Soviet Economic Aid to Vietnam." *Contemporary Southeast Asia*, Vol. 12, No. 4 (March 1991): 360–76.

Chanda, Nayan. *Brother Enemy—The War after the War: History of Indo-China after the Fall of Saigon*. New York: Harcourt Brace Jovanovich, 1986.

Chapman, Jessica M. "Staging Democracy: South Vietnam's 1955 Referendum to Depose Bao Dai." *Diplomatic History*, Vol. 30, No. 4 (September 2006): 671–703.

Chapuis, Oscar. *The Last Emperors of Vietnam: From Tu Duc to Bao Dai*. Westport, CT: Greenwood Press 2000.

Chen Jian. "China's Involvement in the Vietnam War, 1964–69." *The China Quarterly*, No. 142 (June 1995): 356–87.

Cherry, Haydon. "Digging Up the Past: Prehistory and the Weight of the Present in Vietnam." *Journal of Vietnamese Studies*, Vol. 4, No. 1, pp. 84–144.

Churchman, Catherine. "Where to Draw the Line? The Chinese Southern Frontier in the Fifth and Sixth Centuries" in James A. Anderson and John K. Whitmore (eds.), *China's Encounters on the South and Southwest: Reforging the Fiery Frontier Over Two Millennia*. Leiden, The Netherlands: Brill. 2015.

_____. *The People between the Rivers: The Rise and Fall of a Bronze Drum Culture*. London: Rowman & Littlefield, 2016.

Cima, Ronald J. *Vietnam: A Country Study*. Washington, DC: Library of Congress, 1989.

Cooke, Nola. "The Myth of the Restoration: Dang Trong Influences in the Spiritual Life of the Early Nguyen Dynasty (1802–47)" in Anthony Reid (ed.), *The Last Stand of Asian Autonomies: Responses to Modernity in the Diverse States of Southeast Asia and Korea, 1750–1900*. Melbourne: Macmillan, 1997.

Cordier, Henri. *A Narrative of the Recent Events in Tong-King*. American Presbyterian Mission Press, 1875.

Davis, Bradley Camp. *Imperial Bandits: Outlaws and Rebels in the China–Vietnam Borderlands*. Seattle: University of Washington Press, 2017.

Deane, Hugh. "The Chinese Flight from Vietnam." *Contemporary Marxism*, No. 12/13, (Spring 1986).

Diffloth, Gérard. "The Westward Expansion of Chamic Influence in Indochina: a View from Historical Linguistics" in Tran Ky Phuong and Bruce Lockhart (eds.), *The Cham of Vietnam: History, Society and Art*, p. 355. Singapore: NUS Press, 2011.

Do Thanh Hai. "Vietnam: Riding the Chinese Tide." *The Pacific Review*, 31:2 (2018).

Dosch, Jörn. "Vietnam's ASEAN Membership Revisited: Golden Opportunity or Golden Cage?" *Contemporary Southeast Asia*, Vol. 28, No. 2 (August 2006): 234–58.

Dosch, Jörn, and Alexander Vuving. "The Impact of China on Governance Structures in Vietnam." *Discussion Papers* 14/2008, German Development Institute / Deutsches Institut für Entwicklungspolitik (DIE). (2008).

Duiker, William. "Vietnam: a Revolution in Transition." *Southeast Asian Affairs 1989*, Singapore: ISEAS–Yusof Ishak Institute, 1989.

Dutton, George. *The Tây Son Uprising: Society and Rebellion in Eighteenth-century Vietnam.* Manoa: University of Hawaii Press, 2006.

Dutton, George Edson, Jayne Susan Werner, and John K. Whitmore (eds.), *Sources of Vietnamese Tradition.* New York: Columbia University Press, 2012.

Edward Miller. *Misalliance: Ngo Dinh Diem, the United States, and the Fate of South Vietnam.* Cambridge, MA: Harvard University Press, 2013.

Elliott, David W.P. *Changing Worlds: Vietnam's Transition from Cold War to Globalization.* Oxford, UK: Oxford University Press, 2014.

Erlanger, Steven. "Vietnamese Communists Purge an In-House Critic." *New York Times* (April 1, 1990).

Fairbank, John King. *The Cambridge History of China: Volume 1, The Ch'in and Han Empires, 221 BC–AD 220.* Cambridge, UK: Cambridge University Press, 1986,

Favereau, A., and Berenice Bellina. "Thai-Malay Peninsula and South China Sea Networks (500 BCE–AD 200)," based on a reappraisal of "Sa Huynh-Kalanay"-related ceramics, *Quaternary International* (2016), http://dx.doi.org/10.1016/j.quaint.2015.09.100.

Fforde, Adam. *Vietnamese State Industry and the Political Economy of Commercial Renaissance: Dragon's Tooth or Curate's Egg?* Oxford, UK: Chandos, 2007.

Garrett, Clarke W. "In Search of Grandeur: France and Vietnam 1940–1946." *The Review of Politics*, Vol. 29, No. 3 (July 1967): 303–323.

Glover, Ian, and Nguyễn Kim Dung. "Excavations at Gò Cấm, Quảng Nam, 2000–3: Linyi and the Emergence of the Cham Kingdoms" in Trần Kỳ Phương and Bruce M. Lockhart (eds.), *The Cham of Vietnam: History, Society and Art.* Singapore: NUS Press, 2011.

Goloubew, Victor. "L'Âge Du Bronze Au Tonkin Et Dans Le Nord-Annam." *Bulletin de l'École Française d'Extrême-Orient*, Vol. 29 (1929).

Goscha, Christopher E. "Building Force: Asian Origins of Twentieth-Century Military Science in Vietnam (1905–54)." *Journal of Southeast Asian Studies*, Vol. 34, No. 3 (October 2003): 535–60.

_____. *The Penguin History of Modern Vietnam.* New York: Penguin, 2016.

Greene, Graham. "Is there a Way Out in Indo-China?" *The New Republic* (April 4, 1954).

Grossheim, Martin. "'Revisionism' in The Democratic Republic of Vietnam: New Evidence from the East German Archives." *Cold War History*, Vol. 5, No. 4 (November 2005): 451–77.

Hall, D.G.E. *A History of South East Asia.* New York: Macmillan & Co., 1981 .

Hardy, Andrew. "The Economics of French Rule in Indochina: a Biography of Paul Bernard (1892–1960)." *Modern Asian Studies*, Oct., 1998, Vol. 32, No. 4 (October 1998): 807–848.

Herman, John. "The Kingdoms of Nanzhong: China's Southwest Border Region Prior to the Eighth Century." *T'oung Pao* 95 (2009): 241–86.

Higham, Charles. *Early Mainland Southeast Asia: From First Humans to Angkor.* Bangkok: River Books, 2014.

_____. *The Bronze Age of Southeast Asia*, Cambridge, UK: Cambridge University Press, 1996.

Hilgers, Lauren. "Vietnam's First City." *Archaeology* (July/August 2016).

Hoang Anh Tuan. *Silk for Silver: Dutch-Vietnamese Relations, 1637–1700.* Leiden, The Netherlands: Brill, 2006.

Holcombe, Charles. "Early Imperial China's Deep South: The Viet Regions through Tang Times." *Tang Studies*, 1997:15–16, 125–56.

Holmgren, Jennifer. *The Chinese Colonization of Northern Vietnam: Administrative Geography and Political Development in the Tongking Delta, First to Sixth Centuries A.D.* Singapore: ANU Press, 1990.

Hong Kong Daily Press Office. *The Directory and Chronicle for China, Japan, Corea, Indo-China, Straits Settlements, Malay States, Sian, Netherlands India, Borneo, the Philippines, Etc.*, 1910.

Horn, Robert C. "Vietnam and Sino-Soviet Relations: What Price Rapprochement." *Asian Survey* Vol. 27, No. 7 (July 1987).

Hue-Tam Ho Tai. *Radicalism and the Origins of the Vietnamese Revolution.* Cambridge, MA: Harvard University Press, 1996.

Huynh Kim Khanh. "The Vietnamese August Revolution Reinterpreted." *The Journal of Asian Studies*, Vol. 30, No. 4 (August 1971): 761–82.

Joiner, Charles A. "The Vietnam Communist Party Strives to Remain the 'Only Force.'" *Asian Survey*, Vol. 30, No. 11 (November 1990): 1053–65.

Kahin, George McTurnan. *Intervention: How America Became Involved in Vietnam*. New York: Knopf, 1986.

Keiji Imamura. "The Distribution of Bronze Drums of the Heger I and Pre-I Types: Temporal Changes and Historical Background." Departmental Bulletin Paper, Archeology Laboratory, Faculty of Letters, Graduate School of Humanities and Social Sciences, University of Tokyo, 2011.

Khoo, Nicholas. *Collateral Damage: Sino-Soviet Rivalry and the Termination of the Sino-Vietnamese Alliance*. New York: Columbia University Press, 2011.

Kiernan, Ben. *Viet Nam: A History from Earliest Times to the Present*. Oxford, UK: Oxford University Press, 2017.

Kim, Nam C. "Lasting Monuments and Durable Institutions: Labor, Urbanism, and Statehood in Northern Vietnam and Beyond." *Journal of Archaeological Research* (2013) 21: 217–248.

_____. *The Origins of Ancient Vietnam*. Oxford, UK: Oxford University Press, 2015.

Kim, Nam C., Lai Van Toi and Trinh Hoang Hiep. "Co Loa: an Investigation of Vietnam's Ancient Capital." *Antiquity* 84 (2010): pp. 1011–27.

Le Dang Doanh. "The Evolution of Vietnam's Institutional Reforms—Progress and Challenges" in Borje Ljunggren and Dwight H. Perkins (eds.), *Vietnam: Navigating a Rapidly Changing Economy, Society, and Political Order*. Cambridge, MA: Harvard University Asia Center (forthcoming).

Lentz, Christian C. *Contested Territory: Ðien Biên Phu and the Making of Northwest Vietnam*. New Haven, CT: Yale University Press, 2019.

Lewis, Mark Edward. *The Early Chinese Empires (History of Imperial China): Qin and Han*. Cambridhe, MA: Harvard University Press, 2010.

Li, Tana. "An Alternative Vietnam? The Nguyen Kingdom in the Seventeenth and Eighteenth Centuries." *Journal of Southeast Asian Studies*, Vol. 29, No. 1 (Mar., 1998).

_____. "The Eighteenth-Century Mekong Delta and its World of Water Frontier" in Nhung Tuyet Tran and Anthony Reid (eds.), *Vietnam: Borderless Histories*. Madison: University of Wisconsin Press, 2005.

_____. "A Historical Sketch of the Landscape of the Red River Delta." *Trans-Regional and -National Studies of Southeast Asia*, Vol. 4, No. 2 (July 2016): 351–63.

_____. "Jiaozhi (Giao Chỉ) in the Han Period Tongking Gulf" in Nola Cooke, Tana Li and James A. Anderson (eds.), *The Tongking Gulf Through History*. Philadelphia: University of Pennsylvania Press, 2011.

_____. "The Ming Factor and the Emergence of the Viet in the 15th Century" in Geoff Wade and Sun Laichen, *Southeast Asia in the Fifteenth Century: The China Factor*. Hong Kong: Hong Kong University Press, 2010.

_____. *Nguyen Cochinchina: Southern Vietnam in the Seventeenth and Eighteenth Centuries*, 2018.

_____. "Swamps, Lakes, Rivers and Elephants: a Preliminary Attempt towards an Environmental History of the Red River Delta, c. 600–1400." *Water History* (2015) 7:199–211.

_____. "Towards an Environmental History of the Eastern Red River Delta, Vietnam, c.900–1400." *Journal of Southeast Asian Studies*, Vol. 45, No. 03 (October 2014): 315–37.

_____. "A View from the Sea: Perspectives on the Northern and Central Vietnamese Coast." *Journal of Southeast Asian Studies*, Vol. 37, No. 1 (February 2006).

Lieberman, Victor, and Brendan Buckley. "The Impact of Climate on Southeast Asia, circa 950–1820: New Findings." *Modern Asian Studies* 46,5(2012) pp. 1049–96.

Lipson, Mark, et al. "Ancient Genomes Document Multiple Waves of Migration in Southeast Asian Prehistory." *Science*, Vol. 361, No. 6397 (July 6, 2018): 92–95.

Lockhart, Bruce M., and William J. Duiker. *Historical Dictionary of Vietnam*. Lanham, MD: Scarecrow Press, 2006.

Logan, William S. *Hanoi: Biography of a City*. Seattle: University of Washington Press, 2000.

Manguin, Pierre-Yves. "The Archaeology of Fu Nan in the Mekong River Delta: The Oc Eo Culture of Viet Nam" in Nancy Tingley (ed.), *Arts of Ancient Viet Nam*. New Haven, CT: Yale University Press, 2009.

_____. "Early Coastal States of Southeast Asia: Funan and Srivijaya" in Guy, John (ed.), *Lost Kingdoms: Hindu-Buddhist Sculpture of Early Southeast Asia*. New Haven, CT: Yale University Press, 2014.

Mann, James. *About Face: A History of America's Curious Relationship with China from Nixon to Clinton*. New York: Knopf, 1999.

McLeod, Mark W. "Nationalism and Religion in Vietnam: Phan Boi Chau and the Catholic Question." *The International History Review*, Vol. 14, No. 4 (Nov., 1992): 661–80.

Miksic, John N. *Historical Dictionary of Ancient Southeast Asia*. Lanham, MD: Scarecrow Press, 2007.

Miksic, John N., and Goh Geok Yian. *Ancient Southeast Asia*. London: Routledge, 2016.

Moïse, Edwin E. *Tonkin Gulf and the Escalation of the Vietnam War*. Chapel Hill: University of North Carolina Press, 1996.

Momoki Shiro. "Dai Viet and the South China Sea Trade: From the 10th to the 15th Century." *Crossroads: An Interdisciplinary Journal of Southeast Asian Studies*, Vol. 12, No. 1 (1998): 1–34.

Nguyen, Lien-Hang T. *Hanoi's War: An International History of the War for Peace in Vietnam*. Chapel Hill: University of North Carolina Press, 2012, p. 42.

_____. "The War Politburo: North Vietnam's Diplomatic and Political Road to the Tet Offensive." *Journal of Vietnamese Studies*, Vol. 1, No. 1–2 (February/August 2006): 4–58.

Nishino Noriko. "An Introduction to Dr. Nishimura Masanari's Research on the Lung Khe Citadel." *Asian Review of World Histories*, 5 (2017).

O'Connor, Richard A. "Agricultural Change and Ethnic Succession in Southeast Asian States: A Case for Regional Anthropology." *The Journal of Asian Studies*, Vol. 54, No. 4 (Nov., 1995): 968–96.

O'Harrow, Stephen. "From Co-loa to the Trung Sisters' Revolt." *Asian Perspectives*, Vol. 22, No. 2 (1979).

Obermeyer, Ziad, Christopher J.L. Murray and Emmanuela Gakidou. "Fifty Years of Violent War Deaths from Vietnam to Bosnia: Analysis of Data from the World Health Survey Programme." *British Medical Journal*, June 19, 2008.

Osborne, Milton E. *Strategic Hamlets in South Viet-Nam*. Ithaca, NY: Cornell University Southeast Asia Program, 1965.

Oxenham, Marc F., Hirofumi Matsumura and Nguyen Kim Dung (eds.), *Man Bac: the Excavation of a Neolithic Site in Northern Vietnam*. Canberra, Australia: ANU E-Press, 2011.

Oxenham, Marc F., et. al. "The Da But Culture: Evidence for Cultural Development In Vietnam during The Middle Holocene." *Indo-Pacific Prehistory Association Bulletin*, Vol. 25 (2005).

Papin, Philippe. "Hanoi et ses territoires." *Bulletin de l'École française d'Extrême-Orient Année* (1995): 201–30.

Path, Kosal. *Vietnam's Strategic Thinking during the Third Indochina War*. Madison: University of Wisconsin Press, 2020.

Pelley, Patricia. "'Barbarians' and 'Younger Brothers': The Remaking of Race in Postcolonial Vietnam." *Journal of Southeast Asian Studies*, Vol. 29, No. 2 (1998).

Peycam, Philippe M.F. *The Birth of Vietnamese Political Journalism: Saigon, 1916–1930*. New York: Columbia University Press, 2012.

Phạm Lê Huy. "A Reconsideration of the Leilou-Longbian Debate: a Continuation of Research by Nishimura Masanari." *Asian Review of World Histories*, Vol. 5 (2017).

Pham Minh Huyen. "Northern Vietnam from the Neolithic to the Han Period" in I. Glover and P. Bellwood (eds.), *Southeast Asia: from Prehistory to History*. London: Routledge, 2004

Phan, John. "Re-Imagining 'Annam': A New Analysis of Sino-Viet-Muong Linguistic Contact." *Chinese Southern Diaspora Studies*, Vol. 4 (2010).

Piper, Philip J. "Human Cultural, Technological and Adaptive Changes from the End of the Pleistocene to the Mid-Holocene in Southeast Asia" in Marc Oxenham and Hallie Buckley (eds.), *The Routledge Handbook of Bioarchaeology in Southeast Asia and the Pacific Islands*. London: Routledge, 2015.

Porter, Gareth. "The Transformation of Vietnam's World-view: from Two Camps to Interdependence." *Contemporary Southeast Asia*, Vol. 12, No. 1 (June 1990): 1–19.

Qiang Zhai. *China and the Vietnam Wars, 1950–1975*, Chapel Hill: University of North Carolina Press, 2000.

Reaves, Joseph A. "Vietnam Reveals Cambodia Death Toll." *Chicago Tribune* (July 1, 1988).

Reilly, Brett. "Before the First Indochina War: Redefining The Origin Of Vietnam's Civil War." Association of Asian Studies, 2017 Annual Conference.

_____. "The Myth of the Wilsonian Moment." Wilson Center Blog, https://www.wilsoncenter.org/blog-post/the-myth-the-wilsonian-moment (June 17, 2019).

_____. "The True Origin of the Term 'Viet Cong.'" *The Diplomat*, https://thediplomat.com/2018/01/the-true-origin-of-the-term-vietcong (January 31, 2018).

Reinecke, Andreas. "Early Cultures (First Millennium B.C. to Second Century A.D.)." *Arts of Ancient Viet Nam: from River Plain to Open Sea*. Asia Society, 2009.

Riedel, James. "The Vietnamese Economy in the 1990s." *Asian Pacific Economic Literature*, Vol. 11, No. 2 (November 1997), p. 60.

Ross, Robert. *The Indochina Tangle: China's Vietnam Policy, 1975–1979*. New York: Columbia University Press, 1988.

Sasges, Gerard. "State, Enterprise and the Alcohol Monopoly in Colonial Vietnam." *Journal of Southeast Asian Studies*, Vol. 43, No. 1 (February 2012): 133–57.

Schafer, Edward Hetzel. *The Vermilion Bird*. Berkeley: University of California Press, 1967.

Schütte, Heinz. "Hundred Flowers in Vietnam 1955–1957." *Südostasien Working Papers No. 22*, Department of Southeast Asian Studies. Berlin: Humboldt-University, 2003.

Schweyer, Anne-Valérie. "The Birth of Champa." Conference Paper for *Crossing Borders in Southeast Asian Archaeology*, September 2010, Berlin.

Sheehan, Neil. *A Bright Shining Lie: John Paul Vann and America in Vietnam*. New York: Random House, 1988.

Shiro, Momoki. "Dai Viet and the South China Sea Trade, 10th–15th centuries." *Crossroads: an Interdisciplinary Journal of Southeast Asian Studies*, Vol. 12, No. 1 (1998): 1–34.

Solheim, Wilhelm. "A Brief History of the Dongson Concept." *Asian Perspectives*, Vol. 28, No. 1 (1988–89).

Sophie Quinn-Judge. *Ho Chi Minh: the Missing Years*. London: Hurst, 2003.

Southworth, William A. "Coastal States of Champa" in Ian Glover and Peter Bellwood (eds.), *Southeast Asia from Prehistory to History*. London: Routledge, 2004.

Springhall, John. "Kicking out the Vietminh: How Britain Allowed France to Reoccupy South Indochina, 1945–46." *Journal of Contemporary History*, Vol. 40, No. 1 (2005).

Stevenson, John. "Vietnamese Ceramics and Cultural Identity: Evidence from the Ly and Tran Dynasties" in David Marr and Anthony Milner (eds.), *Southeast Asia in the 9th to 14th Centuries*. Canberra: Institute of Southeast Asian Studies, School of Pacific Studies, Australian National University, 1986.

Sun Laichen. "Imperial Ideal Compromised: Northern and Southern Courts across the New Frontier in the Early Yuan Era" in James A. Anderson and John K. Whitmore (eds.), *China's Encounters on the South and Southwest: Reforging the Fiery Frontier Over Two Millennia*. Leiden, The Netherlands: Brill, 2015.

Taylor, Keith. "Authority and Legitimacy in 11th Century Vietnam" in Anthony Milner, David G. Marr (eds.), *Southeast Asia in the 9th to 14th Centuries*. Singapore: Institute of Southeast Asian Studies, 1986.

_____. *The Birth of Vietnam*. Berkeley: University of California Press, 1983.

_____. "The Early Kingdoms" in Nicholas Tarling (ed.), *The Cambridge History of Southeast Asia Volume 1: from Early Times to c.1800*. Cambridge, UK: Cambridge University Press, 1993.

_____. *A History of the Vietnamese*. Cambridge, UK: Cambridge University Press, 2013.

_____. "Surface Orientations in Vietnam: beyond Histories of Nation and Region." *The Journal of Asian Studies*, Vol. 57, No. 4 (November 1998).

Thayer, Carlyle A. *Vietnam People's Army: Development and Modernization*. Research Monograph, Sultan Haji Bolkiah Institute of Defense and Strategic Studies, Brunei Darussalam, 2009.

_____. "The Tyranny of Geography: Vietnamese Strategies to Constrain China in the South China Sea." *Contemporary Southeast Asia*, Vol. 33, No. 3 (2011): 348–69.

_____. "Vietnam's Foreign Policy in an Era of Rising Sino–US Competition and Increasing Domestic Political Influence." *Asian Security*, Vol. 13, No. 3 (2017): 183–99.

U.S. Government Printing Office. *Congressional Record: Proceedings and Debates of the United States Congress. (1966)*. Washington, DC: U.S. Government Printing Office, August 19, 1966.

Van Staaveren, Jacob. *Gradual Failure—the Air War over North Vietnam 1965–66*. Washington, DC: Office of Air Force History, 2002.

Vann, Michael G. "Building Colonial Whiteness on the Red River: Race, Power, and Urbanism in Paul Doumer's Hanoi, 1897–1902." *Historical Reflections / Réflexions Historiques*, Vol. 33, No. 2 (Summer 2007).

Vickery, Michael. "Champa Revised" in Tran Ky Phuong and Bruce Lockhart (eds.), *The Cham of Vietnam: History, Society and Art*, Singapore: NUS Press, 2009.

_____. "Funan Reviewed: Deconstructing the Ancients." *Bulletin de l'Ecole Française d'Extrême-Orient*. Tome 90–91, (2003).

_____. "A Short History of Champa" in Andrew David Hardy, Mauro Cucarzi and Patrizia Zolese (eds.), *Champa and the Archaeology of Mỹ Sơn (Vietnam)*. Singapore: NUS Press, 2009.

Vu Hong Lien. "Mongol Invasions in Southeast Asia and their Impact on Relations between Dai Viet and Champa (1226–1326 C.E.)." PhD thesis. University of London, 2008.

_____. *Rice and Baguette: A History of Food in Vietnam*. London: Reaktion Books, 2016.

Vuving, Alexander L. "Grand Strategic Fit and Power Shift: Explaining Turning Points in China-Vietnam Relations" in Shiping Tang, Mingjiang Li, and Amitav Acharya (eds.), *Living with China: Regional States and China through Crises and Turning Points*. London: Palgrave Macmillan, 2009.

Wang, Nora. "Deng Xiaoping: the Years in France." *The China Quarterly*, No. 92 (December 1982), pp. 698–705.

Whitlow, Robert H. *U.S. Marines in Vietnam: The Advisory & Combat Assistance Era, 1954–1964*. Washington, DC: United States Department of Defense, Department of the Navy, Marine, Corps, Headquarters, History and Museums Division, 1977.

Whitmore, John K. "Ngo (Chinese) Communities and Montane–Littoral Conflict in Dai Viet, ca. 1400–1600." *Asia Major*, 2014, Third Series, Vol. 27, No. 2, Maritime Frontiers In Asia: Sino-Viet Relations, ca. 900–1800 CE (2014): 53–85.

_____. "The Last Great King of Classical Southeast Asia: 'Chế Bồng Nga' and Fourteenth-Century Champa" in Trần Kỳ Phương and Bruce M. Lockhart (eds.), *The Cham of Vietnam: History, Society and Art*, Singapore: NUS Press, 2011.

_____. "The Two Great Campaigns of the Hong-duc Era (1470–97) in Dai Viet." *South East Asia Research*, Vol. 12, No. 1 (March 2004): 121.

Wicks, Robert S. *Money, Markets, and Trade in Early Southeast Asia: the Development of Indigenous Monetary Systems to A.D. 1400*.

(Studies on Southeast Asia.) xii, Ithaca, NY: Southeast Asia Program, Cornell University.

Wilcox, Wynn. "Transnationalism and Multi-ethnicity in the Early Nguyen Anh Gia Long Period" in Nhung Tuyet Tran and Anthony Reid (eds.), *Vietnam: Borderless Histories*. Madison: University of Wisconsin Press, 2005.

Wolters, O.W. "On Telling a Story of Vietnam in the Thirteenth and Fourteenth Centuries." *Journal of Southeast Asian Studies*, Vol. 26, No. 1 (1995): 63–74.

Womack, Brantly. *The Politics of Asymmetry China and Vietnam: the Politics of Asymmetry*. Cambridge, UK: Cambridge University Press, 2006.

Woodside, Alexander. *Vietnam and the Chinese Model: a Comparative Study of Vietnamese and Chinese Government in the First Half of the Nineteenth Century*. Cambridge, MA: Harvard East Asian Monographs 140, 1988.

Yang, Bin. "Horses, Silver, and Cowries—Yunnan in Global Perspective." *Journal of World History* Vol. 15, No. 3 (Sep., 2004): 281–322.

Yao, Alice. "The Dian and Dong Son Cultures" in *Handbook of East and Southeast Asian Archaeology*, pp. 503–12.

Yao, Alice, and Jiang Zhilong. "Rediscovering the Settlement System of the 'Dian' Kingdom, in Bronze Age Southern China." *Antiquity*, Vol. 86 (2012): 353–67.

Yao, Alice, Jiang Zhilong, Chen Xuexiang, and Liang Yin. "Bronze Age Wetland/Scapes: Complex Political Formations in the Humid Subtropics of Southwest China, 900–100 BC." *Journal of Anthropological Archaeology*, Vol. 40 (2015): 213–229.

Zhang Xiaoming. "Deng Xiaoping and China's Decision to go to War with Vietnam." *Journal of Cold War Studies*, Vol. 12, No. 3 (Summer 2010).

_____. "The Vietnam War, 1964–1969: A Chinese Perspective." *The Journal of Military History*, Vol. 60, No. 4 (Oct., 1996): 759.

Zinoman, Peter. *The Colonial Bastille: A History of Imprisonment in Vietnam, 1862–1940*. Berkeley: University of California Press, 2001.

Index

Agent Orange, 227
Agriculture
  garden-based, 123
  in Cochinchina, 191
  in Dai Viet, 64
  Le Thanh Tong and, 113
  rice-based, 51, 98
  salinated arable fields, impact of, 269
  sophisticated, evidence for, 20
  surplus, 19
Ai Lao (upland state), 48
Ai Lao people, in Hua Pan/Houaphanh, 112, 115
Alcohol, 166
  consumption of, 110
  illegal distilling, 182
  monopoly, 182
  state-backed monopolies, 190, 195
  tax on, revenue from, 182
  transport and sale of, monopolies on, 183
Amaravati (Champa state), 60, 61
American War
  1963–1965, 232–237
  1965–1975, 237–245
  end of, 237–245
Anderson, Jamie (historian), 46
An Duong (legendary king), 22, 39
Ang Cheng Guan (historian), 224
Angkor, 66, 86, 88
  Bayon Temple, 63
  expansion of, 61
  Khmer city of, 63
  King Jayavarman and, 61, 63
  Zhenla incorporated into, 53
Angkor Borei (archaeological site), 51, 52
Angkor-Cham mandala, 63
Annam, 8, 9, 36, 169, 171, 176, 182, 194, 198, 206, 209
  "Chambers of People's Representa-

tives" for, 195
  communist activists in, 197
  Emperor of, 184
  French control of, 177, 181
  French fighting in, 181
  idea of, 189
  Nghe An Province, 186
  protectorates of, 180
  students from, 187
  Tang rule in, collapse of, 80
  World War II, impact of, 204
Annamese culture, 189, 190
Annamite mountains, 33
Annamite People, 192, 194
  become Vietnamese, 200–209
Annan duhu fu (Protectorate of the Pacified South), 36
ARVN (Army of the Republic of Vietnam), 225, 229, 230, 232, 234, 242
ASEAN. see Association of Southeast Asian Nations
Associated State of Vietnam (ASVN), 209, 212
Association of Southeast Asian Nations (ASEAN), 261, 265
ASVN. see Associated State of Vietnam
Au Co (fairy princess), 39, 134
Au Lac (legendary kingdom), 22, 39
Austroasiatics, 15, 75, 227
  language, 30, 56
  speakers, 56
Austronesian, 15, 55–56, 59, 227
  languages, 56, 60

Bac Thanh (nineteenth century name for Hanoi), 147

Bach Bang River, 28, 71, 72, 74, 95
Bahnaric (language group), 56–57
Baldanza, Kathlene (historian), 105, 118
Banoy, Sri, 63
Banque de l'Indochine (BIC), 171, 183
Bao Dai (last Nguyen emperor), 171, 193, 208, 219–221
  "Empire of Viet Nam," 205
  French government association with, 209
  and Ngo Dinh Diem, 204, 212
  returned to Hue from France, 198
  treaties with France, 204
Bao Ninh (writer), 274
Bassac River, 131
Ba Trieu (legendary leader), 10, 31
Beau, Paul (French governor-general), 184, 187
Beijing, 157, 160, 161, 176, 210, 224, 236, 243
  Forbidden City in, 148
  French navy attacked, 177
  Gia Long sent officials to, 7–8, 147
Ho Chi Minh in (August 1959), 225
  Imperial Palace, 107
  instructions to Gia Long, 8–9
  Japan attacked, 200–201
  leaders in, 251
  Le Duan visit to, 249
  Tran Thang Tong sent emissaries, 94
  Tran Thang Tong visit, 95
Bhadravarman (Champa ruler), 58–60
BIC. see Banque de l'Indochine

Billault, Adolphe, 159
Binh Thuan province, 144
Binh Xuyen gang, 207, 219, 220
Black Flags, 167, 170, 172–178, 181
  business model, 177
  Chinese troops joining, 175–176
  French and Chinese representatives against, 173
  and French authorities, 172, 173
  against Garnier's forces, 174
  Liu Yongfu, 188
  members of, 172
  rebels, 169, 172
  "Black Tai" people, 48
Bon River, 28, 53, 58
Boulevard Amiral Courbet, 11
Boulevard Gambetta, 11
BRIAM. see British Advisory Mission
Brick tombs, 21, 28, 29 32
British Advisory Mission (BRIAM), 228
Bronze, 18–20
  arrowheads, 19, 57
  culture, source of, 37
  drums, 13, 14, 24, 25, 27, 28, 44, 46
  implements, 28
  long-buried, 13
  peoples used, 18
  techniques of working with, 18
  tools, 44
Bronze Age, 14, 18, 50
Buddhism, 99, 102, 154–155, 209, 215
  Caodaism and, 216
  Funan and Champa, arrival in, 41
  Gia Long placed limits on, 147–148
  Indian roots of, 81
  Le Thanh Tong and, 114
  Mahayana, 62, 63, 216
  Minh Mang and, 151

spreading of, 52
  superstition of, Chu Van An opposed, 101
Theravada, 154, 216
Buddhist monarchy, 77, 78

Cambodia, 23, 50, 51, 153, 157, 160, 165, 198, 236, 243, 258, 268
  Angkor in, 61
  "associated states" of, 209
  borders of, 227
  Case–Church Amendment, 244
  Cham flee to, 144
  China and, 251, 266
  communist regime in, 251
  counterinsurgency quagmire, 253
  French in, 164
  invasion of, 251, 252, 254, 255
  Khmer Rouge in, 255
  Minh Mang annexed, 154
  protectorates of, 180
  territories, 52
  Theravada Buddhism in, 216
  Thieu Tri's reign, external crises, 155
  Vietnamese forces recaptured (1834), 153
  Viet supremacy in, 155
  withdrawal from, 257, 260
Cam Ranh Bay, 265
Can Lao (political party), 219
Can Vuong
  movement, 178
  rebellion, 177, 178
  revolt, 187
Cao Bang, 84, 85, 124, 253
Cao Bien. see Gao Pian
Cao Dai, 199, 207, 219, 220
  religions infused in, 214–215

religious community, 202
"saints," 215
Cao Dai Tien Ong, 215
Cao Dai Tien Ong Dai Bo Tat Ma Ha Tat, 215
Ca River, 14
Case–Church Amendment, 244
Catroux, Georges, 201
Cau River, 85, 117, 118
Central Highlands, 55, 233, 237, 238, 243, 244, 268
An Khe in, 137
bauxite reserves in, 266
controlling, importance of, 227
indigenous population in, 56
Cham coast, 56, 62
Champa, 54–67, 78, 80, 82, 86, 88, 94–99, 111, 112, 116, 127, 133, 144
Angkor's conflict with, 61, 63
Buddhism in, arrival of, 41
coast, 79
culture of, 60
emergence of, 37
fleet, 74
records of raids on, 79
"Cham World," 137
Che Bong Nga (ruler of Champa), 65–66
forces, 65
Chi Linh (home of Tran Hung Dao)
China, 7, 10, 268
and Cambodia, 251, 266
and Vietnamese civilization, 12
France acquired trading rights in, 155–156
France renounce colonies in, 206
Guangdong Province, 8, 21, 35, 106, 143, 247
Ming, 271
Mongols rule in, 97
Qing, 141, 154, 169, 173, 176, 178
rising influence in Laos, 266
rising influence in Laos and Cambodia, 266
Song, 63, 80, 84

symbols of resistance against, 12
Xi'an, 21, 23, 24, 25
Cholon, 165, 230, 246, 255
Christianity, 129, 134–135, 139, 156, 167
Gia Long attitude towards, 148
Churchman, Catherine (historian), 28
Chu Van An (thirteenth century scholar), 100–101
CIA, 220, 221, 227, 228
Climate, 16, 26, 37, 43, 92, 98
global changes in, 97
in Southeast Asia, 77, 97
shift, 87
Coast, 24, 55, 89, 106, 116, 136, 144, 210, 213, 232
central, 121, 137, 148, 238, 244
Cham, 56, 62
Champa, 79
DRV, 234
en route to Macau, 134
Cochinchina, 125, 158, 164, 167, 171, 176, 177, 180, 182, 184, 185, 199, 203, 208, 209
and Christianity, 134
annexation of, 247
Chinese business syndicates in, 190
colons, 195, 209
Commission for, 158
French, 165, 166, 179, 202
French law in, 172
French troops in, 206
government, 165, 166
governor of, 172, 173, 174, 218
incorporating in Empire of Viet Nam, 204
modernization of agriculture, 191
newspapers in, 193
operations in, 159
rice-growing land of, 199
students from, 187, 194
"Treaty of Hue," 175
Vietnamese Revolutionary Youth League in, 196

Colani, Madeleine (archaeologist), 16
Co Loa (archaeological site), 19, 20, 22, 27, 30, 72, 73
Co Loa state, 19, 20
Colonialism, 193
Franco-Vietnamese collaboration and, 195
French, 135, 160, 167, 190, 247
Western, local cultures and, 10
Colonization (1874–1887), 178
COMECON. see Council for Mutual Economic Assistance
Comintern, 192, 196, 197, 198, 199
Commandery, 25, 32
Jiaozhi, 24, 31
Rinan, 57, 58
Con Dao (Poulo Condor), 189
Confucian, 101, 127, 150
classics, 83, 183
classic texts, 148
colonial ideology, 134
culture, 154
duties and rituals, 183
elite, 185
family genealogy, 133–134
Gia Long, 148
ideas, influence of, 111
identity, 111
Le Quy Ly, 102
Le Thanh Tong, 114
male-dominated society, 161
Ming China, 271
morality, 114, 187
norms and rules, 8, 109, 147, 162
oppressors, 159
orthodoxy, 152, 155, 157
population of "Dang Ngoai" north, 147
protocol, 8, 108
role as "son of heaven," 151
rulers, 130, 141
scholar-officials, 152, 167
scholars, 141, 151
schools, 107
style, 108
theory, 108
traditions, 181
values of loyalty, 83
Confucianism, 99,

114, 116, 128, 150, 189, 190, 195
arguments rage over, 40
armed, 192
Caodaism and, 215
orthodox, 149
Phan Boi Chau, 188
roles for, 99
tenets of, 40
Tran dynasty and, 41
Confucian World, 166
Copper, 45, 115
Chinese coins, 130
coins, 25, 171
in Yunnan province, 18
money, 130
Corps Expéditionnaire Français d'Extrême-Orient (CEFEO), 207, 208
Corruption, 126, 182–183, 260, 264, 270
eliminating, 228
of Dong Kinh, 125
of Jiaozhi (name), 125
of Malay name, 125
Varenne of, 195
corvee (forced) labor, 188
Cosier, Henri, 184
Council for Mutual Economic Assistance (COMECON), 252
COVID pandemic, 270
Crony capitalism, 270
Cuu Chan. see Jiuzhen

Da But, 17
Da But village, 17, 18
Dai Co Viet (tenth century state), 73, 74, 77, 78, 79, 80
Dai La (early name for Hanoi), 36, 37, 44, 47, 72, 73, 73 78. see also Hanoi
Dai Nam (name of country 1838–1945), 9, 10, 154, 157, 159–160, 163, 178
attack on French, 169
Catholic missionaries in, 156
court, 156, 159, 172
France aggressive policy in, 173–174
Ham Nghi, 171
Qing China, relationship with, 169
"Treaty of Hue," 175
treaty with France, 172

Tu Duc Emperor, rule of, 166–167
Dai Ngu (name of state under Ho Dynasty), 105, 106
Dai Viet, 9, 47, 55, 61–67, 81, 82, 87, 93–101, 104, 106, 108–116, 118–121, 124, 125, 133, 134, 146, 147, 149, 152, 153, 154, 159, 165
and Dali kingdom, 48
Cham attacked, 65–66
Christians in, 109
civilizing mission, 111
conflict with Angkor, 61
court, 84, 90, 95, 111, 173
culture, 99, 105
fascist parties, 233
Indrapura, attacked by, 61–62
Le Thanh Tong, 116
lowland ruler of, 48
Ly Nhan Tong, 85
Ly Thai Tong, 48–49, 63
Ming occupation of, 109
Mongols' invasion, 63–64
nationalism, 111, 199
Nguyen Trai and, 133
politics, 141
population growth in, 88, 92
relationship with Ming state, 65
relations with neighbors, 88
slave raids, 88
Song's invasion, 83
southern boundary of, 115
Tran Dynasty of, 66
Tran Nhan Tong, 65
troops, 48
Dai Viet groups, 202, 204, 206
Dai Viet National Socialist Party, 199
Dai Viet Restoration Association, 202
Dai Viet Su Ky Toan Thu, 134
Da Lai (tenth century name for Hanoi), 71
Dali (upland state), 47–48, 87
frontiers right to lands, 48
kingdom, 47, 48

Mongols' invasion, 93

Danang, 33, 134, 156, 157, 159, 205, 206, 210, 213, 236

Dang Ngoai (Trinh-ruled northern Dai Viet), 125–129, 131, 146
  Confucian population of, 147
  Dutch East India Company in, 126
  European impact on, 127
  identity, 126
  northern frontiers of, 128
  Trinh Sam, 139

Dang Trong (Nguyen ruled central Dai Viet), 125–131, 138–140, 146
  annexation of, 129
  Chinese communities in, 128
  disarray in, 138
  fighting with Cham, 129
  junks trading in, 131
  Nguyen Phuc Khoat, 130, 137
  people, 147
  Phu Xuan, 138
  Trinh forces withdrawal from, 138–139

Daoism, 40–41, 99
  and Cao Dai religion, 214–215
  and Caodaism, 215
  arguments rage over, 40
  roles for, 99

d'Argenlieu, Georges Thierry (French high commissioner), 206

Davis, Bradley Camp (historian), 167, 173

Deforestation, 93

"Delta World," 137

Democratic Republic of Vietnam (DRV), 205–208, 222–228, 232–237, 241–244, 247
  armed forces/troops, 205, 210, 225, 232, 234, 237, 241, 244
  authorities, 207
  coastal defenses, 234
  leadership, 212, 222, 226, 249
  military planners in, 227
  state media, 227, 249

Deng Xiaoping, 192, 252

de Puymanel, Olivier (French engineer), 144

Dian Lake, 44, 45

Diaz, Monsignore, 159

Dien Bien Phu, 209–213, 223
  Viet Minh victory at, 212

Dinh (village communal hall), 114, 128

Dinh Bo Linh (Founder of Dinh Dynasty), 62, 68, 69, 72, 73, 75

Dinh Chi (Cauldron handle) dyke, 92

Dinh Dynasty, 74

Dinh Lien, 62, 73

Dinh Phe De, 73

Doi moi (renovation), 256

Dong Do (eastern capital, fifteenth century name for Hanoi), 104, 105, 106, 110

Dong Kinh (name of Hanoi in fifteenth century), 110, 116, 117, 118, 122, 123, 124, 125, 140, 141, 145, 146, 157

Dong Nai River, 50

Dong Son culture, 14–15, 30

Dong Son drums, 14, 19, 28, 52

Dong Son village, 13, 17, 18, 19
  bronze drums found at, 14
  culture of, 14–15
  graves, 14

Dong World, 42–49, 137, 211, 268

Doumer, Paul (French governor-general), 180, 182, 183–184

Drums, Bronze, 13, 14, 24, 25, 27, 28, 44, 46

Duong River, 31

Dupuis, Jean (arms trader), 167–168

Dutch, 125–127
  Chinese civil war and, 208
  representative, 126–127
  traders, murder of, 126
  traders and mercenaries, 129–130
  used Dang Ngoai, 126

Dutch East India Company, 126

Dutch East Indies, 196, 202

"Empire of Viet Nam," 204

English, 125
  traders, 142

Famine, 88, 96–98, 132, 140, 157, 203–204, 250
  during Mac dynasty, 119, 122
  families experienced, 268
  in 1290–1292, 96

Feng. *see* Phong

Ferry, Jules (French politician), 173–174

First Opium War, 155, 158

Flag, 216
  Bao Dai's "Empire of Viet Nam," 205
  Buddhist, 230
  national, 204–205
  of northern DRV, 247

Floods, 49, 113, 124, 132, 140, 157
  catastrophic, 88
  Dinh Chi, 92
  Ma River, 13
  protection, 50
  protection ditches and dykes, 38, 44
  records of, 92
  Red River, 35, 36

Fontaine, Auguste-Raphaël, 183

Forest, 16, 21, 28–29, 56, 208, 227, 254, 269

B-52s carpet bombed, 237–238
  elephant, 57
  ethnic groups in, 43
  herbicide spray, 229
  plantations in, 215
  products, 29, 37, 44, 57, 98

France, 150, 158–160, 164, 165, 167–170, 179, 181, 182, 189, 190, 193, 194, 195, 196, 200, 204, 214
  acquired trading rights in China, 155–156
  administered colonies in India, 163, 165
  annexation of Cochinchina by, 247
  attack on Danang, 156
  Bao Dai returned

from (1932), 198
  Battle of Waterloo, 158
  Chamber of Deputies, 184
  competition with British colonies, 165
  developments in, 201
  Doumer returned to (1902), 184
  Ferry, Jules, 173–174
  Franco-Prussian war, 167
  Geneva conference, 211–212
  Greater France, 167
  Ho Chi Minh's activism in, 192
  "honorable exit" from Indochina, 211
  King Louis XVI of, 142
  metropolitan, 171, 190, 208
  renounce colonies in China, 206
  Treaty of Hue, 175
  Treaty of Saigon, 169
  treaty with Dai Nam, 172
  Vietnamese laborers during First World War, 192

Franco-Confucian culture, 190

Franco-Prussian war, 167

French, 158–160
  and representatives against Black Flags, 173
  authorities, 11, 172, 173
  Cochinchina, 165, 166, 179, 202
  colonialism, 135, 160, 167, 190, 247
  colonists, 11–12
  colony of Pondicherry, 143
  control of Annam, 177, 181
  Dai Nam attack on, 169
  Empire, 9
  fighting in Annam, 181
  government association with Bao Dai, 209
  in Cambodia, 164
  merchants, 143
  missionaries, 156, 157–158
  Résident Supérieur, 183

rule, end of, 209–213

French Indochina (1887–1907), 178–185

Funan, 49–54, 59
  Buddhism arrival in, 41
  civilization, 49
  construction and cultural creation in, 53
  culture, 50
  primary orientation, 52
  rival state of, 58
  rulers, 52

"Funan World," 137

Gao Pian (Tang military commander), 38

Garnier, Francois (adventurer), 168–169, 173, 174, 179

Geneva Accords, 220, 221, 222

Gia Dinh (eighteenth century name for Saigon), 7, 129, 140, 143, 147, 164, 248
  Turtle Citadel in, 153

Gia Long. *see* Nguyen Phuc Anh

Giao (region of Dai Viet), 68, 69, 71, 72, 73

Giao Chi. *see* Jiaozhi

"Go East" campaign, 187

Goscha, Christopher (historian), 194, 210, 211, 235, 273

Gracey, Douglas (British general), 205–206

Great Clans of Nanzhong, 46

Greater France, 167

Great Viet, 9, 73

Great Yue, 70, 73

Greene, Graham (novelist), 211
  The Quiet American, 214

Guangdong Province (China), 8, 21, 35, 106, 143, 247

Guangxi Province, China, 21, 24, 35, 43–44, 48, 79, 94, 106, 120, 124, 142, 147, 157, 173, 188

Guangzhou, China, 34, 36, 71, 142, 194, 201, 214
  authorities in, 189
  communism and Confucianism in, 193

Pearl River Delta, 31
Pearl River south of, 28
port of, 61
refugees fled into, 37
South China Sea, 32
Whampoa Military Academy, 193
Youth League, 203

Hai Ba Trung, 10, 26
Hainan Island, 32, 129
Haiphong, 28, 71, 95, 169, 172, 184, 191, 201, 202, 207, 243
Hai Van Pass, 33, 57, 58, 61, 113, 115, 139
Ham Nghi (deposed Nguyen emperor), 176, 177, 180
Emperor, 180
enthronement of (1884), 171
rebel court, 178
Han brick tomb builders, 28
Han Dynasty, 25, 39, 134
Hanoi, 7, 10, 15, 16, 32, 36, 91, 92, 93, 94, 95, 110, 168–170, 173, 175, 176, 187, 193, 222, 235, 241, 248, 258
as colonial city, 184
authorities, 168, 201
Bac Thanh, 147
Ba Dinh Square, 80
capital in, 218, 247
central, 179
Christmas bombing, 244
citadel, 179
colonial French community in, 188
death of Ho Chi Minh, announcement of, 242
Doumer's remodeling of, 179–180
Ecole des Beaux-Arts d'Indochine, 191
foundation of, 76
French garrison in, 188
French representatives in, 172
French-run museum in, 13
French-troops marched out of, 213
Governor-General Palace in, 205
Ho Hoan Kiem lake, 133
leadership, 232, 236, 241, 243, 244

Le Duan, 240
Ly citadel, 79
National Convention Center, 266
nationalists marched (Oct 1954), 11
new building construction in, 190
newspapers in, 193
pollution in, 269
railway line between Haiphong and, 183–184
Red River, 14, 17, 28, 77
Red River Delta, 168
renaming of streets in, 11
School of Public Administration and Law, 231
temple to honor Confucius, construction of, 82–83
Thang Long, 133
tombs, 28
Tonkin Public School, 188
viceroys in, 146
Viet Minh militants attacks, 207
Vietnam National Convention Center guards, 261
Xuan Hong lived in, 162
Ha Tien, 136, 139, 143, 216
Hiep Hoa (Nguyen emperor), 174, 175
Hinduism, 54, 62
Hmong (ethnic group), 43, 211
Hoa, 246
Hoabinhian (stone age culture), 16, 19
Hoa Binh province, 16, 86
Hoa Hao (village), 216, 217
Hoa Hao sect, 199, 202, 207, 216–217, 219
Hoa Lu (Dai Viet citadel), 62, 68, 69 72, 73, 74, 76
Duong Ding Nghe, 71
rebellion in, 89
rulers, 75, 78
Hoang Dao Thanh (historian), 11
Hoan Kiem Lake, Hanoi, 133, 170, 179
Ho Chi Minh, 195, 198, 201, 202, 205, 213–214, 223, 224, 225, 231, 242

activism in France, 192
communism, 193
family and political networks of, 197
travelled Yan'an, 200
Vietnamese Revolutionary Youth League, 196
Ho Chi Minh City, 10, 50, 250, 255, 269
Ho Chi Minh Trail, 225, 227, 233, 235, 237
Ho Dynasty (1400–1407), 106
Hoi An, 28, 54, 121, 124, 126, 127, 141
Ho Quy Ly. see Le Quy Ly
Horses, 20
cast statues of, 27
in Central Asia, 45
military, 87
trade in, 45
Yunnan, 45
Houaphanh province, Laos, 48, 112, 115
Ho Xuan Hong (poet), 161–162
Hua, 246
Hue (city), 8
Hue, Treaty of 1863, 159
Hue, Treaty of 1884, 175
Hue Tam Ho Tai (historian), 193
Hung kings, 39, 134
Hung Kings Festival, 39
Hung Kings Temple, 39
Hung Vuong (first of the mythical Hung kings), 39
Hunting, 16, 18, 25, 44

Ia Drang Valley, Battle of, 237, 238
Ice Age, 16
Ikshvaku dynasty, 59
India, 20, 41, 49, 54
Andhra Pradesh, 59
France administered colonies in, 163, 165
Funan's orientation towards, 52
trading networks in, 30, 126
trading posts in 158
Indochina Communist Party (ICP), 198, 199, 203, 205, 209
Indochina Union,

179, 180, 218
Indochinese Federation 1946–1954, 206
Indrapura (Champa state), 60, 61–62, 82
Iron Age, 14, 50
Irrigation, 27, 35, 38, 44, 61, 92, 191
Islam, 127, 151, 216

Japan, 10, 11, 97, 126, 134, 188, 201–202, 203, 266
attacked Beijing and Shangai, 200–201
beat the Russians (1904/5), 202
French compete with, 202
modernization in, Chinese study, 187
Nguyen and diplomatic relations with, 124–125
Vietnamese radicals tour to, 186
Jayavarman (ruler of Angkor), 61, 63
Jean Marie Antoine de Lanessan (French governor-general), 181
Jiaozhi, 23–26, 28, 29, 30, 31, 125
Jiaozhi commandery, 24, 31
Jiaozhi Department, 24, 25, 31
Jiaozhi Prefecture, 73
Jiaozhou (province of Han), 24, 31–36, 58, 61, 74, 106, 107
Jin (state), 32, 58
Jiuzhen, 23, 24, 28, 30
Jiuzhen commandery, 24
Johnson, Lyndon (US president), 233

Katuic (language group), 57
Kauthara (Champa state), 60, 62, 67
Kelley, Liam (historian), 147, 274
Khmer, 57, 60, 62–63, 137, 154
bnam (language), 49
communities, 152, 155
court, 149
farmers, 143
kingdom, 61, 149
lands of Mekong Delta, 146
leaders, 131
nationalists, 152
territories, 149

throne of, 139, 149, 155
Khmer Empire, 53–54, 127, 129, 131
Khmer (Cambodian) monarchy, 127
Khmer Rouge, 251, 252, 255, 258
Khuc Thua My (ruler of Annan), 70–71
Kissinger, Henry (US official), 242, 243
Kublai Khan (Mongol leader), 63, 93–96

Lac Long Quan (dragon lord), 39, 134
Land reform, 209–210, 211, 227
communists', 222
five waves of, 223
Le Quy Ly, 101
Wang Mang and, 25
Language(s), 15, 74–75
Austroasiatics, 30, 56, 75
Austronesian, 56, 60
Bahnaric, 56–57
bnam/phnom, 49
Chinese, 107
Sinitic, 29
Tai, 43–44, 47, 49, 92
"Tai-Kadai," 30
Vietnamese, 99, 134–135, 191
Lan Sang (upland state), 79
Laos, 48, 79. 80, 119, 153, 165, 198, 211, 225, 227, 235, 243
Ai Lao people, 112
and Indochina Union, 179, 182
associated states of, 209
borders of, 165, 227, 241
Case–Church Amendment, 244
China's rising influence in, 266
French attacks, 210
Phuan people, 111
Last Glacial Period, 16
Le Chieu Trong (last king of Le Dynasty), 145
Le Dinh, 75, 76
Le Duan (DRV leader), 224, 226, 232, 240, 242, 248, 249, 255, 256, 271
Le Dynasty (1428–1789), 66–67, 76, 120, 130, 141, 145, 148, 160, 163

1428–1527, 109–118
founder of, 133
restoration of, 123
Trinh Tung and, 122
Lefèbvre, Dominique
(French mission-
ary), 156
Le Hoan (founder of
Early Le Dynasty),
73–76
Le Loi (founder of Le
Dynasty), 66, 107–
110, 113, 121, 132–
133, 177
Leninism, 197, 258,
259, 271
Le Quy Ly (over-
thrower of the Tran
Dynasty), 98, 101–
103, 104, 105
Le Thai To. see Le Loi
Le Thanh Tong (Le
Dynasty king, born
Le Thu Thanh),
113–117, 133
Le Van Duyet (nine-
teenth century ruler
of south), 152
Liang (later) dynasty,
34, 35, 38
Liang state, 34, 47, 60
Lingnan region, 21,
35, 37, 70
Linyi (coastal state),
31, 32, 33, 35, 37,
58, 59–60, 61, 62
Li Tana (historian),
87, 107, 115, 122,
125
Liu–Song
dynasty, 32, 58
emperor, 33
state, 52
Liu Yan (ruler of
Southern Han), 70–
71
Great Yue, 70
Southern Han em-
pire, 70, 71
Liu Yin (ruler of
Lingnan), 70
Liu Yongfu, 188
Logan, William S.
(historian), 179
Long Bien (archaeo-
logical site), 30–31,
34, 35, 61
Luang Prabang, Laos,
115, 141, 181
Lung Khe (archaeo-
logical site), 30–31
Luo (ethnic group),
26
Luoyang, China, 25
Luo-yue, 27
Luo-Yue drum own-
ers, 28
Ly Bi. see Ly Nam De

Ly Bon (rebel), 34–35
Ly Cong Uan. see Ly
Thai To
Ly Dynasty, 12, 112,
121
1009–1226, 75–90
Ly Cong Uan, 76
Ly Long Trat, 88
Ly Nam De (rebel
emperor), 10, 32–38
Ly Thai Tho (nation-
alists), 11
Ly Thai Tho Street, 11
Ly Thai To (founder
of Ly Dynasty), 10,
76, 77, 178
Ly Thai Tong (born
Ly Phat Ma second
ruler of Ly Dynas-
ty), 48, 78, 80
Ly Thanh Tong
(born Ly Nhat
Ton), 80–81, 82, 83
Ly Thuc Hien (gover-
nor of Jiaozhou), 33
Ly Thuong Kiet (Ly
Dynasty general),
82, 83, 84, 85
Ly Truong Nhan (re-
bel governor of Jiao-
zhou), 33

MAAG. see Military
Assistance Advisory
Group
Mac Dynasty (1528–
1593), 119–122, 163
Mac family, 121
Maddox, 234
Mahayana Buddhism,
62, 63, 216
Mai Chau, upland
area, 42–43
Majapahit (kingdom
on Java), 64
Malaria, 26, 27, 28,
37, 64
Man Bac (archaeologi-
cal site), 18–19, 30
Mandala, 59, 61, 62,
63
Manguin, Pierre-Yves
(archaeologist), 51
Ma River, 13, 14, 17,
28, 42, 104
Market-Leninism, 263
Ma Yuan (Han gener-
al), 26, 47
Mekong Delta, 7, 51,
52, 58, 129, 131,
136, 142, 153, 155,
166, 172, 191, 217,
232, 238, 240
communist-ruled
areas, 213
conflict in, 143
cross-border raids
into, 251

environmental man-
agement of, 53
ethnic groups in, 152
flatlands of, 49
former Khmer lands
of, 146
Funan culture
across, 50
Funan World, 137,
138
newcomers settled
in, 246
provinces, 225, 269
Mekong expedition
(1866), 168
Me Linh, 26, 69
Military Assistance
Advisory Group
(MAAG), 221
Miller, Edward (his-
torian), 228
Ming Dynasty (Chi-
na), 5, 98, 105, 246
Minh Mang (second
Nguyen emperor),
150–155, 158
Moise, Edwin (histo-
rian), 234
Monarchy, 140, 183,
185, 198, 209
Buddhist, 77, 78
Khmer (Cambodi-
an), 127
Trinh and, 195
Mongols, 43, 48, 63–
65, 93–96, 100, 106
armies, 93
invaded and occu-
pied Dali, 47, 93
invasion force, 64
Kublai Khan, 63,
94, 95
pincer movement, 64
Prince of Yunnan, 94
rule in China, 97
Mon-Khmer (lan-
guage group), 51, 56
Mount Ba The, 49, 53
My Son (archaeologi-
cal site), 54, 58, 59,
60, 61–62, 64

Nam C. Kim (archae-
ologist), 19
Nam Dinh city, 89,
100, 169, 174
Nam Viet, 8, 9, 72, 147
Nanyue, 22–24, 39,
45, 147
Nanzhao (upland
state), 37, 38, 44,
47, 78, 84, 87
Nanzhong (upland
state), 45
Napoleon III, 158, 167
Navarre, Henri
(French general),
210

Ngang Pass, 58
Nghe An Province,
48, 62, 78, 97, 107,
135, 161, 186, 193,
197, 201, 213, 223
ngô (ethnic Chinese),
116, 117–118, 124
Ngo Dinh Diem
(president), 198,
202, 204, 212, 213,
219, 227, 231
Ngo Quyen (victor
over Southern Han),
11, 71–73, 74, 95
battle, 72
declared king, 72
idea of state, 72
Ngo Quyen Street, 11
Ngo Si Lien (Le Dy-
nasty historian),
114, 133–134
Nguyen Ai Quoc
(pseudonym for Ho
Chi Minh), 192, 214
Nguyen Du (poet),
160–161
Nguyen family, 9,
104, 118, 119, 121,
123, 139, 146, 147,
149, 251
Nguyen Hue (Tay
Son Rebel, ruler of
Dang Ngoai), 10,
139, 140–142, 145
Nguyen Hue Offen-
sive, 243
Nguyen Lu (Tay Son
Rebel, ruler of
south), 139, 140,
143
Nguyen Nhac (leader
of Tay Son Rebel-
lion, ruler of Dang
Trong), 138, 139,
140, 143, 144
Nguyen Phuc Anh
(first Emperor of
Nguyen Dynasty,
known as Gia Long),
136, 138, 142–146
alliance with Thai
king, 142
choice to create
"Viet Nam," 8–9
forces, 139
naming of state, 8–9
self-title, 7
sent officials to Bei-
jing, 7–8
Nguyen Phuc Khoan
(last adult ruler of
Dang Trong), 131,
137
Nguyen Phuc Khoat,
130
Nguyen Sinh Cung.
see Ho Chi Minh
Nguyen Thai Hoc (na-

tionalist), 195, 196
Nguyen Trai (fifteenth
century official), 10,
108–109, 111, 112,
132, 133–134
Nguyen-Trinh alli-
ance, 121
Nguyen-Trinh plan,
120
Nhat Le River (fron-
tier between Nguy-
en and Trinh), 123,
124, 125, 129, 138,
145
Nhat Nam. see Rinan
commandery
Nha Trang, 55, 59,
60, 61, 62, 67, 127,
144
Ninh Binh province,
17, 18, 68, 169
NLF (National Liber-
ation Front), 226–
227, 229, 234, 238,
239, 242, 243
Nôm (writing script),
99, 135
Nom poetry, 161–162
North Vietnam, 12
Nung (ethnic group),
48, 80, 84, 86
Nung Tri Cao (up-
land leader), 48, 80

Oc Eo (archaeologi-
cal site), 49–53
One Pillar Pagoda,
Hanoi, 80
Operational Plan 34A
(OPLAN-34A), 233,
234
Operation Rolling
Thunder, 235–236
Opium
smuggling, 182
state-backed mo-
nopolies, 190
tax on, revenue
from, 182
transport and sale of,
monopolies on, 183
Opium Wars, 155,
158, 159, 163

Pajot, Louis (amateur
archaeologist), 13
Panduranga (Cham-
pa state), 60, 61, 62,
64, 67, 153
Pass of the Clouds.
see Hai Van Pass
Patenotre, Paul
(French diplomat),
176
Path, Kosal (histori-
an), 251
Pays Montagnard du
Sud, 227

Pearl River, 17, 21, 28
Pearl River Delta, 31
Persia, 32
Petrus Ky, 165
Phan Boi Chau (nationalist), 186–194, 196, 202, 231
armed Confucianism of, 193
family and political networks of, 197
"Go East" campaign, 187, 201
Liang Qichao's advice, 187
open letter, 188
radical, 213
travelled southern China, 188
Phan Chu Trinh (nationalist), 186–189, 190, 192, 194–195, 214
Phan Dinh Phung (court official and rebel), 181
Philippines, 10, 17, 55, 56, 242
Phoenix Program, 239, 241
Phong (region of Dai Viet), 69, 71, 72, 73
Phung Nguyen (Bronze Age culture), 18–19
Phung Nguyen communities, 19
Phung Nguyen site, 18, 50
Phu Quoc (island), 136
Phu Tho Province, 18, 39
Phu Xuan (old name of Hue), 121, 138–139, 140, 141, 144, 145–146
Pierre-Joseph-Georges Pigneau de Béhaine (French bishop), 136
Piracy, 58, 88, 168
Po Nagar (Mother Goddess) temple, 61, 128
Population
Catholic, 159
Chamic, 124, 127
Confucian, 147
Dai Viet, 88, 92, 109
Hoa, 253, 256
indigenous, 56
Khmer, 151
Mekong Delta, 155
Phuan, 115
Saigon, 208
Viet Hoa, pre-war, 253

Vietnamese, 202, 240, 270
Portuguese, 121, 126, 134
explorers, 125
traders and mercenaries, 129–130
vessel trading, 134
Pottery, 17, 19, 44, 50, 51, 56, 59, 93, 97
Poulo Condor. see Con Dao
Province of Jiaozhi, 107

Qin Dynasty, 20
Qing China, 141, 154, 169, 173, 176, 178
Qing Code, 148
Qing Emperor, 130
Qing Empire, 167, 176, 187, 189
Qin Shihuangdi, 20
Quang Trung Emperor, 141, 142, 147
Quoc ngu (national script), 135, 164, 165, 188, 189, 193
Quy Nhon

Red River Delta, 7, 18, 23, 24, 31, 38, 44, 45, 46, 47, 50, 51, 61, 66, 68, 69, 75, 104, 105, 117, 121, 123, 124, 128, 132, 133, 140, 141, 145, 146, 157, 163, 167, 168
agricultural development of, 92
culture of, 15
flatlands of, 119
highlands around, 111
Ming invaders welcomed in, 106
rival clans in, 89
rival families of, 88
southern fringes of, 107
Tran family base in, 101
wealth of, 20
Re-education, 233, 248
Reilly, Brett (historian), 206
Republic of Cochinchina, 207
Republic of Vietnam (RVN), 221–222, 224–229, 238, 247, 251
American War, 232, 233, 235, 237, 239, 240–243, 244
anti communist

campaign in, 227–228
army of, 225
Diem-led, 228
former officers of, 248
military planners in, 227
officials, 250
spraying herbicide, 227
Résident Supérieur, 180, 181, 183
Returned Sword Myth, 108, 132–133
Rhodes, Alexandre de, 135
Rice, 18, 29
cultivation, 25, 52, 53
exports, 190, 200
fields, 42, 44, 68, 91, 92
growers, 88, 92
harvesting, 77, 82
learning to cultivate, 17
paddy systems dating, 44
Phung Nguyen communities, 19
production, 254–255, 269
trade, 51, 130
traders, 239
Rice-based agriculture, 51
Rinan commandery, 57, 58
Riviere, Henri (French naval officer), 173, 174, 179
Roman Empire, 30
Rubber, 183, 190, 191
global supply of, 196
prices, 196
tappers, 197
Rudravarman (Champa ruler), 53, 60, 82
Rue Henri Riviere, 11
Russia, 243, 265, 266
RVN. see Republic of Vietnam
RVN Law 10/59, 225

Sa Huynh (archaeological site), 55, 56
Saigon, 7, 9, 127, 129, 139, 143, 145, 156, 157, 165, 168, 169, 187, 190, 191, 194, 229, 235, 243, 247, 248, 255
battle in, 136
beer, 250
British Advisory Mission, 228

British Gurkha troops, 205
business bankruptcies in, 196
capture of, 163
French Cochinchina, 165, 179
French troops left, 221
Gia Dinh, 147, 153, 164
government, 219, 232
Independence Palace, 218
Khmer king fled to, 149
leadership, 233
liberation, 205
MAAG in, 209
new building construction in, 190
officials in, 219
plantations in, 215
population of, 208
port of, 159, 160
sister city of, 246
subordinate viceroy in, 146
US embassy in, 236, 241
Saigon, 1862 Treaty of, 164, 167
Saigon Municipal Council, 199
Saigon River, 246
Samsung, 267
Sanskrit, 52, 54, 59, 60, 63
Sarraut, Albert (French governor-general), 189
Sasges, Gerald (historian), 182
Second Opium War, 159, 163
SEPES. see Service des Études Politiques et Sociales
Service des Études Politiques et Sociales (SEPES), 220
SFDIC. see Société des Distilleries de l'Indochine
Shambhuvarman (Champa ruler), 60
Shi Xie. see Si Nhiep
Siam, 88, 181–182
SICAF. see Société Indochinoise de Commerce, d'Agriculture et de Finance
Silk, 247
Chinese, 126
for silver trade, 126, 127
industry, 127

Tonkinese, 126
Silver, 127, 168, 176
coins, 130
currency/money, 130, 171
Japanese, 126
Mexican, 171
taels, 171
Sima Qian (Han period historian), 45
Si Nhiep, 31
Sinitic World, 51, 60
Sipsong Chu Tai, 112
Slave raids, 88
Slavery, 58, 79, 96, 117
Socialist Republic of Vietnam, 248
Société des Distilleries de l'Indochine (SFDIC), 183
Société Indochinoise de Commerce, d'Agriculture et de Finance (SICAF), 183
Song China, 63, 80, 84
Song dynasty, 73–74
Song Empire, 48, 63, 69, 73, 77, 94
South China Sea, 16, 32, 56, 61, 129, 257, 261, 265, 266
Southern Han empire, 70, 71
South Vietnam, 12, 198, 218, 222, 247
Soviet Union, 209, 212, 232, 233, 236, 238, 242, 251, 252, 255, 257, 259, 271
Spanish
government, 159
ships, 125
troops, 159
Speedy Express Operation, 210
Spirit worship, 40, 41, 215
State of Vietnam, 212, 219, 227
Stilt houses, 14, 42, 51, 128
"Street-name heroes," 10
Streets, 10–12
in Hanoi, 11
Sui Dynasty, 60
Swarnabhumi, 59
Swarnadvipa, 59

Tai (ethnic group), 43, 44, 79, 86, 93, 97, 107, 111–112, 129, 134, 203
Tai-Kadai (language), 30

Taiwan, 55, 233, 256
Tang Dynasty, 35, 37, 40, 60–61, 70, 72, 101
Tax, 102, 130, 131
abolished, 107
codes, 110
collecting regime, 191
indirect, 182
rates, 182
revenues, 110
rules, 182
to Cochinchina government, 166
Tay Do (western capital), 104, 105, 106, 110, 120
Taylor, Keith (historian), 27, 36, 78, 81, 90, 114, 143, 178, 223, 273
Taylor, Maxwell, 228
Tay Son (district), 132
forces, 144
leaders, 140
navy, 144
rebellion (1771–1802), 137–146, 149, 246
rulers, 161
Tay Son War (1771–1802), 137–146, 161
Telegraph, 164, 169, 177
Temple of Literature, 83
Tet Offensive 1968, 141, 241, 242
Thailand, 10, 43, 44, 48, 50, 56, 79, 136, 235, 242
Thang Long (name of Hanoi from eleventh century), 7, 64, 66, 76, 77, 78, 82, 86, 89, 93, 100, 101, 104, 133
Thanh Hoa Province, 14, 23, 24, 98, 101, 104, 121, 132
Thanh Thai (Nguyen emperor), 181, 183, 184, 231
Thieu Tri (third Nguyen emperor), 155–156
Thu Bon River, 54, 58
Tonkin, 110, 125, 126, 131, 170, 175, 176, 179, 181, 182, 183, 187, 194, 195, 196, 199, 201, 202
Tonkin Gulf, 16, 261, 264
Tonkin Gulf Incident, 234–235

Tonkin Gulf Resolution, 235
Tonkin Public School, 188, 189
Ton That Thuyet (Nguyen official), 174, 175, 176, 177–178, 181
Trade, 20
cross-border, 261
in horses, 45
international, 98, 130, 165, 166, 256
maritime, 20, 58
regional, 20, 30, 32, 36, 53, 65, 123, 130, 131
rice, 51, 130
rice-based, 51
route, 64, 84, 112, 137, 169, 172
silk for silver, 126, 127
South China Sea, 61
tribute, 82
Tra Kieu (archaeological site), 28, 59, 60
Tran Du Tong (king of Dai Viet), 65, 98
Tran Dynasty (1226–1400), 41, 66, 97, 100, 101, 105, 108, 109, 118
Tran Hung Dao (thirteenth century general), 11, 91, 93, 94–95, 96, 97, 106, 112
Tran Hung Dao Street, 11
Tran Minh Tong (king), 49, 97, 98, 101
Tran Nhan Tong (king of Dai Viet), 63, 65, 94, 95, 96, 100
Tran Thai Tong (first king of Tran Dynasty), 91, 92, 100, 118
Treaty of Hue, 175
1863, 159
1884, 175
Treaty of Saigon, 169
1862, 164, 167
1874, 169
Tribute trade, 82
Trinh clan, 121, 123–132
Trinh family, 118, 119, 140
Trinh Kiem, 119, 121–122
Trung Quoc, 10
Trung Sisters. see Hai Ba Trung
Trung Sisters' uprising, 44

Truong (region of Dai Viet), 69, 72, 73
Truong Chinh (DRV leader), 205, 223, 232
Truong Phuc Loan, 137, 138
Truong Vinh Ky, 165
Tu Duc Emperor, 156–158
"Twelve Tai Districts" (Sipsong Chu Tai), 48
Twelve Warlords, 68, 72

UCI. see Union Commerciale Indochinoise
Union Commerciale Indochinoise (UCI), 183
Uplands, 20, 28–29, 30, 36, 41–48, 56, 60, 66, 69, 77, 79, 104, 108, 153
Bahnar group, 138
Cham World, 137
dong world, 43
ecological niches, 43
elites of Phong in, 72
geology of, 45
groups/people of, 41, 46–47, 119, 129, 134, 167
international trade in, Champa and, 98
Khmer communities, 155
Lao, 141
leaders, 46
Mai Chau, 42–43
Ming civilization, 107
minorities from, 75
Nanzhao kingdom, 78
of Yunnan, 44
rebels, 170
Red River Delta, 167
rice growers, 90
Tai language, 92
USSR. see Soviet Union

Van Don (port), 88, 95, 97, 110, 117
Van Lang (mythical kingdom), 39, 101
Vann, John Paul (American military adviser), 229
Van Xuan, 34
Varenne, Alexandre (French governor general), 193
Versailles Peace Conference, 192, 214

Vichy government, 201
Vickery, Michael (archaeologist), 51
Viet Cong, 207, 226
communications by, monitoring of, 229
guerrillas, 241
Viet Hoa, 246–247, 249
culture, 256
entrepreneurs, 256
pre-war population, 253
Viet Minh, 201, 203–208, 210–212, 217
Chinese communists and, 211
committee, 205
forces, 204, 206
front organization, 203
leaders, 205
militants launched attacks in Hanoi, 207
rebuilding of networks by, 203
victory at Dien Bien Phu, 212
"Vietnamese," 9
Vietnamese civilization, 12
Vietnamese language, 99, 134–135, 191
Vietnamese nationalists, 11, 206, 208
Vietnamese Revolutionary Youth League, 193, 196
Vietnam Nationalist Party. see VNQDD
Vietnam Workers Party (VWP), 210, 223, 232, 250
Viet Quoc, 208
Viet Thuong, 8
Vijaya (Champa state), 60, 62–65, 62–67, 80, 82, 94, 113, 115, 139, 140
Vinh Loc, 42, 101, 104
Vinh Te Canal, 151
VNQDD, 195, 196, 206
Vo Nguyen Giap (DRV general), 205
VWP. see Vietnam Workers Party

Whampoa Military Academy, 193
Whitmore, John (historian), 106, 113
Woodside, Alexander (historian), 148
Wu (new state), 31–32, 51–52

Wu Di (Han emperor), 23

Xi'an, China, 21, 23, 24, 25
Xianbei, 52
Xiangkhouang, 115
Xianglin (district of Rinan), 57, 58
Xingzhonghui, 189
Xiyu, 23
Xue Zong (governor of Jiaozhi), 29, 30

Yangtze River, 15, 17, 18, 20
Yangzhou, 58
Yao, Alice (archaeologist), 19, 44
Yellow Flags, 167, 168, 175
Yellow river (China), 17, 20, 39, 40
Yen Bai Province, 48
Y Lan (mother of king Ly Nhan Tong), 83, 86
Youth League, 193, 196, 203
Yue, 15, 21–22 27
identity, 73
suppression campaign against, 21–22
Yunnan province, 18, 20, 43, 87, 165, 168

Zhao Tuo (ruler of Nanyue), 22–23
defeated King An Duong, 39
"Emperor of Nanyue," 22
Zhao Xing, 23
Zhao Xing (ruler of Nanyue), 23
Zhenla, 53
Zhou Enlai (Chinese leader), 192, 194, 201, 226
Zhu Di (Ming emperor), 105–106
death of, 107
Zinoman, Peter (historian), 197